A.P. McCoy

A.P. McCoy

My Autobiography

A. P. McCoy with Donn McClean

The right of A.P. McCoy to be identified as the author of
this work has been asserted in accordance with the
Copyright, Designs and Patents Act 1988.

First published in Great Britain in 2011 by Orion Books
An imprint of the Orion Publishing Group Ltd
Orion House, 5 Upper St Martin's Lane,
London, WC2H 9EA
An Hachette Livre Company

1 3 5 7 9 10 8 6 4 2

A CIP catalogue record for this book
is available from the British Library.

Hardback ISBN 978 1 4091 3166 3
Trade Paperback ISBN 978 1 4091 3167 0

Printed in Great Britain by
CPI Group (UK) Ltd, Croydon, CRO 4YY

The Orion Publishing Group's policy is to use papers that are
natural, renewable and recyclable products and made from wood grown in
sustainable forests. The logging and manufacturing processes are expected to
conform to the environmental regulations of the country of origin.

www.orionbooks.co.uk

To the light of my life Eve, my fantastic wife Chanelle
and to the greatest parents Claire and Peadar.

Acknowledgements

Big thanks to everyone who helped me to tell my story. To David Manasseh for planting the idea in my head in the first place; to all at Orion Publishing, Alan Samson and Susan Lamb and Lucinda McNeile and Martha Ashby; to Donn McClean, for helping me write my story; to everyone who gave up their time to help fill in the blanks, including Martin and Carol Pipe, Jonjo O'Neill, Dave Roberts, TJ Comerford, my mum and dad, my sisters Roisin and Anne Marie; to Patricia Davis and Mary O'Reilly for transcribing the tapes, to Rachel Cullen and Jane Burke for proof-reading and sense-checking; to Gee Bradburne for sourcing the photographs.

Personality Speaking

'So, it's time, ladies and gentlemen,' Gary Lineker was saying, pausing momentarily to add to the drama, 'to announce the winner of the 2010 BBC Sports Personality of the Year.'

It was all a bit surreal. Here was I, Anthony Peter McCoy from Moneyglass in County Antrim, sitting in the front row of the LG Arena in Birmingham among some of the great sports people of our time – David Beckham, Ryan Giggs, Cesc Fabregas, Lee Westwood, Phil Taylor, Andrew 'Freddie' Flintoff, Graeme McDowell – people I watch on television, superstars, sports stars. And me. I shouldn't have been in the front row. I shouldn't even have been in the back row. I should have been at home on the couch, watching it all on television.

I couldn't win it, that was for sure. A jockey, Sports Personality of the Year? Some chance. I had been lucky enough to win the Grand National that year on Don't Push It, but lots of jockeys had won the Grand National, and none of them had come close to the big award. Nor had any of the best jockeys of the modern age. Sir Gordon Richards hadn't won it, Lester Piggott hadn't won it, Frankie Dettori hadn't won it, and Frankie is a real personality.

People began to get behind me though: a campaign began, interviews and feature articles were arranged for me. To be honest, it was all a little embarrassing. I am not big on interviews really; there is only so much you can say. Different interviews, different interviewers, but the same questions, the same answers. Your first winner doesn't change no matter how many times you are asked, your favourite food, your mother's name. I'm sure readers and listeners were sick of seeing and hearing me. That said, if people were going to organise these interviews for me, and if they thought that it was all going to be good for racing, the sport that has given me so much and allowed me live the life of my dreams, then the least I could do was go along with it.

I never really thought that I could win it. I never really allowed myself to think that I would. We live in our little horse-racing cocoon. I love racing, almost everyone with whom I associate loves racing, but racing is a minority sport. Racing doesn't have the following that, say, football or golf enjoy. There was a chance that people within racing were deluding themselves. A jockey couldn't win it in front of football players, golfers, athletes, boxers. Racing's position in the pantheon of sports is not high, and I am sure that everyone involved in the world of darts thought that Phil Taylor was a shoo-in.

I knew that the racing public was behind me. I knew that lots of people had made lots of phone calls, that many of them would have had huge phone bills that night. Getting closer to the day, different people started telling me that they thought I would win it, even people from outside of racing. I made my way down to the actual event with the swimmer Karen Pickering, and she told me that she thought I had a great chance. That made me think, I might actually have a chance.

Then I walked into the place and saw this room full of sports people, household names, television stars, and I thought: no chance. I am honoured even to be in the same room as them. I was thinking, they're probably looking at me thinking, who's your man? To be numbered in the top 10 was huge, to think of being named number one was just crazy.

'To present the award,' Sue Barker was saying, 'please welcome back Cesc Fabregas and former winner Andrew Flintoff.'

'The Flood' by Take That blared through the arena, the crowd applauded, Cesc Fabregas and Freddie Flintoff made their way coolly down the steps towards the stage in front of us, and my heart did a little somersault. I looked at my wife Chanelle, petrified; she looked back, smiling.

'I think I've won,' I said.

I don't really know where that came from. I wasn't even certain that the thought had fully formed in my head, but the words came tumbling out.

'What?!' she replied, bursting with terror and exhilaration at the same time.

'I think I've won.'

There, I said it again.

Cesc Fabregas had been called up on stage again to present the trophy. The BBC knew that I was a big Arsenal fan and I thought that they had asked him to present the trophy because I had won. Two plus two equals 15. I thought all of this in the fraction of a second between Cesc appearing and me blurting out this thought to Chanelle. I could have been miles off the mark. Cesc could have been teed up to present the trophy to whoever won it, Jessica Ennis might have been an even bigger Arsenal fan than me, Phil Taylor could have gone on holiday to Spain once. Who knew? Reason had long gone out the window.

'All votes have been counted and independently verified,' said Gary, 'so eh, Andrew, if we can ask you to reveal, who was in third place please?'

Freddie opened the envelope. I have to say, I was hoping he wouldn't call out my name. Third would have been great, but when you finish third you can't win.

'In third place,' said Freddie, 'is Jessica Ennis.'

The music blared, the audience applauded, and Jessica made her way graciously and gracefully up to the stage.

'Congratulations to Jessica,' said Sue Barker. 'And Andrew, the runner-up please.'

'In second place...' said Freddie.

I held my breath. Second was better than third, second was better than I had done in 2002, but if you finish second, you still don't win. Same as if you finish third then.

'... is Phil "The Power" Taylor.'

It's difficult to say Phil Taylor without putting 'The Power' in the middle.

More music, more applause. I was delighted for Phil. He seemed to be thrilled as he made his way up to the stage, kissing everyone, including Freddie Flintoff. Cesc gave him his trophy and he stood there on the stage beside Jessica Ennis, beaming.

'And the BBC Sports Personality of the Year for 2010 please, Andrew,' Gary said.

A horrible thought struck me. What if I didn't win it now? If I didn't win, I wasn't in the first three. It would be worse than 2002, I would have gone backwards, racing would have regressed. How big an eejit would I look then? All this effort, this campaign, all these interviews, the cardboard cut-outs, the reminders to racegoers to vote for you, the race names, the 'Vote AP' Gold Cup. What if, after all of this, I had finished fourth or fifth?

And it was possible. Graeme McDowell or Lee Westwood hadn't been mentioned yet. Graeme McDowell, the US Open champion, the man who had, just two months earlier at Celtic Manor, holed the putt that won the Ryder Cup for Europe. Lee Westwood, the new world number one, the man who had knocked Tiger Woods off the top spot just six weeks previously. It was impossible to think that none of them would make the top three.

'The 2010 BBC Sports Personality of the Year...' said Freddie.

I looked over at the autocue, and there it was. AP McCoy. My name. Me. The 2010 BBC Sports Personality of the Year is AP McCoy. It was written there. For a second I didn't believe it. Silence. Why wasn't Freddie saying anything? Was he going to say it? Was it a mistake? Was I dreaming this? Was it really my name? Then Freddie spoke.

'... is AP McCoy.'

CHAPTER 1

Troubled Times

I am often asked by journalists where I got my stubbornness, my single-mindedness. It's hard to tell really. It's not really a family trait, but it has always been there in me. As a kid I was shy, I didn't like talking to people, I didn't really like doing things that involved people, and I tried not to; maybe that's where my stubbornness began. Like going to school. Nightmare.

I wouldn't interact with unfamiliar people if I could avoid it. Even when strangers came into our house, friends of Mum and Dad's, I would prefer not to have to even stay and say hello. And I can remember sitting on the rug in the sitting room with my mother on Friday nights when I was about 10 or 11, watching television, when all the other kids would be outside playing.

I wasn't mad into horses when I was very young. Snooker and football were my big passions. Arsenal was my football team from as early as I can remember. I remember watching the 1979 FA Cup Final, when Arsenal beat Manchester United 3–2. I was five years and one week old; I think it is my earliest-ever memory. I can still see Alan Sunderland sliding in to knock the ball over the line to make it 3–2. Maybe that's why I'm such a big Arsenal fan now, or maybe it's because so many Irish lads played for them then: Liam Brady, David O'Leary, Frank Stapleton and Pat Jennings, a Northern Irish man, from Newry in County Down, or maybe it's a combination of the two factors. Whatever the reason, I carry the burden of being a lifelong Gunners fan.

Belfast-born Alex Higgins was another one of my childhood heroes. Higgins won the World Snooker Championship in 1982 when I was almost eight, and Dennis Taylor, from Coalisland in County Tyrone, won it in 1985 when I was almost 11, beating Steve Davis in the final on the last black in the final frame. You couldn't have written sports drama like it. In Northern Ireland we don't have many world champions in any sport, so to have two in the space of four years in one sport was fairly amazing. If you were an impressionable lad growing up in Northern Ireland at the time, if you had even a peripheral interest in sport, you were into snooker.

Moneyglass in County Antrim was never big horse country. Horse racing was something that, if people knew about it at all, they knew that other people did it. For my sisters, racing was something that wasted two of our four television channels on a Saturday afternoon.

My dad was unusual then: a Moneyglass man who had a passion for horses. Peadar McCoy, a carpenter by trade but in reality a man who could turn his hand to pretty much anything, had no family history steeped in horses or in racing, but he always had a hankering to have horses of his own. So much so that, when he built the bungalow behind his parents' house, the house in which we would ultimately grow up, he also built three stables out the back. A three-bedroom bungalow and three stables: as much room for horses as there was for people.

It was in 1970 that my dad bought his first horse, a mare called Fire Forest, a relative of the 1962 Grand National winner Kilmore. The mare was in foal at the time to the local stallion Steeple Aston. My dad didn't know it, but there was another interested party, the late Billy Rock, who trained racehorses at Cullybackey, about 11 miles from Moneyglass. When Billy heard that the mare had been sold to a carpenter from Moneyglass, and that she was in foal to Steeple Aston, he came up to meet my dad to talk about buying the resultant foal. So began a friend-ship and a camaraderie that would last from that day until the day that Billy died in April 2003, far, far too early, at the age of 59. And it was a friendship that was to have a more profound impact on the life and the career of Peadar McCoy's eldest son than he could possibly have imagined.

My mum Claire is originally from Randalstown, a small town about six miles from Moneyglass. Mum and Dad got married in 1968, and moved into the bungalow with its three bedrooms that my dad had built beside his parents' house. As the years went by, the bedrooms began to fill up: Anne Marie was the first of the little McCoys to arrive in 1971, she was hunted up by Roisin the following year and then, after a delay of two years, I came kicking and screaming into the world on 4th May 1974. Jane arrived in 1976, Colm joined us three years after that, and then Kelly completed the sextet when she arrived in 1986.

We lived in the bungalow until I was about seven. Then my dad's father died and left the home house to his sister Bernie, but she and my dad decided that they would swap houses, so my dad with his entourage would live in the big house while my aunt Bernie would live in the bungalow. The home house wasn't a massive house or anything, but it was bigger than the bungalow, so it all made a lot of sense. Also, there was a small shop attached to it, just a little local shop, but my mum was able to make a few pounds from it. My sister Roisin now runs a hairdressing salon from what used to be the shop, but they still have a Vivo shop beside it. My brother Colm lives in the bungalow now, my sister Anne Marie runs a pub with her husband about two miles away, so most of us haven't gone too far.

I've always been close to them; we are a close family. Of them all, Kelly was the sibling that I probably didn't know that well. I left home in April 1990 when she was four, and you probably don't have that much interest in hanging out with your four-year-old sister when you are 16 and want to conquer the world. But Kelly was over in London doing a course in 2009, and she came and lived with me, Chanelle and Eve for six weeks. That was great – we got to catch up a lot and I got to know her much better. She's a great kid; she's the smartest of the lot of us I'd say, by a long way.

Like I say, I was a quiet child, except maybe when I lost my temper, which I didn't do that often thankfully. My sisters say that I could dictate the mood of the entire house. If I was in good form, then everyone was happy, but if I was grumpy or fighting with someone, they say that everyone else in the house was in bad form as well. I tried to run away from home many times, but I never got very far. I remember one day having a big row with my mum.

'That's it, I'm leaving,' I screamed at her.

'Away you go,' said Mum.

That was a little unexpected, but I couldn't back down. So I threw some stuff into a bag and headed off. I was eight. I got as far as Kelly's field, which is a fair bit away from the house; it was a fair hike for eight-year-old legs. Very far I thought, as you do as an eight-year-old, but you could see it from the sitting-room window in the bungalow. I was behind the tree in the field, but Mum could see me all the time. When it grew dark, though, I thought of the warm fire in the house, and my bed. I had cooled down a little. Kelly's field was cold and scary, so I tucked my tail firmly between my legs and made my way home.

There was one day that Mum took me to Ballymena in the pram. Roisin and Anne Marie were at school, so it was just the two of us. Out for a day's shopping in Ballymena with your mum, as you do, when there was a bomb scare. Bomb scares weren't that uncommon in Northern Ireland towns in those days. Mum went to get me, but I wasn't there, neither me nor the pram. Some woman, when she heard there was a bomb scare, just grabbed my pram and ran with me away from the danger area. And it wasn't as if Mum was that far away, she was standing beside me, but when she turned around to get me, I was gone.

Mum was beside herself. It turns out the woman had brought me down to the far end of the town as Mum searched all over the place for me. There was a photo of me in the paper the following day, me in my little blue anorak with the yellow hood, a baby lost in the bomb scare in Ballymena. Eventually Mum found me. I'm not sure if she ever got her shopping done that day.

*

Growing up in a Catholic area in Northern Ireland in the 1970s and 1980s, The Troubles were never going to be far from your doorstep. I remember the night the IRA blew up the police barracks in Toomebridge, which is about a mile and a half down the road from Moneyglass. I was really young at the time – I couldn't have been any older than six or seven – and I was up on my uncle's farm. I went through a phase when I was a kid of wanting to be a farmer, and I used to go up to my uncle's farm in the evenings. This particular evening I was up there with my uncle on his farm on the top of a hill overlooking Toome bridge, and we suddenly heard this really loud bang. We looked down into Toome bridge and saw the place just going black.

It was just the time and the area in which we were living. A bomb going off was really nothing new, and we were young enough that we didn't really think of the possible consequences for others; it was just one of those things that happened in Northern Ireland. We knew no different.

You would regularly hear helicopters at nighttime, and when you went outside and looked up, you would see them with their spotlights, scouring the fields and farmyards for God knows what. There were army trucks around all the time, soldiers with guns over their shoulders. The police would often just decide to set up a checkpoint outside our shop for no apparent reason, and they would stop cars just driving down the road; it wasn't close to the border or anything, they would just decide to stop cars going through this Catholic area. They'd get lads out of their cars, get them to open their boots then search their cars with sniffer dogs and everything. They never found anything. Right, on you go.

One evening, Mum was driving her sister Marie and her children home from our house with all of us in the back of the car, the yellow Volkswagen Passat, about seven of us, all sitting on top of each other, no seat belts and certainly no booster seats. Marie lived about two miles away, across the River Bann into Derry. This particular evening, as was often the case, there was a checkpoint on the bridge going over the river and a big traffic jam, so instead of waiting, Mum decided that she would drop her sister off at the bridge, her sister could walk over the bridge, and Mum could drive home and ring Marie's husband Sean to tell him to come and collect her on the Derry side.

All very fine and sensible, except that the last thing you do when you are in line for a checkpoint is a U-turn. Mum had hardly reversed the car when we were surrounded by soldiers. Guns pointing and shouting and everything. Mum was trying to explain to a soldier what she had been doing, but he wasn't really listening, he was too busy shouting at her and pointing his gun in her face. As this was going on, Marie got out of the car, walked around to the soldier and tapped him on the shoulder. Another bad move. The soldier got the fright of his life and could easily have shot Mum and the lot of us in the back of the car. Thankfully he didn't and we weren't headline news that night.

There was another night Marie was in her house in Derry (Sean was away), when there was a knock on the door. Two fellows were standing outside, telling her that they wanted her car.

'What do you mean, you want my car?' Marie asked.

'We want your car,' they said.

'Well you're not having my car,' said Marie.

'Look, we need your car,' they said.

'You can't have it.'

With that they pulled out a handgun.

'We're taking your car. You can pick it up tomorrow in the car park at the nightclub up the road.'

So they took her car. Marie went up to the nightclub the following day, and there was her car, fully intact, exactly as it was when she had parked it outside her house the previous evening.

I suppose looking back on it now, it was all fairly scary, but we were never really frightened at the time. Like I say, it was all we knew. We lived in a predominantly Catholic area, but there were Protestant families around with whom we were friendly. Billy Rock, for example, who was to have such a profound impact on my life, was Protestant. The fact that he wasn't Catholic was completely irrelevant, except for the banter.

A lot of the lads who worked at Billy's were Protestant as well, but they were great – religious persuasion wasn't relevant. Your ability to handle a half a ton of thoroughbred on a Saturday morning was much more important to them than what church you attended on a Sunday morning. I was only ever really a child when I lived in Antrim, but in my 15 years there, I never experienced discrimination against me because I was Catholic.

Billy used to tease me all right. He used to tell me that he would dress me up in all the Orange Order regalia on 12th July and bring me to one of the Orange Order marches, then bring me home and leave me at my mum and dad's front door in Moneyglass in all my gear.

The fact that we had the shop, with space for cars in front of it, meant that we had to be a little careful. I would often hear cars pulling up outside the shop in the dead of night and car doors opening and closing, and then one car speeding off. The following morning the bomb squad would be out at the car that had been left behind, checking it with their remote-control gadgets, and us inside in the house just yards away from the car.

Mum thought that we couldn't be seen to serve a member of the British Army in the shop, or an RUC man. If you did, and it became known, then you could have been in trouble. It wasn't a problem for Mum anyway. Generally she thought the RUC men weren't that nice to her. One evening at about eight o'clock, a policeman came in, and Mum told him she couldn't serve him. The fact that there was a Post Office in the shop meant that she was obliged to serve him, but the Post Office closed at eight o'clock, she explained. The following morning the policeman came in to buy a stamp, which Mum sold to him, a little reluctantly. If he had been looking for a bottle of milk, he mightn't have been so lucky.

An IRA activist stayed with us once. I would have been only a child at the time. He was a friend of our family; his family was friendly with our family, so we put him up for a couple of days. However, the fact that he was on the run from the police complicated matters a little. Dad was away working one day and Mum had been out for the day. On her way back home, she realised that the whole area was teeming with police and army men, sniffer dogs and everything, all searching for our lodger.

He lay low, hiding under the bed in the room. That must have been a fairly fretful time for my mother – an IRA fugitive under the bed in her house. I'm not sure what the penalty for hiding an IRA man on the run was, but it wouldn't have been pretty. Eventually the search units moved on and Mum could breathe again. As soon as she composed herself again, she went down to the room and hauled him out from under the bed.

'See here now,' she said. 'I may sympathise and all, but I am not going to jail for anybody, not for you, not for Ireland, not for anybody. And if they do lift me, I'm telling you I'll sing like a bird. So you best be getting yourself out of here and moving on.'

So he did.

CHAPTER 2

Between a Rock and a Hard Place

If Dad wanted me to take an interest in horses, he never told me as much. He never pushed me towards horses, but he did expose me to them. What I did after that was up to me.

Neither of my older sisters showed any interest. My brother Colm rode a little when he was younger, but he had no real enthusiasm; he only rode because I made him. You have a certain amount of authority over your six-year-younger brother, so I used to get him to ride with me. When I was 14 or 15, he would have only been eight or nine, but I would make him ride one of the ponies and I would ride the other. It was more fun riding with someone than on your own, but I used to get him to do all the things I was doing on my pony, all the jumps, which was hard for a little guy. I might have soured him against riding, I don't know. He was never really into it, he was more into boxing. Luckily he hasn't boxed me on the head yet for the years of older brother direction/coercion.

There is a photograph of me at home sitting on Misclaire, a mare that Dad bred out of Fire Forest. Misclaire is actually the dam of Thumbs Up, who was also bred by Dad, and who was trained by Nicky Henderson to win the 1993 County Hurdle at the Cheltenham Festival, with Richard Dunwoody on board. That was a good day, the day that Richard Dunwoody rode a horse bred by Peadar McCoy to win a race at the Cheltenham Festival! Anyway, I can't be any older than three in the photo, and I'm sitting up on this mare, bareback, holding onto her mane and her neck, my little spindly legs barely reaching halfway down her frame, and my dad just holding her head collar.

I remember every Easter when I was very small going down to the horse fair in Toomebridge. The travelling community would come along to buy and sell their horses, and I used to love going down with Dad just to look at the ponies. I just always had an interest in horses, even before I started to ride them.

When I was eight, Dad brought me down to the local riding school owned by Mrs Kyle (I'm not sure that she had a first name, we just knew her as Mrs Kyle), and I found that I quite liked riding. Mrs Kyle said that I had a natural talent (she probably said that to all the parents just to keep them coming back with their kids!), but I enjoyed sitting on a horse, feeling this power beneath me, a living animal with that strength, the strength to carry you and run and jump, but an animal that you could semi-control with your hands and your legs.

Soon I was asking Dad for a pony of my own. I was nine. Dad first borrowed a little white pony from one of our neighbours, Pat Liddy, and, once he was happy that I could handle the pony and that this wasn't just some passing fad, he bought me a pony of my own.

She was a horrible pony. She was a good-looking, but an absolutely horrible thing. There was a lot of thoroughbred blood in her, which probably explained her good looks, but it was also probably most of the problem. She was just wild. She would bury you as soon as look at you.

We got her riding away anyway; Dad thought that she would calm down once we started riding her and she learned to settle, but the opposite was the case. The more we rode her, the fitter she got, the stronger she became, and the more energy she had to bury you. Looking back, it's probably surprising that I wasn't put off riding by her. It was always with an air of trepidation that I approached her because I knew she was going to bury me. But I never thought of stopping. It wasn't that I decided to persevere, I just never really thought of not riding her – I just never really considered it as an option.

We called her Seven Up because that was about the number of times she would drop me in one session. And it wasn't just me. Dad got some of the lads who worked at Billy Rock's to come down and ride her for a bit, and she buried them as well. She didn't discriminate.

Eventually we got rid of the pony and Dad got me another, a lovely little mare that I named Chippy, after Liam Brady. Chippy was fast, and she was a great jumper. I got my hands on a few poles and I did them up, painted them black and white and made a show-jumping course out at the front of the house for myself on this grassy patch between two busy roads. Chippy and I spent many a long evening and many a Saturday afternoon going around the course, faster and faster, trying to better our previous world record.

We went to lots of gymkhanas, and because Chippy was so fast and such a good jumper, we did very well. I accumulated a fair stock of trophies and rosettes, but they didn't really do much for me. I didn't get any great sense of achievement from winning a rosette; it was just the riding and the competing that gave me a buzz. Also, there was a lot of standing around at gymkhanas waiting for your turn. It all happened a little too slowly for my liking.

School presented a difficulty for me as well. It wasn't the lessons or the learning, I didn't mind the lessons and I was able enough to learn – it was the very act of going to school. I hated it long before I ever really knew what a horse was but, as the years went by and as my interest in horses and ponies grew, I thought school was a severe waste of time, something that kept me from horses.

After my first or second day at school, I decided that I wasn't going to go any more, that it wasn't a good idea at all, and so began a struggle between me and school and Mum and the attendance officer and the principal that lasted a childhood.

The school bus used to pass very close to our door, but I used to do all I could not to get on it. Sometimes it would actually come up the little roadway to our house and stop outside our front door, and Mum would literally be trying to squeeze me out the front door with me clinging onto the door frame.

So Mum used to have to drive me. It still didn't fully solve the problem though. It wasn't that I didn't want to get on the bus, the bus wasn't the problem, school was the problem. Very quickly I figured out that Mum's car wasn't any better than the bus. Four-year-old brains can tick over quite quickly.

There was this little pouch in the back of Mum's yellow Volkswagen Beetle and, on what must have been only my third or fourth day of going to school, I climbed into it. I was small enough to fit my whole body in. The plan worked perfectly. Mum couldn't get me out. She tried everything to prise me out, but to no avail, and she had no option but to drive back home again with me still in the back of the car.

I must have been a nightmare for my parents. It was a struggle every morning – from one day to the next I'm sure they had no idea whether they were going to succeed in getting me to go to school or not. I tried most tricks. I remember hiding my schoolbag behind the cement slab that lay beside the back door. I figured if I didn't have a schoolbag, I couldn't go to school.

Dad used to go down to Billy Rock's yard on Saturday mornings. He didn't go down every Saturday or anything like it, he wouldn't want to be making a nuisance of himself. He is a shy man, my dad, maybe that's where I got it when I was younger, or at any rate he's a shy man when he doesn't have a few pints in him.

Dad would probably go down to Billy's maybe once a month just to see him and to watch the horses work. They grew to be really good friends, and later on, when I left home and started to make my way in the world, they became even closer. I started going with my dad down to Billy's when I was about 10, and I was fascinated. This was a real racing yard, with real horses, big horses, thoroughbreds, racehorses who could gallop and jump, and all I wanted to do was get up on one of them.

Billy was actually born to be a football player, not a racehorse trainer. His father was chairman and president of Ballymena United, and he was a selector on the Northern Irish football team. Billy was apparently a very good player when he was younger. When he was 15 he was offered a trial with Everton, but just before he went over to Liverpool, he injured his back playing summer league. When he recovered a little, he joined Coleraine and played in the Irish League, but his back never really got better, and he had to stop playing altogether when he was 20.

But football's loss was racing's gain. He spent a summer with Mick O'Toole and then he began riding point-to-pointers for Hugh Dunlop and, when he got too heavy for riding, he started to train horses instead of ride them.

I would be on at my dad all the time. Can we go down to Billy's this Saturday? Can we go down to Billy's this Saturday? I remember the weeks that I knew we were going down: I would sit in school counting the days to Saturday, then counting the hours. It was all I could think about. I would be sitting in school with some teacher going on about long division or something equally irrelevant, and all I would be able to think about was going down to Billy Rock's.

I wasn't even riding the horses at first; I was just going down to watch them with my dad. But I was hoping that some day I would get to ride one of them. And I did. The horses were just going around the indoor school one day and Billy asked my dad if I wanted to sit up on one. It would have been like asking a dog if he wanted to chew on a meaty bone. I couldn't believe it, me riding a real racehorse. At first it was just around the indoor school, the barn in which the horses used to circle, to stretch their legs before they went out to exercise; then I got to ride one or two on the road, just doing roadwork, just walking on the roads.

Gradually my involvement at Billy's grew. I started to go more frequently and ride more horses. I used to get on to my dad to take me there every Saturday, and I started riding horses around the gallops.

I had a million falls. In the beginning, I kept falling off. There was this horse called Eddie Wee, one of Billy's very best horses, he won the two-mile Champion Chase at the Punchestown Festival in 1987 as an 11-year-old. He was coming back from injury at the time, so in the beginning I used to ride him quite a lot. He had leg problems, but he was a good horse, and while coming back from injury he was as fresh as hell. He used to buck like mad and he would regularly get rid of me. The lads at Billy's used to laugh their heads off at me, trying to stay on this mad, fresh thing, but it didn't bother me. I wasn't hurt, I wasn't embarrassed, I just wanted to get up on him and ride him again.

Billy was the type of man who would push you; he'd just chuck you up on some yak and see how you got on. I would regularly get buried. I used to dread telling him about some of the horses, about how bad or how fresh they were. I thought I should be staying on them anyway, and it just made me more determined. And I would always do what Billy told me to do, no matter how frightened I was or how certain I was that I was about to get buried – if Billy told me to get up on one, I got up on one.

It was a similar story later on when I started riding for Martin Pipe. Martin would tell me how the horse was, what I should do, how I should ride him in the race, and I did it. I figured that it wasn't my place to question him. Even if I disagreed with him, even if I thought that the horse should be ridden differently, I figured that Martin had his reasons, and it wasn't my position to question them or to doubt him. Maybe I got that from my time with Billy; I trusted Martin's judgement just like I had trusted Billy's all those years before. If either of them had told me to ride a horse over a cliff, I would have ridden the horse over the cliff.

I think Billy used to test me. In the beginning, the other lads would probably pick the quieter ones to ride, so I'd be left with the lunatics, me the patsy. But as time went on, Billy would put me on the more difficult horses. He probably thought that I was able for them and that I could handle them and learn something at the same time.

The more I rode horses at Billy's, the less attention I paid to the ponies. Poor Chippy. I didn't rush home from school any more to ride her. It wasn't that I didn't ride her, I did, and I still quite enjoyed jumping around the course I had built at the front of the house. But it wasn't the be-all and end-all for me any more. It was like moving from the paddling pool to the deep end, it was for real now. I wasn't sitting in school bursting to get home to ride Chippy. It was racehorses for me now. It was all about Saturday mornings, going down to Billy Rock's.

I started to pay attention to horse racing. I started watching it on television, reading about it in the papers, watching horses, watching jockeys. I'm not sure how, but I managed to convince Mum to buy *Pacemaker* magazine for me every week. It wasn't cheap, £2, which was a lot of money back then for a magazine. Racing took over my whole world. I would come home from Billy's on a Saturday afternoon, throw my stuff on the ground, go into the sitting room with my whip, get up on the leg of the sofa and ride a three-mile chase, whip flailing on the run-in and everything. I rode plenty of Gold Cup and Grand National winners on the leg of that sofa before I was 14.

As time went on, I started to go down to Billy's more often. I started going to point-to-points on Saturdays, leading up Billy's horses. That was fantastic. There was such a sense of being involved. Of course, I wasn't riding, I was only 13, riding a horse in a point-to-point was way beyond my 13-year-old ability, but leading the horses around the parade ring before the race, leading them in afterwards with the sweat and the steam and the rider covered in muck, being involved like that, I was living the dream.

There was only one way this was going. As time passed I only grew more interested in horses, more interested in Billy's, and less interested in school. Sometimes during the week, Billy would say that he had a few horses working after racing, and would I come along. I used to ask my dad if it was okay for me to go. I would never ask Mum, because I knew for sure what the answer would be.

Of course she would find out, and the rows would start. Mum would be trying to get me to go to school, but all I wanted was to go down to Billy's or go to the races. I would go to the races with Billy, or I would go in the lorry with the lads and the horses, and I would just be there to help out with the horses after racing. When I got a little older, I used to ride them in work on the racecourse after racing. You wouldn't get away with that now, I was only 13 or 14, so I shouldn't really have been riding on a racecourse, even if it wasn't in a race, but I didn't really know about that and, even if I had known, there is no way I would have cared.

Dad didn't say much. I suppose he was conflicted. He wanted me to pursue my dream of riding horses for sure, he knew how good Billy was for me, he knew how much I was learning, but at the same time there was probably a part of him that saw the benefit of me going to school, and there was a large part of him that didn't want to go against my mum. Most of the time, as Mum screamed at me and I screamed back, he would just sit there and say nothing.

The lads in school started to call me Lester. I used to play Gaelic football for the local GAA club, and the lads didn't call me Anthony or AP, just Lester. I loved that, I loved playing Gaelic football, and I loved going to play indoor soccer on Monday evenings – I thought I was the next Liam Brady or George Best. I was also going to be the next Alex Higgins or Dennis Taylor down at the snooker club, and I went through a phase of intending to be the next Barry McGuigan when the local youth club started getting the lads to do a bit of boxing. But racing took over, so football, snooker and boxing had to do without their Northern Irish world champion. I left the boxing to my brother Colm.

Everyone knew that when I wasn't at school, I was down at Billy Rock's riding horses. The lads knew it, the teachers knew it. PJ O'Grady was a fairly new principal at St Ulcan's, my secondary school, when I started going (or not going) there and he was on a mission to make his mark. He was a good guy, he looked a bit like Norman Wisdom, but he was the principal of my school, so it was my duty to have a mixture of fear, respect and loathing for him.

The parent–teacher meetings generally went okay. I was quiet in class, I wasn't disruptive, I didn't want to be there when I was there and I suppose I did my best to remain unnoticed. I didn't cause trouble, so the teachers generally seemed to be happy enough with me. Most of them probably didn't really even know that I was in their class.

I was at one of these parent–teacher meetings with Mum, probably moping around a little, not too happy about being there, when PJ O'Grady came up to me and Mum.

'He has to do his GCSEs,' I heard him say to Mum. 'Whatever happens, at the very least he has to do his GCSEs.'

I didn't pay too much heed. How were my GCSEs going to get me riding winners?

'And what do you want to be when you grow up?' he asked me.

'I want to be a jockey,' I mumbled, fairly inaudibly.

'A joiner?' said Mr O'Grady. 'Well there you go, you need your GCSEs if you want to be a joiner.'

I looked up at him sternly.

'I don't want to be a joiner,' I said. 'I want to be a jockey.'

'Well,' Mr O'Grady hesitated. 'You'll still need your GCSEs,' he said uncertainly. 'Look what happened to Lester Piggott. If he had done his GCSEs, he probably wouldn't have ended up in jail.'

I bit my lip, I didn't say anything, but I was livid. How could he say that about Lester Piggott, probably the best jockey in the world, ever?

Going home in the car I let fly to Mum, I couldn't believe that the principal would say that. I couldn't believe that anyone would say that. Who did Mr O'Grady think he was? How many Derby winners had he ridden? None, that's how many. Mum had to calm me down.

Life moves on though. PJ and I have since buried the hatchet. He's a good man, he only wanted what was best for me, or what he thought was best for me. Of course he was right, it was the right advice, it just wasn't what I wanted. We get on great now, and he follows my career very closely.

Back then, to tell someone in Moneyglass that you wanted to be a jockey was like telling them that you wanted to be an astronaut. That's how far removed from reality it was. Nobody around home was into racing. It wasn't a real career choice, it wasn't a real goal. I want to be a jockey when I grow up. Grand, now tell me what you really want to be. (Good lad, pat on the head.) Dreamer.

When I was at school, I quite liked Maths, I was quite good at it. I always thought that it was important to be able to count and add, and I didn't mind woodwork or metalwork or PE. But I just had no interest in them, and I never did my homework. If I did it at all, it was on the bus on the way in to school in the morning.

'Have you got your homework done?' Mum used to ask. Every single morning.

'Yeah,' I would mutter in response, knowing full well that she knew full well that I hadn't. I figured she thought she had to ask.

Looking back now, I don't really regret not going to school, or leaving at such a young age. It isn't the same for everyone and of course a young aspirant rider is better having a qualification behind him or her before embarking on the road into the unknown, but given how lucky I have been, given how well things have worked out for me, I wouldn't change a thing. I went to Jim Bolger's in 1990; if I had stayed in school then for another year or two, who knows how things would have panned out? I might not have got the opportunities that I did get, and my career might have taken a different path.

And I'm not sure that I would want to go back to school when I finish riding. Horses and racing is what I know, I have a lifetime's experience in racing, so why would I throw all that experience away and go back to do something new, when I would have to learn it from scratch? No, whatever I do after I hang up my boots, I'm sure it will be something with horses or racing.

Back then, there was an issue with the attendance officer as well, who had beaten a path to our door to discuss the issue of my sporadic school-going with my parents. Mum used to have to cover up for me. There were penalties for parents who didn't send their children to school for the requisite number of days, and Mum would often pretend that she didn't know where I was. It was okay when I eventually left to go to Jim Bolger's, even though initially I only went for two weeks. Mum was able to say that I was with a trainer in the Republic of Ireland, in a different jurisdiction, that she didn't hear from me. I'm sure the attendance officer thought that they were the worst parents in the world. If she did, she couldn't have been further from the truth.

I was all the while on the lookout for her as well. Once I was down at Billy's and this strange car pulled up at the gate. I was certain that it was the attendance officer, so I told Billy as much and went off to hide. Billy went down and gave the guy an earful.

'What are you doing?' Billy enquired. 'This is private property!'

'What do you mean?' asked the poor guy, petrified. 'I'm from the Electric Board, I'm just checking the electricity supply.'

'Ah right,' said Billy. 'On you go son.'

Billy didn't see the point of me continuing with school, and Billy's opinion meant the world to me. I took heed of everything he said, he couldn't do any wrong in my eyes, he was like a second father to me. When I was fighting with Mum about school, a lot of my sentences began with 'Rock says'.

'Rock says, Rock says,' my mother would repeat. 'I'll give you Rock says!'

Billy obviously saw something in me, a talent for riding horses, and he was convinced that I was going to make it as a rider. I didn't need any more information. If Billy Rock thought that I could make it as a jockey, then that was enough for me to believe it, and to work towards fulfilling his expectation.

As well as the horses, Billy was also big on the artificial insemination (AI) of cows. He was one of the main men for AI in cows in Northern Ireland, he worked for the Department of Agriculture and he set up a business importing semen from The Netherlands and Canada and re-selling it. He only had about 15 or 20 horses so, ironically, I'd say the majority of Billy's income came from AI, not from training racehorses. His theory was that, if I didn't make it as a jockey, if he was wrong about me or if injury or circumstances meant that I couldn't make a living as a jockey, he figured that he would teach me how to do AI, and I could make a living out of that.

Billy used to tell me to tell my mother not to worry, that if the jockey thing didn't work out, I could make a living bulling cows. He might even have been teaching me just to put my mother's mind at rest. Who knows? Billy was a very clever man. In reality, though, I never considered it as a real option. It was a safety net for sure, but I never really thought about the possibility that there would be a need for a fallback position. If you are doing a high-wire act, it's always good to have a safety net underneath you in case you are going to fall. However, if you are not going to fall, you don't actually need a safety net.

Foolishly and naively, I never really thought of the possibility that I wouldn't make it as a jockey. Foolishly and naively, I don't think Billy did either.

CHAPTER 3

How Far Away is Kilkenny?

The summer holiday of 1989 couldn't come soon enough. I felt like Huckleberry Finn as I faced into a summer of riding, racing and horses with Billy Rock.

The problem was that Billy's was about 11 miles from our house. Dad could take me on Saturdays, but during the week he was obviously working, so I had to make my own arrangements. It turned out the guy who owned the butcher's shop that was about two or three miles from Billy's used to drive past our front door on the way to his shop every morning, so I used to get a lift with him. Dad bought me a bike, a really good racing bike that had belonged to a friend of a friend of his who was emigrating to London, so I used to bring the bike with me, put it up onto the butcher's truck, and cycle the two or three miles from the butcher's shop to Billy's.

Unfortunately this arrangement didn't last the entire summer. For some reason, the butcher stopped going, or stopped taking me – maybe he couldn't put up with my incessant chattering every morning, he just couldn't shut me up – so I had to make my own way. It wasn't a problem; I just cycled the 11 miles. Billy could have been 111 miles away, I still would have cycled it.

A side-effect of working at Billy's was that I was earning money. Billy paid me £100 a week, which was huge money for a 15-year-old boy in rural Antrim back in the late 1980s with not much to spend it on. I didn't go out that much, I didn't really go to discos or pubs. If I went out at all, it was down to the local hall for a game of snooker. But you couldn't spend too much money in there, so I stayed relatively well off.

My older sisters, on the other hand, were mad into going out and they were always broke. I used to lend them money, but I made sure that they knew it was a loan, not a gift, and I used to keep track of all they owed me in a ledger. I took great pleasure in counting my money and checking the ledger to see how much they owed me, although I don't think they were that impressed.

I remember I lent money to Anne Marie to buy a suit for a wedding – £90 it cost her, funded entirely by me – a right little money lender, I was. A couple of weeks later, there was no obvious sign of her paying the money back, so I told her that the next time she took the suit off, I was taking it and selling it, and that I would put the proceeds towards the settlement of her debt.

*

Billy had five or six other lads working for him, which was a bit of a problem because Billy used to tell me what he wanted done and get me to tell the lads. He'd head off in the afternoons and leave me with the instructions on what he wanted done, so I'd have to tell the lads. I wasn't comfortable with it at all; it wasn't as if I had an air of authority about me either, and I certainly wasn't their boss. I did it though. I just told them that this was what Billy wanted done and I went on about my business.

Billy had a few horses at the time that were absolute lunatics. Unrideable they were, some of them. There was Eddie Wee, who was just fresh while coming back from injury, but there were others who were plain mad. I remember a horse called Joey Kelly, who was moderate but mad, and another, Dr Jekyll, who was well named, as he was also a bit of a lunatic. He won a couple of point-to-points all right, but he never won on the track.

Conor O'Dwyer and Brendan Sheridan and the late Anthony Powell used to ride most of Billy's horses on the track. Tom Taaffe rode a few as well, and Tony Martin rode some of his bumper horses. And they sometimes had difficulty with Billy's horses as well, so I didn't feel so bad. There was one day, in September 1990, when Anthony Powell rode Joey Kelly in a maiden hurdle at Down Royal, and he all but got run away with. Joey Kelly almost ran off the track – it didn't matter what Anthony did, he couldn't steer him.

A few years later, during the Punchestown Festival, there was a group of us in a Chinese restaurant in Naas, when Conor started telling a story about that day. There were a few of us just out for a bite to eat on one of the evenings. I hadn't been that long in the UK, I'd say I had been there just a couple of seasons, been champion jockey once or twice. Anyway, different people were telling different stories, and Conor pipes up, 'Here, I'll tell you a good one about your man there,' pointing at me, sitting in the corner, minding my own business.

Apparently that day at Down Royal, Conor and Anthony decided that they had had enough of riding Billy's horses that would all but run off the track, so they had a go at him.

'We're not riding these horses any more Willie,' they said. Conor called him Willie. 'They're unrideable. Someone is going to get injured.'

'Ah, what's wrong with ye?' Billy retorted. 'Wee Anthony has no problem with them. Wee Anthony rides those horses at home all the time.'

That was the start of Wee Anthony. If ever Conor or Anthony Powell had a problem with one of Billy's horses after that, Billy would always just say 'Wee Anthony doesn't have a problem with it.'

It got to the point where Conor was convinced that there was no such person as Wee Anthony, that he was a mythical figure that Billy had conjured in order to wind the lads up. Later on, after another particularly hair-raising ride, Conor had reached the end of the road.

'I'll tell you what you can do with this horse,' he told Billy. 'Get Wee Anthony to ride it. If Wee Anthony is that fucking good, there's no point in myself or Poweller riding it any more, is there?'

Conor thought no more of it. Later on, he did get to know about this young lad, Anthony McCoy, who was riding a bit for Jim Bolger, and he knew that Anthony McCoy went to England, joined Toby Balding, and was champion conditional, but it wasn't until near the end of the following season, when I was in the running to be champion jockey, that Conor heard about the Billy Rock connection.

Anthony McCoy – Wee Anthony! Wee Anthony had shown up.

*

I was spending more time at Billy's than I was at home. I always found Billy to be really easy company. I spent a lot of time with him that summer. He wouldn't have had that many horses in, it was predominantly a National Hunt yard and most of the good horses would have been off for their summer breaks, so I used to go around in the van a lot with Billy in the afternoons, going to different yards and farmers.

I could talk to him, he really was like a second father to me, and he was a knowledgeable, intelligent man who took no shit from anyone, it didn't matter who they were. He never spoke to me about riding technique, he never really tried to teach me how to ride, whether to ride long or short, tuck yourself in, loosen your grip, straighten your back, none of that, but I was starting to try to develop my own style by watching the top riders on television.

I watched as much flat racing as National Hunt, and I loved watching Steve Cauthen ride. The Kentucky Kid, Cauthen sprung to fame as Affirmed's jockey. In 1978, Affirmed and Cauthen won the American Triple Crown, the Kentucky Derby, the Preakness Stakes and the Belmont Stakes, when he was just 18. Remarkably, Affirmed was the last horse to win the Triple Crown.

Robert Sangster brought Cauthen over to the UK in 1979. Cauthen brought an American style with him, toes in the irons, low crouch, and he was a superb judge of pace. Time has always been a huge factor in American racing, how fast a horse can go in a race, how fast he can work; everything is timed, much more so than in the UK or Ireland at that stage, so when Cauthen was riding from the front, he was lethal. They used to say that he had a clock in his head.

I loved watching Mick Kinane ride as well. He was the most perfect jockey I had ever seen. You would rarely see Mick make a mistake, he would always have his horse in the right position through a race; he was stylish, strong in a finish.

Over jumps, of course I was a huge Richard Dunwoody fan; you couldn't have been a fan of National Hunt racing and not been a Richard Dunwoody fan. I also loved watching Conor O'Dwyer ride, although I never told him that. I suppose because he was riding Billy's horses a lot, I took particular interest in him. I thought he was a brilliant rider. He always gave a horse a ride, but if it wasn't the horse's day, he didn't subject it to a hard race. He didn't beat a horse up to finish fifth or sixth when he could give him an easy time and finish seventh or eighth, just keep him for another day.

I picked up a lot of things from watching other jockeys. For some reason, I always wanted to look good on a horse. It would be drilled into me later on when I went down to Jim Bolger's ('You might not be able to ride like a jockey, but the least you can do is try to look like one'), but even before I went to Jim's, I was always conscious of how I looked. I would have just my toes in the irons, like Steve Cauthen. The bottom of my stirrup would be on my toe as opposed to the ball of my foot. It just felt more stylish. Back straight.

I used to go around Billy's on a horse on sunny days and look at my reflection in car windows, checking myself out, making sure I was looking good. I don't know why, but I always believed, even as a child, that I could ride. Billy also thought I could ride. He used to call me the next John Francome.

Things were good that summer of 1989. I was down at Billy's every day, riding horses, doing what I loved doing, and getting £100 a week. It was at the start of that summer that Billy started talking to me about the possibility of going down to Jim Bolger's. He knew that, if I was going to make it as a jockey, he wasn't going to have enough horses for me. More than that, in order for me to have a chance of making it, he thought that I would have to leave Northern Ireland. He took me aside one day and told me as much.

'If you're really serious about being a jockey,' he told me, 'it's not going to work here. For a start you're too small to take out an amateur licence and go riding in point-to-points. You're too light. You're talented enough to go and join one of the big yards, take out an apprentice licence, ride on the flat, but obviously you would have to leave me here and leave your home. You need to decide what you want.'

As far as I was concerned, there was no decision to be made.

It must have been tough for Billy though. Here was I, this supposed talent that he had cultivated and nurtured, that he had seen progress, wholly and completely under his influence, and here he was telling me that I would have to leave, that he wasn't going to be able to help me get beyond a certain point, and that this point was rapidly approaching.

Billy knew John Oxx quite well. John Oxx is one of the top flat trainers in Ireland, and it would have been logical for Billy to ask John to take me. It would have been an easy phone call for Billy to have made: 'Hi John, I have the next riding sensation here, will you take him on for a couple of weeks, see what you make of him?' I'm sure John Oxx would have at least given me a trial.

But Billy thought that The Curragh might not be the place for a young wet-behind-the-ears aspiring jockey from Northern Ireland to learn his trade. I suppose he thought that life's temptations on The Curragh would be too great, too much of a distraction for a 15-year-old from deepest Antrim whose only real forays beyond the stable door were to a snooker hall or a football pitch.

Even then, Jim Bolger had a reputation. He was a top-class trainer of racehorses, a reputation well earned through his achievements with his horses, mainly with fillies at that time, like Give Thanks, Condessa, Park Express, Flame of Tara and Polonia. As much as he was regarded as an outstanding trainer, though, it was also well known that he operated a strict regime for the lads who worked for him. For starters, you went to Mass every Sunday and every morning during Lent. That was the type of regime it was. And you weren't allowed to drink or smoke. 'You can drink and you can smoke, I have no issue with that,' he used to say. 'You just won't be working here if you do.'

More than the rules, though, it was the fear of God that Jim struck in you. You would know that Jim was coming down to the yard because all the lads would scarper, just like the little fish do when a shark is approaching. There was no upside to being seen by Jim, only a potential downside. And those unfortunates who didn't have the wherewithal or the time to make themselves scarce grabbed a shovel or a fork or a yard brush and made themselves look busy. 'There's only one rule around here,' the older lads used to say. 'Always know where Jim is.'

Billy arranged for me to go down to Jim's for a two-week trial at the end of the summer. I was as excited as hell. Here I was, about to start working in a real racing yard, a top yard, working for Jim Bolger. Of course I knew how good a trainer Jim was, of the success that he'd had already as a trainer – and there was much more to follow in subsequent years – and I believed Billy when he told me that this was my stepping stone to making it as a jockey.

Mum and Dad drove me down to Jim's place on a Sunday evening in August. The journey from Moneyglass to Kilkenny is long enough, even with all the motorways and the bypasses and the general upgrading of the infrastructure in the Republic of Ireland, but back then it was a nightmare of a journey. Even so, Mum and Dad wanted to come with me to see my set-up.

It was about five o'clock on a sunny summer's Sunday evening when we finally found Jim Bolger's place. We had a quick look around, immaculate yard, and then we were given directions to Mrs Delaney's house, my digs. It was a far cry from home, about 14 or 15 lads staying there. Bedlam.

Mum was sad leaving me that evening. I wasn't too bad, I knew it was only for two weeks, so I just got on with it. I was desperately homesick during those two weeks, but I knew I was going home at the end of it however I got on, and I knew that I was getting great experience, so I just put my head down and kicked on.

One of the biggest problems was getting from the digs to the yard. They were about two miles apart, and only a couple of the lads in the digs had a car. There was a pub down the road from the digs, The Bus, and a couple of us used to walk down to The Bus in the morning and try to get a lift from someone up to the yard. Luckily, I struck up a good friendship with one of the lads, Conor Everard, quite quickly. Conor was a good rider, and Jim gave him plenty of opportunities. He won the Phoenix Stakes in 1996 on Mantovanni for Jim, and he won the

Golden Pages Handicap on Graduated. Conor and I became really good friends, and it wasn't just because he had a car, although that was no deterrent. He had one of these old vans with no seats in the back, so he used to pile a load of us into the back every morning and drive all of us to the yard.

I thought my two weeks went well. I didn't see Jim that much; all of my dealings were with the head man in the yard, Dave Downey. Like at Billy's, I just did whatever I was asked to do, groom a horse, rake or sweep a yard, muck out a box. I didn't mind. I do remember Jim talking to me once.

'What's your name?' he asked.

'Anthony McCoy,' I told him.

'Anthony McCoy,' he repeated slowly and thoughtfully. 'Billy Rock tells me you're going to be the next John Francome.'

I wasn't sure if it was a question or not. Even if it was, I wasn't sure what the correct answer was, so I just said nothing.

'We'll see if you are.'

I went home after my two weeks were up, back to working with Billy, and didn't really think much more about Jim's. I was with Billy for what was left of the summer until, ultimately and inevitably, September came around again and with it the start of the new school year, and with that the rows with my mother.

I went back to school for the first week, then I took one day off the second week to go to Billy's, I took two or three days off the third week, and by the fourth week, I was more or less gone. Mum tried really hard to get me to stay at school, but it was no use. I was 15 and I knew my own mind. I couldn't see the point. I was going to be a jockey and I couldn't see any way in which going to school was going to help me down that road.

There was the attendance officer to contend with, and I know there was trouble there. I have no idea how my mum got around that one, but as far as I was concerned, it didn't matter. I was going to be a jockey, and I had every confidence that my mum was going to be able to sort out the attendance officer.

Mum told her that I had left home, that I was gone to the Republic, down with Jim Bolger in Kilkenny. Kilkenny was a million miles from Moneyglass in those days, different jurisdiction, so maybe the attendance officer figured that I wasn't her problem any more, if I was down south. She obviously didn't know that I was in Cullybackey, just 11 miles up the road.

I worked with Billy all through that winter, getting put up on these mad horses, getting bucked off, but I still believed that I could ride them. April came around quite quickly, and with it the prospect of working for Jim Bolger on a more permanent basis. Billy had been on to Jim again, who was happy to give me an apprenticeship after my two-week trial.

I was sad about a lot of things. I wasn't yet 16, yet here I was heading out into the big world. Even at the time, I did appreciate the enormity of it all. I thought of all my friends at home, I was probably never going to spend that much time with them again. I thought about the fact that I was probably never going to live at home again with Mum and Dad, or with my sisters or my brother. Kelly was only six at the time, she was a child, so I was going to miss seeing her growing up.

So all of that was going around in my head, but overriding it all was my burning ambition to make it as a jockey. Billy was right about that, as he was about a lot of things: if I was going to make it, I needed to leave Moneyglass. I could see that quite clearly. I hadn't even thought about going to England at this stage, I just knew that I needed to leave home.

Mum was sad. Even to this day, she blames Jim Bolger for stealing my childhood from her. Not from me, but from her. She says that if she had her time again, she wouldn't have let me go. I'm not sure that she would have been able to stop me, nor that she would have wanted to stop me, given how strong my desire was, but she still regrets the fact that I didn't grow into an adult at home under her gaze.

I consoled myself and her with the notion that, if it didn't work out, I would come back home. I always had the safety net of going back to work with Billy, either riding out or bulling cows, or maybe a combination of both. But in reality, I knew myself. There was no way I was going to return from Kilkenny a failure, no matter how badly things worked out. I would have perished on Jim Bolger's gallops rather than return home with my tail between my legs. As it turned out, I nearly did.

CHAPTER 4

Master of Cool

These days, it takes about three and a half hours to get from Moneyglass to Jim Bolger's yard in Coolcullen, County Kilkenny. Back then, though, it took about five hours, and that was if you didn't get held up at the border. If you thought Moneyglass was remote, welcome to Coolcullen. Jim himself used to regularly get lost on his way home after he first moved into the place. He says that if someone arrives at the front door and tells you he was just passing, that person is apt to be a liar.

Jim was and is one of the best racehorse trainers in the world, but he is unusual in that he is a trainer who has built up a really strong breeding operation. A lot of the horses that are owned by Jim's wife Jackie – the horses that you now see racing in her familiar white and purple silks – have been bred by Jim himself.

Jim set up his breeding operation because he figured that he was losing out by not doing so. Here he was, he thought, training these horses that he had bought, winning top races, but then, when he went back to the sales to try to buy brothers or sisters to these horses, he couldn't afford them, precisely because their siblings had done so well under his care. The value of the entire family had gone up. So Jim thought, why not breed them himself? If he did, he would be the breeder with the mare whose offspring would be more sought-after and therefore more valuable because of the exploits of the foals that had gone before.

Originally from Oylgate in County Wexford, Jim studied accountancy for a while, but didn't complete his final exams. He started off training show jumpers, figured he wasn't good enough to compete at the highest level, and switched his attention to racehorses. Actually, he used to train out of the Phoenix Park in Dublin, as did Christy Grassick and Noel Chance and a couple of others, before the Pope's visit to Ireland in 1979, and in particular the Mass, preparations for which put an end to the training of racehorses there. Jim moved to Coolcullen in County Kilkenny, which is quite ironic, given Jim's passion for Wexford hurling and the arch-rivalry that exists on the hurling pitch between Kilkenny and Wexford.

In the early days, Jim majored on fillies, simply because, he says, he couldn't afford to buy colts. But he won most of the top racing prizes in Ireland with those fillies, as well as races in the UK, France, Italy, and later on, Hong Kong. Later, in 1992, he proved that he could train colts as well when he won the Irish Derby and the King George with St Jovite, and he trained two of the best colts of the last decade in champion two-year-old Teofilo and Derby winner New Approach.

At the time Jim didn't really have the reputation for producing talented young riders or horsemen or women that he has now, so it was a fair call from Billy to try to get me an apprenticeship with him. There was also the reputation that Jim was developing for valuing discipline. There were two ways to do things at Jim's, Jim's way and the wrong way, and if you chose the latter, you didn't generally last very long there.

Robbie Supple and Dean Gallagher were away riding in the UK, and they had spent time in Jim's, but a star-studded list of horse people was to follow. Aidan O'Brien was there when I was there. Aidan later took over the reins at the world-renowned Ballydoyle stables shortly after Vincent O'Brien retired, and he is widely recognised as one of the best racehorse trainers in the world. Aidan was great with horses, and Jim loved him. Aidan used to ride all the difficult ones, and if there was a problem with something, Jim would get Aidan to sort it out. They say that Aidan is the only person who ever left Jim's who Jim was sorry to see leave.

Christy Roche was there, the stable jockey. Also there were Seamie Heffernan Kevin Manning, David Wachman, Willie Supple and Ted Durkan. Paul Carberry was there as well, although, unlike the rest of us, Paul probably succeeded in racing in spite of the time he spent at Jim's, not because of it. Paul Nolan arrived at Jim's the day Aidan O'Brien left, Paddy Brennan would arrive later. The Jim Bolger Alumni reads like a Who's Who of horse racing.

It was tough arriving at Jim's that day in April. This was different to the two-week spell that I had spent there the previous August. That was a temporary thing, I knew it was ending and I knew that I was going home; it was almost like a holiday. I had thrown a couple of things into a bag and headed off. This time, I was leaving home. I took most of my possessions with me. My room at home was no longer my room. This was for real, this was life, this was make or break, sink or swim.

It was very difficult in the beginning. I was dreadfully homesick. For the first couple of nights, I cried myself to sleep. I missed home desperately, I missed Mum and Dad, I missed going up to Billy's, I missed the familiarity, I even missed my sisters. I was in a man's world, a 15-year-old, left to fend for himself, fight for himself, make his own way, get himself noticed.

Mrs Delaney's place hadn't improved any in the eight months since I had last been there. It was still a free-for-all in the kitchen in the morning. You'd try to grab a cup of tea and a piece of toast. A cup of tea was usually okay, but it was always touch and go if you did or didn't get a piece of toast. The slow movers didn't eat and the slow eaters got even thinner.

Conor Everard was still there, so I used to get a lift with him most mornings. Conor was one of my good mates there, as were Calvin McCormack and TJ Comerford. TJ was a local lad, he lived just up the road from Jim's. He went looking for a summer job at Jim's when he was 12, but didn't get it. He went back again the following year, intent on asking Jim himself. He cycled up to Coolcullen one Friday evening at the end of the summer of 1987, jumped over the gate, ignored the sign that said beware of the dog, and knocked on the big red door. Fortunately, Jim himself answered.

'And who are you?' he enquired.

'TJ Comerford. My family has a farm up the road.'

'And what do you want?' asked Jim.

'I was wondering if you would have any jobs going,' said TJ hesitantly.

'When could you start?'

'I suppose I could start on Monday.'

Jim looked at TJ disapprovingly.

'And what's wrong with now?'

TJ stared back blankly. Nothing, he supposed. Five years later, he was still there.

TJ spent a couple of years with the trainer Mary Reveley in the north of England after he left Jim's, he rode for her when she had all those good horses, Cab On Target and Morgans Harbour and Seven Towers, before going home and working for Aidan O'Brien down in Ballydoyle, which is where he is now. He was and is a very good friend. He was groomsman at my wedding and he comes over to stay with me for about a month every year.

Conor wasn't a great fellow for getting up in the mornings, and I was desperate that I wouldn't be late, so I'd be trying to get a lift off one of the other lads, or walking down to The Bus and trying my luck. It was all a bit stressful every morning, wondering how I was going to get to Jim's.

You couldn't be late, that was for sure. And you had to look good. Boots cleaned, real riding boots, not Wellington boots or anything, and you had to wear jodhpurs, none of your jeans here. As I said, Jim was anxious that you looked good even if you couldn't ride to save your life.

You'd have your four or five horses to muck out in the morning before work, then you'd tack up first lot and get ready to ride out, then the yard had to be swept and raked before breakfast. Then you rode out another two or three lots, then you swept and raked the yard before lunch. Then you came back after lunch and did your horses, and the yard had to be swept and raked again. So basically before you scratched yourself, the yard had to be swept and raked. Everything had to be spotless. There was no such thing as, ah it'll wait, or I'll do it after lunch. That just didn't work.

There would be plenty of craic in the mornings, plenty of banter, lads slagging each other, but that would all stop as soon as Jim showed up. It was remarkable; lads who were full of chat when Jim wasn't there would go as quiet as church mice. It was like the headmaster had just walked into the room.

So we'd be circling there, just walking around the yard before going out, and there wouldn't be a peep. Twenty-five or 30 horses, 25 or 30 lads, young fellows who should be full of the joys of life, and not a word. You could hear the birds singing. Every morning you could hear the birds singing.

All the horses' tack had to look good as well. Shiny bridles, clean saddles, bridles fitted properly. I've been to other yards where lads would be riding out with bridles hanging off horses, but not at Jim's. And every horse had to be ridden. Even walking around before going onto the gallop, he wanted every horse ridden, no big loop in the reins, no laid-back sauntering around, you had to ride even when you were walking, horses' heads down. Jim wanted horses to use their muscles even when they were walking around before going out to exercise. There wasn't much you could do if the horse wanted to put his head in the air, but Jim wanted every horse's head down so, as far as he was concerned, if your horse's head wasn't down, it was your fault.

Jim would know all the horses. I suppose you should know all the horses individually if you are training them, but I was impressed that he did. And if he saw a new lad on one of the horses, as happened frequently, he would stop them and take them out the back of the canteen to have a chat with them, to welcome them.

'What's your name?'

'Anthony McCoy.' We had been here before.

'How are you? How are your parents?'

'All fine, thanks.'

'You're back now for good, are you?' he said. 'Well, this is where the real work starts.' The Gospel according to Jim.

He was very nice in the beginning, that's for sure. Very pleasant, he'd talk to you about being a jockey, about being an apprentice, about what you could expect working for him, the rides you would get. Then you signed up to be his apprentice, and he had you.

He didn't get everybody though. I saw lads coming in for the first time at seven o'clock on a Monday morning and leaving at breakfast time.

I learned so much there. Things that I learned at Jim's are still with me today. Simple things, like having your boots clean. I don't ride out that much these days, but when I do, I make sure my riding boots are clean. I would hate to be looking down at dirty boots. And you see lads riding out in mucky filthy boots, and you're thinking, would you not just clean your boots? Why wouldn't you just give them a wipe before coming to ride out?

Or fitting a bridle properly. Sometimes I'd be riding a horse in a race, not just in work, and the bridle would be hanging off him. I have to ask the starter to come over and fix the bridle and I'm thinking, Jim would be going ballistic. If you hadn't the bridle fitted properly just for riding out at home, he'd go ballistic. If it happened at the races – well, it just wouldn't happen with one of his horses.

Or making ground up a hill. I remember making ground up the hill at Clonmel one day. It was only my third or fourth ride. I made ground going up the hill on the far side, I thought it was the right thing to do, and I got a bollocking from Jim when I came back in. It's something I'll always remember. I don't make ground going up a hill if I can avoid it.

'Is it harder to run up a hill or down a hill?'

'Up a hill, boss.'

'Well why would you try to make ground going up the hill then? Do you think that's harder for a horse or easier?'

I was mad keen to learn everything when I first got to Jim's, I lapped everything up, I was a hoover for knowledge. However, as time went on and I got a bit older and thought I was getting a bit wiser, there were times when I hated it. Jim had a reason for everything that he did or he had you do. Like after my first ride on the racecourse, I thought great, here we go, I've had my first ride, now my next one will be soon, and then another and then another and I'll be on my way. But no. That wasn't Jim's way. You'd have one ride, that would keep you sweet, whet your appetite, but then you'd wait another three or four months before you had your next ride. You'd have to work hard to earn your next ride. You'd be champing at the bit, dying to know when your next ride would be, but you had to be patient, that was Jim's way. There was a television documentary made about Jim in 2010 and they called it Jim Bolger, Master of Cool. It was well-named.

You'd get a bollocking for the slightest thing. Jim loved giving people a bollocking, and he had a way of doing it that would really annoy you. I was only a kid at the time, but I saw him make grown men cry. He'd pick you out after you did the slightest thing wrong, and he'd get you to take your horse out the back.

'Why did you do that?' he'd go.

'Dunno, boss.'

'You're a gobshite. What are you?'

He would get us to repeat it.

'I'm a gobshite, boss.'

I'm not joking. It seems incredible thinking back on it now. Grown men standing there like school children.

'You're a fool. What are you?'

'I'm a fool, boss.'

One of his favourite punishments was getting you to work on Sunday. You'd get the slightest thing wrong, that's it, you're working this Sunday. And if you protested at all, if you started claiming that you had been unjustly treated, you'd get the next Sunday as well. And the next and the next if you kept protesting. You could end up working for three months in a row without a day off just for one misdemeanour.

Some lads suffered more than others. Seamie Heffernan was a desperate man for getting into trouble, and he was even worse at answering back. I saw Seamie line up about six Sundays' work in a row in just one disagreement with Jim. Actually I don't think Seamie had a Sunday off that year.

Of course, you wouldn't get paid for working those Sundays. Not that we got paid much as it was: £90 a week, less £35 to Mrs Delaney for your digs. It was a different life then, £55 for the week. We were broke all the time. And you were apprenticed to Jim for three years, so you had no prospect of moving on or progressing somewhere else. Once you had signed on the dotted line, you had to wait at least three years before you could move on. You had signed up to the whole lot, £90 a week and all, although I don't think the bollockings were in the contract.

And yet, if someone was to ask me now, if they had a young fellow or girl who was trying to get into racing, where they should send their kid, I would say Jim Bolger's. No question. The grounding that I got there was invaluable, a solid foundation for a career in racing. He probably wouldn't admit it, but I think Jim has mellowed. He said to me recently that he wouldn't get away now with the way he treated his staff then. That said, in all my years with Jim, I never saw anybody telling him where to get off.

Gordon Strachan has spoken about the time that he played for Aberdeen when Alex Ferguson was manager. He talked about the mixture of fear and respect that Ferguson used to engender in his players. In one sense, you were afraid of your life to make a mistake, but in another, you wanted to play well for him. If you made a mistake in the first half, you knew you were in for a bollocking at half-time.

He said that you'd come into the dressing room at half-time and sit on the bench, looking down at the ground. You'd fix your gaze on a spot on the ground, and you wouldn't move your head in case you attracted the manager's attention unnecessarily. You'd hear his footsteps, then you'd see his shiny black polished shoes as he came into the dressing room. Everybody would freeze and go silent... He'd pace up and down in front of you, go past you, come back, stop at you, then the shoes turned in so that they were pointing right at you. You knew you were in for it.

I can imagine that playing for Sir Alex was similar to riding for Jim. You were afraid of your life to do something wrong, but rather than halting your progress or paralysing you, it was that mix of fear and respect that spurred you on to perform. Interestingly, that Aberdeen team of the 1980s broke the dominance in Scotland of Celtic and Rangers that went before and that continues today, winning three Scottish League titles, two Scottish Cups and a European Cup Winners' Cup.

Jim had some great lads working for him as well. As well as the riders, Aidan O'Brien, Christy Roche and their like, Dave Downey and Pat O'Donovan were there as well, and they were brilliant. If someone were to ask me to train horses for them in the morning, if Sheikh Mohammed or John Magnier were to ring me (highly likely, I know) and ask me to train their horses for them, I'd say get me Dave Downey and Pat O'Donovan. I don't care what it costs, I want those two lads.

Either of them could run any yard in the country.

After a while I moved digs, from Mrs Delaney's to Mrs Murphy's. It was a better set-up at Mrs Murphy's. There weren't 14 lads scrapping over a piece of toast in the morning for starters. There were only seven of us there at one time: Pat O'Donovan was there when I moved in, Willie Supple was there, also Adrian Regan, Ted Durcan, Paul Carberry and Calvin McCormack.

The craic was good. Our social scene, such as it was, centred mainly around The Bus as it was close. We used to walk down in the evenings and just hang out, play pool. I didn't drink or smoke. I never really wanted to smoke, it never appealed to me and, for better or for worse, I never really liked the taste of alcohol. Even now, I don't drink. Of course, despite Jim's rules, there were lots of lads who drank and smoked off campus, so to speak, but I didn't.

I remember being in The Bus a couple of nights, with the lads trying to get me to try different drinks and to keep drinking them, but I never really liked the taste of any of them, so I didn't bother. I just thought, not for me, and then I thought I would probably be better off without it anyway. And I think I was probably right. I'm quite glad now that I didn't like the taste of alcohol and that I decided not to drink. I don't think it's good for your body, it can't be, and I think that my body is in better condition now than it would have been if I'd been drinking and smoking.

There was a nightclub in Kilkenny, Itchycoo Park, or just 'The Coo' to the locals, to which we used to go regularly. There were enough lads with cars to take us all, so we'd all pile in, all the lads off to Kilkenny for the night. Usually we'd drop into the local chipper in Kilkenny, Supermacs, afterwards for a burger and chips, and then it was back into the car and home. That was if you didn't get lucky, which was pretty much every night.

The lads were great, but the competition for rides was intense. Christy Roche was a stable jockey, so he rode everything he could ride. Willie Supple was champion apprentice, and he was kind of second jockey after Christy, so he rode everything else. After that, there was a host of hungry wannabe jockeys scrambling around for the scraps. Seamie Heffernan was well enough established, so he was probably ahead of the rest of us, then there was Paul, who was Tommy Carberry's son and had been riding as an amateur, so you probably felt that he was ahead of you as well. There was a guy called Mick Martin who used to come in every summer whom Jim used to love, he was going to be an apprentice as well, and I always felt that he got more of a chance than I did. Then there was the rest of us. There were about 10 apprentices, including Tommy O'Leary, Stephen Kelly, Declan Quirke, Conor Everard, Ted Durkan and Calvin McCormack. How the hell was I ever going to get a ride?

I never thought of giving up, despite how bleak my prospects looked sometimes. There were plenty of times I thought that I should be leaving, that I wasn't going to get the opportunities at Jim's, but for one thing, I was apprenticed to him for three years, so I couldn't go anywhere else and get rides. For another, Billy Rock had sent me there; he had said that this was the right place for me, so it must have been. On top of that, I always believed that I was as good as the other lads who were getting rides. In my own head, I just had this idea that I was as good as anybody and that eventually the opportunities would come. I was right.

CHAPTER 5

Getting Going

Here's how it worked: if you were riding the following day, a message came down to the yard for you to call the office. Every morning, when you knew that we had runners the following day, you held your breath. Maybe today. But every morning was a disappointment. It was like standing in a line in the schoolyard, seeing other lads getting picked for the football team, and desperately hoping you'd be next. Then one Friday morning, on the last day of August 1990, I was next.

Nordic Touch was an easy horse to ride, but he wasn't very good. He had run 10 times already that season, his first season racing, and he hadn't won. He had finished second on his previous run though, for Willie Supple at Tralee just three days before I was to ride him at the Phoenix Park, and he was well enough fancied. It didn't really matter; I was just delighted to have got the call, thrilled to have a ride.

I went to the races in the lorry with the horses; I was leading up other runners as well on the day. Nordic Touch was due to carry 7 st 2 lb but, because I hadn't ridden a winner (or a runner) before, I was allowed to claim 10 lb off him, so he would only have 6 st 6 lb on his back. I wasn't sure what weight I would have been, I knew I was close to that, so I didn't have any breakfast that morning, and I remember weighing out, 6 st 4 lb, perfect, a 2 lb saddle and I was right.

I walked the track before racing with Tom Gallagher, the travelling head lad, father of former jockey Dean Gallagher, and Christy Roche. Christy was riding another horse in the race – he obviously couldn't do the weight on Nordic Touch – and I remember Tom telling me to keep an eye on Christy.

Dad and Billy made their way down from home to the races that day, which was great. I remember getting my photograph taken with them, and Jim had organised for me to have my photograph taken in my silks as well. Later, after I was champion jockey a couple of times, when Jim was ever asked if he had spotted my potential early on, I have heard him say that he must have thought that I was good because he organised for me to have my photograph taken when I was having my first ride. I'm not sure about that one. I'm not sure that he thought I was that special, that he didn't organise to have photographs taken of all the lads when they were having their first ride.

Of course I was nervous, I was nervous the whole day, but Willie Supple brought me into the weigh room, introduced me to the valets, made sure I was all right. Then I weighed out, went out to the paddock, got legged up, got down to the start, into the stalls and whoosh! It was all over.

I don't remember anything about the race. Six furlongs, a minute and 11 seconds up the Phoenix Park, it doesn't last very long. Keep an eye on Christy, track Christy. Are you joking? It was all I could do to keep an eye on myself. Tactics? No chance. I just sat on the horse for a couple of furlongs, then tried to ride a finish. Fourteen runners, we finished seventh. I never rode Nordic Touch in a race again, and he never won one. Eighteen runs in his career, no wins.

I thought I was off and running then, I thought now I'd had my first ride, they would start to flow. But no. That wasn't Jim's way. I was six weeks mucking around the yard before I got another message to phone the office. It was a frustrating six weeks before my next opportunity. When it came, it was at The Curragh at the end of October in a nursery, a handicap for two-year-olds, on Nordic Wind. I remember that race well because Willie Supple beat me on another horse of Jim's owned by Michael Smurfit, Heavy Beat.

I was gutted. My overriding feeling wasn't one of excitement, my second-ever ride and I've finished second; I was disappointed that I hadn't won, disgusted with Willie Supple for beating me by a length, when he knew that I had never ridden a winner.

If I was progressing at Jim's, it was very slowly. I was asked to ride a lot of the difficult horses. I didn't think too much of it at the time, it was no different to how it was at Billy's and I was probably the only fool who would ride them, but I suppose with hindsight it wasn't a bad thing, it might have been a measure of how capable the head lads thought I was.

There were these ponies in a field down the road, wild ponies, mad ponies, and we always talked about getting on them and trying to ride them. It's ridiculous, there we were, working with horses all day, riding some of the best racehorses in the country, and all we could talk about was going down to this farmer's field and trying to ride the wild ponies in it.

One day we did. Carberry and TJ and a couple of the other lads and I headed down and said that we'd ride them. We nicked a load of bridles out of the yard so that we could put them on the ponies. When I think about it now – it was crazy. To take bridles out of Jim Bolger's yard to put them on a couple of wild ponies! We did manage to catch them, and we did manage to ride them, but if they looked wild in the field as we just looked at them, they were even wilder when we tried to ride them. No major surprise there then. None of us managed to stay on for very long, we all came off, but it was all a good laugh, which was fine as long as Jim didn't know about it.

Then Carberry turned white and started vomiting. He must have fallen awkwardly. We got very worried for him, but we couldn't tell anybody as we couldn't let anybody know that we had been riding these ponies. So we carried him home to Mrs Murphy's and put him to bed. He didn't look good though, he was still as white as a sheet. Everybody was very concerned, we thought about calling a doctor or an ambulance, but that would have been a disaster – Jim would have found out and we would have been in serious trouble. So we thought we'd take the risk on Paul's behalf, leave him in bed and hope he'd get better. Unfortunately, he didn't. He continued being sick, and he started pissing blood. We had to call an ambulance for him at two o'clock in the morning. Luckily he was okay, but we weren't.

There were some good horses at Jim's at the time. Star Of Gdansk, owned by Henryk de Kwiatkowski, won his maiden at The Curragh on his racecourse debut on Derby weekend in 1990, and he went on to finish second, beaten just a head by Fourstars Allstar, in the Irish 2000 Guineas the following year, and to finish third behind Generous in both the Epsom Derby and the Irish Derby. He was probably the first top-class colt that Jim ever had. All his best horses before Star of Gdansk were fillies.

Jet Ski Lady won the Oaks in 1991 at 50/1, the soft ground at Epsom playing to her strengths and Christy Roche kicking on early, sure of her stamina. Then St Jovite came along. He was an unbelievably classy colt, he always showed lots of ability at home, he won his first three races as a two-year-old in 1991, then he finished second behind Dr Devious in the 1992 Epsom Derby before beating him in the Irish Derby, winning by 12 lengths in a record time. Then he went and won the King George.

Before St Jovite, Jim had a reputation as a trainer of fillies, not of colts, although Jim always maintained that if you could train fillies you could train anything. St Jovite proved to the world that Jim knew how to handle a top-class colt. I remember, later on after Jim had trained Teofilo to win the Dewhurst in 2006, a racing journalist asking Jim if Teofilo was the best colt he'd ever had. Jim looked back at him square in the eye, deadpan, and said: 'Sure. I've only had two.'

Jim had some good National Hunt horses about the place at the time as well, like Condor Pan, who had won the Bula Hurdle at Cheltenham in 1988, and Nordic Surprise, who won the Irish Champion Hurdle at Leopardstown in 1991 as a four-year-old, and Chirkpar, Dr Michael Smurfit's horse, who finished second in the 1991 Triumph Hurdle and who beat Morley Street in the Irish Champion Hurdle in 1992.

He had two really good two-year-olds that I used to ride out in 1994, my last year with Jim, Desert Style and Eva Luna. Desert Style was a gorgeous colt, a real racehorse, owned by Maktoum Al Maktoum, Sheikh Mohammed's eldest brother, whereas Eva Luna was a plain-looking thing with a big white face, owned by David and Catherine Shubotham, but I think Jim had a share in her as well. Both of them were going for the Heinz 57 Stakes in August 1994, the big Group 1 two-year-old at Leopardstown, now the Phoenix Stakes and now run at The Curragh, and both of them were unbeaten. Desert Style had won his maiden and a winners' race, while Eva Luna had won all four of the races she had contested, including the Group 3 Railway Stakes at The Curragh on Derby weekend, in which she had beaten a good colt of Robert Sangster's, Helmsman.

On the Friday before the Heinz, Jim took me aside.

'You know those two horses are running in the Heinz on Sunday?' he said to me.

'I do, boss.'

'Which of them do you think will win it?' he asked.

'The colt will win, boss.'

I liked Desert Style better. He was a much better-looking horse than Eva Luna, and I thought he was a classy colt, but Jim wasn't happy with my answer. He looked at me disapprovingly.

'You're a fool,' he said. 'I don't even know why I asked you.'

Sure enough, Sunday came along, the Heinz 57 Stakes, down the old straight six furlongs at Leopardstown (the one on which part of the M50 now sits), both horses ran well, but Eva Luna beat Desert Style. Eva Luna won the race under Kevin Manning with Desert Style finishing five lengths behind her in third, the Dermot Weld-trained Sharp Point splitting the pair of them.

I knew what was coming.

Monday morning, first lot, we're walking around before going out onto the gallops, Jim comes down, all is quiet, watches us for a little while, then calls me, tells me to pull my horse out the back.

'Were you watching the racing yesterday?' he asks.

'I was, boss.'

'Do you know what won the Heinz?'

'I do, boss.'

'Did I not ask you on Friday which horse would win the Heinz?'

'You did, boss.'

It was like you were spiralling out of control, down the helter skelter, nothing you could do about it, absolutely helpless, into the pit of abuse that was inevitably awaiting your arrival.

'And what did you tell me?' he asks me.

'I told you that the colt would win, boss,' I said.

You just had to go along with it. There was no point in trying to stop yourself, no point in trying to fight the force of gravity.

'Now wouldn't I be some trainer if I was listening to you?' he said. I was sure that one didn't need an answer. 'You're riding those two horses every day since they came into the yard, and you can't tell me which of them is better. And I'm only looking at them, and I know that the filly is better than the colt.'

'Yes, boss. You're great, boss. You're the best trainer in the world, boss.' Of course I didn't say any of that out loud. My inner thoughts were very brave. Ironically, Eva Luna didn't win another race.

I was getting the odd ride for Jim, but I wasn't getting any closer to riding a winner. Strange how your expectations change. Before you get a ride, all you want is a ride, then when you get one or two, all you want is a winner. As I would later discover, as soon as you get one or two winners, all you want is one or two more, one or two hundred more, one or two thousand more.

Jim would always tell you that the horse you were riding had a good chance of winning, but I'm not sure about that. I'm sure he was just getting a handicap mark for them. You'd ride a couple of two-year-olds at the end of the season, they'd finish down the field, and Jim would put them away for the winter so that they would have a handicap mark when they returned as three-year-olds the following year. Then they'd win as three-year-olds, they'd win a couple of races, and Jim wouldn't be able to resist.

'And you couldn't win on him last year as a two-year-old,' he'd say.

'That's because you never trained him,' you wouldn't say.

Legal Steps was just another juvenile that I used to ride at home. She didn't race as a two-year-old, but she was ready to run early in her three-year-old year. She was declared for a 12-furlong maiden at Thurles on 26th March 1992, and I got the call up to ride her.

She wouldn't have impressed you at home, that's for sure. She had no gears, which is probably why she was running in a 12-furlong maiden on her racecourse debut as a three-year-old and not a six-furlong maiden. We had another filly in the race as well, Northmaid, a filly who had run reasonably well to finish third in a maiden at Navan the previous October. Christy was riding her, she was a 4/1 shot, while my filly was a 20/1 shot, and not too big a price at that.

I don't remember too much about the race. I remember a girl called Sarah Walsh led me up, and I remember winning by a long way as there were no other horses around me when I passed the winning post in front. It took a while to sink in. All I had wanted was to ride a winner, but then, when it happened, I couldn't believe it. It was as if, after it happened, I looked back and thought that I never fully believed that I could ride one, that I could never get on a horse that would be good enough to win a race.

I remember going back to Jim's in the lorry that evening and thinking that I was halfway there. A winner in the bag, now I'm a jockey, now I'm on my way to making a career out of this. This is just the beginning.

The lads were great. Paul, Calvin and I had started around the same time; Paul had already ridden his first winner on a horse called Petronelli two years previously, so I was a fair way behind him, but Calvin hadn't. I'm not sure that Calvin ever rode a winner for Jim actually, but they were both delighted for me, as were all the lads. There was good banter, and there was plenty of competition for rides, but also great camaraderie at Jim's.

It had been a long time coming. It was two years after I had joined Jim before I rode my first winner. Imagine telling a young lad now, joining a yard for the first time, that he wouldn't ride a winner for two years. He'd say thanks and good luck, I'm off somewhere else.

There are lots of good young riders who come along these days, ride a winner, ride another winner, dying to get going, ride another, then another, then suddenly their claim has been reduced to 5 lb, then to 3 lb. A young rider's claim is a huge asset. A young rider is allowed to claim off the horses that he rides in order to compensate for his inexperience. So if a 5 lb-claimer is riding a horse that is set to carry 10 st 10 lb, that horse will only have to carry 10 st 5 lb. Good young riders who are able to claim are in huge demand.

But while that is great for the young rider, it can also be a problem. The more winners you ride, the more your claim reduces. If you keep riding away and keep riding winners, suddenly your claim is down to 5 lb, then 3 lb, then gone. You are competing on a level playing pitch with the top professionals. If you ride out your claim before you get properly established, then you can be in trouble. Your career can perish on the rocks, like a firework, dazzling light, then gone. Better the slow burn. Of course, when you are a young fellow, it is difficult to see the big picture; all you want to do is to get going, to get rides, to get winners.

Jim could see the big picture though. I had 22 more rides that season, but no winners.

CHAPTER 6

Broken Leg, Shattered Dreams

Kly Green was nothing special, but he did have the potential to be a decent two-year-old in the winter of 1992/93. He was a Green Desert colt – owned, like Jet Ski Lady and Desert Style, by Maktoum Al Maktoum – who was always a bit fresh and keen in the morning, and consequently he was one of those horses that I used to ride out a fair bit. This particular morning, 2nd January 1993, he was fresher and keener than normal.

I had just returned from spending the New Year at home in Moneyglass. Christmas on, New Year off, or vice-versa, that was how it worked at Jim's. I had enjoyed spending the time at home, being with my family for a couple of days, but at the same time I was looking forward to getting stuck back into work and to getting more rides on the track.

It was freezing cold that morning. There was frost on the ground and the air cut your face. Because some of the lads had been off over the Christmas period, the horses hadn't been out as much as they normally would be, and that wasn't ideal for a fresh horse like Kly Green. He was mad keen from the moment that I tried to put a saddle on him, he bucked and plunged all the way to the gallop, he bucked and plunged at the top of the gallop and, as we set off gingerly down towards the bottom of the gallop, he continued bucking and plunging.

He musn't have seen the wooden fence at the bottom of the gallop or, if he did, he must have thought he could take it on, because he didn't stop. He just went headlong into the fence. Wham! He hit the fence and came to an abrupt halt. He must have hurt himself but, I have to admit, his welfare was the last thing on my mind. I had no chance. I was slung like a stone in a catapult off Kly Green's back and onto the ground.

As soon as I hit the ground I heard the snap. There was no mistaking it. The snap of bone. Even now, when I fall or when I see other lads fall, you know immediately if a bone has been broken, you can hear the snap. It's a horrible sound. The pain shot up from the bottom of my leg and flashed through every cell, like a lightning strike on every single part of your body. I had one of those out-of-body experiences, a pain that is so severe that, for a fraction of a second, you don't really believe that it is happening to you.

I had never known pain like it before. I felt weak and nauseous, the blood drained from my face and the energy drained from my body. I looked down at my leg, I could see my thigh and my knee, but it looked like I had another knee right in the middle of my lower leg; my leg was bent in two places instead of one. I looked away.

I lay there on the ground, grimacing with the unbearable pain and shivering in the rawness of the morning. The lads knew that it was bad very quickly, and someone ran back to the yard to get some horse blankets to put over me. Nobody dared move me; I didn't dare move myself. An ambulance was called. Seamie Heffernan went off to tell Jim, and the boss arrived along a couple of minutes later.

'How do you know it's broken?' was his first question.

It must have been about 45 minutes before the ambulance arrived. Those 45 minutes seemed like 45 hours to me. The cold had got into my body; it must have been minus three or minus four as I lay there on the ground, a January morning in deepest Kilkenny. I was numb with the cold, and yet I was in more pain than I had ever been in my life. I can understand now how people can pass out with pain, but I didn't. I just lay there on the ground, steeling myself, crying, trying to bear it for what seemed like an eternity.

Then the ambulance guys arrived and put a mask on my face. That was an unbelievable feeling, the relief. I could trace the gas's journey from my mouth down through my body, a soft anesthetic moving easily through every cell, relieving the pain as it moved. I tried to relax and allow the gas to do its job.

After a couple of minutes, they were able to move me into the ambulance. I remember the ambulance journey to Kilkenny Hospital, I remember every bump, every pothole in Jim's place before we got to the road, and I remember getting onto the road and feeling so much better as the pain began to subside and my body began to thaw out.

Once I got to the hospital, the x-ray showed that both my tibia and my fibula had been broken, both of them smashed, although you didn't need an x-ray to see that, you could tell by the way my lower leg had been bent around. The care and attention that I received was top class, but there were no pins in those days, so they put a Plaster of Paris cast on my leg, right from the bottom of my ankle to the top of my thigh.

I was in hospital for a couple of days before I returned to Mrs Murphy's house, but there wasn't much point in me being there as I wasn't able to go into the yard, I wasn't able to ride, I wasn't able to do much, except get this twisted coat hanger down between my plaster and my leg to scratch the itches. My parents thought I would be better off at home, so they came down to collect me, and I spent the next four months recuperating in Moneyglass.

I didn't do much there either, but at least I was at home. It was nice to spend lots of time with my mother again, although I'm sure I got on everybody's nerves a bit, sprawled out on the sofa all the time, me and my gammy leg, annoying my family, demanding attention, watching television. Actually, I watched a lot of television, I couldn't do much else, but I couldn't even watch racing; there was no At The Races or Racing UK channel back then, so I became an expert in daytime television. If you have any of the problems that Sally Jesse Raphael covered during that time, I'm your man.

I did watch the Cheltenham Festival from the couch. I watched Mark Dwyer and Jodami beating Richard Dunwoody on Rushing Wild, who was trained by Martin Pipe, in the Gold Cup, and I watched Peter Scudamore ride Granville Again to win the Champion Hurdle, making up for the previous year's misfortune when he fell at the second last when he was travelling like a winner.

Granville Again was significant in that he was the first Champion Hurdle winner that Martin Pipe trained. Martin Pipe was champion trainer in the UK at the time, he was prolific. Champion for the first time in 1989, he and Peter Scudamore were busy rewriting the record books of British National Hunt racing, and I was able to admire his achievements from afar. There was a feeling around that he was good at training bad horses, that he could win lots of races at the gaff tracks with bad horses, but that he hadn't proven that he could train top-class horses. Granville Again disproved that hypothesis, as would many others that followed.

Of course, I didn't realise the significance for me of Granville Again's win in the Champion Hurdle at the time. If you had told me, stretched out on that sofa, wholly immobile, with a Plaster of Paris cast going up to my groin and in need of a stick to get from the sitting room to the bathroom, that just four years later I would ride Martin Pipe's second and final Champion Hurdle winner, I would have had you institutionalised.

It wasn't the Gold Cup or the Champion Hurdle that was my main focus at that Cheltenham Festival anyway. It was the County Hurdle, the last race on the last day, in which Thumbs Up was running, the horse trained by Nicky Henderson and ridden by my childhood hero Richard Dunwoody but, more importantly, bred by Peadar McCoy out of his mare Misclaire, the first horse on which I ever sat.

Billy had actually trained Thumbs Up to win a bumper at Down Royal in 1991, before Nicky Henderson bought him for Michael Buckley, whose horses used to race in black and white quartered colours, but now race in the all-white with the black cap that you see high-class horses like Spirit Son and Finian's Rainbow carrying these days.

Because the County Hurdle was the last race, it was after the terrestrial television coverage of the meeting had finished, so we all went down to Toal's Bookmakers in Toomebridge to watch it on SIS. Plaster of Paris or no Plaster of Paris, I wasn't going to miss this one.

Thumbs Up was a 16/1 shot, but we thought he had a chance. He was a novice racing against handicappers, but he was racing off bottom weight of 10 st with Richard Dunwoody on his back, well worth the 2 lb overweight he was putting up.

He was always going to win. He travelled like a dream down to the last and, although he made a mistake there, he had enough in reserve to pull right away up the run-in. We cheered like we owned him as he pulled away up the hill. In truth, it felt like we did. I was delighted for Dad. Cheltenham is huge, whether you are a jockey or a trainer or an owner or a breeder. Your ultimate goal is to have a winner at the Cheltenham Festival, and it was a huge deal for Dad, a tiny breeder with just a couple of mares, to do that.

I was back at Bolger's by May. It was nice being at home and all, it was great to spend time with my family, and Mum was sad to see me go again, but time passes slowly when you are laid up, there are only so many times you can read the *Racing Post* and the *Sporting Life* cover to cover. I probably knew more about every horse that was running than I do now, I became a bit of a form fiend, studying every race: a selling hurdle at Plumpton, a two-year-old five-furlong race at Redcar, I paid attention to them all. But I was anxious to get going. I was afraid that in my absence other lads would have passed me out in the pecking order at Jim's, such as it was.

The other issue was my weight. I was 7 st 7 lb when I got up on Kly Green that January morning, five months previously. I was 9st 2lb by the time I rolled back into Jim's. To be honest, I hadn't thought about my weight too much when I was off. I hadn't needed to think about it before; my main concern was being able to carry my saddle, so I didn't really see it as an issue. Turns out, though, my mum's fry-ups were great at the time for a hungry patient, but not great for an aspiring flat jockey.

I did get back down to be able to ride at 8 st 6 lb by the time Bubbly Prospect ran at Gowran Park that August. He was set to carry 9 st, so with my 8 lb claim he was down to 8 st 6 lb, which I did comfortably. It didn't make that much difference to Bubbly Prospect, he wouldn't have won if I had chopped both my legs off and ridden at 5 st 6 lb, but at least it was a ride.

I was struggling with my weight though. I was heavy for a flat jockey, a 19-year-old flat jockey who wasn't naturally going to get any lighter. I'm not sure if it was my injury that did it or not, I'm not sure that I wouldn't have put on weight anyway, but it certainly didn't help. Richard Hughes is tall, he could easily have let his weight go and ridden over jumps, but he kept it in check and can ride at 8 st 6 lb or 8 st 7 lb on the flat. People say that he is light-boned, and I'm sure he is, but maybe he has made himself light-boned because he has always kept his weight in check. I'm not sure that I wouldn't have been able to do the same if I hadn't been on the flat of my back for five months eating my mother's fry-ups.

At the time, I wanted to be a flat jockey; they have an easier life, a longer career. The difficulty is that flat jockeys have to be lighter than jump jockeys. In the big races on the flat, horses generally carry around 9 st. Top weight in a handicap is generally between 9 st 10 lb and 10 st, bottom weight can be 7 st 12 lb. By contrast, bottom weight in most handicaps over jumps is 10 st, top weight can be 11 st 12 lb or 11 st 10 lb, and all horses in the top conditions' race, the Grade 1 races like the Gold Cup and the Champion Chase, carry 11 st 10 lb. So if you are struggling to ride at anything less than 9 st when you are 19, you really don't have much of a future riding on the flat.

I hadn't even considered the possibility of becoming a National Hunt jockey. If I had wanted to be a National Hunt jockey, I could have stayed at Billy Rock's, lived at home, taken out an amateur licence and ridden in point-to-points initially before trying to make it as a conditional and as a professional. I wouldn't have had to endure the hardship that was part of leaving home at 15.

While the top jump jockeys are pushing and cajoling some slow beast worth a couple of grand over big, black birch obstacles and around three and a quarter miles on bottomless ground at Sedgefield in the dead of winter, the top flat jockeys are sunning themselves in Dubai, riding in the evening at what they call the Dubai Spring Carnival. Would I trade? No way.

Who knows what kind of a flat jockey I would have made? I might have been useless. And however good I might have been, it is impossible to think that I would have been lucky enough to achieve all I have achieved as a jump jockey.

My three-year term with Jim was coming to an end, and I was thinking about leaving him and trying to make my way in the world as a National Hunt jockey. Jim had jumpers at the time, some good ones as well, like Nordic Surprise, Chirkpar, Elementary and Vestris Abu, but it wasn't an option to stick around Jim's and try to be a National Hunt rider. It was a flat yard with flat horses.

'You're some fool,' Jim said to me when I told him. 'You, a jump jockey? I heard you crying like a baby when you hurt yourself here in January. That happens to jump jockeys every day of the week. You're not tough enough to be a jump jockey. You're just getting going here, you're just getting started. There will be plenty of opportunity for you here.'

Jim could be quite persuasive. He was one of those people who made you believe him. You believed that what he was telling you was true, that his way was right. If you want to get on in life, do what I am telling you to do. I signed on for another year, although I did manage to get him to agree that I would take out a National Hunt licence and that he would give me some rides over hurdles.

In one sense, I couldn't believe that I had committed to another year after the three years that I had endured. In another though, I could sort of see the bigger picture. As an apprentice, a trainer had to hold your licence. You had to be apprenticed to a licensed trainer. I could have had Billy Rock hold my licence, I could have gone back home and tried to make my way from there, but deep down I could see that the right thing to do was to stay with Jim. And after you had done your three years, it was a year-to-year thing, you only had to commit to another year, and that didn't seem too long.

Jim was true to his word though. On 23rd October, he put me up on Zavaleta in the Autumn Nursery at Leopardstown. Zavaleta is actually a half-sister to Affianced, dam of Irish Derby winner Soldier of Fortune. Seamie Heffernan had ridden her to win the Birdcatcher Nursery at Naas the previous week, she was sent off the 3/1 favourite for the Leopardstown race, and she duly won like one. I never had a moment's anxiety, we won by an easy two lengths.

It was an amazing thing then, riding another winner. Zavaleta was my second winner, my first since Legal Steps 19 months previously, and I felt a million dollars again. The following day, the *Sporting Life* described me as the next Alan Munro. That was a huge compliment. Alan Munro was riding all those top-class horses for Paul Cole at the time. Two years earlier he had ridden the superstar Generous to win the Epsom Derby, the Irish Derby and the King George, he rode those top Fahd Salman-owned horses like Zoman, Great Palm and Bright Generation, in those cool dark green colours. More than that, though, he was a really stylish rider. He rode American style, toes in the irons, low crouch. To be compared to Alan Munro at the time was huge for me.

After Legal Steps, I thought that I was on the road; I thought that the winners would flow. They didn't. Nineteen months is a long time to be waiting for your second, even if you did spend a couple of months on the sidelines through injury. When it did finally arrive, I was thrilled, and I thought again that the winners would flow. Guess what – they didn't.

If Jim's strategy was to keep me sweet by putting me up on Zavaleta at Leopardstown, it worked. I did ride her again in a nursery at Gowran Park before the 1993 season was out, but the ground was very soft that day, too soft for her, and we could only finish third. I was desperate for another winner, but I still thought that I was making progress, and I thought that I was an all right rider. I never told anyone that I thought I was okay, but I felt fairly secure looking at the other lads in the yard, Ted Durcan or Seamie Heffernan, or Mick Martin or David Wachman; I thought that I would be well able to hold my own against any of them as a rider.

I got heavier that winter. I was 19 going on 20, and it was difficult to keep my weight in check. As the 1994 season dawned, the rides didn't seem to be getting any more plentiful, but the quality of them seemed to be increasing. Gallardini was a good horse for me. I rode him to win a decent enough handicap at Navan in May. I remember top Meath Gaelic footballer Colm O'Rourke was there that day. He has been a good friend of Jim's for years, he was mixed up in a couple of horses with him down through the years, and I was a bit star-struck meeting him. I also rode Gallardini four days later to win an apprentices' handicap at Leopardstown. He provided half my total of four wins on the flat that season. But I only had 16 rides. Even now, I'd settle for a strike rate of 25 per cent.

I also rode over jumps though. My first ride over hurdles was on a horse called Riszard in a two-and-a-half-mile hurdle at Leopardstown on St Patrick's Day, 1994. Riszard was a good horse, owned by Star of Gdansk's owner Henryk de Kwiatkowski. He had won the Queen Alexandra Stakes at Royal Ascot the previous summer, but he hadn't managed to win in five attempts over hurdles. Even so, he wasn't that big a price in a good race at Leopardstown that day. We were travelling well going to the second last, I was tracking Anabatic, and I thought Riszard had plenty left to give. Then Anabatic got the second last wrong, came down and left us with nowhere to go. Riszard cannoned into the back of him and came down as well, me on top of him. As it turned out, we might not have won the race anyway, as it was won by Imperial Call, who would go on to win the Cheltenham Gold Cup exactly two years later under Conor O'Dwyer.

I was gutted, but if I had been expecting words of consolation from my boss, I would have been disappointed. Fortunately, I hadn't been. All I got was a bollocking, which I was expecting, interestingly. Apparently I should have known that Anabatic was going to fall. What was I doing tracking a horse that was going to fall? My world was full of rhetorical questions. Riszard ran in a maiden hurdle at Gowran Park a month later, and Jim let me ride him again. We made no mistake this time, winning easily enough. I was delighted, my first winner over hurdles.

Other trainers were showing a bit of an interest in me, but Jim didn't like me riding too much for outside yards. That said, he did let me ride Huncheon Chance for Ian Ferguson in a maiden hurdle at Down Royal, and we duly won. It was great to ride a winner in Northern Ireland, at my local track, and it was great to ride a winner for Ian, whom I had encountered plenty as I went around the Northern point-to-point circuit with Billy Rock.

Six days later, I rode Huncheon Chance to win on the flat at Sligo, and the following month, I rode him again to win over a mile and six furlongs at Bellewstown, beating the Mick O'Toole-trained Celibate by a head. Two years later, when Celibate was trained by Charlie Mann, I actually rode him to win a novices' chase at Cheltenham's October meeting.

Things weren't going badly at all, but I was losing my battle with the scales. Huncheon Chance was set to carry 9 st 10 lb, I was able to claim 8 lb, which brought his weight down to 9 st 2 lb, and I couldn't have done much lighter. I knew that my days of riding on the flat were numbered and I was right. Huncheon Chance was actually the last winner that I rode on the level.

I was realistic enough to know that, if I was to have a future in this game, the future would be over jumps.

CHAPTER 7

Any Jobs?

I knew that, if I wasn't going to continue as a flat jockey, there was no future for me at Jim's, so I started to tell people that I was interested in joining a National Hunt yard if the right opportunity became available. Ireland is small, there were only three or four race meetings at most on a normal week during the winter, and Charlie Swan and Conor O'Dwyer seemed to have the best yards and the best rides sewn up anyway. I was resigned to the fact that I would probably have to move to the UK. It wasn't ideal, but I didn't mind too much – I was happy to go wherever the opportunities were.

Fortunately, I had a lot of people looking out for me. I had got to know a lot of good people in Irish racing at the time. Dessie Scahill for one, Ireland's leading racecourse commentator, reckoned there was a job for me with Jimmy Fitzgerald. Norman Williamson, who would ride Master Oats to win the Gold Cup and Alderbrook to win the Champion Hurdle for trainer Kim Bailey in 1995, told me that there was a job going with Kim, and Paddy Graffin, who used to ride up in the north of Ireland and was then training, and who now works for the Turf Club, said he'd try to set me up with a job with Martin Pipe. And there was Eddie Harty, who had ridden Highland Wedding to win the Grand National in 1969 for trainer Toby Balding, who thought there was a job going at Toby's. James McNichol, who looked out for good horses for Toby in the North, also recommended me to Toby.

Unfortunately, before any of these jobs could become a reality for me, Jim got wind of my intentions. Irish racing moves in small circles, and you can be sure that, within it, most people know about most things. Jim wasn't happy. There were more bollockings, as Jim dug deep into his persuasive powers to try to get me to stay. He presented every rationale that he could. There was the Abusive Rationale ('You're some fool, thinking you can just up and leave here and be a National Hunt jockey'), the Dismissive Rationale ('You're not tough enough to be a National Hunt jockey'), the Persuasive Rationale ('Spend another year here, then you'll be a stronger and better rider, better equipped to go it alone') and the Emotional Blackmail Rationale ('I spend four years teaching you how to ride, and then you're going to up and leave and let somebody else benefit?'), but none of them worked this time.

I have huge respect for Jim Bolger, for all he did for me. Billy Rock was right, the time that I spent at Jim's was the making of me. I learned so much there, not just about horses and about riding, but about people as well, about life. I didn't fully realise it back then, but the more time went on, the more I came to appreciate the value of the time I spent at Jim's. I am sure that I would not be the rider or even the person that I am now were it not for Jim Bolger. Back then though, I knew that it was time to move on.

Jim and I get on great now, and when I am in Ireland, I make a point of trying to go down to see Jim, call into the yard, have a cup of tea with him from his bone china teacups and catch up. If nothing else, it's a good exercise in keeping my mind at peace, reminding myself how lucky I am that I escaped. When I am driving through the gate, I get flashbacks of how it used to be, of the feeling I used to get going in through those gates, knowing I was there for the day, for the year, for the next three years. It's nice now to be going in, knowing you're not going to get put up on a mad unbroken yearling, that you're not going to get thrown off 14 times, that you're not going to get a bollocking (although that one isn't absolutely certain) and that you will be able to walk out again in an hour or two.

Things happened quite quickly when I decided to leave Jim's. Toby Balding was over looking at horses with Eddie Harty that summer, and they came to Wexford to see me ride on 19th July. I only had one ride that evening, Havin' A Ball in the 6.30, the mare's maiden hurdle, and I finished second on her, beaten three-quarters of a length. Even back then, I hated finishing second. I was in the weigh room after the race, throwing the race about in my head, how could I have made up that three-quarters of a length, when Eddie came in and told me that Toby was outside.

Toby was one of the top trainers in the UK at the time. He couldn't really compete with Martin Pipe or David Nicholson, but he always featured among the top trainers. In 1991–92, he had finished second in the trainers' championship, with only Martin Pipe ahead of him. As we stood there chatting at Wexford that evening, I knew that he hadn't had such a good time of it during the season that had just ended, just 17 winners, but I figured that that was just a blip, the fundamentals were still good, and I was right.

Toby had trained Morley Street, who was actually a full brother to Granville Again, to win the Champion Hurdle in 1991, and to win three Aintree Hurdles in a row. He had also trained Beech Road to win the Champion Hurdle in 1989, and Cool Ground to win the Gold Cup in 1992. More importantly from my point of view, however, he was the springboard from which Adrian Maguire was able to launch his riding career in the UK. Adrian joined Toby as his conditional rider at the start of the 1991–92 season. That season, he rode 71 winners and was champion conditional rider. The following season, he rode 124 winners, including the Gold Cup on Cool Ground for Toby. Then he joined David Nicholson, and had been half of the main story of the 1993–94 season, when he and Richard Dunwoody had fought out the jockeys' championship all the way to the very last day of the season, Dunwoody eventually winning the title by three wins, 197 to 194. But the competition nearly killed the two of them.

Adrian's story told me that Toby gave young riders an opportunity. As well as that, he had good horses and he didn't really have a stable jockey. Kim Bailey had Norman, Martin Pipe obviously had Dunwoody, so however the ball had hopped, if I had joined either of them I would have been playing second fiddle to the stable jockey, and that might not have been ideal. The other thing was that Toby had access to Dave Roberts, the jockeys' agent. Jockeys' agents weren't as significant then as they are now, but Dave was the top man, he was really the only man, and even then I realised that it could be very helpful to have a man like Dave on your side, helping you to get rides.

I liked Toby from the start. He came across as a good guy, he was friendly and open, and he seemed to be willing to give me a chance. Come over and see how it goes, he told me. If you don't like it, if we don't get on, you can come back. You've got nothing to lose. He was right. Finbarr Leahy had been given the job with Kim Bailey, there wasn't much movement on the other jobs as far as I could see, and I knew that my time in Ireland was up. The potential downside of joining Toby wasn't very big, but the potential upside was huge.

I rode in Ireland for another couple of weeks. I rode Havin' A Ball again in a hurdle race at the Galway Festival – we got beaten a short head by Richard Dunwoody on the Aidan O'Brien-trained Ballyhire Lad. I was gutted. Dunwoody had been my childhood hero; to me he was the best National Hunt jockey that there had ever been, so to have beaten him in a hurdle race at the Galway Festival would have been huge. I thought I had him beaten going up the run-in, but it just happened that when we hit the line, Ballyhire Lad's head was down, Havin' A Ball's head was up.

I remember that day for another reason: Graham Bradley. I was sitting in the weigh room after the race, probably looking like I had the weight of the world on my shoulders – even then a narrow defeat used to get me down – when Brad came up to me.

'Don't worry,' he said. 'You'll get Dunwoody again. You gave the mare a great ride.'

He only said a couple of words, but they gave me a huge lift. For a senior jockey, one as good and as well-respected as Graham Bradley, to take the time to come up to me and tell me that I had given a horse a great ride was a huge deal.

That was the type of fellow that Brad was. He was always very helpful to a young lad who was trying to make his way. He was generally a happy character, always in good humour, always there with a craic or a joke. I didn't know him at all when I first moved to England, but when I started playing golf – there were a few of us who used to play golf together – Brad was in our group, and gradually I struck up a solid friendship with him.

Graham Bradley was not without his flaws, everyone knew that. In 1982 he had been suspended from race-riding for two months after walking into the betting ring at Cartmel and betting £50 on a horse running that day. Obviously, jockeys are not allowed to bet. It was a blatant and flagrant contravention of the rules. In 1987 he had been suspended for three months for making insufficient effort on a horse called Deadly Going in a race at Market Rasen.

Later, in 1999, he was one of a number of people who were arrested and charged as part of a long-running investigation into alleged race-fixing. The charges were later dropped, but the damage to Brad's career, and to some of the others who had been charged, was significant. Throughout that time, I remained a staunch supporter of Brad's. I vouched for him in court, along with several other weigh-room colleagues; I lived with him for a spell while I was waiting for a new house to be ready. That was right at the height of the race-fixing investigation. My new house was actually ready before the investigation concluded, but I didn't move into it, I remained in Brad's house with him, partly because I could see how low he was and I thought that he probably didn't need to be going home to an empty house, and partly because it wouldn't have looked good for him if I had been seen to be moving out just when the investigation was nearing completion. Then all the charges against him were dropped and it was okay for me to leave.

Brad retired from riding in 1999, and began to concentrate on building up his bloodstock business. He bought horses for, among others, Liverpool footballers Robbie Fowler and Steve McManaman. They had some good horses with Martin Pipe, horses like Seebald and Auetaler, and through Brad, and the fact that I was riding for Martin Pipe at the time, I got to know both of them very well.

Then in November 2002, Brad was banned from racing for eight years, later reduced to five on appeal, after being found guilty of passing information for reward to the convicted drugs baron Brian Wright. That was a bad day; the ban placed everyone in a difficult situation. Brad had lots of friends in racing, but when you are a licensed professional in racing, you are not supposed to be associating with disqualified persons. I was a licensed professional, I was champion jockey so, even though Brad was a good friend of mine, it put me in a difficult situation.

You get to a point at which you have to do what's right for you, and selfishly, I knew that it wouldn't be good for me to be seen to be hanging out with Brad. There were more senior jockeys to me, people who had known Brad for longer than I had, who were nervous about associating with Brad, so I was nervous about him calling me or if I was ever with him on my own. If there was a golf day and he was there, fine, there were other people there, or if we were all down in the pub together, we were all in the same boat. I felt comfortable when there were other people around. But I felt that I couldn't go down to his house, and I was on tenterhooks if I spoke to him by phone. It was horrible.

Maybe I should have acted differently. Maybe I should have been a better friend to Brad. I'm sure he was disappointed with me, and probably with other jockeys as well. Maybe I or we weren't as supportive of him as I or we should have been. To this day, I think that there are a lot of people in racing who have done much worse things than what Brad did. I think he was a bit of a scapegoat. He was an easy target after he admitted that he had passed information on horses to Brian Wright when he was a witness in a court case involving a different man.

I still see Brad now, I'd still play golf with him, he remains a fellow for whom I have time and he is still a good fun guy to be around. But our relationship now is nothing like the one we had before he was warned off. That's fair enough – I couldn't expect that it would have been.

CHAPTER 8

Smoking Pipe

I finished second on a mare trained by Peter Casey, Bellecara, in a handicap hurdle at Gowran Park on 6th August 1994, beaten a head by Brendan Sheridan on Sense of Value. That was a killer. I knew that Bellecara was going to be my last ride in Ireland for a while. If things worked out well with Toby, there was a chance that I wouldn't be back for a long while, if at all. I would have loved to have gone out on a winner. Alas, just like Willie Supple and Richard Dunwoody before him, Brendan Sheridan hadn't read the script that I had written.

It wasn't difficult for me to leave Ireland. I wasn't really sad leaving Jim's, I was going to miss some of the lads for sure, but I certainly wasn't going to miss going into Jim's every morning. My overriding feeling was one of excitement, this was the next step for me in my career, and I knew that it was a big step forward in the right direction. The possibilities were limitless; England was a big place with lots of horses and lots of racing.

The contrast between Toby Balding's and Jim Bolger's could hardly have been starker. At Toby's, everything was so much more relaxed: jeans and wellies were the order of the day, Toby was one of the lads, not this headmaster-type figure who put the fear of God in you. There was no need for silence as you walked around before going out in the morning, no need to know exactly where Toby was, no need to scarper when you heard him coming. You rode the horses on a loose rein, it didn't matter if the bridle wasn't fitted properly, lads smoked on horseback and chatted away to each other without a care in the world.

You mucked out with a muck sack, not a wheelbarrow. So you'd be putting this bag on your back to carry it, a bag full of horse shit, and the smell on your clothes would be permanent. You tried to have an old coat in which you could muck out, so you could sling the muck sack up on your old coatbut; in truth, the smell got to all your clothes.

Unlike Jim's, where the yard and the gallops were private and self-contained, Toby's place was in the middle of the village of Weyhill. His yard actually backed onto a housing estate. We used to have to walk the horses a mile and a half or two miles down the road just to get to the gallops, public roads with cars and trucks passing. And the lads would quite easily chat or smoke away as they walked down the road.

I was hardly in Toby's a week when I got a call from Paddy Graffin to tell me that Richard Dunwoody had organised for me to meet with Martin Pipe. I had completely given up on any audience with Martin Pipe. I had almost forgotten about it. I wasn't sure what to do. I ignored it for a while, did nothing, as I was apt to do in those days when it came to making big decisions, career decisions. But Toby's secretary, Shirley Vickery, was going out with Martin's son David at the time, and she was on at me. 'So when are you going to meet Martin?' She'd ask me every time she saw me.

Toby was great about it. He was very fair in that way; he knew that it would have been crazy for me not to go and meet with the champion trainer. Go on down and have a chat with him, see what you think, he said.

I was nervous going into Martin's. Of course I was in awe of him. Me meeting Martin Pipe? It was all a bit surreal. I couldn't have imagined being in the same room as Martin Pipe six months previously. Martin was already a racing legend, he had already rewritten the record books and, less than six months earlier, he had trained Minnehoma to win the Aintree Grand National.

As I drove to Nicolashayne, I was thinking, this could be the best thing ever, I'm going to see Martin Pipe and I might even get a job with him. The interview went well, we got on well, despite my star-struck state, and he offered me a job. I could have said yes right there and then, I probably would have had my bags in the car if I had known that he was going to offer me a job. But I told him that I would have to go home and think about it, talk about it with Toby. He was fair enough about that. But as I drove out of Pond House that day, there was no doubt in my mind that I was going to be going back a couple of days later, that that was where my immediate future lay.

I told Toby that Martin had offered me a job, and I asked him what he thought I should do. Toby was different to Jim. I could imagine Jim going, 'You fool! You'd get lost in Martin Pipe's.' Toby was much more circumspect.

'You have to do what is right for you,' he said. 'But I think it would be best for you to stay here. If you join Martin Pipe, you know, you will probably ride 30 or 40 winners this winter and you will probably be champion conditional rider. But long term, it might not be the best thing for you.'

My head was wrecked. Toby had taken me on, given me a job when nobody else had. When I had arrived at Toby's, I was happy, I was staying there for the foreseeable future. Then Martin Pipe offers me a job. You couldn't turn down a job with Martin Pipe, could you?

For a few hours I had been definitely leaving Toby and definitely joining Martin. It was a no-brainer. If you were stable jockey to Martin Pipe, you were champion jockey. It was a given. You remained injury- and suspension-free, you kept yourself right, and you were champion jockey. That was why Richard Dunwoody gave up the pick of the David Nicholson and Nicky Henderson horses. Before he joined Martin, Dunwoody had been in the enviable position where he could choose between two of the most powerful yards in the country, Saturday trainers, trainers who always had big runners in the big races on Saturdays during the National Hunt season, and at Cheltenham. He didn't give up those yards so that he could ride better horses. He gave them up so that he would ride more winners, so that he would be champion jockey.

By the same token, if you were Martin Pipe's conditional rider, you became champion conditional. That meant that you would ride 30 or 40 or 50 winners in a season. Even Toby had said it.

That said, I could have been champion conditional with Martin all right, but what then? I could be a slower burn at Toby's. I would ride fewer winners all right, but my claim could last longer, I could spread my claim over a longer period of time, hopefully remain in demand as a claiming rider for longer, have a chance to gain experience and establish myself before I would have to compete with Dunwoody, Williamson and Maguire on a level playing field. And I would have the assistance of my agent Dave Roberts.

I'm not sure if I would have had Dave in my corner if I had joined Martin, but I'm fairly sure that I wouldn't have. Not initially anyway. Toby had made it fairly clear that he would introduce me to Dave. Dave had been so successful for other jockeys, like Adrian and Richard Guest, and now he had Norman Williamson and Mick Fitzgerald and others, and you're thinking, that is the place to be. If I was in the office with Shirley in the mornings at Toby's, the first thing she would do would be to play the recorded messages on the answering machine, and the first message would always be from Dave Roberts: that horse is running at Folkestone, I have Adrian or Norman or Fitzy or whoever. I wanted to be on that team, I wanted my name to be one of the names that Dave would rattle off.

Toby told me that it was not impossible that I would be champion conditional if I stayed with him, that he had some nice horses running that season, and that Adrian Maguire had been champion conditional with him. I thought sure, but that's Adrian. Adrian was a one-off, Adrian was a prodigy. I was no Adrian Maguire.

I went around for two days with all of this kicking around my head, my brain fried. Other major decisions that I had made in my life up to that point – the decision to leave school, the decision to work at Billy's, the decision to join Jim Bolger, the decision to leave Jim Bolger, to go to the UK – had all been easy. This one wasn't.

In the end, I thought that, with an eye on the long term, I was better staying with Toby for now. Toby seemed delighted when I told him, it was the right decision. I phoned Paddy Graffin to tell him, I was embarrassed doing so, but Paddy was great, he said that I had to do what was right for me, and he thanked me for letting him know.

I phoned Martin Pipe. That was a difficult phone call. I couldn't believe that I was phoning this racing legend to tell him that I didn't want to work for him, but I did. He made it easy for me, he just said thanks very much for letting him know, and wished me the best of luck.

I hung up the phone. I still couldn't believe that I had turned down a job at Martin Pipe's. That was it now, I thought, you get one chance at a job with Martin Pipe, and that was mine. I was certain that I would never ride for him after that. I could hardly have been more wrong.

CHAPTER 9

Jump Start

I didn't really think about what other people thought of me, but there was a little bit of talk about me when people heard that I was joining Toby Balding, simply because Adrian Maguire had joined Toby just three years previously, and he had been champion conditional rider that year with an unprecedented 71 winners.

I did have confidence in my ability to ride though. A lot of that confidence came from Billy Rock, and it continued at Jim's. Nobody at Jim's ever said anything to me, nobody ever told me that I was a brilliant rider, that wasn't the way it worked at Jim's, that isn't the way it works in any yard, but I kind of knew from some of the lads that they thought I was all right.

Pat O'Donovan always seemed to think that I could ride as he always put me on the difficult horses. I always got on well enough with Christy Roche and with Aidan O'Brien. Like at Jim's, I was never told I was a good rider, but I sensed by the way they never spoke down to me that they thought I was okay.

Then, when you had the likes of Dessie Scahill, Pat Healy, Paddy Graffin, Eddie Harty and Norman Williamson putting in words for you, trying to get you jobs, you think that they think you are all right as well. They wouldn't be putting themselves out, they wouldn't be recommending you to somebody if they didn't think you could do the job. It was just a case of getting the right job and hoping that you would be able to make your way. It's a fickle business. It's important to be able to ride for sure, but it's also important to be fashionable; if you are not in vogue, you can struggle quite badly.

Toby was always a trainer who had 40 or 50 winners in a season. He had won a couple of Champion Hurdles and a Gold Cup. So to go from those heady heights to 17 winners in a season was a fair drop, but that was all he had in 1993–94, the season before I joined him. It wasn't ideal. Beech Road and Morley Street were still there, but they were getting on in years and obviously weren't as good as they had been. Cool Ground had joined David Elsworth. Toby did have some nice young horses coming along, but I was all the while hoping that I had made the right decision, that some of the young horses would come on and be all right. I was also hoping that Toby would be true to his word and that I would get plenty of rides.

Britain is different to Ireland, there is more racing in Britain. It is a bigger country, there are more horses, more trainers, twice as many racecourses and more racing, which gives a young rider more opportunities. There are, at a minimum, two or three race meetings a day in the UK, whereas in Ireland, especially during the winter, there could be only three or four a week.

It all got going very quickly for me. Just a week after I arrived, on 13th August 1994, I had my first ride in the UK on Arctic Life, trained by John Jenkins, in a novices' hurdle at Stratford. Paddy Graffin was friendly with John Jenkins, and he got me the ride. Arctic Life didn't run badly, we chased the odds-on favourite Wilkins for the whole of the two-and-three-quarter-mile trip, but we couldn't catch him, and finished second. Still, it was great to be up and running.

I started to get rides. I wasn't champing at the bit as I had been in Ireland, frustrated as hell, waiting for the message to call the office, Jim restraining me like a seasoned professional rider would restrain a young thoroughbred.

Chickabiddy was no world-beater, she had been beaten 30 lengths in a selling hurdle on her previous run, but I was delighted to get the ride on her in a poor handicap hurdle at Exeter on 7th September 1994. She wasn't trained by Toby either, she was trained by Gordon Edwards. Mick Fitzgerald had ridden her a few times before, but Fitzy was out with an injured wrist at the time, so Dave Roberts got me the ride.

She wasn't a big mare, but she travelled well for me, she jumped well, we moved up from the back going to the second last, took it up at the last, and she kept on well up the run-in to win by a length.

That was great. My first winner in England. It was a wonderful feeling, riding a winner, getting off the mark in my new life, starting to establish myself. Everything was happening more quickly for me than it had in Ireland, people seemed to know who I was, Dave Roberts was doing a fantastic job for me and I was getting rides. I hoped that another winner would follow soon afterwards, and it did, Anna Valley, an ordinary filly of Toby's that had run 30 times and had won just once, in a two-and-three-quarter-mile handicap hurdle at Worcester on 24th

September. It didn't matter to me that the winning owner barely netted two and a half grand, it was my second winner, just over two weeks after my first, and it was the last winner on which I could claim 7 lb. After that, I was only good for 5 lb.

It was great though, my second winner in the UK, my first winner for Toby. Two winners in three weeks. It got me thinking, if I could ride two winners every three weeks for the entire season, then that wouldn't be such a bad season. That was a realistic target.

Five days later I was booked to ride a horse called Wings of Freedom for John Jenkins in a conditional jockeys' handicap hurdle at Cheltenham. Me riding at Cheltenham. I couldn't believe it. Okay, so it wasn't the Festival, it was Cheltenham in September as opposed to Cheltenham in March, but it was still Cheltenham, the same turf, the same hill, the same winning post, the same weigh room, the same winner's enclosure.

I had never even been to Cheltenham before. Venues can often disappoint you, not being the same in reality as they appear on television, but Cheltenham didn't. If anything, it was better. I walked the track beforehand as I always tried to do before riding, especially at a track at which I hadn't ridden before, and all the tracks in the UK were new to me. It was something that had been engrained into me at Jim's, something he always wanted his riders to do. As with a lot of things at Jim's, it made complete sense.

I remember riding a front-runner, Dakota Girl, at Hereford that November. I had never been to Hereford before, so my intention was, as ever, to get there early and walk the track. But I was travelling with Toby, and Toby was a great man for Just In Time management. On this occasion, though, we got stuck in traffic, and literally got to Hereford with minutes to spare. No time to walk the track. So here was I, riding a front-runner at Hereford and not even sure if we were going clockwise or anti-clockwise. (Clockwise, by the way.) It worked out okay, I figured out which way we had to go, we led from early and, although we were passed, she stayed on well for me to win. But it was not an experience that I wanted to repeat.

Wings of Freedom was good. I held him up out the back, made ground going down the hill, challenged at the last and he kept on really well up the hill to win by a neck. Fantastic. First ride at Cheltenham, first winner at Cheltenham, back to the winner's enclosure and everything, the one I used to see on television. It wasn't thronged like it is in March, they weren't stacked up on the steps around the winner's enclosure and there wasn't a big cheer when I punched the air before dismounting. There was just polite applause, but it was still Cheltenham and it was another winner for me.

So I had ridden more winners in six weeks in the UK than I had ridden in three years in Ireland. In my head I was thinking that if I had come to England a year or two earlier, I would have been a year or two further down the road, more established, more experienced, more winners under my belt, but that is probably not the case. My years spent at Jim's, even though I didn't see it at the time, were a brilliant grounding. They were my foundation, equipping me for a career as a jockey.

Things could actually have been completely different if I had moved to England a year earlier. I could have got lost. It was as if I was an instant success in England, but it wasn't as simple as that. I felt that I had learned the hard way and that I was now reaping the rewards that I deserved. I thought that I was more experienced than your average rider who had just ridden a handful of winners. The foundation for my career had been well laid: I had worked for five years to become an overnight success.

The following week I went to Newton Abbot and rode my first double, Bonus Boy, a 20/1 shot for Bob Buckler in a bad conditional jockeys' selling handicap chase, and Ask The Governor for Toby in the handicap hurdle. It could have been a treble, because I was four lengths clear on Southampton in the claiming hurdle earlier in the day when we fell at the final flight. A double was good, but a treble would have been great.

I blamed myself for Southampton's fall; I thought that I had put him on the floor. That was the start of it, no matter how good a day I had, there was always something that had gone wrong. The day that I rode five winners at Market Rasen and my overriding feeling going home was that it should have been six, that I shouldn't have fallen on the last one. And if it had been six, I'm sure I would have been kicking myself that I hadn't had a ride in the seventh race, that I hadn't had the opportunity to ride every winner on the card. I have never gone through the card, I have never ridden every winner at a meeting, but if I ever did, I'm sure I would find some negative. I know I would look for one.

There was no Sky Plus then, there were no Racing UK or At The Races replays, so you couldn't go home and torture yourself, slowing down the fall, looking for what you did wrong. In a way, that was good. Sky was the ruination of me, it gave me the opportunity to watch every ride, the losing rides, looking for what I did wrong, beating myself up.

I would like to think that I am better now at dealing with defeats or falls, but I'm not sure. I don't spend hours in front of the television at night these days watching my falls, play, rewind, play, rewind, trying to find the exact moment at which I made a bollocks of it, but I still find it difficult. I am probably better at dealing with all of that since my daughter Eve was born, but the defeats and falls do still play on my mind and get under my skin.

There is always something you could have done differently. If a horse gets beaten, or if a horse falls, there is always something that you can find that might have made a difference. You didn't do the right thing because you were beaten. Obviously, whatever you did, it wasn't the right thing. And it's not a case of convincing yourself that it wasn't your fault. People try to cheer you up, tell you that you couldn't have done anything differently, but that's bullshit, you know they probably don't mean what they are saying and, if they do, they don't know what they are talking about. They are just saying words. You feel like telling them to piss off, but you don't because you know they mean well.

Even now, the last thing I think about before I go to sleep at night is that defeat, that fall. I will be closing my eyes and it will be the first thing to come into my head, just replaying it in my mind, what I did wrong, why I fell, why I got beaten. Sad I know.

*

Bonus Boy was my first winner over fences. I hadn't had much experience of riding over fences, and I'm sure I was hanging off him. I wouldn't like to see the video of that race, that's for sure. Riding over fences is quite different to riding over hurdles. Fences are obviously a lot bigger and when I was inexperienced, I used to try to jump for the horse, to jump over the fence with him. As you get more experienced, though, you realise that it's up to the horse to jump the fence. If he jumps, he jumps, and if he doesn't, that's just the way it is. You can't jump the fence for him. Of course, you can help him, and I try to do that, but it's up to the horse to jump.

I remember a little while later in my career that there was a notion doing the rounds that I was a better hurdles jockey than a chase jockey. It didn't bother me, there might have been something in it, but if there was, it was only because I hadn't had much experience of riding over fences. I hadn't been an amateur, I hadn't ridden in point-to-points, I had been essentially a flat jockey in Ireland, so the only way I could gain experience was by schooling and by riding in chases. Gradually I hope I got better.

The *Racing Post* report the day after my Newton Abbot double described me as a rising star. That was probably a bit premature, but you read these things, you take heed of them, everybody has an ego, and you are affected by them. Of course it's nice to read things like that as long as you don't start dwelling on them.

I was on some trip though, it was some change. In Ireland, even at my pinnacle, such as it was, I would have been lucky to have had two or three rides a week. Now, after just about six weeks in England, I was going racing most days, I was riding three or four days a week, one or two or three rides a day. The more winners I was riding, the more rides I was getting. It's a self-perpetuating circle, the more rides you get, the better rides you get, the more winners you ride and the more rides you get.

The other thing was that I was now riding against jockeys who were legends in my eyes, and I was sharing the weigh room with them. Richard Dunwoody, Adrian Maguire, Norman Williamson, Mick Fitzgerald, Jamie Osborne, Graham Bradley, they were names that I used to read in the paper, jockeys that I used to watch riding on television on a Saturday, celebrities, and here was I, sharing the weigh room with them. It was difficult not to be star-struck and to resist the temptation to run up to them and ask them for their autographs. It would be like sharing a changing room with Eric Clapton, Barack Obama, Al Pacino, Michael Jordan, Tiger Woods and David Beckham, then going out to try to beat them in a race. Not that Fitzy looks anything like David Beckham, but you get the drift.

Facilities were generally better in the UK as well. One thing that was very noticeable: if I had been doing light in Ireland on a Saturday, I would often go up to the sauna in the apprentice centre in Kildare on a Friday night with Conor Everard, and see Johnny Murtagh and Christy Roche and some of the other top flat jockeys there, buckets of ice on their head, all trying to shed a few pounds for the weekend's racing. In the UK, even back then when I first came over, I would say that around half of the racecourses had their own sauna, so you could just go to the races early and have a sweat. No need to be going up to Kildare on a Friday night.

There was one other major difference between Ireland and England for me: in Ireland I was Anthony McCoy, in England I was Tony. As soon as I crossed the Irish Sea, I was Tony. Even the newspaper reports changed. Not that there were many newspaper reports about me when I was in Ireland, I didn't even get a mention after I rode my first winner Legal Steps, but after I rode Zavaleta to win at Leopardstown, I was still Anthony. By the time I had ridden my first winner in the UK on Chickabiddy, I was Tony.

It was just the way it happened. The lads at Toby's started to call me Tony; I suppose they thought it was easier. I did say to one or two of them that I preferred Anthony, but it made no difference. You don't push these things in stables; if you do, you usually just make things worse. Actually a reporter asked me one day, early on, if I was Anthony or Tony. I said Anthony, everybody else said Tony, I said whatever.

My family calls me Anthony, Chanelle calls me Anthony, Jim Bolger always calls me Anthony, Aidan O'Brien calls me Anthony, all my friends from Jim's call me Anthony, Conor Everard and Willie Supple and TJ Comerford, my friends from home all called me Anthony, which makes sense, it's my name. That said, some of the people that I knew at home, who used to call me Anthony, now call me Tony. Strange one that. Maybe they think that I prefer Tony. I don't. Former jockey Tony Dobbin's family all call him Anthony as well, so I suppose he just ended up with it too.

I don't really care at all now, lots of people call me AP, and I prefer that to Tony, but I suppose if people are talking about you and writing about you and wanting you to ride their horses, you don't really care what they call you.

So I had ridden seven winners by the end of October. I didn't say it to anyone, but in my own little head I was thinking, you know I could do well this season, I could do well in the conditional jockeys' championship. I did kick myself a little, thinking that if I had gone to Martin Pipe's I would probably be even further down the road to the conditional jockeys' title, but even at Toby's, I was thinking, you just never know, I could do all right.

Philip Hide and Rodney Farrant were leading the conditional jockeys' championship at the time, but I wasn't too far behind them with seven winners. Seven winners in six weeks, I was thinking, that's more than one a week. If I could continue to ride one winner a week, that wouldn't be a bad total at the end of the season. Already I was thinking about totals at the end of the season, numbers of winners. I wasn't in the UK a wet week, and already I wasn't thinking about big meetings or big races, I was just thinking numbers. That would be 30 or 40 winners, and that would nearly be enough to win the conditional jockeys' championship. And if I could ride two winners a week, well then I'd surely win it.

So I thought, two winners a week, that's a fair target. Of course I never said it to anyone, not a soul, I just started thinking these thoughts myself, getting carried away in my own little Walter Mitty world. Here was I, just over from rural Ireland, still wet behind the ears, a whole two winners on my CV before I got on the ferry in Rosslare, and I'm thinking about winning the conditional jockeys' championship. Crazy. Who do you think you are, Adrian Maguire? I didn't even think that, in the depths of winter, when the racing got more competitive and the big horses and big races rolled around, I might not even get two rides a week, never mind two winners.

All the while, Dave Roberts was working away on my behalf, booking me rides, getting me on horses for outside yards. I don't think I was annoying him too much, I wasn't onto him every hour, every day, wondering what I was riding or why I wasn't riding more horses, or why Adrian was riding a horse that I thought I should have been riding. I don't think I was ever like that with Dave. Even today, if I am not riding a horse I think I should be riding, I don't ask Dave why. I assume that Dave has a reason, and if Dave has a reason, that's good enough for me. By the same token, if I get beaten on a horse that he has put me on, or if he puts me on a poor jumper, I don't get onto him and give out. Dave always has his reasons, and I trust Dave's reasons implicitly.

The craic was good at Toby's, the lads were good, everyone got on well together. I hung out mostly with Brian Clifford and Richard Davis, who used to come in and ride out a bit. Richard was tragically killed in a fall at Southwell in July 1996. The horse he was riding, Mr Sox, fell at the first fence and Richard lost eight pints of blood before suffering heart failure. It was a devastating day.

You couldn't have met a nicer bloke than Richard. He wasn't much older than me and he couldn't have been more helpful. I'm not sure that if I was in the same position, if some little upstart might have a chance of taking some of my rides, that I would have been as helpful.

He used to ride out at Toby's three or four days a week, so I became pretty friendly with him. I actually won the novices' chase in which he suffered his fatal fall. The last fence was dolled off when we came around on the final circuit, which is never a good sign, and I can remember coming in afterwards and asking the doctor if Richard was okay. The doctor said he wasn't in great shape but he was all right, that he was on his way to hospital. There was never any mention of him being badly injured or being in a critical condition.

I'll never forget that day. I was driving back home to Toby's from

Southwell. I remember stopping at the traffic lights in Newbury and getting a phone call from a fellow called Sean Ellery, who was a good friend of Richard's.

'Dickey is dead,' he said.

Sean used to call Richard Dickey, as in Dickey Davis.

'What?'

'He died on the way to hospital.'

It was as if I had been hit by a brick. I sat there, stunned. I can remember the tears running from my eyes, thinking I had just left him a little while ago. The traffic lights must have gone green because the cars behind me started beeping, and I had to try to drive off through my tears.

It was the first experience that I'd had of anything like that, of the job and how dangerous it was. It was tragic, terrible for Richard's family. We all went to his funeral; it was all obviously very tough to take in, someone with whom you had been working and with whom you had become friendly, and actually seeing it happen.

Richard's death had an effect on all of us, on all the jockeys and on a lot of people associated with jockeys. It had a profound effect on Dave Roberts, who had been looking after Richard as well, and he beat himself up a lot, convincing himself that he was partly to blame, having booked the ride for Richard. He nearly gave up being an agent. But Richard's family was brilliant. It was a tragic situation, desperately sad for them, but they weren't at all bitter, never trying to blame anyone. Richard died doing what he loved was their way of dealing with it. I still think of Richard a lot. I have a picture of him up on my wall at home.

Some of the other lads used to come in to ride out as well. Jimmy Frost, who had ridden Morley Street to win the Champion Hurdle for Toby in 1991, was still riding, so he used to come in to ride out or to school, Adrian used to come in sometimes, and Dunwoody used to come in a bit.

It wasn't ideal that there were other jockeys coming in to school; it meant that they were in line for some of the better rides for some of Toby's better horses, but you didn't mind too much when it was the likes of Adrian or Dunwoody. Adrian had taken over as stable jockey to David Nicholson, The Duke, at the time, but you knew that when he wasn't required by The Duke, he would be riding for Toby, and that was fair enough. You also knew that Toby would use Dunwoody when he was available, also fair enough. You couldn't expect to compete with Adrian Maguire or Richard Dunwoody.

There was one day, though, that I had a ride at Bangor for an outside yard and Toby wouldn't let me go. I loved going racing, obviously, all I wanted to do was ride in races, but when you go racing it obviously means that you can't work in the yard in the afternoon. This particular day, Dave had booked me just one ride at Bangor, but Toby decided that I wasn't going. I couldn't believe it. He figured that it wasn't worth it, driving three hours to ride one horse then driving three hours back again.

It was worth it to me. I would have driven for days for one ride, but Toby said that he wanted me in the yard, and he was my boss, so I had to ring Dave back and tell him that I couldn't go. It wasn't a good day. It wasn't good for Dave, he had to call the trainer back and tell him that I couldn't ride, and it can't have been good for Dave's confidence in me. So if he books me on another horse tomorrow, is there a chance that I won't be able to go and ride that one as well?

I don't know if there was a sense that I was getting too big for my boots, that Toby felt the need to put me back in my box, like Jim would have done. Maybe he genuinely needed me at afternoon stables. Maybe he felt that I was riding out my claim too quickly, or that he wanted me to claim off his horses, not to be wasting my claim riding winners for other yards. Anyway, he obviously had his reasons and I didn't go to Bangor that day.

I was getting plenty of outside rides though. I was riding a bit for John Jenkins, Paddy Graffin had a good association with him, and he started me off there, and I was also riding a bit for John White and Gary Moore. Adrian rode a lot for John White during the early part of the season, during the early autumn before The Duke's good National Hunt horses would have been out, and I was more or less riding John's horses that Adrian couldn't ride.

I didn't ride out for any other trainers in the mornings though. I was pretty much tied to Toby's. I'd muck out my four horses in the morning, then ride out, then do afternoon stables if I wasn't going racing. As the year went on though, I was getting to go racing more and more, I was getting more rides, so towards the end of the season I was hardly ever in the yard in the afternoons. I still had to muck out in the mornings though; you couldn't forget who you were.

I did a fair bit of schooling at Toby's as well, but I don't think I was very good at it. I still didn't have very much experience of riding over fences. It's like everything, the more you experience something, the better you get at it. It wasn't that the fences frightened me, I just didn't really know what I was doing. The more I did it, the better I got, but I would say that it wasn't until after about a year in England that I felt fully comfortable riding a horse over a fence.

It didn't stop me riding in chases on the track though, and thankfully it didn't mean that trainers were slow to book me for their chasers. I was riding winners over fences as well as over hurdles, and that was the main thing. It's better winning ugly than looking pretty and losing. In any walk of sport, you can forgive and be forgiven an awful lot when you win.

I just kept trying to improve. I didn't go to riding lessons or go back to riding school, I just watched other jockeys riding over fences, tried to take the good bits from the riders that I respected, tried to put it all into practice myself when I was schooling and when I was race-riding. I felt that I knew what I should have been doing, I just needed to put it into practice. I just needed to do it and get good at it. I knew that I could fix it myself. I usually think that I can fix things myself. Somebody telling me how to do something is not necessarily the right thing for me.

Toby loved his horses dropped out the back and delivered with a well-timed run late in a race, so that was how I rode that year. Later on, when I started to ride for Martin Pipe, it was totally different. Martin's horses were usually fit as fleas, so he wanted them ridden handily, up front, to exploit the potential fitness advantage that his horses enjoyed over their rivals. In fact, the two styles couldn't have been more different, but I was happy to ride out the back for Toby.

There was one horse in particular that I loved riding like that, a horse called Blair Castle. He was a good horse off the flat, he had won a couple of races on the flat and he had finished fifth in a Britannia Handicap at Royal Ascot, so he had bags of speed. I remember winning three races on him in the summer of 1995, two at Worcester and one at Market Rasen. I just settled him out the back in all three races, made ground steadily, and got there just in time, just giving him a squeeze. I never had to get serious with him yet I never won by more than two lengths on him.

He was a bit of a monkey though. On his next two races he didn't seem to want to go through with it; he got there all right at the second last, but didn't seem to want to win. So next time at Bangor, and again at Exeter later in the summer, I jumped him off smartly, got a good start, set out to make all, and we never saw another rival in either race until we were pulling up after crossing the winning line. So I rode him seven times in two months that summer, winning five times and finishing second once and third once.

My season seemed to take off just after Christmas. Up until Christmas I was up there with Philip Hide and Rodney Farrant, challenging at the top of the conditional jockeys' championship, but after Christmas, for some reason, somebody hit turbo-boost on my career. I don't know why that happened. Maybe people were generally thinking, rightly or wrongly, that I could ride a bit, and I was in demand. Outside trainers were looking for me more often, and I noticed that Toby was putting me up more often as well, putting me on some of the better horses in the better races. Adrian was still Toby's number one, whenever his commitments to The Duke allowed him ride for him, but Toby was starting to put me up on horses that beforehand might have been Jimmy Frost's or Jaimie Railton's ride.

I seemed to be getting more opportunities, I was riding a lot more frequently and I was going racing nearly every day. I had had my 5 lb claim reduced to 3 lb when I had won on Eskimo Nell at Warwick on 26th November, and I lost my 3 lb claim altogether when I won a handicap chase at Nottingham on Romany Creek on 28th February. That was my ninth win over fences, the 55th winner of my career, my 53rd winner of the season in the UK, and I was clear in the conditional jockeys' championship.

If I had broken my leg that day, I was probably still assured of the conditional jockeys' title, but I refused to believe it. Although Adrian's tally of 71 in 1991–92 was off the scale, and you would win the conditional jockeys' championship with 30 or 40 winners in a normal year, I refused to believe that the title was wrapped up. I was all the while looking over my shoulder, expecting Philip Hide or Rodney Farrant to go on a roll and catch me. Rodney ended up with 29 winners that season, Philip ended up with 34. That total would have been enough to win the title in a normal year but, thankfully, that year wasn't a normal year. Nevertheless, my overriding feeling the whole time was fear of losing the title, not excitement at the prospect of winning it. That was to become a common theme for me.

Now I had no claim, the rides could have dried up. Thankfully, they didn't. The momentum continued, demand for me continued to increase. I had my first ride at the Cheltenham Festival that March, Supreme Master in the first race on the first day. He was a 100/1 shot, but I didn't care, the Cheltenham Festival was going on and I was involved. It was totally different to riding there the previous September: the crowds were there, the whole world was watching, the atmosphere was amazing, in the weigh room before the first race, walking out through the throng of people, cantering to the start, the hum of the grandstand behind me. I finished 16th on Supreme Master.

Bizarrely, Cheltenham day two, I was at Nottingham. I went there to ride The Boiler White for Tim Thomson Jones in a Class F handicap chase. Champion Chase day at Cheltenham and I'm riding in a Class F handicap chase at Nottingham. It was a bit of a comedown all right, there was nobody at Nottingham, no crowds, no cameras, just a couple of people and their dogs – I wondered if the race was worth running at all. As it happened, though, we won, so actually it was well worth it.

I was back at Cheltenham the following day, the final day of the Festival, for two rides, Brave Tornado in the Triumph Hurdle and Beech Road in the Gold Cup. It was amazing. Brave Tornado actually had a chance; I had won the Grade 2 Finesse Hurdle on him at Cheltenham's January meeting, so it was fantastic to be going out in the Triumph Hurdle, the first race on Gold Cup day, with some kind of a chance of winning the race.

Things didn't work out too well for us though. We got hampered at the first flight, and we were too far back in the field and always playing catch-up, but we finished seventh, promoted to sixth when Dr Leunt was disqualified because he had crashed through a rail at the top of the hill.

Beech Road had no chance in the Gold Cup. He was the Champion Hurdler of 1989, but six years' worth of water had passed under the bridge between the 1989 Champion Hurdle and the 1995 Gold Cup. He was a 13-year-old when he lined up in that Gold Cup, another 100/1 shot and deservedly so, but I had won a handicap chase on him at Cheltenham that January, and he was my first ride in the Gold Cup, so he was special to me.

I couldn't believe that I had a ride in the Cheltenham Gold Cup, the biggest race in National Hunt racing. It's different to the Grand National, which is the most famous race, it's the public's race, the race that everybody knows. I have no doubt that not many of my friends at home would have known that I was riding in the Gold Cup, but if I had a ride in the Grand National, everybody would know.

The Gold Cup is the purists' race I suppose, the race that the best staying steeplechaser should win. The Grand National is a handicap, the best horses don't even run in it. Neither Kauto Star nor Denman, the two best staying chasers of this generation, ever ran in the Grand National, although Denman did flirt with it a little. They would have been shouldered with a big weight, they would have been giving weight away to all their rivals. In the Gold Cup, though, every horse carries the same weight, and the best horse on the day, as opposed to the best-handicapped horse, usually wins.

It was unlikely that Beech Road was going to be the best horse on the day, but I didn't really care. It was more important to me at the time that I was riding in the Gold Cup, that I was a part of it all. A conditional rider, my first season riding in the UK, and here I was with a ride in the Gold Cup. The parade beforehand was something I had never experienced before, walking up in front of the stands in order as the guy on the PA system told the packed grandstand who all the horses were. Beech Road, trained by Toby Balding, ridden by Tony McCoy.

Beech Road jumped around okay, but we were never in with a chance of winning, we were never even close, but he kept at it, and we eventually finished seventh of the nine finishers, a distance behind the winner Master Oats, ridden by Norman Williamson. Norman had also won the Champion Hurdle on Alderbrook on the Tuesday, so it was some week for him and for the horses' trainer Kim Bailey.

As it happened, I did get a ride in the Grand National the following month, Chatam for Martin Pipe. Amazing how the world works sometimes. I didn't think that I would ever ride for Martin Pipe. I had turned down the job with him, I had chosen my path, chosen to stick with Toby instead of joining the record-breaking perennial champion trainer, and I thought that that was it, that that had been my one shot and I had missed. So when Dave Roberts called to tell me that I was riding Chatam in the Grand National, I was blown away.

I was ecstatic about having a ride in the Grand National. As I said, the most famous National Hunt horse race in the world, probably the most famous horse race in the world full stop, the race that I used to win more than any other race when I was a kid riding Chippy or the arm of the sofa, and here I was with a ride in it. For real.

There are several races run now over the Grand National fences, but I had never ridden in any of those races, so I had never ridden over those unique fences before. So that was something which I was really looking forward to, as well as the very fact that I would be riding in the Grand National. Then there was the fact that I would be having my first ride for Martin Pipe.

Minnehoma was running again, Dunwoody riding again, but he was 12 years old and he had 11 st 4 lb to carry, as opposed to the 10 st 8 lb that he had carried to victory the previous year, so it wasn't going to be easy for him. Martin also had Riverside Boy in the race, to be ridden by

Irish perennial champion jockey Charlie Swan, and Errant Knight, to be ridden by Mark Perrett.

Chatam wouldn't have been everybody's cup of tea. He had won a Cathcart Chase at the Cheltenham Festival in 1991 and the Hennessy Gold Cup the following season under Peter Scudamore, but he was a bit of a thinker; he might not have been the ideal type of horse that you look for in a Grand National ride. Maybe that was why I got the ride, maybe some of the other lads didn't fancy it, maybe I was the only fool left in the weigh room who would ride him. I didn't care. I fancied it all right.

The buzz beforehand was incredible: the Grand National start is just in front of the stands, and you can hear the buzz from the crowd and the enclosures as you circle at the start. Of course I was nervous, you are always a little nervous before any big race, but a little bit of nerves is a good thing, it means you are switched on, but I was as excited as hell.

Chatam gave me a good ride. We were hampered slightly by a faller at the third fence, the big ditch, and he was down on his nose at Becher's Brook, but he picked himself up well and jumped okay until we got to the 12th fence, the one before you rejoin the main racecourse and come up in front of the stands. We were well behind at the time when he got in tight to the fence, went through the top of it and came crashing down. That was the end of my first Grand National adventure, the first of many, but it had been quite exhilarating.

The whole season had been quite exhilarating actually. I ended up as champion conditional rider with 74 winners. Actually, that total saw me finish seventh in the overall championship, behind Dunwoody, Williamson, Maguire, Osborne, Niven and Bridgwater. It was difficult to believe that I was getting even close to those riders.

I had beaten the record of 71 that Adrian Maguire had set for conditional riders just three years previously. I had turned down the job that I thought would have made me champion conditional as a matter of course, in order that I would be a slower burn, yet I had just gone ahead and won the title anyway. I had ridden in the Gold Cup and the Grand National, and I was in demand. For some reason, I was fashionable, a lot of trainers were wanting me to ride their horses. Things could hardly have been going better.

If there was ever any danger of me running away with myself, I could rely on one man to anchor me back down on solid ground. I was at the Galway Festival that August; I went over to ride Crosula in the Galway Plate for Martin Pipe on the Wednesday. I also rode Mystical City for

Willie Mullins in the Galway Hurdle the following day, and I picked up a couple of other rides along the way.

One of the first people I met when I arrived on the first day was Jim Bolger. I was in the little team room beside the weigh room, having a cup of tea. I was after the conditional jockeys' championship, I was riding in Britain, and Jim wasn't my boss any more, but I still felt like a stable lad when I met him. He extended his hand.

'Well done,' he said, as he shook mine.

'Thanks, boss,' I said. I still called him boss.

'But don't be thinking you were right to leave me when you did,' he said.

I stared back at him blankly, helpless. I could have been back in the yard at Coolcullen, getting a bollocking over a piece of woodchip that was out of place.

'Don't think you were right and I was wrong,' he continued. 'You still would have been much better off staying with me for another year, and then going to England.'

I just nodded, speechless. There was no point in arguing, and I was powerless anyway.

'Well done though,' he concluded. 'I'm very pleased for you.'

CHAPTER 10

Ton Up

There had been rumours doing the rounds for a little while that Richard Dunwoody was not going to be Martin Pipe's stable jockey the following season. I first heard them at Cheltenham: that things weren't too harmonious in the camp, relationships were strained, Dunwoody wasn't happy, Pipe wasn't happy. That type of thing. You don't take any notice of these things usually, just racecourse gossip. So I didn't pay too much heed to the rumours – it didn't affect me anyway. So things weren't great between Dunwoody and Pipe, that's the way these things go. Relationships falter.

I was at Hereford on the evening of 1st June when Dunwoody had a bad fall on James Pigg in the second race and took a right kicking. He had to give up the rest of his rides that night, including the ride on Crosula in the novices' hurdle. There were a couple of us sitting in the weigh room when it became apparent that Dunwoody wasn't going to be able to ride for the rest of the evening; Norman Williamson was there, David Bridgwater was there, Brendan Powell was there.

'Well, we'll know very soon who's going to be Pipe's stable jockey next season,' Brendan said.

I looked over at him. We all looked at him.

'Whoever rides Crosula,' he said, as if he was explaining the theory of relativity to a group of five-year-olds. 'Whoever Pipey asks to ride Crosula, that person will be his stable jockey next season.'

Shortly after Brendan published his hypothesis, Chester Barnes, Martin's assistant trainer, came to the weigh room, had a word with the door man, and the door man shouted in:

'Tony McCoy, Chester Barnes wants to talk to you.'

Brendan burst out laughing. There were roars of laughter all round as I made my way to the door.

'It's you, McCoy! You're going to be Pipe's stable jockey next year!'

Sure enough, Chester asked me if I could ride Crosula.

I won on Crosula, I just kicked him out in front as instructed and he was never headed. We won by a distance.

Despite Brendan Powell's theory, I still never thought that Martin would ask me to be his stable jockey. There were too many other top-class riders around for me to even be in the frame. Charlie Swan had been talked about a lot. Actually, there was talk of Charlie getting the job when Peter Scudamore retired, and when Dunwoody got the job, the talk was that Charlie would be next.

Charlie had ridden a bit for Martin in the interim; he was based in Ireland but he came over to the UK for the big meetings and he was riding a few of the Pipe horses. It would have been a big commitment for Charlie though: he had a great position in Ireland, he was king pin, he was the best, he was riding for Aidan O'Brien and he was riding Danoli and he was riding just about anything he wanted to ride after that. He rode 119 winners in Ireland the previous season, which was quite a tally given how little racing there is in Ireland relative to Britain. To put that total into context, Franny Woods was next best with 69 winners. So Charlie would have been giving up a lot in Ireland to come over and ride for Martin and, in the end, it never happened.

Before 1995, the first year of summer jumping in Britain, National Hunt racing took a break for the summer months and National Hunt jockeys took it easy, I'm sure. I wasn't around then. At the end of my first season in the UK, summer jumping began. No break, no let-up.

Martin had a strong team of jumpers for the summer. The ground is obviously firmer during the summer than it is during the winter, so it can be harder on horses' legs, and a fall on good or firm ground is usually harder on jockeys than a fall on soft ground, which is why there was no National Hunt racing during the summer until 1995. Even though there is now National Hunt racing 12 months a year, the good horses usually don't come out until October or November, when the ground gets softer and the big races appear on the horizon, and they are usually roughed off for the summer in April, off for a well-earned summer break. So it is generally a different type of horse that runs during the summer, a horse that likes fast ground for sure, and Martin had plenty of them.

I started to get a few rides for Martin, but other jockeys did as well. David Bridgwater got plenty. David was kind of riding as second jockey to Nigel Twiston-Davies at the time as well. He was riding a few winners for Martin, but so was I, and the racecourse rumour was that the job as stable jockey was between the two of us.

On 11th June I rode a double for Martin at Uttoxeter, Crosula again in a handicap chase and Shikaree in a novices' hurdle. As I was coming back into the winner's enclosure on the horse, Martin came up, walked alongside me, put his hand on my leg and looked up at me:

'What about the job then?' he asked.

I looked down at him. What about what job? I had no idea how to deal with that curveball. How could I answer? What about the job that I haven't been offered yet? And if he was offering it to me, what was I going to do? Was I big enough to take on such a job? Was I good enough? Was the job bigger than me? Would I be able to handle being in such a high-profile job, just out of the short trousers of my career, just one season in the UK under my belt, the job that had been held by Richard Dunwoody and by Peter Scudamore before him, two legends of National Hunt racing? I think I just smiled.

I met Martin again after racing that day.

'Come on now, we'll have a chat about this job,' he said. 'Would you be interested in the job?'

'Of course I would be,' I said, taking care to continue in the conditional, as he had started. 'I'd be very flattered to be offered the job.'

'Would you be interested in being our retained jockey?' asked Martin.

Jesus, this was for real now. The Martin Pipe job, the most sought-after job in National Hunt racing, was there in front of me on a platter. All I had to do was reach out gently, pick it up and put it in my pocket. It was mine if I wanted it, it appeared.

'It's obviously a very big position,' I said. 'I'm obviously flattered for me even to be considered for such a job. The worries I would have though would be that some of your owners would think that I didn't have enough experience for the job, that they would want Richard Dunwoody or Norman Williamson or Jamie Osborne to ride their horses, not Anthony McCoy.'

Martin just stood and listened as I babbled away.

'Maybe I'd be better off just riding the horses,' I said. 'You know, just riding away and seeing how we go. Not being your stable jockey, you know, no retainer, just riding some of your horses.'

My fear was that it wouldn't work out, and that it would be a disaster. I was going along fairly well as I was, riding away for Toby and riding for a lot of outside yards. I was after riding over 20 winners in the first month of the new season, I was leading the jockeys' championship. Not that that counted for a whole lot at the time, it was only summer jumping, the real season hadn't got going, but it was still a fair measure of how well I was doing, and once I was riding winners I was happy.

Follow this through. If I joined Martin, I wouldn't be able to ride for many, if any, outside yards. Martin had so many horses, so many runners that you were rarely free to ride for other trainers. Then trainers stop using you, they start to use other riders, and suddenly you are devoted exclusively to Martin. Not that that is a bad thing. On the contrary, it's a very good thing if things work out, it's the fast track to being champion jockey, but if it didn't work out I imagined that it could be a very lonely place.

Imagine joining Martin and some of his owners not wanting me. You didn't need a vivid imagination to envision that scenario; I had just completed my first year in the UK, champion conditional but still a conditional. Imagine they wanted Dunwoody. Again, no vivid imagination required.

So some owners in Martin's want Richard instead of me, then other owners ask, hold on a second, how come Dunwoody is riding that guy's horses and the young fellow is riding mine? Then another owner wants Dunwoody, then another, then another. Suddenly I am only riding a small proportion of the horses in the yard. Stuff like that doesn't go unnoticed, and we know that in this game, fashion is as important as substance, perception is reality. It's a fickle business.

Gradually the notion goes around that McCoy isn't good enough for some or most of Pipe's owners. He's not that good at all, really. A flash in the pan. Then there you are, high and dry, no claim, out of fashion, a pair of drainpipe trousers, and your whole first season has been for nothing. Champion conditional, my arse. What use is that? You are just another journeyman jockey fighting for rides, struggling for recognition.

It can all unravel very quickly.

I asked Dave Roberts and Toby for their advice. Toby told me that Richard had struggled at Martin's, that he had never really fitted in. I kind of knew that anyway, there was always a feeling around that Richard and Martin's relationship was never as harmonious as the relationship that Martin had had with Richard's predecessor Peter Scudamore. That also worried me. Maybe Martin was a difficult man, maybe he was a tough boss and it wouldn't work out. So despite the fact that it was the best job in the world, no question, I was reluctant to take it.

I'm not sure why it didn't really work out between Richard and Martin. People said that Richard didn't really suit Martin's style. Richard liked to ride a race, he liked to think about how best to ride a horse in a race, sit in behind, take his time. That wasn't what Martin wanted. Most of Martin's horses were bounced out in front and never headed. From my point of view, Martin Pipe was so far ahead of his time, there was no advantage to be gained from riding a race. His horses basically just killed off the opposition because they were fitter than everyone else's horses. The only reason you went flat out the whole way was because the other horses couldn't live with you, they weren't as fit as you. So if you knew that you were going to win by going flat out from the start, why would you ride the horse any other way?

Richard was used to riding for The Duke and for Nicky Henderson, they were probably different types of horses that he was riding there, more chasing types, horses that needed more time, to be patiently ridden. That wasn't Martin's style at all.

Maybe their personalities clashed as well. Both had big personalities, that's for sure. I'm sure Richard wanted to do things his way, ride horses his way, and I'm sure he was frustrated that Martin couldn't see the benefit. By the same token, I'm sure that, if Martin knew that his horses were fitter than everyone else's, it would have been frustrating as hell for him to watch Richard ride a waiting race, not kicking on from the start.

I have to say that, much and all as I thought Richard was a brilliant rider, Martin's attitude made more sense to me. If you knew that by riding a horse in a certain way it would probably win, why would you ride it any other way?

When I started riding for Martin, I just did what he told me to do. I thought, who am I to argue with Martin Pipe? It's safe to say that he knows what he's doing. If he is asking me to do something, if he is telling me to ride a horse in a certain way, there is a reason for it. I never questioned it.

That was later though. When Martin offered me the job this time, I actually didn't give him a response. I told him that I would go off and think about it, but I never went back to him with an answer. I didn't know what to answer, so I just let things drift. I was quite happy with things as they were. I was riding away for Toby, I was riding away for other trainers, I was riding away for Martin. I was very happy with how things had developed.

Toby told me that I could ride all his horses. That was a big step forward. It meant that I wasn't going to have to step aside if Adrian or Jimmy Frost or anybody else was available. It was a big vote of confidence in me from Toby. I was starting to ride a bit for Paul Nicholls and Philip Hobbs as well. Paul Nicholls and Philip Hobbs were not the Paul Nicholls and Philip Hobbs that we know today –Paul Nicholls champion trainer every year since 2005, Philip Hobbs always in the top five – but they were good trainers, it was great to be riding for them. So it was all ticking along quite nicely from where I was standing.

I'm sure that Martin wasn't happy with the way it was ticking along though. He was never a trainer who was going to be happy just to use the best jockey who was available. He always wanted a stable jockey, he had always had one ever since he became a trainer with whom the world had to reckon, and I suppose I knew that it was inevitable that he would have to appoint one, whether it was me or not.

I suppose David Bridgwater and I were sharing the Pipe rides, but I was probably doing a little better, I was generally riding some of the more fancied ones, and most of them were winning. That was the thing about a Martin Pipe horse, often you just had to point it in the right direction, keep it upright and it would win. You didn't have to be a superb jockey or anything, they were all so well-schooled, they were all so fit, your grandmother could have won on most of them.

On 21st June I rode Crosula in a handicap chase at Worcester and he ran out with me at the third fence. There was nothing I could have done about it, he was just free and fresh and he took me outside the wings. The stewards enquired into the incident. I suppose they had every right to hold an enquiry as Crosula had never done anything like that before and he was the 4/6 favourite for the race. At the very least, the stewards had to be seen to be asking the question. It was good for the optics. Lots of punters would have backed Crosula and it wouldn't have looked good if they hadn't even enquired into the incident. They can't have thought that I would have done something like that on purpose.

My relationship with Martin, or at least with Martin's horses, such as it was, seemed to change after that. Maybe it was just a coincidence, maybe it was getting to that point anyway, maybe he had decided that he couldn't be waiting around for this young whippersnapper to make a decision. It just happened that, from that point, I wasn't riding that many horses for Martin, and the ones I was riding weren't that well-fancied. David Bridgwater seemed to be getting more rides for him, and more of the better ones. There was nothing I could do about it; the trainer, or the owner and the trainer, decides who rides the horses, not the jockeys. I just put my head down and continued to try to do my best. Then one morning, a couple of days later, I picked up the *Racing Post* to read that David Bridgwater had been appointed as Martin's stable jockey.

I had only myself to blame. Opportunities are not lost, they are taken by others. Martin had offered me the job, I had said that I would think about it, then I just never went back to him. What was I thinking? Did I just think that I could continue riding his best horses without going back to him and saying, yes, I'll take the job Martin, thanks very much? I did. I'm embarrassed even now thinking back on it.

I didn't even give him an answer. It was cheeky, it was rude, it was thoughtless, it was short-sighted. Martin must have thought that I was stupid. How could anyone in their right mind, who had been over riding for just one season, not want to be Martin Pipe's stable jockey? Ah he's got no brains, as Jim would say.

I didn't tell anyone that I had been offered the job, I felt so stupid. Dave Roberts knew and Toby knew, but nobody else What would I have said? Oh, Martin Pipe offered me the job as stable jockey, but I'm champion conditional so I just told him I'd think about it and I never went back to him. My burning ambition was to be champion jockey, I was offered the job that would almost automatically make me champion jockey and I said I'd think about it. Billy Rock would have kicked my arse.

People had been asking me about it all right, had I been offered the job, was I Pipe's stable jockey, and they asked about it even more when it was announced that David Bridgwater had got the job. I thought it best just to say nothing and move on. I wouldn't have known where to begin explaining it.

I was disappointed that David had been given the job, but not devastated. I was leading the jockeys' championship at that stage. Adrian Maguire was out with a broken arm, and Richard Dunwoody was easing off, having decided that he wasn't going to be haring up and down the country to ride every horse he could, that he was going to concentrate more on quality than quantity, and that he would probably be riding a bit in Ireland. So during the summer, David Bridgwater and I were making hay. I was about 20 winners ahead of him when he got the Pipe job, but I was sure that I wasn't going to be able to maintain that lead, not with the firepower that David now had at his disposal.

In one sense, I was happy not having the Pipe job. As I said, I worried about the pressure from Martin himself and the pressure from owners. That said, during the four or five weeks that I rode for him that summer, I thought it was the greatest thing in the world. It seemed like a fairly easy job, just get on the horse and point it in the right direction, and I found Martin really easy to deal with. There was a sense of closure when David got the job. At least I knew where I stood.

Although I was leading the jockeys' championship, I had no notion of winning the title. I knew Adrian was coming back, and even though Dunwoody had said that he wasn't going to be going pell-mell for the championship, I knew that, Dunwoody being Dunwoody, he wouldn't be able to resist. More than that, though, David Bridgwater was now Martin Pipe's stable jockey, and that was the golden ticket to the championship.

I did decide that I would put my head down and ride as many winners as I could though. I decided not to take a holiday, that I would just ride through the whole season and see how I went. But the stewards had a different view. They gave me and six other riders seven days for going the wrong side of dolled off hurdle at Taunton in November. It was ridiculous, we went left when the rules said we should have gone right, but left was the most sensible and safest way to go as there was hardly enough room for us to go right. The only reason Jamie Osborne was able to go right was because he was tailed off and he could go there on his own, which he did, and was duly awarded the race.

We appealed, of course, and went to Portman Square in London to appeal against the suspensions, to appeal to the Jockey Club's sense of common sense. Alas, they didn't see it our way, our appeals were thrown out and we all had to sit on the sidelines for seven days. I missed the Hennessy Gold Cup meeting at Newbury as a result. I wasn't happy. And I was even less happy when I went back to Taunton for their next meeting and saw that the course plan had been changed, that we were now going the left side of the hurdle if it was dolled off instead of the right, the way we had actually gone, and I thought, what a fucking joke.

The introduction of summer jumping in 1995 was a brilliant thing for me. I thought that, if I could ride as many winners as possible during the summer, during the bad racing before the season really gets going, before the good horses come out and before some of the other jockeys have got tuned in again after the summer, if I could sit on top of the table for as long as possible, then that would be something, people might not see me as a one-season wonder, a flash in the pan. Every time they looked at the table, they would see AP McCoy on top of it, and that could help me, it could make them think that, if I was leading the jockeys' championship I might be all right. So I said that I would keep going for as long as I could, until the petrol and the momentum of the early season ran out and the big boys got rolling, or until the Pipe yard kicked into gear and David Bridgwater took off.

I had ridden 74 winners as a conditional the previous season, and I had had a great year, so I thought, if I could ride 100 winners this season, that would be fantastic.

It was desperate for Adrian but it was a help to me that he was out injured. It is an ill wind that doesn't blow someone some good. Adrian rode a lot for John White, and John was always a great man to have his horses going during the summer from day one, so with Adrian out, I got to ride a lot of John's horses. John placed his horses really well and he had them fit and ready to go during the summer. That summer was the John White/Martin Pipe show, as were many other summers that followed, and I was fortunate to be in John's corner when I wasn't in Martin's. So I was riding for John, and obviously for Toby and for Paul Nicholls and Philip Hobbs, I had a good set-up, and the winners continued to flow. I had ridden 50 winners by the first week in October and was setting a fair pace in the jockeys' championship.

I was at Ascot on 16th December, riding Call Equiname for Paul Nicholls to win the Kennel Gate Hurdle, and I rode Morley Street, who was tailed off in the Long Walk Hurdle, but I didn't have a ride in the last race, the two-mile hurdle. Martin had two in the race, David Bridgwater was riding Pridwell and Jonathan Lower was riding Kissair, on whom he had won the Triumph Hurdle at Cheltenham the previous March.

Jonathan was riding at Uttoxeter earlier in the day, and was due to get a helicopter to Ascot for the last race to ride Kissair, but the fog was really bad, so Jonathan was grounded. Bridgie switched from Pridwell to ride Kissair; he obviously thought that Kissair had a better chance even though Pridwell was a shorter price, and Chester Barnes – who was at Ascot on the day, Martin wasn't there – asked me if I would ride Pridwell.

I won on Pridwell. It was my first ride for Martin since Bridgie had been announced as the stable jockey. There were lots of important things going on here: it was significant that I was asked to ride Pridwell, and it was obviously significant that we won. A winner is always significant. Before that day, I was thinking that I would probably never ride for Martin again. After that day I was thinking, maybe this is meant to be.

Toby was going okay, and Paul Nicholls was getting going and Philip Hobbs was improving the type of horse that he had. Philip's brother, Peter, who had been his stable jockey, had just retired and Philip was using the best available, Dunwoody, plus Graham Bradley sometimes as well, but I seemed to be his first choice. So between the three yards, I would have had about 100 horses to ride.

I was more or less first choice for Paul as well, and I used to go up there and school a bit. My days of mucking out at Toby's were over, I was beginning to get more and more established and my mornings were spent either riding out or schooling. Paul always had a nice type of horse. He had had See More Indians before I arrived, a top-staying novice chaser, winner of the Feltham Chase at Kempton on King George day, and subsequent Gold Cup winner See More Business was there when I arrived. I rode him in all three of his novice hurdles that season, all three of which he won. Subsequent Champion Chase winner Call Equiname was also there. I won four novice hurdles on him, including that Kennel Gate Hurdle at Ascot on 16th December.

I rode my 100th winner of the season on Amber Valley, a horse trained by Dai Williams, at Nottingham on 17th January. Made all, unchallenged: it could have been a Martin Pipe horse. It was incredible, I had set myself a target of 100 winners for the season, a really ambitious target I thought, dream stuff. A century of winners, my first century, would really be something, so to reach that goal on 17th January, with over three months of the season still to go, was fantastic.

I started to think then that I had a chance of winning the jockeys' championship. I didn't say it to anyone, and any time anybody asked me about it, I said no, no chance, sure it's only a matter of time before Pipe kicks into overdrive and Bridgie won't be able to count the numbers of winners he'll be having.

In truth, I was waiting for that to happen, for Martin to start churning out the winners, two, three, four a day and for Bridgie to close in on me and go past me, but it wasn't happening, I was maintaining my lead over him, and I had a steady flow of winners coming from Toby, Paul and Philip. On top of that, Norman and Adrian had both missed a lot of the season through bad injuries, and Richard was true to his word, going over to ride in Ireland a lot, clearly not interested in winning the championship. It was obvious that the title was between me and Bridgie from as early as January.

I just needed to keep up the momentum, keep all my trainers happy. Naively perhaps, I thought that it would be possible to do so.

Winning the 1996 Mumm Melling chase at Aintree on Viking Flagship, the only time I ever rode him. (That's Richard Dunwoody on Sound Man behind me!)

Winning the 1997 Arkle on Or Royal

Jumping the final flight in the 1997 Champion Hurdle on Make A Stand. We never saw a rival.

En route to winning the 1997 Scottish Grand National on Belmont King

The only flying dismount of my life, on Blowing Wind after winning the County Hurdle in 1998. Frankie Dettori needn't worry – I won't be doing that again!

Me winning on Pridwell in the Martell Aintree Hurdle, 1998 (Mirrorpix)

Gloria Victis, the best novice chaser I have ever ridden.

Back to the winners' enclosure with Edredon Bleu after scraping home in the Queen Mother Champion Chase.

On the pint-sized Northern Starlight, winning the 2000 John Huges Chase over the big Aintree fences.

Valiramix, so sad that he
was never able to realise
his true potential.

Lady Cricket

If I was a horse, I would probably be Deano's Beeno.

Euphoric after breaking
Sir Gordon Richards' record
on Valfonic

Soaring on Seebald

Uttoxeter, 27 August 2002, my
agent Dave Roberts was on hand
to see me riding my 1700th
winner on Mighty Monefalco,
beating Richard Dunwoody's
record number of wins by a
National Hunt jockey. (*Racing Post*)

Going, going, going, gone! Falling off Golden Alpha when clear at the second last fence in the 40th Anniversary Chase at Cheltenham, December 2002. (Mirrorpix)

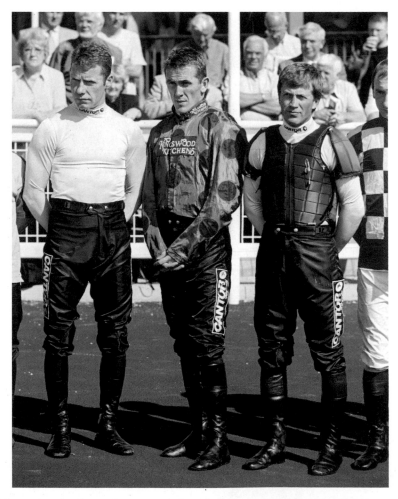

Three Musketeers: Fitzy, me and Carl observing a minute's silence on the first anniversary of 9/11. We were all sponsored by Cantor, who lost 658 employees that day, more than any other World Trade Center tenant.

Winning the 2005
Powers Gold Cup on
Like-A-Butterfly

Baracouda, one of the
best long-distance
hurdlers of all time

Winning the 2002 King
George VI Chase at
Kempton on Best Mate
(Mirrorpix)

Jubilant after winning
the 2006 Champion
Hurdle on Brave Inca

CHAPTER 11

Number One

Monicasman was a nice horse, I finished second on him in a decent novices' hurdle at Sandown in February and I won on him at Newbury's meeting in early March, just over a week before the Cheltenham Festival. After the race, his trainer Alan Jarvis asked me if I would ride him at Cheltenham, that he was going in the Sun Alliance Hurdle. He would have had a chance, so I was happy to ride him.

My book of Cheltenham rides was building up nicely. I was leading the jockeys' championship, I had ridden 120 winners before Cheltenham, so it was right that I should have been in demand, but it doesn't always work out like that; you don't always get what you think you deserve in this game, so I was delighted to be putting a couple of rides in the bank. Then Adrian Maguire got injured in a four-horse pile-up at Leicester, and things changed.

I felt desperately sorry for Adrian. It was the second year in a row that he was going to miss the Festival, having missed it the previous year after his mother died just before the meeting started. Even though it did mean that there were spare rides to be had, you had to feel sorry for Adrian. Everybody did. The Duke had a strong team of horses going to Cheltenham that year, as he did most years, and with Adrian now unavailable, he was looking for other jockeys. Dave called me.

'The Duke has been on looking for you to ride a couple of horses for him at Cheltenham,' he said.

'That's great,' I said. I hadn't ridden for The Duke before, so this was another huge step forward.

'Zabadi in the Triumph Hurdle,' said Dave, 'Barton Bank in the Gold Cup and Jack Tanner in the Sun Alliance Hurdle.'

'Fantastic.'

'What about Monicasman?' asked Dave.

Monicasman was a good horse, but Jack Tanner was a different matter altogether. He was a really exciting novice that The Duke had got from Ireland, and he had a big chance of winning the Sun Alliance Hurdle. As well as that, I'm not sure that I was in a position to pick and choose; I don't know that I could have said, great, I'll ride Zabadi and Barton Bank, but I won't ride Jack Tanner. It was an all-or-nothing deal from The Duke and, no offence to Monicasman or to Alan Jarvis, but if you have to choose between three good horses of David Nicholson's or one good horse of Alan Jarvis's, you're going to choose David Nicholson all day long.

It wasn't ideal, you don't like letting trainers down, telling them that you'll ride their horse in a race and then say actually you won't, you've been offered a better horse to ride. But it happens sometimes. And it wasn't as if it was the day before Cheltenham or anything, it was about a week before the Festival; and it wasn't as if Alan Jarvis was going to have difficulty getting another rider to ride Monicasman. I was sure he would understand; Adrian was out and The Duke had asked me to ride three of his horses. He had to know that this was an offer I couldn't really turn down.

Dave rang Alan Jarvis to tell him, and I thought that was the last I would hear of it. I was wrong.

The next day I received a call from Ann Jarvis, Alan Jarvis's wife. She was livid. 'You said you'd ride our horse and now you're going back on your word.' That type of thing, replete with expletives. Fine, she was upset, I understood. It's not great to be going back on your word, and she was more upset than I thought the trainer would be, but at the same time I understood. I wasn't happy either with the fact that I was un-committing to something.

Jack Tanner ran well in the Sun Alliance Hurdle to finish fourth behind Urubande. As it happened, Jamie Osborne rode Monicasman, but he ran out with him at the first flight. Zabadi was a bit disappointing in the Triumph Hurdle, he could only finish eighth, while Barton Bank ran well enough in the Gold Cup to finish a distant fourth behind Imperial Call, ridden by Conor O'Dwyer. It was great for Conor. His first Cheltenham Festival winner and it was a Gold Cup. Actually, Conor only ever won four races at Cheltenham: two Gold Cups and two Champion Hurdles.

I was riding Kibreet for Philip Hobbs in the Grand Annual Chase. The Grand Annual used to be the third-last race on the last day at the Cheltenham Festival. Gold Cup, Foxhunter, Grand Annual, Cathcart, County Hurdle, that was the way it used to go, so I was running out of opportunities to ride my first Cheltenham Festival winner. It was great to be as heavily involved as I was, it was great to have so many rides, it was great not to be going to Nottingham with its tumbleweed on the Wednesday and it was great to be involved in the big races – I had had my first ride in the Champion Hurdle on Absalom's Lady (66/1, finished 14th of 14 finishers) – but, me being me, I craved a winner.

Kibreet had a chance in the Grand Annual. It was a competitive race, a 13-runner two-mile handicap chase, but he was a super jumper who would gallop all day for you. I had ridden him a couple of times that year, including on his previous run at Sandown, when he had done well to finish second to High Barron after getting hampered when Martin's Lamp fell in front of us at the second fence down the back straight.

The plan was to be handy on him; he was such a good jumper and he stayed two miles so well that it made sense to be up there in the van, making full use of his fluent jumping. Easthorpe and Jason Titley led for most of the way, and I sat in behind him until we ran down the hill on the far side to the third last fence, when I gave Kibreet a squeeze and asked him to stride on. He jumped the third-last well, went on around the home turn, jumped the second-last and ran down to the last fence, clear. I couldn't hear anything coming behind me. If we jump the last fence well, this could be it – this could be my first Cheltenham Festival winner.

He did jump it well, and I sat down to ride him up the hill. I didn't look left or right, just put my head down and rode him out, intent on getting to the winning post in the shortest possible time. I knew that he would stay on well, that it was unlikely that anything would come from too far behind us. Nothing did. Kibreet ran gallantly and gamely all the way up the hill and carried me to my first Cheltenham Festival win, four lengths clear of Easthorpe.

I was on top of the world. It wasn't a Gold Cup or a Champion Hurdle, it wasn't an Irish winner, which is always trumpeted and cheered all the way back into the winner's enclosure. It was the third-last race, the Gold Cup was over, there were plenty of people in the bars, but there were also plenty of people in the stands and at the winner's enclosure to cheer me in, and I loved it. I was floating on air. First Festival win. Another massive milestone, another childhood ambition fulfilled.

It was important for me to ride a winner at Cheltenham that year. I was leading the jockeys' championship, but I hadn't ridden any of the big winners. You need the big high-profile winners as well as the copious amounts of them. It was only my second season riding, it was only my second Cheltenham Festival, but you don't want to be going to too many of them and coming away without a winner.

It's like anything: success breeds success. It's fantastic to ride a winner at Cheltenham, like I'm sure that it's fantastic to score a goal in the Premiership, but the longer you go without riding a winner there, the longer you go without scoring for your new club, the more the pressure mounts and the more difficult it seems to get. Then you ride one, then you score one, then you relax and the winners or goals flow.

Adrian was still out by the time Aintree rolled around, so I kept the ride on Kibreet, even though Dunwoody was riding a lot of The Duke's horses in Adrian's absence. Back to his old boss.

I was delighted to keep the ride on Zabadi. I fancied him going to Cheltenham; he had been impressive in winning the Adonis Hurdle at Kempton, usually a good pointer to the Triumph Hurdle, on his last run before Cheltenham. I thought that he was my best chance of riding a winner all week, but, having ridden him at Cheltenham, I fancied him even more for the Glenlivet Hurdle at Aintree. He was a nice horse, an Aga Khan-bred horse who had won on the flat for John Oxx in Ireland, and I thought that Aintree would suit him better than Cheltenham did; the flatter track would play more to his strengths.

It did. I held him up out the back, he picked up nicely in the home straight and he quickened away well from the final flight to win nicely.

I had some other nice rides at Aintree that year. I rode Barton Bank again for The Duke to finish second to Scotton Banks in the Martell Cup, and I rode Top Spin to win the three-mile handicap hurdle, the last race on the Thursday, for John Jenkins. That was some thrill. Top Spin was a horse who had to be dropped out and ridden patiently, so I dropped him out, stone last of the 19 runners, and made my ground gradually. As it turned out, luckily, we timed our run perfectly and just got up on the line to beat Dunwoody on a horse of The Duke's, Jathib, by a neck.

I rode Viking Flagship in the big two-and-a-half-mile chase, the Mumm Melling Chase. That was a big day. It was my first really high-profile top-class ride. I had ridden Beach Road and I had ridden Morley Street, both Champion Hurdle winners, but they were well past their prime by the time I got to ride them in races. Even Barton Bank was beyond his peak.

Viking Flagship, by contrast, was still in his prime. He had won the Champion Chase in 1994 and 1995, but he was still only nine, and he had run a cracker at Cheltenham that year as well, he and Sound Man going at each other from a long way out, and softening each other up for Klairon Davis to arrive at the last and do the pair of them. It was still a huge run from Viking Flagship to finish second.

It was a massive thing for me that The Duke had asked me to ride Viking Flagship at Aintree, and I was determined to repay his faith. Klairon Davis and Sound Man were in the race again, the first three from the Champion Chase taking each other on again. We took it up from Coulton at the third-last and powered clear to win really impressively. It was a great feeling, coming back into the winner's enclosure at Aintree, The Duke there, everybody all smiles, a Grade 1 winner, another Aintree winner. It was the only time that I ever rode Viking Flagship, but it was great to get to ride him and to win on him. He was some horse.

After the race Mum called to say that my sister Roisin had had a baby girl, Annie, her first grandchild. My first Grade 1 win, my first niece, 29th March 1996, that's one birthday I won't forget.

I rode Deep Bramble in the Grand National that year. He wasn't a straightforward ride, he could be a little bit quirky, and a lot of the lads wouldn't have fancied him in a Grand National or as a safe conveyance, but he was a classy horse, he had a chance of winning the race in my eyes, so I was delighted to ride him. He had been good when he was trained by Michael Hourigan in Ireland, he had won an Ericsson Chase, the modern-day Lexus Chase, and Paul Barber had paid a decent price for him to bring him to the UK to be trained by Paul Nicholls.

I did get a great spin off him before he went lame. I don't think we would have won, I don't think we would have beaten Fitzy on Rough Quest, who had finished second to Imperial Call in the Gold Cup at Cheltenham that year and who looked thrown-in at the weights in the National as a result, but I'm sure we would have been placed. Unfortunately, Deep Bramble never raced again.

I was leading rider at Aintree that year with three winners. Jonathan Lower had also ridden three winners, but I had more seconds than him (Barton Bank and Clifton Beat in the second-last race) so I was deemed to be the leading rider at the meeting and I was presented with the trophy.

In my head, though, I still didn't think that the jockeys' championship was secure. There were still eight weeks to go in the season, which didn't finish until the end of May that year, and I was still waiting for Martin Pipe to unleash his end-of-season arsenal that would give David

Bridgwater the turbo-boost that would allow him to catch me.

I did go to Punchestown for two days though. By the time the Punchestown Festival began on 23rd April, I reckoned that I was far enough clear to allow myself two days in Ireland, that I could go a couple of days without riding any winners in the UK and still not lose the title.

Punchestown was just a three-day meeting back then, not the five-day extravaganza that it has become, and I was riding at Chepstow on the first day, where I rode two winners, so I was happy enough heading off to Ireland.

I had a remarkable couple of days at Punchestown. I rode Mulligan for Mouse Morris to win the first race on the Wednesday, the two-mile novices' hurdle. I rode a treble on the Thursday: Mayasta, who was trained by Frank Berry and owned by JP McManus in the two-mile handicap hurdle, Have To Think for Arthur Moore in the three-mile handicap chase, and Shaunies Lady for Aidan O'Brien in the Champion Four-Year-Old Hurdle. Aidan had four in the race, as was his wont, and I think I was on the third string.

Mayasta was actually my first ride for JP McManus, my first time putting on those famous green and gold hooped silks, the silks that I wear so often these days, the ones I wore when I won the Grand National on Don't Push It, as well as in so many other races. Actually, Mayasta is the dam of Synchronised, bred by JP's wife Noreen, on whom I won the Midlands National in 2010 and the Welsh Grand National in 2011. It just shows you how long I am on the go. It's a bad scene when you win a novices' hurdle on a mare and then win a Welsh National on her son!

So I had four winners at the Punchestown Festival, my first time riding there, each of them trained by a different trainer, Mouse Morris, Frank Berry, Aidan O'Brien and Arthur Moore, four of the top National Hunt trainers in Ireland at the time. I was leading rider at Punchestown as well as at Aintree. I didn't expect to be top rider at either. It's amazing when the cards drop right for you: four winners in two days, top rider at the Punchestown Festival, top rider at a meeting I wasn't even sure I was going to attend.

I was standing in the parade ring after the last race after having been presented with my trophy for leading rider when Anna Moore, Arthur's daughter, came up and asked me if I would go up with some of the jockeys to a group of students who had been on a day out at the races, just say a few words about being a jockey. Jason Titley and Graham Bradley were going up and a few of the other lads, she said. Apparently Richard

Dunwoody was supposed to go up as well, but he had had to leave early, so they needed somebody to fill in for him. I was second choice after Dunwoody. Nothing new in that then!

I said no problem, I wasn't rushing away after racing. On the contrary, I was planning on going out with the lads, so I was happy enough to stick around for a bit. Anna introduced me to the girl who had organised the students' day at the races, Chanelle I thought she said her name was, a pretty blonde girl who was very nice, if a little stressed at the time.

And so it began.

CHAPTER 12

Chasing

I shouldn't have asked Chanelle to hold the trophy for me. That was the first of many mistakes that I made-with her. I'm still making them.

She came up to me and tapped me on the shoulder. Here's your trophy back. She didn't add, you jumped-up little shit, who do you think you are, a jockey are you? Well why haven't I heard of you? Hold your own trophy.

But I'm sure she was thinking it.

Chanelle Burke grew up in Loughrea in Galway, the third of five children. Her dad Michael is a qualified vet, he trained with Dermot Weld, now one of Ireland's leading trainers, at University College Dublin, the pair of them sharing a house in Dublin for five years, and he has always been into horses and racing. He set up his company Chanelle Veterinary in 1979 and established Chanelle Pharmaceuticals six years later. Chanelle's mother's father, Jimmy Kelly, was a jockey; he rode for Paddy Mullins's dad. Her mother Mary grew up in a house in which her dad was a jockey, they always had horses and they used to go racing a lot. Her dad's family was also always into horses and into racing, and her mum and dad have always had horses down through the years, so she went racing a lot when she was a child.

She rode a bit as well. She rode out on The Curragh for two summers, she rode for Michael Halford and she rode her dad's horse Bamapour to win at the Galway Festival in 1995 and at Gowran Park two weeks later. Bamapour joined Martin Pipe in 1997 and I rode him to win 11 times.

Chanelle studied marketing and finance in Dublin, then went backpacking for a year and came home to work in London for Wyeth before she joined the family pharmaceuticals business, which had always been the plan. After two years working for Wyeth, she called her dad: am I ready now? Okay, you're ready, so she returned home to work with her dad in his pharmaceuticals company.

Chanelle set up a racing society in her college, and she organised a day out for the students at Punchestown in 1996. She knew some of the jockeys, she knew Anthony Powell well, and he'd helped her to organise some of the jockeys coming up to say hello to the students after racing.

After the talk, we all went in to Naas to a nightclub. I was talking to Chanelle for most of the night and thought I was making progress, until I realised that she was trying to set me up with her friend Ursula. Apparently she didn't really fancy me. Hard to believe, I know.

I was staying at the Ambassador Hotel on the Dublin Road, and she was on her way back to Dublin, so she said she would give me a lift back to the hotel. But when we were walking back to her car, she made me walk on the other side of the road. I couldn't believe it. She didn't want to be seen to be hanging out with a jockey. As I got out of the car at the Ambassador Hotel, I asked her for her number.

'What do you want my number for?'

'I'll give you a call,' I said. 'We could meet up for a drink.'

'Sure I'll see you the next time I'm racing.' She really wasn't interested.

'When are you racing again?' I asked her.

'Well I'll be at The Curragh for the Guineas,' she said.

I made it my business to be at The Curragh for the Guineas, and I met her in the champagne bar. Everyone seemed to be going to a 21st birthday party in New Ross after racing, and I managed to get myself onto the invite list, such as it was. We got on better that night; I managed to get her number for starters.

I rang her lots after that. I still didn't think she was that interested in me, but I persevered, I enjoyed talking to her. She was going to the States for the summer, and I was on at her to come over to see me in England before she did, but she had no notion of coming over, so I concocted a story that I was interested in buying a pony, and that I was going over to Loughrea to see a few, could she help me out? I figured it was important to see her before she went to the States.

I rang her almost every week when she was in the States. She had hooked up with this Aussie surfer dude, she told me about him, she seemed to want me to know that she only wanted to be friends with me, but I figured that the Aussie was just for the summer, so I kept calling her. I'm sure I was a bit of a nuisance, but we got on so well, I figured it was worth persevering. She came home at the end of August to repeat an exam, and I went over to Ireland to see her the following day. I think I told her I had to see a horse in Jim Bolger's or something. I couldn't say that I was just going home to see her. I didn't want to seem too keen.

She drove me back to the airport. I'll never forget it. She stopped at the drop-off zone and ripped my heart out.

'Look,' she said, 'I think you're a lovely guy, but I just don't fancy you.'

'Right,' I said. What do you say?

'Save your phone bill,' she said.

'Sure I'll call you,' I said. 'Just as a friend.'

'Look,' she said, 'you're busy, I'm busy, you have enough friends, you don't need another friend.'

It was looking grim. I had gone from 8/1 to 100/1 in that conversation. Surfer dude was on the slide as well, he was looking like an uneasy favourite, but it's no good if your main rival isn't going well if you're not travelling well either.

The following week I decided that I would give it one last go. Roll the dice one more time. I called her and asked her to come to the Partridge Ball at Toby Balding's with me, just as a friend. She was a student, I was paying for her flight, of course she was going to come, but she made it clear that it was just as a friend. Nothing more.

I was riding on the Saturday when she arrived over, so I asked Andrew Balding, Toby's nephew, Ian Balding's son, now a bloody good trainer, if he would collect her at the airport. I had marked Andrew's card, I really like this girl, she's coming to the ball with me, but she has no interest in me. I know, I can't believe it either.

Andrew was brilliant. He sang my praises, told Chanelle how good a guy I was (Andrew is good at acting as well), took her back to Kingsclere, looked after her, introduced her to everyone. We had a great night at the ball, Chanelle was great with everyone, and we got on really well, as we always did, and had a kiss at the end of the night.

I went into her room the following morning (honestly) and sat on her bed.

'Look,' I said. 'I had a great night with you last night. I know you don't fancy me, but basically, I want to go out with you, and I think if you give me a chance, that you will get to like me as well. I'm not going to chase you any more though. If you decide no, then fine, that's it, you won't hear from me again. I'm going to have a sweat now for about an hour, have a think about it, and let me know what you decide.'

I left her sitting up in her bed, tea and toast in front of her on the tray, and went and got into my piping hot bath. The usual. Chanelle looked a bit stunned when I left her, but at least she seemed to be happy to consider my proposition.

She called her mum. They usually do. She told her about our conversation and that she was surprised she was even considering consenting to see me again.

'If you never never go, you'll never never know,' her mum apparently told her. I'm still not sure what that means, but it was enough for her to nod her head when I came back in after my bath.

'Right, you're on trial.'

CHAPTER 13

Love Actually

Chanelle was going into her second year in college at the time and had three more years to do, so the relationship was going to have to work across the Irish Sea. But it did, initially anyway, despite the fact that, as well as being in different places in the world, we were also in very different places in our lives. I was pursuing my ambition at 100 miles an hour: I'll be champion this year no matter what. Chanelle was at college, having the craic, out most nights, hanging out.

We would see each other every second weekend, there was no Sunday racing in the UK then so I was able to go to Ireland on Saturday evening, or else I would fly Chanelle over on a Friday and she would come racing with me on the Saturday and stay until Monday.

I thought things were good until Christmas 1998, Christmas of her final year in college, when she broke up with me. I suppose it had been tough, there were events that she was going to that I wasn't able to attend because of racing, there were other events that I didn't go to with her just because I didn't want to, and seeing each other for a day or two every two weeks wasn't an ideal way to be going on. I suppose she wanted a normal boyfriend. I was heartbroken though, and it wasn't helped when I learned that she had started going out with Mr Potato Head.

I was on the phone, I flew over to Ireland to see her, all to no avail. I was suspended for a couple of days just before Cheltenham, and I took it into my head that it would be a good idea to try to get Chanelle to come to Dubai with me for those days, so I gave her a call, fully anticipating her response.

'Are you crazy?' she shouted at me down the phone. 'Anthony, it's over. I'm seeing somebody. Forget it.'

No surprise there then. But there was a hint of a smile in her voice, she didn't hang up on me, it was as if she expected me to persist. It's an Irish trait. Do you want a drink? An Irish person will always say no, no matter how thirsty they are or how badly they want a drink. If you met an Irish person out in the middle of the Sahara Desert, and you were carrying a cooler full of water, and you asked them if they wanted a drink, their initial answer would be no. Ah no, you're grand. You have to ask again. That's the trick. Ah go on, you'll have a drink now. Okay, I will so, thanks a million, you're a life-saver.

So I persisted.

'Come on, it'll be great. Just the two of us.'

Half an hour later, she had agreed to meet me at Heathrow the following day and the Dubai flights were booked. She got a flight from Ireland, I drove to Heathrow, and we got the flight to Dubai together. We spent nine days in Dubai, and it was fantastic. It was good for me both physically and psychologically to rest my body, get away from it all, stop thinking about racing, stop thinking about riding winners and spend some time with Chanelle.

Time with Chanelle was always great when I was able to switch off from racing. I suppose I was able to be like a normal boyfriend when I wasn't wasting or thinking about the next winner, or thinking about the two horses on which I should have won.

The only issue with Chanelle was that she didn't tell the fellow she was seeing at home that she was going to Dubai. He would ring her, she wouldn't answer, then she would sneak off to the bathroom to call him back without telling me. Oh yeah, I'm in Loughrea, yeah everything is fine. She had told me that she had broken up with him. The problem with this strategy was that Chanelle's mother knew the guy's mother very well, they were very good friends actually, and they met up while we were in Dubai. You can imagine the conversation, Chanelle's gone to Dubai with Anthony.

Chanelle didn't feel good about it, but it wasn't that big a deal. She probably should have told him straight away that she was in Dubai, she probably should have told him that she was going, but she chose not to. Poor decision, but we all make them. Or maybe her poor decision was in deciding to come to Dubai with me.

That was in early March, just before Cheltenham. Chanelle's final exams were in May, and after that she was going backpacking around the world with Anna Moore for nine months, so she figured there was no point in getting back together. Of course she was right. Chanelle was usually right. I still went over to see her before she headed off, and took her to Ashford Castle for the weekend.

She came home for Christmas and, after plenty of phone calls and lots of persuasion, she agreed to meet me. All she could talk about, though, was this guy Colin from Wales whom she had met and with whom she was heading to South America in January. It took a lot of persuasion, but eventually she came around to my way of thinking, that she'd finished college, she needed to get a job, she could move to England, get a job in London, no more living in different countries, no more seeing each other once or twice a month, we could have a real relationship, we could be like a normal couple. You know it makes sense. Bye bye Colin, bye bye South America. Chanelle moved to London and got a job with an internet company.

I had an apartment in London at the time, so she moved into that, but she paid half the mortgage and got somebody else to move in to pay the other half. It was a landlord/tenant relationship; it wasn't as if she was a kept woman, living in my apartment in London. It worked well. She would come down and stay with me in Amesbury, me and Barry Fenton and Peter Henley, or I would go up to London to see her if I had a day off.

A pattern developed to our relationship though. Riding horses and riding winners and being champion was my priority. It was as if, once I had Chanelle, she ceased to be my priority. When I didn't have her, my priority was getting her back, but when I had her back, my priority was riding winners.

We fought, just a little in the beginning, then a bit more. We got to spend two days of the week together at most, and we spent a lot of the time fighting. It didn't make sense. And the fights were usually my fault. If I had had a bad day – and I could usually find something bad to be down about even on the good days – I was certain to pick a fight with Chanelle. I was certain to engineer a situation in which I could give out to her, make her cry.

It was messed up. We would usually make up directly afterwards; as soon as she cried I would feel sorry for her and want to comfort her, but it didn't stop me picking a fight with her the next time. I loved her, I was mad about her, but that's not the way you should treat someone you are supposed to care about.

It was as if I needed to have control, as if when she cried she was vulnerable and that I was the person who could make her better. The fact that it was me who put her in that state in the first place was irrelevant.

She asked me about it one evening, after we had made up after a particularly bad one.

'Why do you do that?' she said. 'Why do you make me cry?'

I thought about it for a couple of seconds.

'If I have just had a bad day,' I said, 'why should you be happy?'

One Friday evening, Chanelle arrived to find me sitting on the kitchen floor, in the little gap that was between the dishwasher and the fridge, bawling my eyes out. That's the type of shit she had to put up with. Nothing extraordinary had happened that day, it was just that everything was getting to me, the wasting, the treadmill that my life had become, the pressure. But the pressure was coming from me, this fear that I wouldn't be champion jockey. Everything that I did at the time was governed by the fear that I wouldn't be champion, and this particular evening after racing, I got it into my head that I wasn't able to do it any more, that I was going to lose my crown and that that would be it. I couldn't bear the thought of not being champion. I went home distraught, crawled into this little space in my kitchen and wept like a baby.

It was volatile. Sometimes she would come down on a Friday evening and I would hardly say hello to her.

'What's wrong?' she would ask.

'Nothing.'

'Anthony, I have come all the way down from London to see you, and you have barely even said hello to me.'

'Look, nothing's wrong,' I would say, staring at the television. 'I'm just not in good form. I don't want to talk about it.'

Then she would stand in front of the telly.

'Have I done something wrong?' she would ask. 'I need to know. Are you mad at me?'

Bedlam.

She would leave, go back up to London. I don't know how many times she packed up all her stuff and left, headed back to London. There was lots of that, lots of mini break-ups. I would always follow her though, I would always be able to convince her to come back to me. For a while I could anyway.

The reality was that I wasn't able for a relationship, given where I was in my life and where my focus was. All I wanted to do was ride winners, ride big winners, ride more winners than anybody, ever, be champion every year, and I felt that, in order to do that, I had to remain focused, I had to devote everything I had to horses and riding and racing. In my head I wasn't talented enough to be better than everyone else, so I had to work harder than everybody else. There really wasn't room for anything else; there certainly wasn't room for a partner.

I wouldn't go to functions with her sometimes, just for the hell of it, just because I didn't feel like it, just because I wanted to be in control. It would be all organised, Chanelle would be coming up for the weekend and we would have an arrangement to go out with people or to go to an event on Saturday night, then I'd get home from racing on Saturday evening and I'd say, nah, I don't feel like going. We're not going to that. So I'd sit in and watch *Match of the Day*.

Once I was lucky enough to receive an invitation to play polo with Prince Charles, the invite was for AP McCoy and Guest. I just got this thing into my head that she wasn't coming. I told her as much.

'Why not?' she asked, visibly upset, understandably so.

'Because you need to learn, Chanelle,' I said. 'You can't assume that you're automatically going to come to everything with me.'

Chanelle's family thought I was no good for her. Of course, every time we had a fight, Chanelle would be on to her mother or her sisters. Her friends were the same. They had to pick up the pieces, help her pull herself together, help her pack, help her unpack. Why don't you leave him?

We were at a party in Mick Fitzgerald's house a few months later, Fitzy liked to celebrate his birthdays. Chanelle was a bit of a social smoker, she liked to have a cigarette when she was out having a few drinks, but I was totally anti-smoking, and I told her as much. She had assured me that she had given up, that she wouldn't smoke again, even when she was out having a drink.

At Fitzy's party, though, the craic was good and Chanelle snuck out to Fitzy's garage with Johnny Kavanagh to have a sneaky smoke. They stood close to the door, Chanelle asking Johnny to keep an eye out for me, that it would be a disaster if I caught her smoking. What she didn't realise, however, was that there was a little window that looked out from Fitzy's kitchen into the garage. I happened to be in the kitchen at the time. I had a look out the window into the garage and couldn't believe it.

I knocked on the window and, when Chanelle looked up, I just pointed to her. I stormed out of the kitchen and into the garage. I couldn't believe it, she had defied me, she had lied to me –she had been smoking. She got the treble up.

'Right, get into the car.'

She got in, as quiet as a lamb.

'How fucking dare you!' I shouted at her. 'I can't believe you lied to me.'

She protested quietly, something about it was only a cigarette, it was only one, she was just out chatting to Johnny, but I didn't listen. I didn't want to. I was fuming and I wanted to teach her a lesson.

We arrived at my house.

'Right, out of the car.'

She opened the car door.

'I'm going back to the party,' I said. 'I'll deal with you later.'

I'm embarrassed thinking about it now, but I did, I went back to the party and had a good night as Chanelle stayed at home, getting more and more upset. Actually, she found 20 cigarettes and sat outside and smoked her head off. May as well be hung for a sheep as a lamb.

What a shit I was. What a bully. What a control freak. I wasn't in a good place in my life, my head was wrecked, my fixation on being champion, the wasting that was frying my brain, and Chanelle bore the brunt. It was a horrible way to behave, a terrible way to treat the person you are supposed to love. Even so, worse was to follow.

We woke up the following morning.

'Well,' I said to her. 'What do you have to say for yourself?'

'Anthony, look, I'm sorry, I shouldn't have smoked. I won't do it again.'

'No, you will,' I said. 'You told me before that you weren't going to smoke, and then you did, so how am I going to believe you now?'

'I won't, Anthony. Honestly.'

'No, that's not good enough,' I said. 'You need to be taught a lesson. It's over actually. That's it. We're finished.'

'So you're being like this because I smoked a cigarette in Mick Fitzgerald's house?' she said. 'We've been together six years, and because I smoked one cigarette, you're breaking up with me?'

I helped her to pack. I went up to the attic, got her suitcases down, and helped her fill them with all her stuff. It must have taken about two hours, during which there were tears and sobbing and fighting and silences. All the while I remained staunch, it was over, that was it.

I put her cases in the car and I drove her to Didcot train station. All the while Chanelle bawled her eyes out.

'I'm sorry Anthony, I won't do it again. I know I let you down, please give me another chance.'

I'm not proud of how I behaved, and not a lot of people know about this incident, some of my best friends don't even know about it, but it happened and I can't change that.

Chanelle was in convulsions when we got to the station, pleading, begging. No way, I said, it's over this time for good. I got her suitcases, bought her ticket, saw her on to the platform, and left her there.

'Don't bother ringing me,' I said. 'It's over. Have a nice life.'

I left the platform, but I didn't leave the station. After a few minutes I could hear the train coming, so I made my way back to the platform. When I got there, Chanelle was lugging these cases over to the train, still sobbing, tears streaming down her face. I came up behind her and tapped her on the shoulder. She turned around, startled.

'Now,' I said, 'you definitely won't smoke again. That's a lesson to you. You can get back in the car and we'll go home.'

I don't know what I was thinking, I don't know why I did that, it was just the place I was in at the time, I needed to have control. In one way, I felt that Chanelle was so independent of me, she had her life in London, her friends in London, her friends and her family at home. Maybe I thought that she didn't really need me, so I needed to do these things to make her think that she did need me. Who knows? It was messed up anyway. Like I say, I'm not proud of the way I acted then.

Chanelle went to bed when we got home. She got up later and went up to see Adrian and Sabrina Maguire. Sabrina had actually worked at Jim Bolger's when I had been there. I got to know her fairly well and I got to know Adrian a bit from that time as well, but I obviously got to know him a lot better when I moved to the UK. We hung out together a bit and Chanelle and Sabrina got on great.

Chanelle told her what had happened that morning, and Sabrina couldn't believe it. Chanelle actually stood up for me. He obviously cares about me, he's protecting me, he doesn't want me smoking because it's bad for me. Sabrina shook her head. Chanelle couldn't see the wood for the trees, she was obviously too deeply involved to see how messed up my behaviour was.

It took Chanelle about a month after that to do the right thing. I wasn't good for her, her confidence was shot because of me, she had changed from this gorgeous, vivacious, life-and-soul-of-the-party girl into a nervous wreck. Her friends could see it, her family could see it, her dad would have shot me if he could have got away with it, and eventually Chanelle saw it herself, a month after Didcotgate.

'Look,' she said to me one night. 'I am so miserable in this relationship. You are a bad person. You're not the person I fell in love with. I know why you're not, I know the pressure you put yourself under, but I don't want to be with someone like you, I don't want to grow old with someone like you. I'm not going to ask you to make a choice, because you're not capable of making a choice, but I have to do what's right for me, and I don't like the person that I am becoming when I am with you.'

I was devastated.

'Just do me a favour,' she said, 'and leave me alone. If you really care about me, you will leave me alone, you won't try to call me, you will just let me go.'

I couldn't believe it, I couldn't believe she had actually left. Of course I tried to contact her, I tried to talk to her, to get her back. Her friend Mandy was a good gatekeeper though, she was under instruction not to allow me through, and she didn't, not for ages.

I was trying to get her back for ages. I couldn't believe how stupid I had been. Of course Chanelle was right; my behaviour was extreme, out of order, lacking a shred of decency, not to mind any semblance of having feelings for her.

I did get to talk to her after a couple of weeks, but she wasn't coming back.

'Look, Anthony,' she said, 'I know you're not a happy person, and you're never going to make me happy as long as you're not happy. You've got your career, that's the only thing that's important to you, so just go and paddle your own canoe, get your head down. It's not your fault, you're just not able to do what you are doing, to keep your career going the way you want to keep your career going, and have a relationship at the same time.'

This went on for six months. Ironic that I was now the one who was telling her that I could change, that I could be a different person to the person who had treated her so badly, that I could change my whole personality, when I wasn't even willing to believe her when she told me that she wouldn't smoke again.

'All my friends hate you,' she told me during one of our conversations. 'If I consented to start seeing you again, I couldn't tell them.'

Eventually, she did and she didn't. She started to see me, but she told nobody. After a little while I thought that I had better sort that one out. I rang some of her best friends and told them that I knew I had been a shit, but that I was going to treat her properly from then on. I arranged to meet her dad in London when he was over on a business trip, and told him the same thing. That was a tough one, but it was a good thing to have done.

This all happened during the summer of 2003. Career-wise, things were actually quite good. I had been champion again, I was riding away for Martin Pipe, the winners were flowing, and I suppose during the summer I wasn't riding as much, I had more time to give to Chanelle, more time to devote to winning her back again, winning her friends and her dad around. Then the new season kicked in and I reverted to type.

I suited myself a lot. I wouldn't put myself out for Chanelle. Career was number one, I was always looking after my weight, and I wasn't inclined to go to too many social events with her. I preferred to keep things simple, stay in, eat the things that I knew I could eat, watch television, watch recordings of races, get to bed early, up early the following day to have a sweat. There were other times when I just couldn't have been bothered going out. Then I'd have three winners at Ascot and I'd say, okay, let's get some people together and go out in London for the night. It was all about me.

I told her that we should get engaged. I did want to marry her and spend the rest of my life with her, but I didn't propose.

By Christmas 2003 I was flat out again trying to win another championship, immersed in the season, caught up in myself, and Chanelle was not a part of that. I didn't have time to ask her to marry me, I didn't have time to work out what the implications of that would be, or if the timing was right, or even what to say or where to propose, so I bought her a Cartier watch as a Christmas gift. I would never have imagined that anyone would be disappointed about receiving a Cartier watch, but Chanelle was. I suppose she had every right to expect that it would be an engagement ring, given the way I had been talking about getting engaged. My mum told her that I was just buying time.

The following summer of 2004 was quite traumatic career-wise as I gave up my job at Martin Pipe's to ride for JP McManus, and Chanelle was on the sidelines again. We started fighting again, same things, I was suiting myself, not going anywhere with her unless it suited me, getting caught up in my own world, my own thoughts, not letting her in. One of her good friends was getting married that September, and she was desperate that I go to the wedding with her. I said no, I wasn't going. I wasn't racing or anything, I wasn't wasting, I wasn't doing light, I didn't have to be anywhere else, I just didn't fancy it. I said I was going away for three days playing golf with Timmy Murphy.

She couldn't believe it, went to the wedding on her own and fielded all the 'Where's Anthony' questions as well as she could. I'm not sure what she said. He went off to play golf with some of the lads instead and left me to go to the wedding on my own? Yes, he is that selfish.

That was it as far as she was concerned. I had had my last chance and I had blown it. I couldn't be a normal boyfriend, I wasn't a normal boyfriend, and she needed a normal boyfriend, a guy who would go to things with her, think about her, consider her before making any major decisions or most minor ones, pay her the attention she deserved. There was nothing about me that fitted that description.

There was this guy that she knew in London who was hanging around a bit at the time. I think she used to confide in him, tell him when things weren't going well with me. He heard all the bad bits and none of the good bits, and he told her that if ever she left me, he would love to take her out. He told her that, if she felt like she wanted to leave me, but didn't have the strength to do so, didn't have the courage to be on her own, that he would be delighted to go out with her, even for a little while.

The wedding was the final straw for Chanelle, another final straw, the final, final straw as far as she was concerned. The following week I went over to Ireland as I was riding in Limerick, so she picked me up at Shannon Airport and drove me to Limerick. She didn't get out of the car for the whole day. She sat in the car for four hours, cried her eyes out and wrote me a letter.

I got back into the car after racing, and I knew that something was very wrong. I could obviously tell that she had been crying. She cried the whole way from Limerick back to Shannon, hardly said a word. I didn't say much either, I didn't know what to say. We got to the airport, she got out of the car with me and handed me the letter.

'This is where it ends now, Anthony,' she said. 'You know what's in the letter anyway. I'm asking you, and you owe it to me, to leave me alone. I have given you seven or eight years of my life now, and the least you can do is let me go. It doesn't matter how many times you call me, it doesn't matter how many airplanes you jump on, it's over, and it's for real this time. I have fallen out of love with you. I am gone.'

I was devastated again. How had it come to this again? How could I have been so stupid again? I pleaded with her, but there was no changing her mind. My flight was leaving, so I left. I opened the letter on the plane. It was all there. I've fallen out of love with you. I don't even know if I fancy you any more. I feel sorry for you. I would have been a really good wife, we could have been very happy together, but you've blown it, it's gone. I cried.

I called her that night.

'I'm coming to Ireland,' I said. 'There are a lot of things we need to talk about.'

'Anthony, there is nothing to talk about,' she said. 'It's over. It's long gone. Forget it.'

'I'm coming over anyway,' I said. 'We can't just end like this, there are things we need to sort out.'

'There's nothing to sort out,' she said. 'Don't bother getting on a plane. I'm not going to see you. It's over. Goodbye.'

I was going over anyway to ride a couple of JP's horses at Christy Roche's, so I went to Loughrea anyway. I didn't tell Chanelle that I was still coming, I figured that it would be better if she didn't know, that way she couldn't tell me not to come. She was in the office when I arrived.

'This is wrong,' I said. 'I can't live without you.'

'It's gone, I'm gone.'

'It's not,' I protested.

'Anthony, it is.'

We sat and talked for a while, but it wasn't looking good. Then I had to leave to go to Christy's, but I didn't have a car, so Chanelle said that I could take one of the cars that were in the yard, drop it off at the airport on my way back, and that she would have someone pick it up. I wasn't planning on going to the airport, I was planning on coming back, but I knew that I was fighting a losing battle. This could be it; I could have lost her for good.

I got into the car and was a couple of miles down the road when I saw a mobile phone under the dashboard. I shouldn't have, but I picked it up and opened the text messages. I nearly crashed. There was this string of messages between Chanelle and this London guy.

'Anthony and I have broken up. I'll meet you for a drink.'

'Look I know you don't want anything heavy, you're just out of a relationship, but there are so many things that I want to do with you, places I'd like to take you.'

I couldn't believe it. I turned the car around, drove at 100 miles an hour back to Chanelle's house, jumped out of the car, burst into her office and threw the mobile phone at her.

'You really are gone, aren't you?' I said.

She was stunned.

'I really am,' she said. 'I promise you, nothing has happened with this guy. But he is everything you are not. He wants to spend time with me, he wants to bring me out, he wants to go out with my friends, he wants me to go everywhere with me, he wants to meet my family.'

He knew what buttons to press all right.

'And you know what?' she said. 'Even if it's not him, they are the things that I want in a relationship. I just want a nice guy, a normal relationship, I don't want these fights. You have tried, for the last eight years you have tried, and you just can't be that guy. It's not your fault, you just can't have a normal relationship.'

I was devastated.

'I have to be able to do something.'

'No, you don't,' she said. 'You could get me back before, but not any more. There is nothing you can do. You will meet a girl, I have no doubt, who will be the type of girl you need. You just need a doormat, someone who will just go along with you, take the shit that you give. But that person is not me. Just keep your dignity and go, go back to Shannon Airport or wherever you are going.'

I tried to explain why I did what I did, why I acted the way I did. I had always been able to get her back, I had always known what to say, I had always been able to persuade her to come back, and I always knew that, once she was back, I had to be on my best behaviour for a while, go to a couple of her friends' gigs, be the normal boyfriend. This time, though, it was different. I didn't know what to do, I didn't know how I was going to get her back. I really thought I had blown it, I was sure she was gone.

I sat in her office there for about six hours, just talking things through. Christy's horses had to go unridden.

'I know I've said this before,' I said, 'but if you give me one more chance, from today it will be different. I can't do anything to make you believe that it will be different this time, but it will. I know it will. I am in a different place now, I am better able to cope with the pressures of racing, the pressures of wasting. I have a different job, I am better able to give you the relationship that you want.'

I meant it.

'I am going to leave now,' I said. 'It will take me one hour to drive to Shannon. If I get to the airport and you haven't called me, I will get on the plane and you will never hear from me again. I respect you too much to put you through all this shit again. But I swear to you, if you give me this chance, I will make you a very happily married woman.'

All a little dramatic, I know, but I meant every word. Then there was nothing more to be said, there was nothing else I could say to try to convince her.

I left. Chanelle went down to her friend Mandy's house and Mandy summoned the advisory committee, Chanelle's other five mates. Emergency meeting in Mandy's house: cigarettes (yes, cigarettes), alcohol, coffee, the works. Girls, Chanelle's whole life has to be determined within the next hour.

Chanelle's friends are hugely important to her. What they think really matters to her. As it turned out, three of her friends said that she should go for it, call me and live happily ever after, and three of them said that she shouldn't have anything more to do with me. Let him get on his stupid plane and thank God that you had a lucky escape. Eventually, Mandy told her to get out of the house, go for a walk and make up her own mind.

The hour was nearly up by the time she phoned her dad, and her dad just told her to go with her gut feeling. Her gut told her to give me another chance. I was close to Shannon when my phone rang. My heart did a little somersault.

'This is your very last chance.'

We got engaged the following July, and we were married in September 2006.

CHAPTER 14

Baby Blues

I suppose Chanelle and I always knew that we were going to get married. Very early in our relationship, I knew that I wanted to marry Chanelle, I knew that I wanted her to be my life partner. So I had a strange way of showing it. I had a strange way of going about most things back then.

Within a short space of time, I had somehow managed to convince her that she wouldn't be averse to the idea of marrying me as well. I suppose there is no point in marrying somebody if they are not going to marry you back. We started joking about it after we were together for about six months, but it was joking with intent.

After managing to navigate the rocky road that was our relationship, we arrived at JP McManus's charity golf day in Limerick in the summer of 2005. I told her there that I was taking her away for the weekend, not to make any plans. She seemed happy enough with that.

We went back to Loughrea so Chanelle could pack. I had arranged to meet with her dad so that I could ask him for his permission to ask his daughter to marry me. I suppose I'm a bit old-fashioned like that; I thought it was the right thing to do, especially after the heartache that I had caused Chanelle, and her family by extension.

So we arrived at Shannon Airport and looked up at the board. There were two flights leaving at the same time, one to Belfast and one to Venice.

'I hope we're not going to Belfast.'

I suppose the fact that we were going to Venice gave the game away a bit. Once Chanelle knew we were going there, she was sure that I was going to propose. Then after we got there, and after one night had passed without a proposal, she began to think, what if he brings me to Venice and he doesn't propose?

We went for dinner on the second night, me with the ring in my left pocket, so whenever we were walking, I had to make sure that Chanelle walked on my right, which was all a little weird. After dinner I decided that we would go on a gondola; I thought that was the thing to do, go on a gondola, get down on one knee and pose the question.

We got to the gondola and Chanelle asked how much it was.

'A hundred euro,' said the gondolier.

'A hundred euro?' repeated Chanelle, as if she hadn't heard him correctly. 'For how long?'

'Ten minutes.'

'Ah now come on,' she said. 'That's ridiculous. We'll walk up the river instead.'

It was time to step in.

'Come on, let's get in,' I said.

'But it's a hundred euro.'

'We're in Venice,' I said. 'You can't go to Venice and not go for a spin in a gondola.'

'But it's a rip-off.'

'Look.' Time for the unrationalised approach. 'Just get into the gondola.'

Eventually she got in, okay fine, you're right, when in Venice. I didn't have much time, 10 minutes isn't that long, so I got down on one knee in the gondola, careful not to tip it over, and proposed – fantastic, hugs, kisses, tears, the works. When it was all over, Chanelle noticed that the gondolier was looking down at us.

'We just got engaged!' she said to him. 'He just asked me to marry him!'

'That's great,' said the gondolier. Seen it all before.

*

It was in the summer of 2002 that Chanelle suggested that we go for a fertility check. You don't think about your fertility when you are sitting in a piping hot bath for an hour every morning. All you are thinking about is losing a couple of pounds, keeping your weight in check. You are not thinking about kids, the fact that the daily pasteurisation of your body might be affecting you downstairs, about the fact that you are boiling your balls every morning and that it might be having a detrimental effect on your ability to procreate.

We went to see this really brilliant guy in Oxford, Dr Enda McVeigh. It was a bit weird going in to see him all right. No we're not married, we're not engaged, we're hardly going out together a wet week, but we still want to get this checked out. The doctor immediately put us at ease.

He knew who I was, he was into racing, he owned a couple of horses, so he didn't think I was mad. I know the regime you guys go through, it can affect your fertility, there's no harm having a fertility check.

We went back the following week to get the results. I remember going in, and Chanelle was relaxed about the whole thing, more relaxed than me. It doesn't matter what the results are, she told me. Whatever it is, we can deal with it, but it's as well to know. Then we went into the office and they took out our file, Chanelle Burke and AP McCoy, and there, written on the front of the file in yellow highlighter pen, just in case anybody in the world missed it, were two words: 'Severe Case'. Not good.

'Basically, you are probably never going to have kids yourself,' the doc told me. Break it to me gently, Doc. 'Your sperm count is very, very low.'

I was shocked. I don't know what I was expecting really. I probably expected that he would tell me that things weren't great, that I would need to watch the hot baths, that I was lower than average, but I didn't expect that I would be down at zero. The doc spoke about our options, IVF and all that, and said that if there was a swimmer in there, even one, he was the man to get him, but you could tell that he wasn't too hopeful.

Chanelle was busy putting things into perspective. Anthony is a jockey, he rides horses at 30 miles per hour over fences every day of the week, two ambulances follow him around while he works, he could come home in a wheelchair one day. That would be an issue. This is not an issue.

All I could do was apologise to her. You're better off without me. We should probably split up now.

'Don't be ridiculous,' she said. 'I'm not with you because I want to have kids with you. I'm with you because I want to be with you. Of course, we have spoken about kids, but we can figure this out. Everybody has a cross to bear in life, and if this is our cross, then it's not so bad. Maybe we are supposed to adopt, maybe we are supposed to give some other kid a chance in life.'

The other thing the doc said was that it wasn't going to get better. It wasn't like a broken leg or a smashed up face, it wasn't something that got better with time. Even if I had decided there and then that I wasn't going to have any more hot baths, it was not going to improve. Not a jot. The likelihood was that it was going to get worse. So I froze some sperm there and then, and hoped for a miracle.

Chanelle was great. She desperately wanted to have children, we both did. We both love kids, we had already decided that, if we had a girl, we would call her Eve. So this was a real blow to both of us, but it was my fault. Chanelle wouldn't hear of it though, she wouldn't let me wallow in self-pity.

We talked about all our options. As soon as we got married, we would put our names down to adopt everywhere, it didn't matter if we adopted a Russian baby, an Asian baby, a British baby or an Irish baby, we just knew that, if we couldn't have kids, we would want to adopt. We said that, at the same time, we would go down the IVF route. So that was that, decision made, we said we wouldn't speak about it again.

We got married in September 2006, and started IVF treatment in January 2007. By the end of February Chanelle was pregnant. We hit the bullseye – first time. Miracles do happen. It was an incredible feeling. It was like going out in the Grand National on a 100/1 shot and winning. Then winning the Gold Cup and the Champion Hurdle later that afternoon.

We had to be careful though; the doctor did warn us that we had to do the right things. I suppose Chanelle did overdo it a bit that summer; she was busy at work, trying to get everything sorted before she went on maternity leave. I was schooling a couple of horses in Lambourn one morning that August when Chanelle called me to say that she was bleeding, that I should come home. I gave the horse I happened to be riding a kick in the belly and galloped him as fast as I could to my car. When I got there, luckily there was someone there, so I just handed him the horse, jumped into my car and sped home.

I got Chanelle into the car and I drove as fast as I could to Oxford. It was all very frantic. We were rushed into the doctor. The bleeding hadn't stopped. The doctor searched for the baby's heartbeat, but couldn't find it. My clock stopped ticking, all our dreams were suspended in mid-air as the doctor searched again. Our euphoria at being pregnant, and the expectation that we would have a little baby in our lives in a couple of months, a new life, a tiny little helpless person who would be our responsibility, whom we could nurture and look after and love and teach, was all dissolving before our eyes as we stared wide-eyed, helplessly hoping that everything would be okay, but fearing that it wouldn't. Then he found the heartbeat. I almost cried with relief.

Chanelle still hadn't stopped bleeding so they were going to take the baby out. We weren't out of the woods. The baby would be premature, but the doctor thought that she had a better chance of survival now outside the womb than in it. They gave Chanelle the injection that strengthens premature babies' hearts and lungs and took her up to theatre. Half an hour before they were due to operate, Chanelle stopped bleeding.

They kept Chanelle in hospital for a week after that, but everything appeared to have returned to normal, so they sent her home. A month later, she had another bleed. I was on my way to Cartmel when she called me to tell me they were taking her to John Radcliffe Hospital. I had some good rides at Cartmel, but all I wanted to do was go home.

It's amazing how your mindset changes with different events. I remember when my sister Anne Marie was getting married; the wedding was on a racing day, I had five good rides at Bangor and I was thinking, how can I go to a wedding, even my sister's wedding, when I have five good rides at Bangor? But when this was happening to Chanelle, all I wanted to do was go home.

I was worried out of my mind. The doctors kept telling me that everything was all right, that both Chanelle and Eve (she was Eve already) were fine, but it didn't stop me worrying. It's a terrible feeling, the feeling of helplessness, that there's nothing you can do. It's usually me who is injured, people are worrying about me, with me saying I'm fine, because I know I am. It's not quite the same when someone else is telling you that someone else is fine.

Strange thing, when someone else is sick or injured, I always wish it was me. I can cope much better with being injured or sick than standing around trying to care for someone who is injured or sick.

They kept Chanelle in hospital for six weeks until her due date. I was delighted that they did. It meant that she was in the best place possible in case something did go wrong. She just needed to look after herself, she needed bed rest, she needed to have no excuse to be up and about and doing stuff.

Everything was great. Eve was born on 8th November 2007, our little miracle, the child we thought we would never have.

CHAPTER 15

Pipedreaming

I used to get a lot of visitors to my house at Kingston Lisle. I operated a fairly liberal open-door policy, friends and friends of friends were more or less welcome to come and stay with me whenever they wanted. They had to find their own Corn Flakes in the morning though.

Frannie Jeffers was a fairly regular visitor until one night, when he was down at my house with Graham Lee. We'd been to Luke Harvey's pub, The Blowing Stone, for the night, and the two lads just crashed at my place. I was riding out at Andrew Balding's the following day, and I said to the lads before going to bed that they could come with me if they wanted. Graham said he would come, Frannie said give him a shout, if was awake he'd come as well.

I was surprised when I was getting up the following morning at six o'clock, rain lashing down on the roof, to see the light on in Frannie's room. I opened his door, and there's Frannie, sitting bolt upright in the bed, clinging onto the quilt up around his neck, his face as white as a sheet.

'What's going on?' I asked.

'This house is fucking haunted!' said Frannie in his Scouse accent. 'About a half an hour after I went to bed, I heard a noise, so I turned on the light, and there's this old lady standing at the end of my bed, just staring at me.'

I burst out laughing. I couldn't stop laughing. I was laughing so much I had to lie down on the floor. We woke Graham with all the noise and he came in.

'What's up?' he asked.

'Frannie saw a ghost!' I blurted out.

'I'm not joking you,' said Frannie. 'Honestly, there was this old lady at the end of my bed.'

'Frannie,' said Graham, 'if there had been a woman standing at the end of your bed, I'm sure you would have had her in it in jig time.'

After I'd recovered, I asked the lads if they were coming with me to Andrew Balding's or not. It was a fairly miserable morning.

'Too right I'm coming,' said Frannie. 'I'm not staying here on my own.'

A few years later, shortly after I had moved into Lodge Down with Chanelle, Frannie came to stay again. We had this big old wooden front door at the time, with a big lead cross in the middle of it. Frannie arrived at the door.

'Ah no, that's a crucifix,' he said. 'Don't tell me this house is haunted as well, is it?'

As it happened, Graham Lee was staying with us that night as well, so I brought them upstairs to show them their rooms. After I showed Graham his room, Frannie started to unpack his stuff.

'No, this is Graham's room, Frannie,' I said. 'Yours is over here.'

'You don't think I'm staying on my own in this house, do you?' he said.

*

I didn't allow myself to actually believe that I was going to be champion almost until the day arrived that I was, the Stratford meeting that used to end the season. I ended the 1995–96 season with 175 winners, 43 more than David Bridgwater, with Richard Dunwoody the only other jockey to ride more than 100 winners.

It was some feeling. Champion. I had ridden more winners that season than any other rider in the country. Even though I knew that it was looking good for a while, I still never allowed myself to think that I had it in the bag. If I had done that, I was afraid that I would ease up, take my foot off the accelerator, and the last thing I wanted to be doing was taking my foot off the gas. If you start doing that, if you start easing down, there is no telling how easy you could go.

So it took a while for it all to sink in. At least a couple of days, but probably more like a couple of weeks. I was up there with the great riders of National Hunt, John Francome, Peter Scudamore, Richard Dunwoody, Jonjo O'Neill, they had all been champions before me, and now I was champion, I was up there among them. It took some effort to get my head around that one.

One thing that struck me was that I was champion jockey even though I had turned down the job with Martin Pipe. Of course the ball hopped for me during the season. Bridgie had missed a fair bit of the season through injury, Norman and Adrian had also missed a lot of it through injury, while I had a fair run at it.

On top of that, my agent Dave Roberts had done a brilliant job. He was just as obsessed with finding winners for me as I was with riding them. I would get up in the morning, hoping I had a few fancied rides, go racing, ride a winner, ride another winner, not so bad, go home, grand, that's today done, two more winners, hope I have a few fancied rides tomorrow, go to bed, get up the next morning, go racing. See the pattern? I kept the pressure on myself all the time. It was robotic. I was a robot.

Every winner was just a number, just another winner, another notch. Even when I look back now, so much of it is all just numbers. I don't know if my mentality would have been different if I hadn't been champion in my first season as a fully-fledged professional. I don't think so, but you never know. Champion conditional one year, champion jockey the next, then I couldn't not be champion. So I got it into my head that I had to be champion the following season, and the following season, and the following season. Anything less would be a step backwards. If I had had a couple of years between being champion conditional and champion jockey, would my head have been in a different place? Would I have been less fearful about not being champion than I was? Probably not.

There was pressure on me every day to win, self-imposed of course. I just wanted another number to add to the total, another winner, another tick. I obviously got a lot of satisfaction from winning, the same as I do now, but back then the satisfaction lay in the fact that it was another winner, another 1 to add to the total. But the feeling didn't last very long; almost before I had been led back into the winner's enclosure, more often than not I was thinking of what my next winner would be.

I enjoy riding more now than I did then. I had so many other things going on in my head back then. It wasn't just about riding, it was about being champion, riding more winners than anyone else, but at the same time I had a negative attitude towards it. It was actually more about avoiding not being champion than it was about being champion, if you can follow that logic. The fear of not being champion was my overriding feeling, not excitement at the prospect of being champion.

Of course I got a bigger kick out of winning the big races; I got a huge thrill out of winning at the Cheltenham Festival on Kibreet and from winning the Mumm Melling Chase at Aintree on a top-class horse like Viking Flagship, but it was much more important to me to be champion jockey than to win big races. Average jockeys can win big races if they are lucky enough to get on the right horse. You can be lucky on the day. You can't be lucky over the course of a season though. I've seen a lot of average jockeys win big races, but I don't think I've ever seen an average jockey be champion. For me, it was always about being champion much more than it was about winning the big races.

At the beginning of the 1996/97 season, I thought that it was going to be even tougher to retain my title than it had been to win it in the first place. In 1995/96 I'd had a dream start, riding a lot of the Martin Pipe horses. It was the perfect springboard; I had 50 winners in the bag by September.

This year was going to be different though. I would still be riding for Paul Nicholls, Philip Hobbs, Toby Balding and all the other trainers who had used me during my championship season, and I would surely have the wind in my sails that goes with actually being champion, but David Bridgwater would have Martin Pipe, he would have all the Pipe horses from the start of the season, and that was a gale force.

I didn't start off too badly though. I had over sixty winners on the board by the end of September, I was up with the previous season's pace and I was doing okay, clocking up the winners, tick, tick, tick. Then, on the evening of 29th September, Dave Roberts called me.

'You'll never guess what's just happened,' he said. 'David Bridgwater has just quit the Pipe job.'

I was stunned. That couldn't be right. He had the best job in racing, the job that was certain to make him champion jockey if he could just stay largely injury- and suspension-free, the job that would ensure that he rode more winners in the UK than any other person.

'He was riding for him at Newton Abbot today,' I said to Dave. 'He rode Banntown Bill in the handicap chase.'

'I know,' said Dave. 'Then he got into his car and called Martin and told him he was quitting.'

There was silence as I digested it all.

'Sure that's crazy,' I said. 'He would have been driving past Pipey's front door on the way back from Newton Abbot. He could have called in and told him face to face.'

'Yeah,' said Dave. 'But no, he called him. Says he's going to ride for the owner Darren Mercer.'

More silence. I couldn't understand it. Why would Bridgie give up the job? Maybe they weren't getting on that well. Maybe Martin Pipe was just too difficult a man to work for. Maybe Darren Mercer had some really nice young horses coming through, maybe he offered Bridgie a retainer and Bridgie thought that this would be an altogether easier way to make a living. But it was still a difficult one to get my head around.

I just couldn't understand why anyone would want to give up the Martin Pipe job. It's one thing getting sacked, losing the job, but walking away? Why would you walk away from the best supplier of winners in the business? Why would you not try to make it work?

I know that I had effectively had the opportunity to take the job, and I didn't, but that was because I was afraid that I didn't have the experience to make the job mine. But if I had taken it, I would have done everything that I could have done to make it work. Bridgie obviously had a different mindset to me. Maybe being champion jockey didn't register too highly on his list of goals because, if it did, there is no way he would have walked out on the main job with Martin Pipe.

'You know what this means, don't you?' Dave asked.

'What?'

'He's going to offer you the job again.'

'Ah he won't offer me the job,' I said. 'Not after the last time, not after how that one went.'

'Well,' said Dave. 'I've just got off the phone to him, and he told me to put you up on whatever you want to ride of his.'

Sure enough, the news was in the papers the next day. Bridgwater splits from champion Pipe. Bridgie was quoted as saying: 'The reason I am leaving Martin Pipe is that I feel I am too tied down riding for such a big stable and therefore losing too many outside rides.'

Martin was also quoted saying to a journalist: 'It's a strange decision. I'll be looking for a jockey for the future. I've got some runners that even you could win on this week.'

Luckily Martin put me up on them instead of the journalist, and so it began. Martin was true to his word; whatever I wanted to ride, or whatever Dave thought I should ride, Dave just put me up on it, and nearly every one of them won. It was almost embarrassing. Dave put my name down beside the horse, I got up on it, pointed it in the right direction, and it won. Simples.

Martin never mentioned 'the job'. I just started riding his horses – whatever AP wants to ride, just put his name down beside it. That was the arrangement we had. I have heard people speaking since about contracts and signatures and retainers, but I never had one with Martin. In fact, bizarrely, I was never officially his stable jockey. I was never officially appointed as such.

I did speak to Dave about what I would do if Martin did offer me the job, how I would deal with it and how it would leave me with Paul Nicholls in particular. There was never any love lost as far as I could tell between Martin and Paul, they were both ambitious, they were both intent on getting to or staying at the top of their profession, so it made sense that they weren't best friends. I didn't think, therefore, that I would be able to continue to ride regularly for Paul if I committed to Martin as stable jockey. Paul Nicholls wasn't the champion trainer that he is now, but he was a young trainer who was clearly going places – everybody could see that. Even so, he only had about 50 horses. Martin had 150. I wanted to be champion jockey. If there was a choice to be made, for me it was a no-brainer.

There wasn't a choice to be made initially, simply because Martin never asked me formally to be his stable jockey. Of course Paul could see what was going on, everybody knew that I was riding regularly for Martin, but it didn't impinge on my relationship with Paul, or with Philip Hobbs or with Toby Balding, or my ability to ride their horses.

I started thinking that this was happening for me now. I was riding away for Martin Pipe, riding these steering jobs; Martin himself could have won on them, I'm sure, but it was me who was riding them, it was me who was going up one more notch in the championship every time one of them won. I didn't mind – I was racking up the winners. I had been champion jockey the previous season, I had been leading rider at Aintree, leading rider at Punchestown, I had ridden a Cheltenham Festival winner. Things were good.

I knew that it couldn't last though. Martin had a lot of horses who were primed for the summer, who were fitter than their rivals, who could go on summer ground and who were sure to rack up a sequence of wins before the ground got softer and the good horses started to appear. Paul's horses were generally more traditional chasing types, slower burns, a lot of them owned by his landlord Paul Barber who loved the old-fashioned chasers, the big Irish-bred store horses, the point-to-pointers, horses who were not going to even set foot on a racecourse until the ground got soft.

Things continued to go well through the autumn and into winter. Paul was having plenty of runners, but there were no real clashes, no instances when I had to make a big decision over where my allegiance lay. By mid-January I was getting close to 150 winners. Then Martin entered Cyborgo in a novices' chase at Newton Abbot on 20th January. Paul entered Flaked Oats in the same race. Dave called me.

'It has happened.'

'What has happened?' I asked.

'Cyborgo and Flaked Oats are both running in the novices' chase at Newton Abbot on Monday. Which do you want to ride?'

Dave is a great man for presenting you with the information and allowing you to make your own decision. Even when I come to him with a quandary, he never tells me what he thinks I should do. He just listens, hears me out, asks me the right questions and gradually the right path becomes apparent. If he wasn't a superb jockeys' agent, the best in the business, he would have made a great counsellor or life coach.

Flaked Oats was a nice horse, he had won a couple of point-to-points and I had ridden him to win a novices' chase at Fontwell six weeks previously. But Cyborgo was a completely different ball game, he was proven class, he had won the Stayers' Hurdle at Cheltenham the previous March and he was one of the most exciting freshman chasers in training that year. He was a Gold Cup prospect in time. I couldn't not ride Cyborgo.

'You realise that if you ride Cyborgo,' Dave said, 'Nicholls is going to flip.'

'How can I not ride Cyborgo?' I asked him. 'How can I ride a point-to-pointer in front of a Stayers' Hurdle winner?'

'I agree with you,' said Dave. 'I'm just telling you, Nicholls is going to flip.'

I knew it. There had been instances when I had ridden one of Philip's instead of one of Paul's in a race, but that didn't seem to matter too much. I wasn't rejecting one of Paul's good, exciting horses, and I wasn't rejecting it in favour of a horse of Martin's. This was going to be a double-whammy, rejecting Flaked Oats in favour of a horse of Martin Pipe's.

It was a pity. I really liked riding for Paul, and he had some really nice horses. See More Business was a lovely novice chaser; I had ridden him in all five of his races up to that point, four wins, three novice hurdles and a novice chase, and a one-length defeat to another Stayers' Hurdle winner, the top-class Dorans Pride, in the Drinmore Chase at Fairyhouse the previous month. Actually, after I had ridden See More Business to win a Grade 2 novices' hurdle at Sandown in December 1995, I got off him and told Paul that he was the best horse I had ever ridden.

Call Equiname was another lovely, if fragile, horse of Paul's on whom I had won three novice hurdles and a novice chase. See More Business would go on to win a Cheltenham Gold Cup, Call Equiname would go on to win a Queen Mother Champion Chase, but I never rode either of them again after that day.

I have no regrets though. Apart from the micro-situation that existed, in which it would have been very difficult to get off a Stayers' Hurdle winner to ride a point-to-point winner, nice point-to-point winner though he was, the way I looked at it, I wanted to be champion jockey again, above everything else I wanted to be champion, and I figured that it would be very difficult for someone else to beat me if I was riding for Martin Pipe.

'There's your answer then,' said Dave. Wise Dave.

I told Paul that I was riding Cyborgo instead of Flaked Oats. Dave was right. Paul flipped.

'We had a gentleman's agreement,' he said. 'You gave me your word that you were going to ride all my horses.'

'I'm sorry Paul,' I said. 'I'm riding a lot for Martin as well. I had to choose here and I chose to ride Cyborgo.'

'Right, well have it your way.'

I didn't feel good about it. Paul was too ambitious to play second fiddle to Pipey. But I had to let one of them down, one of them was going to be annoyed with me, and this was the right decision for me at the time, given that all I wanted was to be champion again.

Paul Barber came up to me at the races a couple of days later and told me that I would never ride for him again. You gave us your word, and now you have gone back on it. Okay, I get it. But never is a very long time, and I did ride for Paul Barber again, but it took a long time for that particular hatchet to be buried. It didn't help that I won that novices' chase at Newton Abbot on Cyborgo. Philip Hide rode Flaked Oats. Cyborgo and I had him beaten when he fell at the last.

From that day on, I rode for Martin Pipe, full stop. That was the way it was. I never had a falling out with Philip Hobbs; I don't think the Devil himself could have a falling out with Philip Hobbs. Philip is one of the gentlemen of National Hunt racing, he is a brilliant trainer and he is so easy to ride for. He wouldn't have been as forceful as Paul Nicholls at the time as he was a lot more relaxed about these things, but the fact was that I was riding more and more for Martin, and therefore wasn't available to ride for Philip very much. Philip started to use Richard Johnson, and they have struck up a partnership that has thrived to this day.

They are very similar, Philip and Richard. Richard is one of the nicest people in the weigh room and he is one of the best jockeys riding today. He can't do enough for you, he is generous to a fault, always looking out for others, and he is completely unassuming, with no airs or graces, humble even. It is ridiculous that he has never been champion jockey. He has been fourth in the championship once, third once and he has been runner-up 13 times. I can't help but feel partly responsible for that injustice.

Martin never asked me about the job, I never asked him about the job or my status, I just rode for him and that was how it was. Looking back on it now, I think that Pipey played it all very cleverly. If he really did want me to ride for him, he went about it the right way, putting me on winners, putting me on steering jobs, showing me how easy it could be, appealing to my basic need to ride winners. He knew exactly which button to press. Then, when he had me where he wanted me, weak with winners, brainwashed with winners, he puts his star novice chaser, his trump card, into the same race as a good novice chaser of Paul Nicholls, his main competition for my services, probably knowing that I had to ride Cyborgo, knowing that there was no way I would turn my back on such a classy horse and another almost sure-fire winner, and probably knowing how Paul would react if and when I chose to ride Martin's horse over his. Very clever indeed, although he probably didn't need to go through all that palaver. This time, he probably would have had me at 'Hello'.

I was lucky to get a second bite at the Pipe job so soon after turning it down, that's for sure. I was lucky that he still wanted me. And if I had any reservations about the pressures that the job would place on me, those reservations dissolved with time. As I have said, of course I had concerns. Dunwoody had walked away, it just never worked out for him, and now David Bridgwater had walked away. I actually found it very easy to ride for Martin. He was training winners every day of the week and he was putting me up. What was difficult about that? Maybe we just fitted together well. We had a common goal, winners, lots of them, as many of them as possible, and, crucially, we had the same route to that goal. Martin's route.

Make A Stand was one of those horses that you just pointed in the right direction and sat tight. He was an unbelievable horse, incredibly quick over his hurdles. I didn't ride him when he won the big William Hill Handicap Hurdle at Sandown on 7th December 1996, I was busy winning the Rehearsal Chase at Chepstow on Belmont King for Paul Nicholls. Glen Tormey rode Make A Stand at Ascot, and he was electric.

It was remarkable to think that he could win a competitive handicap hurdle like that while still a novice.

I did ride him in the Kennel Gate Hurdle at Ascot in December though, back among novices, which we won doing handsprings – made all, jumped well, unchallenged – and I rode him again when he won the Lanzarote Hurdle at Kempton in January. I got down to ride at 10 st 3 lb in that, so I obviously thought it was worth it. All I had to do was sit on him and he did the rest, kicking off in front, measuring up his hurdles, jumping like a cat, and he was never challenged.

That February I thought he had a big chance in the Tote Gold Trophy, one of the biggest handicap hurdles on the racing calendar. He was only a novice and he was going to have a fair weight to carry, but I thought that he was classy enough to carry the weight. Alas, I didn't get to ride him. On 23rd January I broke my shoulder in a fall off a horse of Philip Hobbs's, Speedy Snapsgem, in a maiden chase at Wincanton. He just got the first fence all wrong and came down. I knew that it was bad. I could feel the pain shooting up through my arm, and I couldn't breathe for a little while as I lay on the ground in agony. The poor horse was killed, so I suppose I was lucky to get away with being carried off with a broken shoulder blade.

I made a quick enough recovery. I was back on 19th February; 27 days isn't bad for a broken shoulder blade, but it was 11 days too late for Make A Stand in the Tote Gold Trophy. Chris Maude rode him and duly won, made all, never in danger, the usual. Although he was only a novice, there was never any talk of him going for the Supreme Novices' Hurdle at Cheltenham after that. He had won a Tote Gold Trophy off 11 st 7 lb, there was only one race that he was going for at Cheltenham, and my Champion Hurdle ride was sorted.

My ride in the Gold Cup took a little more sorting. Cyborgo was an obvious possibility, but he was still a novice and therefore eligible for the Sun Alliance Chase as well. Noel Chance asked me to ride Mr Mulligan for him in the King George that December and he ran a cracker. We would have finished second to the runaway winner One Man but he took an absolute mother and father of a fall at the last fence.

I came in and told Noel that I thought he could win a Gold Cup, and that I would be delighted to ride him in it. I'm not sure that I actually believed that he could win a Gold Cup, but he was my best option at the time, so I was happy to commit to him.

I didn't really think about it too much after that. Mr Mulligan took a while to get over his fall at Kempton, but Noel reckoned he was bang on track for Cheltenham, so I went up to ride him in a piece of work after racing at Newbury 10 days before the Gold Cup, just to get reacquainted.

We were set to work with another horse of Noel's, Marching Marquis, a decent novice hurdler who had finished third in the Persian War Hurdle a month earlier and who was on track for the Sun Alliance Hurdle at Cheltenham. There were a couple of press people who stuck around after racing to watch Mr Mulligan work. It was a pretty big deal, he was high enough profile, and Noel wanted the horse to work well, or at least to look like he worked well. So he told the girl who was riding Marching Marquis to stay with Mr Mulligan. Whatever she did, she wasn't to go past him and leave him five lengths in her wake.

So we set off, me on Mr Mulligan, Noel's lass on Marching Marquis. We went okay down the back straight, but when we turned for home, he wasn't travelling a yard with me. I was pushing and squeezing, just to keep up with Marching Marquis, as the girl on his back sat as quiet as a mouse.

I was disgusted. This yoke couldn't even come up the straight at Newbury alongside a novice hurdler; he had no chance in the Gold Cup. I tried to avoid the press people when I came in and tried to remain positive. Noel was delighted in front of the press. That was perfect, Marching Marquis is a good horse and Mr Mulligan will come on for the gallop, he said. That should put him spot on for the Gold Cup.

I talked to Noel later.

'Noel, he worked terribly,' I said.

'I know,' said Noel. 'He's not a good work horse though. Why don't you come up on Wednesday and school him over a few fences? He's a different horse when you put a few fences in front of him.'

I phoned Dave.

'This yoke worked desperate,' I told him. 'And this is my Gold Cup ride? Noel says I should go up on Wednesday to school him, but I can't see how a couple of fences are going to transform him. Cyborgo couldn't be any worse a ride in the Gold Cup than him. I think I'll get off him and ride Cyborgo instead.'

'Why don't you wait until after you have schooled him on Wednesday,' suggested Dave. 'You don't have to decide before then anyway.'

Wise counsel.

Sure enough, I went to school Mr Mulligan on the Wednesday, and he was like a different horse. The fences did light him up, he jumped really well and he did it all enthusiastically. So I decided to stick with him. He was more or less the same price for the Gold Cup as Cyborgo, and I had already committed to him, so I would have been upsetting people if I were to get off him. And imagine you got off a Gold Cup winner. As it turned out, if I had known that the horse that Mr Mulligan had worked with at Newbury hadn't been Marching Marquis, but some other yoke that wasn't even nearly as good as Marching Marquis, I wouldn't even have bothered going up to school him.

By the time Cheltenham rolled around, I was well established as Martin Pipe's rider. Martin had a marquee at Cheltenham where he entertained guests, clients of his racing service The Pipeline, and he asked all his jockeys to go to have a chat with his clients before racing. He asked me to be there for 12 o'clock, which was fine.

However, Dunwoody and I were getting a few quid from Guinness to do some corporate work for them before racing, and I was down in the Guinness tent before I had to be in the marquee. As it turned out, I got delayed in the Guinness tent and I was late getting to Martin's. I was only about 15 minutes late, but Martin went ballistic.

'There's no point in coming here now,' he said to me. 'You're late. You were supposed to be here at 12 o'clock, not a quarter past. You might as well not have fucking come at all.'

I was livid. Here I was riding all his horses, we were having all this success, here we were at Cheltenham, the biggest week of the year, and he's giving out to me for being 15 minutes late for his Pipeline clients?

I was still spitting fire when I came out of the weigh room before the first race, the Supreme Novices' Hurdle. I was riding Kailash for Martin, so I went over to him in the parade ring, but I hardly said a word to him. Kailash was well beaten when he fell at the last.

I came out for the second race, the Arkle, in which I was riding Or Royal. I thought that Or Royal had a big chance. Mulligan was favourite for the race, the horse on whom I had won at Punchestown the previous April when he was trained by Mouse Morris, who was now with David Nicholson and who was unbeaten in five chases in the UK, and I had been beaten on Or Royal at Ascot on his previous run, but I had hit the front too early on Or Royal that day. He was a talented horse, but he didn't want to be in front too long, so I decided that I would hold him up for as long as I dared in the Arkle.

I didn't tell Martin this. I don't think we had a conversation at all as we stood in the parade ring before the Arkle. I was still furious. Remarkably, in the minutes before he legged me up for the most important novice chase of the year, we hardly exchanged two words.

The race went to plan. I had Or Royal prominent, Jamie Osborne went on on Squire Silk at the second last and gave us a nice lead to the last. After we landed over the last, I asked Or Royal to pick up, which he did, and he kept on well up the hill to get home by a half a length.

My second Cheltenham Festival winner, fantastic, but I was still annoyed with Martin. We were coming back in, down the chute, and Martin ran towards us, delighted, cheering. He put his hand on my leg as we were led up the chute towards the winner's enclosure.

'Well done, AP,' he said. 'Brilliant.'

'Yes,' I said. 'But if you ever speak to me like that again, you can get someone else to ride your horses.'

It was bad. I shouldn't have said it, but the whole incident from earlier was still bugging me. Three hours later, two races later, one Cheltenham Festival winner later, and it was still bugging me. I was very chippy like that when I was younger. I did hold grudges. I would like to say that I didn't, but I did, and it wasn't good.

I didn't regret saying it at the time though. On the contrary, I couldn't wait to say it. I couldn't wait to tell him that he had been out of order. I suppose, as well as being rude in the extreme, looking back on it now, it was a pretty ballsy thing to say. Martin could have dragged me off the horse there and then and told me that I would never ride for him again. Fortunately, he didn't.

'Okay, okay,' he said. He was the bigger person. I'm embarrassed thinking back on it now. Little upstart, only riding a wet week and he thinks he knows it all, telling Martin Pipe where to go. Martin may have been out of order having a go at me like he did, but I had been out of order first, I had been late, and he was probably on edge on the first day of Cheltenham with all that that entailed. If Martin had been a different type of person, however, it could have escalated into an infernal row. I got what I wanted to say off my chest, he said okay, we could move on.

It was easy to move on. The Champion Hurdle was next, the third race of the day. That's the thing about the Cheltenham Festival, once it starts, it is relentless. Wham, wham, wham. Top-class race follows top-class race. The Champion Hurdle is the fourth race of the meeting these days, but it used to be the third. Supreme Novices' Hurdle, Arkle, Champion Hurdle, that's the way it used to go, no chance to stop and draw breath.

There was very little chance to stop and draw breath on Make A Stand's back either. He only knew one way, flat out from the start, lead his field, cat-like over his hurdles, get his rivals in trouble and come clear.

He was an incredible little horse. That season he had won a William Hill Handicap Hurdle, a Kennel Gate Hurdle, a Lanzarote Hurdle and a Tote Gold Trophy before he lined up in the Champion Hurdle, and he was still a novice. If you wanted a definition of what Martin Pipe was all about, you had it there 'equinified' in front of you: a little chestnut runt of a thing who had been running in claimers on the flat the previous season, whom Martin had picked up for eight grand or so, and now he was a Champion Hurdle horse.

Both Martin and I thought that he was a good enough jumper to run in the Champion. Actually, we thought that he was the best jumper in the line-up, even though he was a novice. It was his jumping that made him such a high-class hurdler. He was a lot like Binocular in that way. If the Champion Hurdle had been a flat race, if you had taken away the hurdles and raced under the same conditions without the hurdles, besides the fact that you would have to rename the race, Make A Stand would have finished sixth or seventh. With the hurdles on the ground, though, different story.

We set off in front, and we never saw another rival. Make A Stand was incredible. All I had to do was sit on his back, stay on his back, and he did the rest. Measured up his hurdles, flew every single one of them, taking lengths out of his rivals as he did. At the line, we still had five lengths in hand over the second and third, Theatreworld and Space Trucker.

First I win the Arkle, then I win the Champion Hurdle. I was dreaming.

I was awakened with a thump the following day, however, when Big Strand caught me and Allegation in the very last stride in the Coral Cup. I led almost the whole way. Going to the final flight, I thought it was between me and Richard Johnson on Castle Sweep, but he made a mistake and handed it to us. Or so I thought. I sat down to ride a finish, ride Allegation all the way up to the line, only for this thing to come from nowhere and do me in the very last stride.

I can still see it, me driving for the line and this thing coming from the clouds, Jamie Evans hanging off him. I know he was champion jockey in Australia or whatever, but he was hanging off the horse. If he hadn't been a Martin Pipe horse, there is no way he would have come up the hill. Oh yeah, that was the other thing. He was trained by Martin, which didn't improve my mood.

I watched the replay for days afterwards. I watched where Big Strand was through the race and how he was travelling. I counted the horses in front of him going around the home turn – 12. He was 13th turning for home, not travelling well, and he got up to do me on the line. I was gutted about that. I still am actually. Imagine, the Cheltenham Festival that I'd had, the races I won and all I can do is go home and watch the video of Jamie Evans getting up to do me in the Coral Cup.

The final day was Gold Cup day, and I was giving Mr Mulligan a chance to show that Cheltenham suited him much better than Kempton. By contrast, One Man had stopped fairly dramatically in the 1996 Gold Cup after running all over Imperial Call going down the hill.

I remember Brendan Powell on Dublin Flyer leading; I was sitting fairly close to him, and then allowed my horse to stride on past him going down the far side. I didn't plan to be in front so early, but my horse was a galloper, so I figured I would allow him to stride on.

After that, we didn't see another rival. I kicked him on around the home turn, we got in tight to the second last, One Man closed up a bit, but my horse had loads left, and he picked up again, ran down to the last, jumped that well, and I just had to keep him going up the hill.

It was an incredible feeling, winning the Gold Cup, after all the Gold Cups I had watched on the television at home and when I was at Jim Bolger's. Dawn Run, Desert Orchid, Forgive N Forget, Jodami. I had won the Champion Hurdle and the Gold Cup at the same Cheltenham Festival. Hardly anyone wins the Champion Hurdle and the Gold Cup in the same year. Norman Williamson had done it two years previously on Alderbrook and Master Oats, but before Norman you had to go back to Fred Winter, who rode Eborneezer to win the Champion Hurdle and Saffron Tartan to win the Gold Cup in 1961.

Twelve months and four days earlier, I had never even been to Cheltenham. To think that I was here now, on the racetrack, part of it, contributing to Cheltenham history, creating it, well that was just going to take a little while to sink in.

That evening, we celebrated in style. I went to a Pizza Hut in Cheltenham with Chanelle, and Conor and Audrey O'Dwyer, and I was riding at Folkestone the following day.

CHAPTER 16

Three Strikes

I have only had three clashes with Martin Pipe in my life. The first was on that day at Cheltenham in 1997, ironically the day I won the Arkle and the Champion Hurdle. I suppose it wasn't really a clash. He just gave me a bollocking and I said if you ever talk to me like that again you can get someone else to ride your horses. No big deal.

The second one was a proper clash though, a real row, over a horse called Courbaril, an ordinary enough novice hurdler that Martin trained for Richard Green.

Five days after I won the Gold Cup, I was riding Strong Tel in a novices' hurdle at Uttoxeter when he ran out with me at the first fence, crashed through the wing and gave me a bad fall. This game has a habit of literally bringing you back down to earth just when you think you are invincible. I was knocked out cold.

When you are knocked out and suffer concussion, you are automatically stood down. If you are out for less than a minute, you are stood down for seven days. If you are out for more than a minute, your enforced holiday is 21 days. It's logical, it makes sense on health and safety grounds, but it's a real pain when it happens, when you are on the sidelines feeling fine, bursting to get up and race-ride again but are not permitted to do so.

There was some confusion over the length of time for which I should have been stood down. The doctor on the day said that I was only out for a minute, so I would have been fine with a seven-day holiday, but when they checked into it later, they concluded that I had been out for three minutes, so I had to serve 21 days on the sidelines, which was a bit frustrating.

Thankfully, that is the only time in my life that I have been badly concussed. It was the first time, and it was the worst. I couldn't remember a thing about the fall. There were other times though, like at Kempton on the day after King George day in December 2008, when I took a fairly bad fall off Vale of Avocia in the mares' handicap hurdle down the side of the track and gave my head a bit of a bang. I got into the ambulance, they asked me if I was all right, I said yeah, grand, but by the time I got back to the weigh room I knew that my head was all over the place.

Shane, my valet, asked me if I was okay. I said yeah, just get me a cup of tea, no sugar, which he did. I was riding Twist Magic for Paul Nicholls in the next race, the Desert Orchid Chase, so I put on my colours, got the saddle and stood on the weighing scales where we check our weight before going out to weigh out. Shane told me that I was grand, the weight was right, so I went to weigh out in front of the stewards.

When I got out though, Dan Skelton, Paul Nicholls's assistant trainer, was there, so I just gave him the saddle without weighing out. He went off with the saddle. Then the word came back that I hadn't weighed out at all, so Dan had to come back with the saddle so that I could. He handed me the saddle, I held it for a couple of seconds, then handed it back to him.

'But aren't you going to weigh out?' he asked me.

'What are you on about?'

Eventually, I stood up on the scales with the saddle, the stewards checked the weight, and Dan went off to put the saddle on Twist Magic.

On the way out onto the track, Jamie Moore, who was riding Fiepes Shuffle in the race, realised that I wasn't great, so he just stayed with me on the way down to the start, told me to follow him, which I did. We were walking around at the start though, and I still wasn't sure where I was. Suddenly all the other jockeys were pulling their goggles down, the starter was making his way over to his roster to start the race, and Jamie was shouting at me to pull my goggles down and line up.

I can't remember anything about the race. I know Jamie won the race on the 16/1 shot Fiepes Shuffle, and that I finished sixth of the seven runners on the 13/8 shot Twist Magic. I called Paul Nicholls afterwards to apologise.

This may sound ridiculous, but I think I have programmed myself to not get knocked out cold. I have been concussed again since my fall from Strong Tel, but I don't think I have been out cold that often. It's like, when you know you are going to hit the ground, you know your head is going to take some kind of an impact, you say to yourself, right, whatever happens, I'm not going to let myself go into a sleep. I'm going to make sure that I get up straight away, that I am up and walking around even if I am in a daze. If I am not lying on the ground, obviously unconscious, then I won't have an enforced absence of 7 or 21 days thrust upon me.

Of course, sometimes you will get such a bang that you will be out cold and there will be nothing you can do about it. But sometimes, you can just get a bit of a knock and lie there on the ground, in a kind of a semi-sleep, thinking ah, I'll just lie here for a little while. They are the ones that I think I have programmed myself to avoid. If you force yourself to get up from those ones, then they can't stand you down, they can't say that you were knocked out.

The 21-day holiday that I got after my fall from Strong Tel meant that I was going to miss out on the Grand National meeting at Aintree, which really wasn't good. I was supposed to ride Belmont King for Paul Nicholls, the horse on whom I had won the Rehearsal Chase at Chepstow the previous December. Obviously, Paul had got over the Flaked Oats debacle, although Belmont King wasn't owned by Paul Barber, so that helped.

As it turned out, Belmont King didn't run in the Grand National. He got worked up on the day – it was the year that the Grand National was postponed from the Saturday to the Monday because of the IRA bomb scare – and he didn't run in the rescheduled race on the Monday. I did ride him in the Scottish Grand National at Ayr the following month though, which we won.

I was doing some work for the BBC at Aintree, so I was there, but I obviously couldn't ride Courbaril in the Grade 2 novices' hurdle. Norman Williamson rode him, and he ran well to finish second to Sanmartino.

Courbaril was running in a handicap hurdle at Cheltenham on the Wednesday after I returned. Dave called me on the Tuesday morning as I was on my way to Exeter, where I had five rides for Martin.

'They want Norman to ride Courbaril at Cheltenham,' he said.

'What?' I asked. I could have sworn that Dave had said that they wanted Norman to ride Courbaril at Cheltenham.

'They want Norman to ride him,' said Dave.

'Yeah right,' I said.

I paused for a second, awaiting Dave's laugh. It didn't come.

'Right,' I said slowly. 'Well, we'll see how that one goes.'

This was a bit of a bolt from the blue. I wasn't Martin's stable jockey, I had no contract, he trained the horses, of course he could do what he wanted, he could have whatever rider he wanted, but I was riding all his horses, I was his stable jockey in all but contract. There was an expectation there, an understanding that came from all the rides, all the wins, all the success, the common goals, the common thinking. It was only one horse, it was only Courbaril, it was only a five-grand handicap hurdle, but the principle of the thing was way more important than that.

I called Martin's office, Gail answered.

'Hi Gail,' I said. 'I hear they want Norman to ride Courbaril tomorrow.'

'Oh yes,' said Gail. 'I'll put you on to the boss.'

Martin came on the phone.

'Dave told me that you want Norman to ride Courbaril,' I said. 'What's that about?'

'Well, Richard Green said that Norman rode him well at Aintree,' said Martin, 'and he wants him to keep the ride.'

'Okay,' I said. 'And what do you think?'

'Well...' Martin hesitated a bit. 'This is what Richard Green wants.'

'Right,' I said. 'Well, I'll tell you what you can do now. You and Richard Green can take your Courbaril, and you can stick him as far up your arse as he will go. When I get off your last horse today, I won't be riding for you any more.'

I hung up and got on the phone to Dave.

'Well,' asked Dave. 'How did it go?'

'It went fine,' I said. 'I won't be riding for him again after today. You can take me off all his horses at Cheltenham tomorrow.'

'Are you sure about this?' asked Dave.

'Look, I didn't go looking for Martin Pipe,' I said. 'I never asked to be his stable jockey. If he wants Norman to ride Courbaril, then fine, Norman can ride them all. If I'm not good enough to ride Courbaril, I'm not good enough to ride any of them.'

Dave listened to me, he heard me out, and then he concluded that I was right. Dave said that he'd call Martin to tell him that I was getting off his other horses at Cheltenham the following day. He called me back 10 minutes later.

'He's not happy,' Dave said.

'So what?' I said. 'This is not my doing. They decided they wanted Norman, that's fine.'

Ten minutes later, my phone rang again. Martin Pipe.

'I spoke to Richard Green,' he said, 'and I told him that you were riding Courbaril tomorrow.'

'Oh right,' I said. 'Do you not think you should have done that in the first place?'

'Yeah, maybe I should have,' he said. 'Sorry about that.'

I wouldn't act like that now. No way. I suppose that's because I'm not an impetuous little git now. If someone called me now and told me that I wasn't riding something I was expecting to ride, I'd say fine, no worries, get someone else to ride it. I would expect to get on something else in the race anyway.

At the time, though, I couldn't believe it. You don't think I'm good enough to ride your horse? I would like to think that I didn't mean it in an arrogant way, but of course I did. There was no other way that I could have meant it.

Thankfully, I did get over myself quite quickly. Not more than a year later, one of Martin's owners, Brian Kilpatrick, decided that he didn't want me riding his horses. He was a longstanding owner of Martin's – he owned Sabin Du Loir and Tarxien among plenty of others – but I think he thought that I was being too hard on his horses. I said fine.

Martin did tell me that he could go back to Brian and tell him that I was riding all the horses in the yard, and that if he didn't want me to ride his horses, he should move them to another yard. I appreciated that, but I had chilled out a bit by that stage. One of Brian's horses, Dom Samourai, won the Greenalls Grand National Trial at Haydock the following February with Chris Maude riding him. I would be lying if I said that I didn't mind missing out on winning a fairly big race, but that was the way it was, and I was dealing with it.

As it turned out, I rode four winners out of five rides for Martin at Exeter that day. Also, the following day, I won on Courbaril and everyone was happy. Nothing like a little bit of success to make everybody feel good.

I never fought with Martin over how I rode a particular horse or how I should ride a particular horse. He never gave me a bollocking over a ride. Not once. Eight seasons riding for him, and we never had a row over a ride. I always told him the truth about horses, I always told him what I thought. If I thought a horse was no good, I told him so. And if I gave a horse a bad ride, I knew it and I would tell him as much. I didn't need him to be telling me. I think he appreciated that.

Our third and final row was the worst though. We had two horses for the big William Hill Handicap Hurdle at Sandown in December 1999, Rodock and Copeland. Rodock had won both his races since Martin had got him from France, including the race that is now the Greatwood Hurdle at Cheltenham's November meeting, while Copeland was another French import who had run just twice and who we liked a lot and thought was really well handicapped.

I was sure that whichever horse he ran would win. I told Martin so during the week and he agreed. Then on Friday, he decided that he would run both. I couldn't believe it. Why would he run both? Whichever horse he ran would probably win, and then he could keep the other for another big race off what was a really attractive handicap mark.

Of course, the two horses were owned by two different people, they both probably wanted to run, there was a lot of prize money up for grabs, but that was no use to me, and at that time the only person that mattered to me was me. I couldn't ride both of them.

I had to make a decision. I chose Rodock. I chose wrong. Rodock didn't jump well, I was always further back than I wanted to be. His class got him there, we got up to challenge Copeland at the second last, but Rodock was carrying 19 lb more than Copeland and that was just too much. He battled up the hill valiantly, but we just failed by a short head to catch Copeland and David Casey.

There was no third horse. We finished miles clear of the rest of them. The third horse was in Sandown High Street while we were crossing the line. I came back into the unsaddling enclosure, took the saddle off Rodock in a strop, and muttered something to Martin.

'What the fuck was the point in that? I told you whichever you ran would win.'

I didn't speak to him any more. I wouldn't speak to him. I was out of my head with rage. Actually, I didn't speak to him for weeks. I rode for him all right over the course of the next couple of weeks, but I didn't speak to him. Not a word. I didn't speak to him in the parade ring before races, I didn't ask him how he thought I should ride his horses, and I didn't speak to him afterwards to tell him what I thought. Bizarre behaviour.

The William Hill was on 4th December, and I didn't speak to Martin for the rest of the month. Eventually, before the New Year's Eve meeting at Cheltenham, Martin's wife Carol called me.

'You know, I think you should speak to Martin,' she said. 'He's very upset about this. I know that you're upset with what happened with Rodock, but it's not good for anyone that you are not speaking to each other. We shouldn't have run both horses, but both owners wanted to run.'

Carol just buttered me up, but it worked. I decided that I would speak to him that day at Cheltenham. I don't know what would have happened if Carol hadn't called me. I wonder if you can ride for a trainer for eight years without speaking to him? Probably not. But that's the way it was going. I was so stubborn, I was being a spoilt little shit. I didn't get my own way, he ran both horses, I chose the one that finished second, I got it wrong, I was beaten by a horse that I should have been riding, and I just went off in a huff. As it happened, Karma being Karma and all, I won the handicap chase at Cheltenham on New Year's Eve on Strong Tel, the horse that had tried to kill me at Uttoxeter almost three years earlier.

I finished the season as champion again with 190 winners, 59 clear of Jamie Osborne in second, and I got to thinking, if I hadn't missed those 21 days with concussion, I could have broken through the 200 barrier. Now that would've been something. Imagine riding more than 200 winners in a season. The only jump jockey who has ever ridden more than 200 winners in a season is Peter Scudamore, and he had only done it once. I had a new goal.

CHAPTER 17

Biggest Certainty Ever

Life was okay. I was champion jockey again, I was riding for Martin Pipe, I was riding plenty of winners, Chanelle was sticking around a bit, and I was getting a few quid together.

On top of that, I didn't have to spend every morning riding out. I went down to Martin's place at Pond House to school maybe once a month during the season, and that was it. They had their work riders, they had their routine, I would only have been upsetting that, and that was fine with me. I had spent the last five years getting up at six o'clock in the morning to ride out, so to not be under any obligation to do so now was great.

I rode five winners on the card at Uttoxeter in the early part of summer 1997. I brought Chanelle to the races with me that day, my lucky charm. Only she had been out all night in Dublin with her college mates the night before... I picked her up at the airport, brought her to Uttoxeter with me, and she said she'd have a little snooze in the car until the first race. By the time she woke up, the last race was over, so she said crap, got out of the car and started walking into the racecourse. On the way in, she asked a guy who was leaving how AP McCoy had got on, if he had ridden any winners, and the guy just laughed at her.

I have never gone through the card at a meeting. I went close that day, and I went close again at Ascot on Ladbroke Hurdle day in December 2001. I rode five of the six winners that day. The one that let me down was Westender in the Ladbroke Hurdle itself. It was obviously a big handicap hurdle, but he was 5/2 favourite for it, and he should have won it. He just had an off-day. On his next run he was beaten a neck by Like-A-Butterfly in the Supreme Novices' Hurdle at Cheltenham. If he had put in that run, he would have won the Ladbroke doing handsprings, even off 11 st 10 lb. Alas, it just wasn't to be.

My relationship with Martin was strengthening all the time. I was still surprised at how easy it was to ride for him. Martin himself was aware of the perception that people had of him, as was evident when he sponsored a race at Taunton in January 1997 and called it the Martin Pipe Am I That Difficult? Handicap Hurdle. (Inevitably, he trained the winner of it too.) There were only three rows, as I mentioned, and they were all mostly my fault.

I used to write a report on every horse that I rode for him, what the ground was like, how the horse moved, if he might want blinkers, did he jump well, did he jump left or right or straight, comment on the race, any recommendations for the horse for the future. Like if he raced keenly and got tired, you might recommend that he be settled in behind next time, or that he step down in trip.

Your report on the ground would also be crucial. The official ground might be good, so the form book would say good ground, but it might have been on the soft side or on the fast side, so we needed to know that for the future.

I quite liked doing the reports, and I thought they were a great idea, and even now, if I ride a horse for Martin's son David, I dictate a report to my PA, Gee Bradburne, and she sends it in to his office.

Gee is brilliant. She is one of the key people in my life. Dave Roberts organises my rides, and Gee organises pretty much everything else in my life. Sister of Grand National-winning jockey Marcus Armytage and wife of jockey Mark Bradburne, Gee was a really good rider herself back in the 1980s. She rode two winners at the 1987 Cheltenham Festival, The Ellier in the Kim Muir and Gee-A in the Mildmay of Flete, and tied with Peter Scudamore as leading rider at that year's Festival, although Scudamore got the award because he had ridden more seconds and thirds. In 1988, she rode Gee-A in the Grand National. Injury forced her to retire in 1995, but she is invaluable to me, and has been for years.

I am very fortunate to have so many good people around me in my professional life. My driver Arnie is a star. It's a huge thing for me to have a good driver; it means that I can sleep or catch up on phone calls on the way to or from the races, and I know that whatever conversations I have in the car will never be repeated by Arnie. He is a top bloke. He's a Liverpool fan, but I suppose nobody is without at least one flaw.

It is not an overstatement to say that Martin Pipe revolutionised racing; he single-handedly changed how National Hunt horses were trained. There are not many people who have revolutionised their industry, and there are very few people who had a greater impact on training methodology than Martin. Vincent O'Brien was one, he was a one-off, a pioneer, and Martin was in the same ball park.

Before Martin came along, National Hunt horses were generally trained slowly: lots of slow work, getting fit slowly, they would rarely be fully fit on their seasonal debuts, they would always come on for the run and generally progress through the season with racing as they were getting fitter. Martin was able to get them fit at home. He didn't subscribe to the notion that jumps horses had to be trained slowly. He introduced interval training, he tested bloods, he weighed his horses and found out what their optimum racing weights were, he went to France and started buying French-bred horses, horses that were more precocious than the traditional Irish-bred steeplechaser.

When Martin started off, when Peter Scudamore was riding for him, you almost always saw his horses out in front. It wasn't because they were all necessarily front-runners, but they were just fitter than their rivals, so Martin and Scu figured that they would maximise the advantage that that had by kicking off in front and making the others play catch-up if they could.

There was a lot of negativity about him at the time. Who is this guy, a bookmaker's son who used to train bad horses? There is no way all his horses could be as fit as they are, there is no way they could keep going for as long as they do, through natural training methods. They must be on something. He must be doing something illicit. That was the general racecourse whisper that went on. Everybody heard it, including Martin.

Martin was able to get moderate and bad horses to run way better than they had been able to before. He would get bad horses off other trainers, get them fit and win races with them. Of course that wasn't going to endear him to the trainers from whom he got the horses. It didn't make them look good. People started saying that he was cruel to horses, training them too hard, which couldn't have been further from the truth. Nobody could have treated horses any better than Martin. The reality was that it was far more cruel to send a half-fit horse to the races and ask him to run three miles on heavy ground. That was something that Martin never did.

I found him fascinating from the beginning. He told me that he would go to the races in the early days and see the horses in the parade ring, and just think that they were too fat, that they weren't fully fit. So he resolved that his horses would be fit. It was a basic starting point. No athlete, human or equine, can perform to the best of their ability if they are not fit.

He used to read every book under the sun on fitness. I remember him telling me about Emil Zatopek, who won three gold medals at the 1952 Olympic Games in Helsinki. He won the 5,000 metres and the 10,000 metres, and then, at the last minute, he decided that he would run in the marathon, which he duly won. He broke the Olympic record in all three events. Martin was fascinated by the way he trained using interval training, which is the method that Martin used on his horses.

Another day he told me that Linford Christie only became Olympic champion because he learned how to start properly before going on to explain to me how important the start was in a race, even in a three-mile chase. In his eyes, the start of the race was just as important as the end. If you give away ground at the start, no matter how long the race is, you still have to make up that ground. It makes sense now, everybody thinks that now, but it was revolutionary thinking at the time.

He would always be trying different things, looking at ways in which he could get his horses to run faster. He tried lighter bridles made of nylon instead of leather. He got these blinkers with holes in the back of the cups and had them trialled in a wind tunnel to see if they were more aerodynamic than normal blinkers.

He treated his horses like athletes in every way. He trained them like athletes. He was into their health as much as he was into their fitness. Fitness was crucial to him, but he figured that he couldn't get them fit if they weren't healthy, so he set up his own laboratory in the yard so that he could check every horse's blood and make sure their bloods were right. Pond House was like an Olympic training camp. Horses can't tell you if they are not feeling well, you have to figure it out for yourself, and Martin figured that the key was in their blood tests. If a horse's blood was wrong, that horse went on the easy list.

I remember the evening that he told me about The Cook Report, the television programme that tried to discredit him, to prove that there was something underhand going on. People hiding in bushes, hiding everywhere around the place, trying to find things that weren't there, trying to prove that there was more to this laboratory than just testing bloods in order to ensure that the horses were healthy. They found nothing. They couldn't find anything when there was nothing there. Even so, it scarred Martin. He was a lot cooler with the press and the media in general after that. It was a really low point for Martin. He thought about giving it all up there and then, he told me. It still hurts him.

He was stubborn, he had his moments and he had his ways, but he was no different to me in that regard, and I always found him and his wife Carol, and their son David, the easiest people to deal with. For the big races, we would discuss tactics and agree how a horse should be ridden. But Martin knew that things didn't always go to plan during a race; you might miss the start or make a mistake at a fence early on, or it might be at too fast a pace, or too slow a pace, and he was always happy for me to adapt tactics to what was happening around me.

I am genuinely of the opinion that, if you're employing someone to ride a horse for you, you shouldn't be telling them how to do it. If you're telling them how to ride it, if you are giving them strict instructions, be first or second or third jumping the second fence, then you are not employing the right person. I have never trained a horse in my life, but if I did, and if I was getting Ruby Walsh to ride it, I wouldn't think for a minute of telling him how to do it.

Sometimes Martin's only instructions to me were not to win by too far. I remember on Imperial Cup day, 14th March 1998, travelling from Chepstow to Sandown with him in the helicopter. I was after riding Eudipe to finish third in a good handicap chase at Chepstow, but the business of the day was Blowing Wind in the Imperial Cup at Sandown. Eudipe ran at 1.45, and I rode another horse in the 2.15, but there was plenty of time to get from Chepstow to Sandown in order to ride Blowing Wind in the Imperial Cup, which was due off at 4.05.

There was a big bonus on offer to the connections of any horse who could win the Imperial Cup, and then go on to the Cheltenham Festival, which kicked off two days later, and win any race there. Martin had landed the bonus five years earlier with Olympian, who had won the Coral Cup at Cheltenham after landing the Imperial Cup under Peter Scudamore, and he thought that Blowing Wind was capable of repeating the feat. We didn't discuss tactics in the helicopter on the journey up from Chepstow, but as we approached Sandown racecourse, he leant over, put his hand easily on my shoulder and said quietly: 'Don't win by too far.'

A 15-runner handicap hurdle, one of the most competitive handicap hurdles on the calendar, and all I have to do is not win by too far?

Martin Bosley had a horse in the race called Rubhahunish, about whom Luke Harvey and Carl Llewellyn were raving. I dropped Blowing Wind out the back in the early stages and just allowed him to creep into the race. As we neared the end of the back straight, I could see Luke just ahead of me on Rubhahunish.

'I'm behind you!' I shouted at Luke.

Luke half looked around. I don't know what he said, but it wasn't nice.

I just allowed Blowing Wind to coast up the home straight. He moved up lovely between the last two flights, I sat on him until after we had jumped the last, then I asked him to pick up, which he did impressively, and won with his head in his chest. It was a fair performance for a five-year-old to win an Imperial Cup off 11 st 10 lb, but I never doubted him for a minute, not when Martin was so confident. We did win the County Hurdle as well at Cheltenham five days later, with the 7 lb penalty, not quite as easily, but we won it and landed the bonus.

We had another horse that season, Unsinkable Boxer. He wasn't a young horse, he had won a bumper in Ireland and he had been trained by the owner, Paul Green's son-in-law, Nick Walker, when he first came to the UK. Martin got him as an eight-year-old, going nine, at the start of that season, the 1997–98 season.

I won his first three races on him, at Plumpton, Fontwell and Doncaster, the last one in January, before Martin put him away with a view to bringing him back to win the Pertemps Final at the Cheltenham Festival in March.

I remember going out of the parade ring before the Pertemps, or the Unicoin Homes Gold Card Handicap Hurdle as it was then. We were after winning the Arkle earlier in the day with Champleve, and we were all a little more at ease than we might have been had we not had a Cheltenham Festival winner on the board. Martin was walking alongside me and Unsinkable Boxer as we went down the chute onto the racecourse before what was the last race on the first day of the Cheltenham Festival.

'What will I do with this fellow?' I asked him.

'Ah just ride him away out the back,' said Martin. 'Just ride him how you find him.'

'It's a 24-runner handicap hurdle,' I said to him, smiling. 'You want me to be out the back?'

'Yeah, drop him in,' said Martin, as relaxed as if he was sitting at home in his sitting room about to watch a recording of the race. 'Last if you like. Just pass them all whenever you want to.'

Then he looked up at me. I'll never forget it. He looked me straight in the eye without breaking stride, and he lowered his voice.

'This horse,' he said in a measured even tone, 'is the biggest certainty that will ever walk out onto this racecourse.'

I looked for a smirk or a smile, but there was none forthcoming. A 24-runner handicap hurdle at the Cheltenham Festival, and Martin is telling me that he is the biggest certainty ever. I thought to myself, holy shit. If I didn't feel under pressure beforehand, I sure as hell felt under pressure after that.

Circling at the start, I told Graham Bradley, who was riding a horse of David Elsworth's called Ivor's Flutter, what Martin had said.

So I was riding Unsinkable Boxer just as Martin had told me to, out the back, his words ringing in my inner ear, the biggest certainty that will ever walk out onto this racecourse, pass them all when you like. We were going down the back straight for the final time, we were just bypassing the water jump on the chase track, and I had plenty more horses in front of me than behind me, when I heard this Yorkshire accent.

'Hey up, lad.' It had to be Brad. 'You'd better get a move on then, hadn't you?'

As it turned out, I didn't need to do anything. I just sat on the horse, made sure he was pointing in the right direction, and he just started passing horses. Before I knew what was really happening, we were going to the second-last and we were in front. I hardly broke sweat, he hardly broke sweat, and we cruised up the hill. 'Canter' was the *Racing Post*'s analysis.

There was a bit of a sour note to this one though. All along, Unsinkable Boxer's owner Paul Green had been talking about going for the Stayers' Hurdle. I don't know why, but he had this thing in his head that he wanted his horse to run in the Stayers' Hurdle instead of the Gold Card Handicap Hurdle. He had never had a winner at Cheltenham before; most owners would give their right arm for a winner at the Cheltenham Festival, of any race at the Cheltenham Festival. He had the favourite for a race at the Cheltenham Festival – and I'm sure Martin told him how much he fancied him – but he wants to run in a different race for which he certainly would not have been favourite. It didn't make sense to me.

There is a world of a difference between a Gold Card Handicap Hurdle and a Stayers' Hurdle. You are into a different grade completely when you are going from a handicap to the Stayers' Hurdle.

So we were standing on the winner's podium after receiving our trophies, me, Martin and Paul Green, smiling for the photographers after winning the Gold Card – it is difficult not to smile after you have had a winner at Cheltenham – and Paul turns to me.

'I can't believe we ran him in that race,' he said. 'We should have run him in the Stayers' Hurdle.'

I couldn't believe what I thought I heard. He's just had a winner at

Cheltenham, he's still on the podium, he should have been lapping it all up, appreciating that rare animal that is a Cheltenham winner, and instead he is giving out about not running in a race later in the week, a race in which his horse is not entitled to finish better than about fifth.

I leaned over to Martin. 'Did you hear what he just said?'

Martin shook his head. Just leave it AP.

That was some Cheltenham Festival for me at the end of some season. I had ridden 100 winners by early November. Indeed, when I won the handicap hurdle at Newton Abbot on Sam Rockett on 5th November, I had clocked up the fastest century in a season ever, beating my own record from the previous season. Of course, I was helped by the fact that summer jumping was now in, and that this was my first full season riding for Martin, when I was able to burst out of the stalls on day one, but it was still great to clock up the fastest century ever.

Then I rode my 200th winner of the season on Fataliste in the Adonis Hurdle at Kempton on 28th February. It was fantastic to ride 200 winners, only the second National Hunt jockey ever to do so, and faster than Scu's 200 back in 1988/89.

That season wasn't all a bed of roses, mind you. There was Challenger Du Luc in the King George. I could have won the race on him, and I could have beaten See More Business, but Challenger Du Luc was a horse for whom everything had to go right, he didn't like being in front for any amount of time, I would have had to have dropped his nose in front right on the line. A hundred yards before the line and See More Business would have got back up, 50 yards before the line and See More Business would have got back up.

As it turned out, we were cantering all over See More Business on the run to the second last, so I took a pull, I couldn't have allowed him to take it up so far out, but once I did, I just couldn't get him going again, and we ended up going down by two lengths to See More Business. There was no disgrace in that though; See More Business won a Gold Cup and another King George after that, and on ratings it was by far the best run of Challenger Du Luc's life. Even so, I was gutted.

I actually thought that he would be the ideal Grand National horse: lots of ability, lots of class, a good jumper, but a bit quirky, and I thought the Aintree fences just might be the thing for him. I rode him in the National that April, but he shit himself on the run to the first. I could feel him getting faster and faster under me on the run across the Melling Road, and then when he heard the crash of the other horses at the first fence, he just panicked and forgot everything about jumping.

He didn't even get his take-off gear out, not to mind his landing gear, and he crashed head first into the spruce, turning a somersault and giving me a right belt off the ground.

I never won on Challanger Du Luc. I rode him 13 times and I never won on him. He wasn't one of my more successful projects.

I was feeling pretty good about myself going into Cheltenham 1998. I had won the Champion Hurdle and the Gold Cup the previous year as well as the Arkle, I had been leading rider, and I had already had some really good rides so far this year. Mr Mulligan won the Gold Cup in 1997, but he was a 16/1 or a 20/1 shot, you couldn't have really fancied him. This year I had a much stronger book of rides.

Ironically, I thought that my three best rides were in the last three races on the last day of the meeting: Edredon Bleu in the Grand Annual, Cyfor Malta in the Cathcart and Blowing Wind in the County Hurdle. Any time anybody asked me for a tip in the lead up to that year's Festival, I told them to back my three horses in the last three races. If they had been on different days, I would have been even sweeter on their chances because, realistically, you couldn't be expecting to win the last three races at the Cheltenham Festival. As it turned out, I did.

I didn't really fancy Champleve in the Arkle. He had been jumping hurdles since Martin had got him from France; he only made his debut over fences five weeks before Cheltenham. He won that, a novices' chase at Lingfield, and he won a decent enough novices' chase at Ascot five days later, which essentially justified his inclusion in the Arkle field, but I didn't think he could win it, I just thought he was too inexperienced.

Martin fancied him a little bit and I knew that his owner David Johnson had backed him. David had lots of horses with Martin at the time, and his famous colours – blue body, green sleeves, spotted cap, very similar to Robert Sangster's colours on the flat – were synonymous with Martin Pipe, and they were carried to success by some of Martin's best horses in the 1990s and 2000s. He was a great owner, a great guy to ride for.

I was prominent on Champleve, we took it up halfway down the back straight and we went for home from three out. We were clear jumping the last, but the hill from the last fence to the line is a bugger when you are out in front looking for the line. I had no idea where the line was, I just rode as hard as I could from the back of the last fence. I just kept my head down, I didn't look up. (I rarely look up for the line – I usually see it on the ground as we cross it.)

There was another horse beside me when we hit the line. I looked over as we pulled up – it was Richard Dunwoody on Hill Society. We exchanged a few words. Are you up? Don't think so. I didn't have a clue if I had won or not, I genuinely thought it was a 50-50 call, but I think Richard thought he had won.

The result hadn't been announced by the time I came back into the unsaddling area, but the general feeling was that Hill Society had won. Hill Society's trainer Noel Meade had never had a winner at Cheltenham before, so that would have been nice for him if Hill Society was up, but I wasn't thinking that at the time. I told Martin that I didn't know.

Still no announcement as I dismounted, took the saddle, went back to the weigh room and weighed in. They were showing replay after replay, slowing the replays down, freezing the horses on the line, nose to nose, and still nobody knew. They interviewed Martin, they interviewed Noel, it was good television, but the tension was almost unbearable. I was weighing out for the next race, the Champion Hurdle, without knowing if I had won the Arkle or not. Then the result was announced. First number 16. Champleve.

Brilliant. To win another Arkle, to have a winner on the board at the Cheltenham Festival so early in the week, the easing of pressure that that brings, to win by a short head, to beat Dunwoody by a short head, it was fantastic. I bounced out into the parade ring to ride Pridwell in the Champion Hurdle. Unfortunately, the momentum didn't continue, and we finished fourth behind Istabraq. Pridwell didn't run badly, but his day wasn't too far away.

The 1998 Gold Cup was one to remember, although not for the right reasons. Martin had three in the race: I chose to ride Cyborgo, Jonathan Lower was on Indian Tracker and Chris Maude rode Challenger Du Luc. Michael Hourigan's horse Dorans Pride was favourite for the race, but See More Business, trained by Paul Nicholls with his new stable jockey Timmy Murphy, had been well-backed and was really well-fancied.

I was travelling okay in mid-division going to the open ditch on the far side when I felt Cyborgo go wrong underneath me. The ditch was fast approaching, and the last thing I wanted to do was jump it with a horse who had gone wrong. It could have done him untold damage, he could have fallen, injured himself further, injured me, injured others around him. I had to act quickly, so I shouted something, I'm pulling up, and I moved him to my right to the outside of the fence.

As I did, I heard shouting behind. I could hear another horse on my outside. I thought that he would have had enough time to pull back and go inside me to jump the fence but, unfortunately, he didn't. As I passed the fence by, I could hear Jonathan Lower's voice cursing and blinding. Disaster – I had taken out Indian Tracker, another one of Martin's horses. At that fence he had lost two of his Gold Cup challengers, one gone wrong and the other carried out by the one that had gone wrong. Then I saw another horse go past me to the right of Indian Tracker – See More Business. I had taken Paul Nicholls's horse out as well. As we pulled up, I apologised to Jonathan and Timmy. I couldn't do anything else.

There were all kinds of rumours going around afterwards, that I had done it intentionally, that my aim was to take See More Business out of the race, that it was Martin Pipe's way of getting at Paul Nicholls. Paul was as angry as a swarm of bees that has just happened upon Winnie the Pooh with an empty jar of honey. He had a go at Martin. It was only a verbal go, but it was a furious one, and it was launched in full public glare. As if it was Martin's fault. In fairness to Paul, he did admit later – much later – that it was crazy to think that he was the victim of some elaborate conspiracy. That said, bizarrely, years later in his book published in 2009, he admits that 'part of me still wishes I'd clocked Pipe'.

He was right – it was a crazy notion. Firstly, even if I had wanted to take him out, I would have had to have organised that Jonathan would be on my outside and that Timmy would be on his outside at the point in the race at which I took Cyborgo out of it. Secondly, there is no way I would have wanted to. I would never have done something like that, and there is no way that Martin would have either.

I can understand that Paul and Timmy, and See More Business's owners Paul Barber and John Keighley, would have been frustrated and annoyed, particularly in light of subsequent events. Cool Dawn won that Gold Cup; it was one of the weakest Gold Cups in recent times. See More Business had won the King George and the Pillar Property, and he went on to win the Gold Cup the following year as well. Even though it was an accident, a complete freak occurrence, looking back, I do feel bad for Paul and Timmy.. See More Business was probably a certainty beaten in that Gold Cup. He probably would have won by a fence.

The meeting ended on a high note for me though. Remember those three horses that I thought would win? Edredon Bleu, Cyfor Malta and Blowing Wind? Well, you learn that, in racing, things don't often pan out the way you expect them to, but this one did. They all did win.

Edredon Bleu was trained by Henrietta Knight, the ex-schoolteacher who would later train Best Mate to win three Gold Cups. Henrietta's stable jockey Jim Culloty was out injured. I rode Edredon Bleu for the first time in a handicap chase at Sandown four weeks before Cheltenham, which we won. I told Martin then that he would win the Grand Annual, the two-mile handicap chase at Cheltenham, and that I would like to ride him in it if I could. In fairness to Martin, he had a horse in the race, Indian Jockey, but he was happy enough to let me get off him to ride Edredon Bleu, and we duly won. I actually didn't give him that good a ride, I went too fast on him, but he had won over two and a half miles, he stayed two and a half miles well, and he kept on up the hill.

Cyfor Malta was a special horse. Carol Pipe told me that, from the first day Cyfor Malta arrived into the yard, Martin could talk about little else. Cyfor Malta this, Cyfor Malta that. When he went down to the yard in the morning, the first horse he would go to see was Cyfor Malta. He was a gorgeous-looking horse, an absolute model. If you were buying a racehorse and you were able to design exactly how you wanted him to look, you would design Cyfor Malta. He was a complete athlete, perfect conformation, the most beautiful head. I managed to get him beaten in the Scilly Isles Chase at Sandown on his last run before Cheltenham, just his second run for Martin, but we made no mistake in that Cathcart Chase.

After Cheltenham, on his very next race he went to the Aintree Grand National meeting, for the John Hughes Chase, now the Topham Chase, over the big Grand National fences. Before I went out to ride him in that, Martin told me that my main job was to make sure that he didn't get brought down. He reckoned that, as long as I didn't manage to get him stuck in behind a faller, he would win doing handsprings.

As we were circling around just before the start of the race, I went around all the riders and told them not to get in my way. Timmy Murphy, Norman Williamson, Conor O'Dwyer, Lorcan Wyer, Mick Fitzgerald, Paul Carberry.

'I'm riding a certainty,' I told them. 'Just don't get in my way.'

Going down the side of the track, I was upsides Norman Williamson on Martell Boy and I was tanking. I couldn't believe how well Cyfor Malta was travelling.

I called over to Norman.

'Norman!'

'What?'

'How far is this going to win by?'

Norman didn't say 13 lengths, he came out with something a

little more forthright than that, but if he had said 13 lengths, he would have been right. Martin was right. Again. Cyfor Malta was only five, he was carrying 11 st 1 lb and racing against 21 others, experienced handicappers most of them, but he went around that track as if he was on springs. At no stage did he look like he would fall or get beaten. He was my first winner over the Grand National fences.

The following season, I won the Murphy's Gold Cup on him, the modern-day Paddy Power, the feature race of Cheltenham's November meeting, and we went on to win the Pillar Property Chase back at Cheltenham the following January. He would have been a real player in the Gold Cup that year, that's for sure. Go Ballistic finished second behind him in that Pillar Property Chase, See More Business finished third, and those two horses went on to finish first and second (in reverse order) in the Gold Cup, so you have to think that Cyfor Malta would have had a hell of a chance of winning it. Alas, he got injured after the Pillar Property and he was off the track for two years. A measure of his ability lay in the fact that he was able to go back to Cheltenham in November 2002, almost four years later, after all the problems that he had, and win the Murphy's Gold Cup again (the Thomas Pink as it was called that year) with 11 st 9 lb on his back.

Walking down the chute on Blowing Wind before the last race, the County Hurdle, with Martin walking beside us, around about the same point where he had told me exactly 48 hours earlier that Unsinkable Boxer was the biggest certainty who would ever walk out onto Cheltenham racecourse, Martin looked up at me and told me that Blowing Wind was the only horse that he really wanted to win at that Festival. Great. I'm after riding three winners for him and now he tells me that this is the only one he really wants to win.

Thankfully, Blowing Wind won. As I said, he didn't win the County Hurdle as easily as he had won the Imperial Cup at Sandown five days previously, but he had a 7 lb penalty to carry and the race was probably coming up for him quickly enough after his Sandown exertions.

Martin was delighted. He had landed the bonus as well for winning the Imperial Cup before winning at Cheltenham. I was delighted, this was my fifth Cheltenham Festival winner, I had equalled the previous record set by Jamie Osborne in 1992 (Barry Geraghty would ride five as well at the 2003 Festival before Ruby blew us all out of the water with seven in 2009). As well as that, I knew that lots of people had backed my last three rides in combination doubles and trebles, so it was great that I had won on the three of them, like I thought I might.

When I came back into the winner's enclosure on Blowing Wind, after winning the last race on the last day of the Festival, my fifth winner of the week, my third in a row, in the gathering gloom I decided that I would do a flying dismount. I had never done a flying dismount before and I haven't done one since, but it just felt like the thing to do at the time. It was a moderate flying dismount as flying dismounts go, it wasn't in the Angel Cordero or Frankie Dettori mode, but I didn't make an eejit of myself and I didn't injure myself, so that was the main thing.

I was leading jockey at the Aintree Grand National meeting that year, and at the Punchestown Festival, where I was particularly happy with the ride that I gave His Song in beating French Ballerina by a head in the Champion Novice Hurdle.

Fataliste won again at Aintree, Unsinkable Boxer won again, Cyfor Malta won the John Hughes, I won the three-mile novices' chase on Boss Doyle for Mouse Morris, and I won the Aintree Hurdle on Pridwell, beating Istabraq. I think the ride I gave Pridwell to beat Istabraq that day was probably the best ride I have ever given a horse in my career.

Pridwell was the type of horse who wouldn't do anything unless he wanted to. He could stop on you; he just wouldn't go forward if he didn't fancy it. He liked to be held up in his races, but the ground was very soft at Aintree on the day, Grand National day, the day that Earth Summit beat Suny Bay in a last-man-standing slog (Challenger Du Luc and I fell at the first, remember?), so I kept him fairly close to the pace, just kept nudging away at him, keeping him interested. There were certain stages of the race at which he tried to drop himself out, but I just kept at him, gently asking him to go forward, coaxing him into it, making him feel like he wanted to do it, that he was doing it because he wanted to do it, not because I wanted him to.

We were actually in front from a long way out, but I didn't really go for him until after we had jumped the second-last, when Istabraq and Charlie Swan moved up to join us. They took it up and went on over the final flight, looking all over the winner, but I managed to get Pridwell to dig deep, as deep as he had ever dug before, and we got back up and nutted Istabraq in a head-bob on the line.

That was a remarkable win. Istabraq hadn't been beaten in 10 runs since he had lost on his debut over hurdles a year and a half earlier. He had won a Sun Alliance Hurdle, a Champion Hurdle and four other Grade 1 hurdles. He was a remarkable horse. He won three Champion Hurdles, he probably would have won four had foot-and-mouth not caused the cancellation of the 2001 Cheltenham Festival, and he was only beaten three times in total in 26 completed races over hurdles, finishing second each time.

More than the horse that we beat, though, was the manner in which we did it. I do believe that I made Pridwell win that day. It might sound ridiculous, but I believe that I made him want to win. I coaxed and cajoled him, I think I got him in the right frame of mind during the race before I asked him to race from the second last. He got to a point where he was there at the second last without really knowing that he was in a race, and then he was thinking about not winning, about not wanting to be bothered putting in the effort. Fortunately, when I asked him to go on and get past Istabraq, he decided that he wanted to do it, so he did. I think that I won the mental battle with Pridwell that day. You know when you get Pridwell to win a race like that, you have done a lot of things right. The fact that we beat Istabraq made it all the sweeter.

I got a four-day suspension for excessive use of the whip. I wasn't happy about that. I didn't think that I was excessively forceful. I had a willing partner, he wanted to go forward and was responding to the whip. I would be the first person to castigate anyone if they misused the whip on a horse, and I'm sure I didn't abuse Pridwell. Even looking back on it now, I still don't think I was overly hard on him.

I argued my case to the stewards on the day, but they didn't see it my way and the four days stood. The rules weren't as clear then as they are now. Whip rules have come a long way. They need to be even better, but we're getting there. Back then, the guidelines were not clear, and the ban that I got took away from what I thought was my best-ever ride.

I appealed the decision. I took a day out, went down to London, me and Michael Caulfield, who was representing me, to the old Jockey Club headquarters in Portman Square, and we appealed. I stated my case, they listened, they nodded, and they said right, it's worse than we thought, have two more days. Six in total. That'll teach you to be wasting our time with an appeal. I was disgusted, and I wasn't finished brushing with the racing authorities there either. Actually, it was just the start of it.

Six days after Cheltenham, I went to Ludlow and won a juvenile hurdle on Petite Risk. It was my 222nd winner of the season, the winner that broke Peter Scudamore's record for the greatest number of winners in a season. Another milestone, another big deal. And it was a big deal for me. These milestones, these records, were the things that were driving me. Cheltenham Festival winners were brilliant, five winners at

Cheltenham was fantastic, but statistics and records are the things that set you apart.

I ended that season with 253 winners, beating Scu's record by 32, which was great, but it was immediately past tense. I had to focus on the next goal. I didn't tell anybody, but I began to think that Sir Gordon Richards's record of 269 winners in a season, for a flat or a jumps jockey, which he set in 1947, was within reach. Sixteen more winners than I had ridden that season would equal it, 17 more winners would beat it. Was it within the bounds of reasonable expectation, if everything went right and if I had normal luck and stayed relatively injury- and suspension-free, that I could ride 17 more winners in a season than I had ridden that season? Sure it was.

CHAPTER 18

Whip Rules

I never took a break. If there was racing, I was riding, it was as simple as that. I was only not riding if I was injured or suspended. I could never relax enough to allow myself to take a break. The day after Cheltenham, I was at Folkestone. The day after that, I was at Uttoxeter. The pursuit of winners was relentless.

At the start of the new season, the clock was reset. Everyone's tally was reset to zero, and off we went again. It didn't matter if you had ridden a thousand winners the previous year; once the first day of the season came around again, you started from scratch.

As a consequence, I find that the first few days, the first few weeks, the first few months of the season are always the worst, when you are looking at lads around you who have more winners than you or nearly as many winners as you or who have enough winners so that, if you were to get injured or suspended and miss a large chunk of the season, they could pass you and win the championship. And even later in the season, if you are lucky enough to ride so many winners that you have built up an unassailable lead in the championship, even if you allow yourself to think that there is no way that anybody can catch you, you are still racing against yourself, looking for the next winner, the next milestone, the next record.

I rode Merry Gale in the Marlborough Cup that May, in the summer of 1998. It was a mistake. The Marlborough Cup was a race over timber fences that was staged at Barbury Castle for a couple of years in the late 1990s. Timber racing – racing over fences that are made entirely of wood – is big in America, but it never really caught on in the UK and the race was discontinued in 2001 after about five years.

I had ridden Derrymoyle for Herb Stanley, Merry Gale's owner, to win the Champion Stayers' Hurdle at that year's Punchestown Festival, and he and trainer Jim Dreaper asked me to ride Merry Gale in the Marlborough Cup, so I figured why not.

I had never ridden Merry Gale before. Norman Williamson had, Conor O'Dwyer had, Barry Geraghty had, Richard Dunwoody had, Graham Bradley had, Paul Carberry had, Tommy Treacy had. I didn't stop for a second to think, well why isn't one of those boys riding him? I just said grand.

I don't remember much about the Marlborough Cup. I don't remember Merry Gale giving the fourth fence an almighty belt and giving the pair of us a mother and father of a fall. I do remember that they had just cut the grass though, that they had left the cut grass lying on top of the ground, and I remember lying on the ground trying to breathe, trying to get air into my lungs, gasping. With every breath that I tried to take, almost inhaling this loose grass, I wasn't able to move my head or hand to move the grass away.

I do remember being in hospital afterwards, semi-conscious, one of the vertebrae in my back fractured. That was my memory of the Marlborough Cup: grass in my face, concussion and a fractured vertebra.

I think that ended my interest in cross-country racing. I know the Marlborough Cup was a timber race, not a cross-country race, but it was in the same category for me, and I don't really ride in the cross-country races at Cheltenham or Punchestown now. It was later that year that Ruby Walsh got badly injured riding in the Czech Republic. He was due to ride Risk of Thunder in their big cross-country race, their Grand National, the Velka Pardubicka, but Ruby got injured riding in an earlier race when his leg got caught in a rail that had come loose. I figure now that there are enough risks in what we do every day without going looking for more doing something that you can really take or leave.

My boss now, JP McManus, obviously has lots of runners in the cross-country races, but Nina Carberry and JT McNamara are fantastic cross-country riders; they ride JP's top cross-country horses for trainer Enda Bolger, and I wouldn't want to make a fool of myself anyway. I just thought after the Marlborough Cup that I wasn't going to get badly injured again in a cross-country race. If I get injured in a novice chase, so be it, that's part of my job, but I'm happy to leave the cross-country races to the experts.

I started to draw the stewards' attention with monotonous regularity that summer. I had served my six-day ban for Pridwell, four for the ride and two for the nerve to appeal, and I got another three days for misuse of the whip when I won on Amlah at Stratford in early May. Then, after I returned from my Marlborough Cup injury, on 15th August I got two days for being too liberal with the whip when I got beaten a neck in a three-mile chase back at Stratford on Ozzie Jones, and the following day I got four more days for using the whip with unreasonable force on Coy Debutante in a bumper at Newton Abbot.

It was getting ridiculous. I didn't know what was going on. I hadn't changed my riding style, I hadn't suddenly started being harder on horses, I wasn't suddenly keener to win races than I had been (I couldn't possibly have been any keener), yet here I was, getting days for giving horses rides that I considered to be normal, Coy Debutante in particular – I didn't think I was hard on her at all.

To this day, some people think I'm too severe on horses. I've never thought that I was too hard on them, despite popular perception. Some people have said to Dave Roberts, ah no I don't want McCoy, he'd be too hard on my horse. They don't stop to think, even if they are concerned about me being hard on a horse, that I will ride their horse whatever way they want me to ride their horse.

JP McManus and Jonjo O'Neill often don't want their horses having hard races. JP is as patient an owner as you will ever come across, he doesn't mind how long a horse takes to come to himself, and he certainly doesn't want a young horse having a hard race when he is just starting off. He wants them to have a good experience and the right attitude; he wants them to enjoy it so that they will continue to want to race. He wants them to be looked after, and that's my job. Back then, I was riding for people who wanted to have winners, I was riding horses who were as fit as fleas, it was all about winning, and I was riding more winners than anyone else.

Maybe the stewards figured that they would concentrate on me, make an example of me, demonstrate the implementation of the whip guidelines on me rather than on someone else or on everyone else. If they had been hard on everyone, there might not have been any jockeys left in the weigh room.

Nobody likes to see horses being flailed. Something that lots of people fail to realise is that people within racing don't like to see it either. Most jockeys have grown up with horses, they have grown up with ponies, grooming them, taking care of them. The vast majority of people who work in the industry love horses. The last thing they want is to see them abused.

The whip debate was re-energised again after the 2011 Grand National, when two horses were killed and when a number of horses looked to be distressed after crossing the winning line. Racing is trying to get the whip rules right, which is the right way to go I think.

We have come a long way in the last few years. The whips are a lot softer than they used to be and the guidelines are a lot tighter. But it is important for the perception of the sport that horses are not seen to be abused. It's all about aesthetics, it's all about perception. There will always be people who will look at a driving finish, at jockeys encouraging willing horses and using their whips, and say that it's not right. For that reason, it is important that racing gets its house in order so that the number of people who think this will be minimised.

You will never appease everybody. There are people who say that rugby has gone too rough, that players are too heavy and too fit and hit each other too hard. Or that racing cars have got too fast. There will always be people who will say that a sport is too dangerous.

The bottom line is that racehorses are not abused – quite the opposite actually. At home, they are treated like athletes, given five-star treatment by their trainers and cared for like children by their lads or lasses. However, as I say, it is important that they are not seen to be maltreated by jockeys in public, on the racecourse.

There have been calls for a total whip ban. I don't agree with this. A jockey needs a whip for safety's sake, in case a horse jinks or veers; a whip is a huge aid in straightening him up. At the same time, the whip rules need to be strict. I have recently suggested that maybe the rule in National Hunt racing should be that you can't use your whip after the last fence or the last flight of hurdles. It's black and white; you can easily see whether a jockey is using his whip after the last fence, unlike some of the guidelines that are in place. Also, it would mean that you wouldn't have this whip-flailing finish that is unpalatable to many. I think it might be worth trying.

However, the guidelines are a lot clearer now than they were in 1998. I was getting frustrated with the whole thing. I was getting banned and I wasn't sure what I was doing wrong. I was certain that I wasn't riding any differently to how I had ridden before, when I wasn't getting banned.

I went back to the racing school in Newmarket to try to figure it out. There was this fellow there, Robert Sidebottom, a nice guy, and no disrespect to him, but he was trying to teach me how to ride. Bizarre. I was champion jockey and here was somebody trying to teach me how to ride. I couldn't get my head around it at all.

There were two senior stewards there as well watching proceedings, Malcolm Wallace and Christopher Hall. Of course they were right to be there, they were doing their job, but I remember thinking, what are you all doing here? There were television cameras there as well. It was all being filmed for one of the racing channels and for Channel 4: McCoy goes back to school to learn how to ride. It was all a bit of a circus really.

I can look back on it now and laugh, but I hated it at the time. I was 24 years old and knew it all. I was riding more winners than anyone else, so how could I have been doing anything wrong? If you had asked me then what I thought of the senior stewards Christopher Hall and Malcolm Wallace, I would have said, wankers. I saw it as a witch hunt, everybody out to get me. It seemed like I was the only one getting banned.

It is funny looking back on it because I get on really well with Christopher and Malcolm now. I actually see them both at the Horse of the Year Show every Christmas, and we meet up for dinner every year and we laugh about those days. I can see now that they had a job to do, and they were actually doing it quite well. Back then, however, different story, different attitude, different me.

I had accumulated 15 days in suspensions before I went out to ride Bamapour in a claiming hurdle at Fontwell on 9th November. Under the new totting-up procedure, if you accumulated more than 15 days in suspensions you were referred to Jockey Club headquarters at Portman Square, where you would be hit with another significant suspension. It was like being punished for the same offence twice.

Bamapour was actually Chanelle's dad's horse, the horse that Chanelle had ridden to win those two bumpers at Galway and at Gowran Park in August 1995. He wasn't much good, but I had won on him five times after he had joined Martin. I made it six at Fontwell that day, but we were all out to hold on by three parts of a length. I got a two-day suspension. It pushed me over the 15-day limit, so I was referred to Portman Square. I knew I was in for a lengthy ban, probably no less than 14 days, but possibly as many as 28.

I was in desperate humour going into the Murphy's meeting at Cheltenham. I thought the whole world was against me. I was riding Cyfor Malta in the Murphy's Gold Cup itself, which was the only ray of light in the cloud that I was under. I loved Cyfor Malta. I won on him too.

During the race, all I was thinking of was the race, the next fence, the next turn, allowing Cyfor Malta to find his rhythm, kicking for home and driving up the hill to the line. As we pulled up after winning the race though, and began to make our way back to the winner's enclosure, I started to remember everything else that was going on, the whip bans and the fact that the whole world was against me. I started to get angrier and angrier. I've just won the Murphy's on one of the most exciting young horses in training, and all I can think about is whip bans.

I threw my whip into the crowd. It wasn't a very clever thing to do, it was impetuous, and I'm sure there is some rule under which I could have been fined or banned further, but it felt like the right thing to do at the time: you won't let me use it, so I may as well throw it away. A racegoer gave it to the Channel 4 Racing presenter Derek Thompson and he gave it back to me as he interviewed me live on Channel 4 after the race. Ah thanks Tommo, I must have dropped it on the way in.

I got 14 days under the totting-up procedure. It wasn't so bad, but it was still a lengthy ban, and the fact that I was expecting it didn't make it any easier. Plus there were four more days, suspended, which would be triggered if I received another ban within six months.

I didn't need six months. I was done again for my ride on Eudipe to win the Anthony Mildmay Peter Cazalet Chase at Sandown that January. I got two days for hitting the horse in the wrong place. Again, we wouldn't have won if I hadn't been strong on him. We were under pressure from a long way out, whereas Philip Hide had been motionless on Glitter Isle until the run to the last.

It didn't matter. Just because I won, it didn't mean that I had given it the right ride. It reminded me of Jim Bolger: just because you have been champion jockey, it doesn't mean that you made the right decision in leaving me. Two more days for that ride, and that triggered the four days that had been suspended for going over the 15 days. So that was six more on top of the 29 that I had accumulated beforehand.

There were more bans. I got two days for getting beaten on Northern Drums at Taunton on 15th March, the day before the Cheltenham Festival started, I got four days for winning the Mildmay of Flete at the Festival on Majadou, but I was getting better, I thought. I wanted to get it right, not necessarily to appease the stewards, but because I was sick of getting banned.

I felt I was making progress until I got four days for excessive force on Picasso's Heritage at Bangor on 30th July. I didn't think I had been hard on her. I asked why I had been punished and I was told it was because she had been marked. I knew she hadn't been marked and the vet confirmed this, so I went back to the stewards' secretary and said that the vet had said that there weren't any marks.

'It doesn't matter if there are marks or not,' was the response. 'You hit her too hard.'

The following day at Worcester, I got three days for being too easy on Galix. I eased her before the last as she had no chance of winning. She was out on her feet and I didn't want to subject her to a hard race, but two horses passed me on the run-in, so instead of finishing fourth we finished sixth. Even if I had driven her as hard as I could, I'm not certain that we wouldn't have finished sixth anyway. It was ridiculous. The fourth horse finished over 20 lengths in front of me.

I wasn't in a great place mentally. The bans were affecting me – all I wanted to do was ride horses and win, and you can't do this if you are banned from riding. Things got worse when I rode poor Eudipe in the Grand National that year. He was well fancied, I thought he had a chance, but he fell at Becher's Brook second time around and was killed.

I only rode 186 winners that season. It was a fair climb down from 253 the previous year, but I suppose if you are going to have the stewards on your tail dishing out suspensions if you scratch a horse behind his ear, if you are going to spend the length of two or three annual holidays on the sidelines, then you are not going to ride as many winners as you expect. I did win the championship though. I finished 53 clear of Richard Johnson.

The trainers' championship was a close one though. While the jockeys' championship is decided on the number of winners you ride, the trainers' championship is decided on the amount of prize money you win. Paul Nicholls was coming of age. He won the Gold Cup that year with See More Business and he won the Champion Chase with Call Equiname. But Martin had the strength in depth, and we had also won big pots like the Murphy's Gold Cup and the Mildmay of Flete and the Supreme Novices' Hurdle with the four-year-old Hors La Loi.

Martin loved Hors La Loi, a horse that he had got from the French trainer François Doumen after he had won the Finesse Hurdle at Cheltenham's January meeting with him. I remember telling Martin that the word from Ireland before Cheltenham was that the two JP McManus-owned novice hurdlers, Joe Mac and Cardinal Hill, were catching pigeons at home, and him telling me that they wouldn't see which way Hors La Loi went. He was right. It was a fair performance for a juvenile to beat older novices, even in receipt of the 8 lb four-year-old allowance.

Hors La Loi won £46,000 for winning the Supreme Novices' Hurdle and he won almost £24,000 for winning the Glen Livet Hurdle at

Aintree three weeks later. Martin finished less than £52,000 in front of Paul Nicholls in the trainers' championship. Martin might have found another way – he often did – but it is possible that, without Hors La Loi, he would not have been champion trainer that year.

CHAPTER 19

Too Tough To Cry

I rode my 999th winner on Hero's Fatal in an intermediate hurdle at Cheltenham on 11th December 1999, and I went out half an hour later and rode my 1,000th winner on Majadou in the two-mile handicap chase.

I was delighted to ride 1,000 winners. I really was. I appreciated the enormity of it. Only four jumps jockeys before me had ridden 1,000 winners: Stan Mellor, John Francome, Peter Scudamore and Richard Dunwoody. I was the fifth. And to be in such exalted company was a big deal for me.

I didn't celebrate it though. I don't really celebrate the milestones much. It's ironic because I always regarded the milestones, the numbers of winners, as more important than the individual wins in the big races, but I generally don't really celebrate the milestones, whereas I often do celebrate the big wins. Cheltenham racecourse presented me with a bottle of champagne for riding my 1,000th winner, then 35 minutes later I went out in the next race in the novices' chase on Lady Cricket, and made it 1,001.

I rode Gloria Victis – another one of Martin's promising French imports – for the first time in a novices' chase at Newbury's Hennessy meeting later that month, and I liked him. Then I rode him in the Feltham Chase, the Grade 1 three-mile chase for novices, at Kempton's King George meeting, and I loved him. In the interim, we had been beaten by Decoupage in the Henry VIII Chase at Sandown, but that was over two miles, which was much too short a trip for Gloria Victis. Back over three miles at Kempton, he was different gravy.

We took it up at the fifth-last in the Feltham, and we just went further and further clear, winning by 18 lengths in the end and clocking a time that was almost identical to the time that See More Business clocked in winning the King George over the same course and distance later on the day.

I got off Gloria Victis and told Martin that he was a machine. I had never before ridden a horse that gave me the feel that he gave me, and I have never ridden one since. He just oozed class. He had the lot. He jumped, he galloped, he stayed, he had pace and he had a brilliant attitude. He was only five, he was destined for the top, and he was destined to stay there for a long time.

Gloria Victis's next target was the Racing Post Chase, back over the Feltham course and distance in February, which was an ambitious target for a novice, a just-turned-six-year-old novice who was rated 151 and who would therefore probably have to give weight away to some much more experienced and more proven horses. Neither Martin nor I thought that it would be too much of a problem for him.

Then I went and got myself banned again. I rode a horse of Jonjo O'Neill's, Ciara's Prince, to win at Leicester in mid-February. We led the whole way, he needed plenty of cajoling, but he stayed on well and won by 11 lengths. The stewards thought that I had used my whip with excessive frequency and banned me. They only banned me for two days, but the timing of it coincided with the Racing Post Chase. I couldn't believe it. I couldn't believe that I wasn't going to get to ride Gloria Victis in the Racing Post Chase. I went home that night and cried like a baby.

I didn't stick around to watch the Racing Post Chase. I had got to know the former Liverpool footballer Steve McManaman well through a very good friend of mine, David Manasseh, a football agent who currently acts for Ashley Cole, Peter Crouch and a whole host of others. Steve had moved to Real Madrid from Liverpool at the start of that season, and it just happened that that weekend, Racing Post Chase weekend, the weekend that I was banned, was the weekend that Real Madrid were playing Barcelona at the Bernabeu. Steve said why don't you come over to the match, it might cheer you up a bit. Nothing could compensate for missing Gloria Victis, but as consolation prizes go, they don't get much better than premier tickets for Real Madrid v Barcelona at the Bernabeu.

In some ways I didn't want Gloria Victis to win. It's human nature; if you are not riding a horse that you should be in a big race, of course there will be a part of you that hopes it doesn't win. Deep down, though, I did want him to win. I wanted him to win for Martin and for his owner Terry Neill, but more than that, I wanted him to win for Anthony McCoy. I thought that he was a top-class horse, and you want to see the horses that you think are top class progressing as top-class horses should progress, winning races, then winning top-class races. Also, I knew that I would be on him the next time he ran, so I wanted him to continue his progression.

He did win. That's another one that Richard Johnson owes me.

The dilemma then was whether to run him in the Sun Alliance Chase or the Gold Cup at Cheltenham. He was a novice, so he was eligible for the Sun Alliance, and there is a school of thought that says that you should keep novices to novice races. They are only novices for one season, so it makes sense to exploit that season fully, to race against fellow novices. You can step up in grade and take on the more experienced horses the following season when you are not a novice any more.

That said, Gloria Victis was shaping like a Gold Cup horse. He had clocked as fast a time as the King George winner when he won the Feltham, and now he had won the Racing Post Chase under top weight of 11 st 10 lb. That was Gold Cup stuff. Plus he had only just turned six and was probably still progressing.

I thought it didn't matter what race he ran in. I thought he would win the Sun Alliance, and I thought he would win the Gold Cup. Therefore, given that I had a horse who I thought would win a Sun Alliance Chase or a Gold Cup, the only question was, which race would I prefer to win? I didn't try to influence Martin's or Terry Neill's decision, I deliberately didn't want to, but I was thinking Gold Cup.

We had Lady Cricket for the Sun Alliance Chase, but I also had Looks Like Trouble for the Gold Cup. Norman Williamson was Looks Like Trouble's regular rider, but he had had a falling-out with the horse's owner Tim Collins, so the ride was up for grabs. It was a good Gold Cup ride too. I was asked by his trainer Noel Chance to ride him at Newbury on the Sunday, nine days before the Festival started, and he went well for me. I liked him, but I loved Gloria Victis.

Martin kept asking me what I thought, in which race should Gloria Victis run, but I kept kicking for touch. I knew I could ride Looks Like Trouble in the Gold Cup, but I didn't want that to be an influencing factor, I didn't want Martin to think that I was favouring Looks Like Trouble over Gloria Victis. A couple of days before the Festival started, Martin phoned me – Gold Cup.

Gloria Victis is the best novice chaser I've ever ridden. No other novice chaser has ever given me the feel that he gave me in the Feltham Chase. The pace he was able to sustain, the accuracy with which he was able to jump, the willingness with which he galloped. I was dying to ride him in the Gold Cup.

I went out for dinner with Norman Williamson after the first day of that Festival, on the Tuesday evening – neither of us had ridden a winner. It could only get better for both of us.

It did. Norman won the first race on the second day, the Sun Alliance Hurdle, on Monsignor, the horse that had got up to do me and Golden Alpha in the Champion Bumper the previous year, him and Brendan Powell, at 50/1.

The second race on the second day was the Queen Mother Champion Chase. I was riding Edredon Bleu for Henrietta Knight, Norman was riding Direct Route for Howard Johnson. Edredon Bleu and I had been beaten in the previous year's Champion Chase by Call Equiname, and I had ridden him just twice in the interim, both times at Sandown, both times finishing third.

I don't think Henrietta was too happy with the ride that I gave him on the latter occasion, when we finished third behind Rockforce, giving him two stone. As I dismounted in the winner's enclosure, she spoke before I had a chance to tell her about how I thought the race went.

'Well, that was a bit disappointing,' she said.

She might not have been referring to the ride that I gave the horse, but I immediately concluded that she was. Without taking any time to think (I was a bit chippy like that) I immediately retorted.

'Well, what do you expect when the horse is only half fit.'

Of course, the Elmbridge Handicap Chase at Sandown six weeks before Cheltenham was not Edredon Bleu's day. Champion Chase day was Edredon Bleu's day, and Henrietta was obviously preparing him for that, so he would be at peak fitness on that day.

I didn't speak to Henrietta much between then and Cheltenham, and I could have lost the ride on Edredon Bleu for that comment, I'm sure. Jim Culloty had ridden him in the Haldon Gold Cup and the Peterborough Chase, and they could easily have left Jim on him at Cheltenham, but I think that the owner Jim Lewis, who also owned Best Mate (who finished second behind Sausalito Bay in the Supreme Novices' Hurdle that year, incidentally), liked me riding Edredon Bleu, so thankfully I kept the ride.

Henrietta didn't say much to me as we stood in the parade ring before the race. Then the bell went, the signal for jockeys to mount. We walked over to Edredon Blue and she legged me up.

'Well, he's as fit as I can get him now.'

It was just as well that he was because he needed every ounce of energy that he could muster. Edredon Bleu was unusual in that he jumped a little to his right, he was always angling to go to his right, but he loved Cheltenham, which shouldn't have played to his strengths as a left-handed track. I think it was the set-up of the track that suited him, the undulations, the up and down hills, jump, turn to your left, jump, up a hill, jump, down a hill, jump, jump. Strange thing to say about a Champion Chase winner and a King George winner, but he actually wasn't that classy a horse. But he was hard, he was a fast, low jumper, and what he lacked in class he made up for in terrier-like guts.

I love the Champion Chase. It's run over two miles, the minimum National Hunt distance. You need speed to win it and you need to jump fast. It's the 100-metre Olympic Final of National Hunt racing. I love riding in it; I love the thrill of going as fast as you can over fences. Maybe I'm better when I don't have too much time to think about jumping the fence, when it just happens upon you at sprinting speed and you fire your horse at it and land running, then move on to the next fence.

I always thought that the Champion Chase was just a sprint over fences, where you go as fast as you can, run as fast as you can, jump as fast as you can, flat out for the whole race, the best jumpers, the fastest horses. Before they took away the second-last fence on the Old Course at Cheltenham, I used to tell people who were interested that, if they wanted to see what jump racing was all about, to go down to the second-last fence before the Champion Chase and watch it being jumped.

It is a pity in lots of ways that they moved the fence around the corner into the home straight. A lot of these things are done in the interests of safety and welfare, and if it's safer for the horses and safer for the jockeys, then I suppose I should be saying that I'm in favour of it. But I'm not sure it was a good thing to take that fence away. The same fence caught Don't Push It out at the 2007 Festival, and it may have cost me an Arkle win, but I still wasn't in favour of moving it.

You had to ride Edredon Bleu just on the right side of his comfort zone. You couldn't push him into going too fast early on, but at the same time you had to keep at him a little, just keep him on the right side of the red zone, because he really had to have all or most of his rivals burned off before the home turn. He had had everything off the bridle except Call Equiname in the 1999 Champion Chase, and he beat us for a turn of foot on the run-in. It was a similar story in 2000; we had everything except Norman and Direct Route off the bridle turning for home.

Direct Route jumped the last level with us and Norman went for home. He must have gone a neck up on us, but I knew that Direct Route didn't like to be in front for too long, and I knew that my fellow

Jim Bolger (Patrick McCann)

'TJ' Comerford, friend from years back

With the Macca and Growler partnership, Robbie Fowler and Steve McManaman

Best bosses, JP and Noreen McManus

AP and the Doc

Happy ever after

With the Burke inlaws: Michael, Kelley, Hilary, Michael, Mary, Ulick. My parents-in-law are on Chanelle's left.

Honeymooners

Eveilicious!

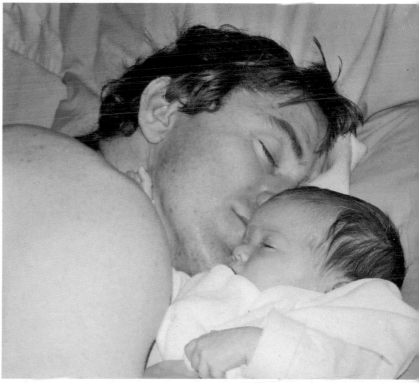

Me and Black Jack Ketchum jumping the final flight on the way to winning the 2006 Brit Insurance Hurdle at Cheltenham (Getty)

Exotic Dancer, super jumper

Albertas Run in full flight – we won the Dalepak Beginners' Chase at Towcester, 2007 (*Racing Post*)

Frankie Dettori presenting me with my Champion Jockey trophy at Sandown on the last day of the 2006/07 season (Ed Whitaker)

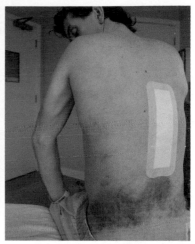

Not a pretty sight (*Racing Post*/Ed Whitaker)

Bow Strada fires me into the ground at Newbury (Getty)

Feeling the effects...
(Ed Whitaker)

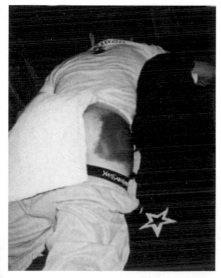

Massive haematoma which resulted from a real kicking at the feet of Image De Marque II at Kempton Park

Master Minded was flawless in the 2008 Tingle Creek Chase

Butler's Cabin crumples at Becher's Brook second time round in the 2008 Grand National (Getty/*Racing Post*)

Rat Pack: (from l to r)
Ruby Walsh, me, James
Nash, Killian McCarthy
and Willie Supple

The Godfather: Carl and me
after Hennessy had won the
2009 Bet365 Gold Cup

Get Mc Out Of Here showed huge
courage to come back from this
mistake at the final flight to get up
and win the Totesport Trophy.

At last, 3000 up as Restless D'Artaix wins the Beginners' Chase at Plumpton on 9 February 2009 (Getty/*Racing Post*)

Lester Piggott presenting me with the trophy to mark my 3000th winner (Matthew Webb)

loved a battle, that he would keep running all the way to the line. So I put my head down and asked him for everything. Direct Route wasn't going any further away from us and, slowly but very definitely, we were getting back on him, inching back the deficit.

Suddenly we were past the line. I had no idea at what point we had hit it, I had just had my head down. I'm sure I rode him until we were well past the line, but that didn't matter, as long as I eked out every last inch of him until we got to the line. I had no idea if we had won or not, Norman had no idea if he had won or not, it was just on the nod. I looked up at the big screen. It appeared as if Edredon Bleu's nose was down on the line, but even on the big screen, even with the freeze-frame and the line drawn in to help you, you still couldn't tell who had won, it was that close.

We did win. Edredon Bleu won. It was a hell of a race in which to be involved; it was one of those signature Cheltenham Festival races that people remember, and it was even better to win it. It was my first Champion Chase and it completed the set, the three big races at Cheltenham: Gold Cup, Champion Hurdle, and now Champion Chase.

The rest of the day wasn't any good though. Lady Cricket ran no kind of race in the Sun Alliance Chase, and one of Martin's horses, Dark Stranger, sporting his first-time blinkers, as I had suggested, won the Mildmay of Flete but with me on Upgrade. That's another one that Dickie Johnson owes me.

The following day was much worse though. Rock bottom. Gold Cup day 2000 was one of the low points of my entire career to date. Gloria Victis travelled well with me through the early part of the Gold Cup, and I allowed him to stride on down the back straight. He was jumping to his right, but we knew that he did that, and he wasn't giving away that much ground. However, after we had jumped the third last, I could feel him coming back under me.

He couldn't have been running out of petrol. He didn't do that. He was such a good traveller and such a good stayer that I knew that he couldn't have been running out of gas. To this day, I think that he had gone wrong before he took off at the second-last fence. He hadn't lost his action or anything, I didn't feel him go wrong underneath like, say, I had felt Cyborgo go wrong underneath me when I pulled him up in the 1999 Gold Cup, but he just wasn't giving me the feel that I knew he was capable of after we had jumped the third-last fence.

It wasn't like him to fall like he did, he was such a good jumper, and he was such an intelligent horse; something had to have been ailing him before he even took off at the fence. Also, he didn't have a hard fall. You never know with these things, the most innocuous-looking falls can have devastating consequences, but this fall was quite soft. The probability is that it wasn't the fall that injured him, that he was gone before he ever took off at the fence. That the leg fracture was on its way, that he had all but fractured it before he took off at the fence, and the impact of landing on the far side of it finished it off.

One of Gloria Victis's characteristics was that he jumped to his right, which is why he was so good at Kempton, a right-handed track, and why left-handed Cheltenham didn't play to his strengths. But often when a horse jumps to his right or left, he does so for a reason, often because something is niggling at him, or because he is protecting himself in some way. Maybe there had been something niggling at Gloria Victis, maybe there was a weakness in his leg that we just never knew about.

I rolled over and looked over at the horse. I don't even know if I was sore from the fall or not, I don't think I was, but my only concern was for Gloria Victis. He lay there on the ground, he didn't even try to get up. It didn't look good. When a horse doesn't move, you fear the worst, but you hope against all hope that he is just winded, that he will spring to his feet in a few seconds. I willed Gloria Victis to his feet, but he wasn't even making an effort.

An ambulance came along and I got into it. I just walked away. That's my way of dealing with these things. I hate looking at a horse being destroyed, any horse. It doesn't matter how good or how bad a racehorse it is, I hate looking at it. So I got into the ambulance, feeling as low as you can feel. I was back in the weigh room when David Pipe came in, tears in his eyes.

'He's gone,' he said. 'They had to put him down.'

The only thing I remember after that is crying all night, crying myself to sleep. You're not so hard that these things don't get to you. You're not too tough to cry.

I have asked myself since: what was I crying about? Why was I really crying? If it had been a selling hurdler that had had to be put down, would I have been as upset as I was? No way. I would have been sad, but I wouldn't have cried all night, that's for sure. So why did I cry myself to sleep? Was I crying for me or for Gloria Victis?

I was gutted at having been beaten in a Gold Cup, especially when I knew I was riding a horse who could have won. But I was more upset for the horse, not only because a beautiful animal had had to be destroyed, but because he was such a good horse. It is always upsetting when you see potential unfulfilled, when a young life is ended before it has been given a chance to reach its true potential.

Gloria Victis could have won as many King Georges as they could have run. He was ideally suited to Kempton, and he was only five when he won the Feltham. He could have won three, four or five King Georges, and he could have won a Gold Cup or two as well. I'm sure that he would have won at least one. Desert Orchid was a Kempton horse as well, and he managed to win a Gold Cup. Kauto Star was at his best at Kempton, and he won two Gold Cups. Gloria Victis could have been a superstar.

I watched the video over and over again. What could I have done? I tortured myself, watched the whole race to the second-last fence, rewound, watched it from the fourth-last, rewound, from the third-last, rewound, from six strides before the second-last. What should I have done differently? I couldn't watch the horse being put down, I had to get away from that place, yet I was happy to torture myself by watching the race over and over again.

I wouldn't do that now. It's strange how your mindset changes. Back then, all I wanted to do was watch the losers, watch the rides that had gone wrong. I convinced myself that I had to do that, that I had to see what I could learn from it. If I had got beaten, I had obviously made a mistake, so I had to go back and figure out what that mistake was so that I wouldn't make it the next time.

I did learn from watching the videos; I did decide that I would ride particular horses a little differently, but I think I was punishing myself by watching the tapes as much as I was. I think I felt that if I watched the race again and again, I would have served the appropriate penance for getting beaten, and then I could move on. Of course, despite my mindset at the time, not every loser was my fault. Sometimes the horse just wasn't good enough.

I remember when I rode Albertas Run against Master Minded in the Amlin 1965 Chase at Ascot in November 2010. Master Minded was obviously going better than us going to the third last, but I knew my horse would keep finding, and I still thought we had a chance. We were meeting the third-last on a very long stride; I thought my only chance of keeping tabs on Master Minded was to ask him to make it, so I did, and he tried, but he just couldn't. He clouted the middle of the fence and turned a somersault. I could have killed the pair of us, and it took us both a while to get over it.

I came in afterwards and met Jonjo. Jonjo looked me straight in the eye.

'You know AP, sometimes you just have to finish second,' he said.

I shook my head. I wasn't convinced.

'We still had a chance.'

These days, I only watch the winners. I have gone full circle. I don't watch the losers. Not that I think I don't have anything left to learn, you are always learning in this game. But now when I get beaten, I know without watching the video if I have done something wrong. I would prefer to watch the winners and gain the confidence that that gives you. Watch what you have done right and know that you can go out next time and do it again. I think watching the winners is much better for me psychologically.

Martin got a lot of stick afterwards for running Gloria Victis in the Gold Cup instead of in the novices' race. All the know-alls were on – he shouldn't have run him in the Gold Cup, what else did he expect? The horse didn't have the experience to run in the Gold Cup.

Firstly, nobody was more upset about Gloria Victis's death than Martin. Secondly, I am sure that, lamentably, the end result would have been the same, regardless of which race he contested. These things happen for a reason. There was this horse that Jonjo and JP got from France in 2010, Rock Noir, a really nice horse who looked like he could be very good. I thought he was going to be a brilliant jumper, but he got worse and worse instead of getting better. He was horrific at Huntingdon, he was horrific in the Arkle.

They let him out into a paddock at Jackdaw's Castle the day after the Arkle, and he got out of the paddock, jumped over the fence, went missing. They found him upside down in a ditch with a broken neck, dead. Nobody could understand it; nothing had happened in the paddock, the other horse that was in the paddock with him was fine. It wasn't until they opened him up to do the autopsy that they discovered he was riddled with cancer. He had a growth the size of a cabbage in his neck, poor fellow.

I am convinced that Gloria Victis had a weakness, that it was only a matter of time before the weakness led to a fracture. It was desperate that it happened in the Gold Cup, but it would have been desperate wherever it had happened, even if it had happened at home on the gallops, and I'm certain that, if he had run in the Sun Alliance Chase instead of in the Gold Cup that year, he still would have met the same end.

Martin Pipe wasn't a conventional horse trainer. That's why he was Martin Pipe, 15 times champion trainer, and not a nonentity. He did things that other people didn't dare do, he did things that other trainers didn't even consider doing. He went against the grain. That's what geniuses do. You don't get to be the best at what you do without pushing at the boundaries of convention.

Martin had run Cyborgo in the Gold Cup as a novice, and nothing was said. He had run Hors La Loi in the Supreme Novices' Hurdle instead of in the Triumph Hurdle, getting the 8 lb four-year-olds' allowance, and people had said, why didn't I think of that? He had run Make A Stand in the Tote Gold Trophy and in the Champion Hurdle as a novice, the horse won both of them and Martin was acclaimed as a hero, a genius. It's a fickle world.

Martin decided that it would be a good idea to run Northern Starlight in the John Hughes Chase over the big Grand National fences at Aintree the following month. I thought that Martin had finally lost the plot. Kids had ponies at home that were bigger than Northern Starlight, so to run him over the biggest fences that you could find in the country was insane. You run small horses at small tracks with small fences, not over the Grand National track.

I remember when I saw Northern Starlight for the first time. I was down at Martin's place at Nicholashayne one morning, schooling a couple of horses for him. I schooled about 15, all fine, I thought that was it, but he called me over and told me that he had one more horse for me to school. He pointed at Northern Starlight. I thought he was joking. I didn't see how he was going to make a steeplechaser out of a kid's pony.

Actually, he had left Northern Starlight until last because he was afraid that, if I schooled him early on, I might get a fall off him and I might not be able to school the rest of them. Anyway, there was no need to worry, he was electric over the schooling fences, he was a super little jumper.

Jumping schooling fences and jumping Grand National fences are two totally different matters, mind you, and I have to say, I wasn't feeling overly confident going out for the John Hughes Chase on this little scut of a thing. He couldn't even see over the fences. There was a picture of us in *Horse and Hound* the following week, taken from behind the first fence. You can see the fence and you can see me, and you can see the two horses and riders on either side of us, but you can't see Northern Starlight. However, as I have said many times, if Martin Pipe thought it was a good idea, then it was a good idea in my book.

Surprise surprise, it wasn't a good idea – it was a great idea. The little horse bunny-hopped over those big fences as if he was on springs, and stayed on resolutely to get the better of Timmy Murphy on Kings Cherry and record a remarkable win.

I ended the season with 245 winners, my second-highest total and over 100 winners clear of Richard Johnson, who was second again for the third year running. Even so, I didn't think that it had been a great year. I had this fixation on Sir Gordon Richards's record of 269 winners in a season. I had had a good year by any standards, but the fact that it was only my second-highest total made me think that I was getting worse. I should have been getting better, my totals should have been going up all the time. Maybe I was never going to beat Sir Gordon's record.

CHAPTER 20

Blowing Out

The weigh room was changing. Richard Dunwoody and Graham Bradley had both retired. Dunwoody had eventually succumbed to medical advice and announced his retirement in December 1999 after spending months seeing specialists, trying to get someone to tell him that it was okay for him to ride again, that if he did he wouldn't run the risk of losing the use of his right arm.

It was a sad day when Dunwoody retired. He had been my idol and my benchmark; when I started riding he was the person I wanted to be, and when I was established, he was the person I wanted to beat. I felt sorry for him when he did end as he didn't want to leave. People said that he walked away from racing, but it would have killed him to have to go racing without being able to ride. Better to not be there, better to be off conquering the South Pole or something.

It was also a sad day when Brad retired, but it was different. His career had been on a downward spiral since he was initially charged in the race-fixing probe in 1998. Those charges were later dropped, but his reputation had been tarnished. He was too good a jockey to be carrying on just scraping for rides. Brad was a brilliant rider and he was great fun, everyone in the weigh room loved him. He was always a person who looked on the brighter side of life.

Other stalwarts of the weigh room had retired or weren't far off retiring: Brendan Powell, Luke Harvey, Simon McNeill, Peter Niven, and there was a new generation emerging, riders like Choc Thornton, Graham Lee, Noel Fehily, Tom Scudamore. These days, I am one of the elders of the weigh room. Actually, I don't even know some of the younger lads these days, which is a bit of a strange situation for me.

I remember when I first arrived into the weigh room, looking at these guys, Dunwoody, Norman, Adrian and Jamie Osborne, lads whose names I used to see in the newspaper, and being a little blown away by the fact that I was sharing a changing room with them. It can be a daunting place. I know what it's like, so I always make a point of saying hello to any new young lad.

Most of the young lads are polite, most of them say hello back and seem to appreciate that I have taken the time to try to put them at ease. Some aren't though. Like Jack Doyle. I didn't notice it at first, I'd just say hello and that would be grand. He wouldn't say much, I thought he was just shy. Then I thought that he was being a bit off with me, but I didn't take much notice until Richard Johnson said to me one day, what's with your man Jack Doyle? Nobody doesn't like Dickie Johnson and Dickie Johnson doesn't dislike anybody, so it was serious when he was saying to me, what's with your man? I don't really bother with Jack Doyle any more. He's probably the only lad in the weigh room that I wouldn't speak to. I just wouldn't waste my breath.

It wasn't just jockeys that I fell out with though.

I rode a horse called Bolton Forest for Charlie Mann in a novices' chase at Stratford on 16th July 2000. I thought I gave it a good enough ride, we took it up at the sixth-last and went clear, but inside the final 200 yards we were just caught by a 20/1 shot called Yer 'Umble ridden by David Dennis. Nobody likes to get beaten, but everyone seemed happy enough with the ride afterwards. Charlie was, and the owners Trevor Phillips and Peter Simpson seemed to be too. We finished second, bad luck to be beaten by a 20/1 shot, but that's racing. I thought no more of it.

I was due to ride another horse for Charlie three days later, Life of Riley, in a novices' hurdle at Worcester. The day beforehand, though, Luke Harvey started slagging me about the ride that I had given Bolton Forest, about Charlie not being happy. I didn't think much of it – you wouldn't want to be taking a slagging by Luke too seriously – until I spoke to Dave, who told me that I wasn't riding Life of Riley, Dickie Johnson was. I wasn't happy about it.

I was at Worcester on the evening, I wasn't riding in Life of Riley's race, but I was gunning for Charlie, so I followed Dickie Johnson out when he had weighed out, when he was going to give Charlie the saddle. I don't mind if someone thinks that I have given a horse a bad ride, nobody is flawless, I have given plenty of horses bad rides and, even if I didn't think I had given Bolton Forest a bad ride, everyone is entitled to their opinion. It was the not telling me that got me.

I saw Charlie.

'All right AP,' Charlie says.

'I'd be all right if I wasn't riding for people like you,' I said.

Charlie looked surprised.

'I hear you weren't happy with the ride I gave Bolton Forest? Funny, I don't remember you saying anything after the race.'

Charlie stumbled around a bit looking for an answer.

'The owners went home and watched the video,' he said, 'and they weren't very happy that you kicked on as early as you did. I have to say, watching the video myself, you did make plenty of use of him.'

'Well that's why you were never any fucking use as a jockey,' I said. My blood was up now. 'You had to go home and watch the video to figure out if you had given a horse a good ride or a bad ride.'

'There's no need to be like that,' Charlie protested.

'Well as far as I'm concerned, you can do whatever you like now,' I continued. 'You won't have to be worrying about me messing up any of your horses again, because I won't be riding for you again.'

Life of Riley won, unchallenged, by 24 lengths.

I phoned Dave that evening to tell him not to put me on any of Charlie's horses again, that I didn't need to be bothering with someone who couldn't work out the difference between a good ride and a bad ride without going home and watching the video. Really mature, I know.

I didn't speak to Charlie for ages. I wouldn't even acknowledge his presence. I did start saying hello to him after about three years, but I didn't ride for him again for about seven. I have no problem with Charlie now, he's grand, it's just the way he is. I quite like him actually. He is what he is. Sometimes you have to put these things behind you and move on.

All trainers are different. Some trainers will spend 15 minutes giving you instructions, going through the small details of how he wants his horse ridden. I don't get that. You employ a jockey, you let them ride your horse. I remember a trainer telling me once that the priority with his horse was to get it to settle in the early stages of the race. He told me that Frankie Dettori rode this horse on the flat on its previous run, and he couldn't get it to settle, but that his missus could settle it at home.

If I could have gone back into the weigh room then, I would have. I wasn't the man for him. If Frankie Dettori doesn't know the job, then I'm wasting my time.

I do ride for a lot of small trainers though, like Jim Best, Rebecca Curtis and Brendan Powell – trainers who know the time of day and what they get with me. Dave decides what I ride; he will figure it all out. Sometimes he will ring me and ask me what I think, but I almost always go with what Dave thinks. Although sometimes he does err on the side of caution, he would prefer to put me on a safe jumper who has a moderate chance of winning than an unproven jumper who has a good chance of winning if he jumps okay. I'd be inclined to go the other way.

I'd never question Dave. I don't think I've ever asked him why I wasn't riding something. He might tell me, but if he doesn't, I won't ask him. If I am not riding a horse that I thought I should have been riding, I just assume that Dave has his reasons.

*

The 2000/01 season was decimated by the foot-and-mouth restrictions that were placed on the movement of animals. The Cheltenham Festival was postponed and then abandoned. I had had 21 days off early in the season with concussion, so my big goal of beating Sir Gordon Richards's record of 269 in a season was probably going to have to wait anyway. So from my point of view, if there was a season to lose meetings because of foot-and-mouth, it was this one.

It was the first time in three or four years that I actually became a little bit more relaxed about riding and about winners. I had the championship in the bag from a long way out; I knew from early on that I wasn't going to be able to beat Sir Gordon's record that season, so I was able to relax. I had a couple of months where I felt that I didn't really need to be counting up the winners, I was just riding away, riding winners and enjoying it.

The cancellation of the Cheltenham Festival wasn't a good thing, that's for sure. They did stage a couple of substitute races at the Whitbread Gold Cup meeting at Sandown at the end of April, but it wasn't the same. There were no Irish horses there for starters, they all stayed at home, and it was Sandown, not Cheltenham.

I won the substitute Champion Chase, the Championship Chase they called it, on Edredon Bleu. It was good to win the race of course, but it did start me thinking that he could have won a second Champion Chase in a row had Cheltenham gone ahead.

Istabraq was on track for the Champion Hurdle. If he had won the Champion Hurdle that year, and he was long odds-on favourite to do so, he would have become the first horse ever to win four consecutive Champion Hurdles. Four horses before him had won three, but no horse had ever won four. You had to feel for his owner JP McManus, trainer Aidan O'Brien and rider Charlie Swan.

I rode Blowing Wind in the 2001 Grand National. It was a desperate day – it had rained all week and it rained all day. On the morning of the race, there was some debate about whether the race should proceed, so soft had the ground become. It was decided to let it go ahead, but it was run in a quagmire. To make matters worse, a loose horse, Paddy's Return, jumped across the field, jumping the Canal Turn on the first circuit, and took half the field out. Luckily I was in third place at the time; I had jumped the fence by the time the carnage began.

Despite the ground, Blowing Wind travelled great. There were only seven horses still standing going out on the final circuit, seven out of the 40 horses that had set out, and Blowing Wind was giving me a great spin. I was beginning to think that this could be my year, the year that I won the National when, on the approach to the third fence on the second circuit, the big open ditch, a loose horse (there were loose horses everywhere by that stage) ran across me, and we had nowhere to go. Blowing Wind had to veer to his right and he couldn't jump the fence. My momentum carried me forward and I came off, landing in the ditch. A similar fate befell Ruby Walsh on Papillon and Philip Hide on Brave Highlander.

I was disgusted. I had never before been in such a good position in the Grand National. Before I was lucky enough to win the race on Don't Push It in 2010, people used to talk about my Grand National hoodoo; about 2005, on Clan Royal, when I was taken out by two loose horses at Becher's Brook on the second circuit when we were travelling well in the lead. They used to talk about 2008, Butler's Cabin, when we were travelling well, again at Becher's Brook second time, when we fell. They used to mention Blowing Wind as well, but it was never really regarded by people as that near a miss. To me it was the nearest miss of all. Blowing Wind was really the one that got away – there were only a couple of horses left in the race.

Blowing Wind ran back the other way down the track, back towards the second fence. Back then, the fences used to go the whole way across the track, there was no space between the outside of the fence and the rail, which was a good thing for me that day. It meant that there was nowhere for Blowing Wind to go. He and Papillon ran into the corner, stopped at the point at which the second fence met the outside rail, and looked around. Ruby and I reached the pair of them before they had a chance to go anywhere else, took a hold of the two of them, looked back up the course and thought, why not.

You can't remount any more in the UK. If you fall or become unseated, that's it, race over. Back in 2001, you could remount though, and as we did, we decided that we would just hunt around together, keep each other company, until the second-last fence, and then race from there. There was a better chance that both horses would complete the course if they had another horse to run with. So that's what we did. We hunted around, took our time. We were sure that there were no horses coming from behind us, but we had no idea how many were in front. We suspected not many, but we didn't know for sure if we were racing for ninth and tenth places or for first and second.

We stayed together until the second-last fence, where I gave Blowing Wind a squeeze, and he just ran away from Papillon. He had loads of energy left. Papillon had won the National the previous year, when he was only 9 lb higher than he had been the previous year, he had a big chance in that year's National as well, and Blowing Wind ran away from him. That confirmed my view that he was the one that got away. As it turned out, only two horses had finished the course in front of us, Red Marauder and Smarty, so Blowing Wind and I finished third.

Maybe I was never going to win the Grand National.

CHAPTER 21

Beating Sir Gordon

When the new season started, it was like flicking a switch inside me. I went from relaxed, riding away, riding winners, winning another championship (with 191 winners), to focused. A laser beam. Beating Sir Gordon Richards's record was now becoming a little bit of an obsession with me. Every time a new season started, it was like, go, light on, I was off, trying to pile up the winners, trying to set a pace that would enable me reach that elusive total of 269.

The 2001/02 season started quite brightly for me. Martin had a nice bunch of young horses plus the usual arsenal of older horses. He had all types of horses that he had got from everywhere, from sellers and claimers, and from France. He had horses for every type of race that was on the British National Hunt calendar. If the Jockey Club had decided to put on a couple of camel races or a couple of egg and spoon races, I'm sure Martin would have got a couple of camels in and invested in a couple of good spoons. That was Martin Pipe for you.

Seebald, a good novice hurdler two seasons previously, a German horse originally, owned by Steve McManaman and Robbie Fowler, kicked off his chasing career and won three on the bounce between May and June. Auetaler, another German horse also owned by Steve and Robbie, won two novice chases during the summer and should have won another, but I managed to put him on the floor in a novices' chase at Newton Abbot in June. Steve and Robbie were great owners, they knew the game, they understood what Martin Pipe was all about, and they loved having runners and winners. Robbie's dad still phones Martin every day for tips, and today I number them both among my very good friends.

It's amazing where this game has taken me. When I was at Jim Bolger's, I would be watching Steve and Robbie on the television, they were proper football stars when I was mucking out and raking the yard and hiding from Jim. I couldn't have dreamed that six or seven years later I'd be best buddies with them.

I had 100 winners on the board by 17th September. It was a new record. Present Bleu's win in a claiming hurdle at Plumpton was my 100th winner. It was unbelievable, the National Hunt season hadn't really got going properly and I had 100 winners on the board.

These days, if I have 100 winners on the board by the time Cheltenham's November meeting rolls around, I am happy. That was the beauty of riding for Martin Pipe, he had the ammunition and I just had to sit on it. You need a strong yard like that if you are going to be riding lots of winners and breaking records. I was just lucky to be in the right place. I rode 189 winners for Martin that season – 189 winners for one trainer in a season. It's mind-blowing. Only three or four jockeys ride more than 100 winners in total in a typical season, and here was I, running on the Martin Pipe treadmill that was going to net me 189 for him alone.

I thought that I was on track for Sir Gordon's record. I thought that I was at least giving myself a chance. A hundred winners by mid-September – I thought if I could ride another hundred by the start of the new year, that would mean that I would only have to ride 70 between January and the end of the season. This is the most competitive stage of the season, when it is most difficult to ride winners. Always has been. Every yard is in full flow. Apart from everything else, Martin's horses didn't have the same fitness advantage over their rivals that they had in the early part of the season.

That would be 20 winners a month. Twenty winners in January, 20 more in February, 20 more in March, and if I could ride 20 more in April, that would do it. Even 10 in April would do it.

The theme continued right up to and during the November meeting at Cheltenham. We won almost everything. I only had one winner on the first day, Manx Magic in the three-mile novices' chase, but I rode three on the Saturday: It Takes Time in the three-mile handicap hurdle and Image De Marque in the novices' handicap hurdle, as well as Shooting Light in the Thomas Pink Gold Cup, the old Murphy's Gold Cup. It was my third Thomas Pink, my second in a row (I had won it the previous year on Lady Cricket), it was Martin's fourth, and it was great.

The momentum continued into the Sunday. I won the first race on Tarxien and I won the big Grade 2 novices' chase on Seebald. That race is often a good pointer to the Arkle; it has been won by some of the top two-mile novice chasers in the past, so by winning it Seebald announced himself as a real player among the novice chasers that season. Fondmort did make a bad mistake at the second last when he was travelling fairly well, but I'm sure we would have beaten him anyway, and we beat the favourite Armaturk well, giving him a stone and four pounds.

Then I went out and won the next race on Westender. We had the race well won going to the last, but I tried to put him on the floor there. He made a terrible mistake from which he did really well to recover, and he got going again up the hill to go on and win well. That was seven winners at the Cheltenham November meeting, the first big meeting of the season.

The roll continued. I could hardly go to a meeting without riding a winner, and I had loads of doubles, loads of trebles. In the next two weeks, I had trebles at Newcastle, Taunton and Newbury, and, as I have mentioned, I rode a five-timer at Ascot on Ladbroke Hurdle day, 22nd December. I was beaten only on Westender in the Ladbroke Hurdle itself. Westender just wasn't right that day, which was a pity, as I would have loved to have gone through the card, to have ridden every winner on a day's racing, especially at Ascot. I have never gone through the card at any meeting, and I suspect I never will now.

Chris Maude retired. Maudey was a big part of my life when he was riding, he was effectively second jockey at Martin's, so he rode a lot of the horses that I couldn't ride, horses of Martin's that were at another meeting, or when I was out through suspension or injury, like Make A Stand in the Tote Gold Trophy, or horses that owners like Brian Kilpatrick didn't want me to ride, like Dom Samourai in the 1998 Greenalls Grand National Trial. He plays an even bigger part in my life now as my valet, the person who looks after me in the weigh room, makes sure I have the right equipment before I go out to ride.

Tom and John Buckingham (John famously rode Foinavon to win the Grand National in 1967) used to be my valets, but John retired from the business shortly after his brother Tom died, and Chris bought the business from him. It's great to have Chris around.

The Bula Hurdle was transferred from Cheltenham to Newbury that season, and I won it on Valiramix. It probably wasn't much of a race in the end, it was only a four-horse race, and Hors La Loi – whom owner Paul Green had taken away from Martin and who had by then joined James Fanshawe (via a spell with François Doumen) – underperformed quite badly.

It didn't really matter, I was really impressed with Valiramix; he probably would have beaten Hors La Loi that day even if he had been in top form. Valiramix was just an ordinary horse the previous season, he had been fairly well beaten by Landing Light in the substitute Champion Hurdle at Sandown in April, but he had filled out and strengthened up remarkably well during the summer. He had become a real racehorse. He was only a five-year-old, rising six, but he was obviously improving all the time as he was growing, and Martin and I thought that he was growing into a real Champion Hurdle horse.

Jim Culloty broke his arm in a fall at Taunton at the end of November, so the ride on Best Mate in the King George was up for grabs. I knew that I had a chance of getting it; I had won a Champion Chase for Best Mate's owner and trainer, Jim Lewis and Henrietta Knight, so I was hoping that I would get the call to ride him. Martin didn't have anything major for the King George, and even if he was going to run something, I was sure that he wouldn't stop me from riding Best Mate.

I did get the call from Henrietta to ride Best Mate, so I went up to her place to school him the week before the King George. I was pretty impressed with him all right. I had seen him close up – Wahiba Sands and I had beaten him and Jim Culloty in the First National Gold Cup at Ascot a month before the King George – but I had never sat on him. He felt good, he popped over the schooling fences effortlessly, he was a really nice mover.

Despite his defeat to Wahiba Sands, Best Mate was the bee's knees. He had been the previous season's leading novice chaser, and he was trying to concede 20 lb to Wahiba Sands in that Ascot race, which was probably an impossible task. Wahiba Sands was a very good horse.

The one worry about Best Mate in the context of the King George was his stamina. The King George is run over three miles, and Best Mate had never been beyond two and a half miles before, so I decided to ride him fairly conservatively. I rode him in midfield, among horses, but we moved up fairly nicely after the fourth last on the run around the turn into the home straight. Florida Pearl had led almost the whole way to that point under Adrian Maguire, he stayed three miles well, Bacchanal was on our outside under Mick Fitzgerald, another stayer, a Stayers' Hurdle winner, so I rode Best Mate to beat them for speed.

We were only about two lengths behind Florida Pearl jumping the third-last, and I asked Best Mate to pick up after jumping it, but the response wasn't immediate. Going to the second-last we were picking up all right, but we weren't reeling Florida Pearl back that quickly. On the run to the last we were still a length and a half behind him. We had dropped Bacchanal all right, but Florida Pearl was picking up as well.

Over the last and up the run-in, the leader wasn't stopping. We were reducing the deficit, but only gradually, not quickly enough. When we crossed the line, three parts of a length behind Florida Pearl, I was still riding Best Mate, I was still asking him to go forward, and I was as frustrated as hell.

Of course I should have ridden him differently, I knew that straight after the race. Actually, I knew it before we had jumped the last fence. Stamina worry? He won three Gold Cups afterwards, for God's sake, he had no stamina issues. Stamina was his forte. But he was thought of as a speed horse before that King George, he was a two-and-a-half-miler who might get three. If foot-and-mouth hadn't scuppered the Cheltenham Festival the previous season, it was the Arkle that Best Mate would have run in, the two-mile novices' chase, not the Sun Alliance Chase over three miles.

Even so, I should have been more aggressive on him. Martin Pipe used to say, they either stay or they don't. There's no point in riding them to get the trip. If they don't get the trip, it doesn't matter how you ride them, they don't get the trip. Ride them as if they stay, and if they don't stay, they won't win anyway. I consoled myself with the thought that we were close enough at the top of the home straight, we had enough time to get past Florida Pearl from there to the winning line, and with the fact that Florida Pearl was a top-class horse that had won five Grade i chases before that. Deep down, though, I knew that I should have won.

I moved house that year, buying a house in Kingston Lisle, just outside Wantage, about 10 miles from Swindon. I thought that it was my house for life, that I wouldn't have to move again.

I had some good times in that house, some good nights, some good parties. It was just down the road from Luke Harvey's pub, and obviously I used to get an assortment of waifs and strays arriving at all hours after Luke had had enough of them. I had a few lads staying with me – David Casey stayed with me for a while, Seamus Durack stayed with me for a while, so there was always good craic in the house.

Seamus Durack was a really talented young rider when he first came over from Ireland, he was champion amateur, but he was desperately unlucky with injury. He broke his leg three times. He broke it so badly at Towcester in May 2005, and dislocated his hip as well, that another jockey Ollie McPhail, when he saw him lying there with his leg out behind him, threw up on the spot. They said that he would never ride again after that (Durack, that is, not Ollie), but he went on the internet and found a doctor who would operate on his hip, drill holes in it or something and get it to grow again. Then he went online again and bought six books on how to build up your muscles, based on dance techniques, and he got back in the saddle. He rode Snoopy Loopy to win the Grade 1 Betfair Chase at Haydock in November 2008. Norman Williamson summed Durack up perfectly – the cleverest idiot he ever met.

I would often come downstairs in the morning and find an array of bodies stretched out over the floor. I'd go into my kitchen to get a cup of tea and meet people that I didn't know. Who are you? Where did you come from? I had a hot tub, a swimming pool and a sauna in the house, so you can imagine the shenanigans.

My dad used to come over to stay with me quite a bit then, even if I was away for the weekend. Luke used to tell me stories about my dad when I was away. Now, Peadar McCoy wouldn't say boo to a goose, he is the quietest man you could ever meet – sober. Get a few drinks into him though, different story. He'd be in Luke's pub and he'd be inviting everyone he met back to my house. There's a hot tub and everything there. It wasn't a hard sell. So people would come back and end up in the hot tub and the swimming pool, my dad encouraging them all.

I had 195 winners by the end of the calendar year, which wasn't bad – I was on track to break Sir Gordon's record. Then the weather set in. Racing was frozen off from the end of December into January, and I was at home tearing my hair out, wanting to get back on the racetrack, wanting to clock up more winners. When racing starts to be abandoned because of the weather, you just don't know how long it will be off. The days ticked by in early January and I was riding no winners.

Thankfully, the freeze only lasted a week. I rode two winners at Fontwell on 7th January and two more at Leicester on 8th January. That was 199. One more for the 200 milestone and then I could kick on again. It was a while in coming. I had plenty of fancied rides at Newbury two days later so I thought it would happen there, but it didn't. It was a disastrous day, capped by a fall from Baclama in the handicap chase.

I got a kick in the head from a following horse. I remember hitting the ground and thinking, not so bad, I'm all right, then, smack! A belt to the back of my head and a pain shooting through my head and then my body. I remember feeling light-headed and thinking, shit, I must have got a kick on the back of the head. I put my hand up to my head, just inside the back of my helmet, and rubbed my head, thinking, Jesus that hurt. I just rubbed it a little to try to ease the pain, then I stood up. Blood everywhere. On my glove, down my sleeve, all the way down my leg. Not good. I still have the scar on the back of my neck to remind me of it.

The next day I went to Huntingdon and won the handicap chase on Native Man, trained by Jonjo O'Neill, wearing the famous Anne Duchess of Westminster colours, yellow with the black band, as worn by Arkle. That was my 200th winner of the season. Just 70 more to go.

It was within touching distance now, and the bookmakers were making me odds-on to break Sir Gordon's record, but I didn't allow myself to think that I was on a downhill run. So many things can happen in National Hunt racing: abandonments, suspensions, concussions, injuries. You can be sailing away, flying high, then go out and ride in a Class F selling hurdle and your season can be over. You are only ever one bad fall away from the end of your season.

The closer you get, though, the more you think, God I've got this far, please don't let me get injured now, just let me stay in one piece. It had been my fastest 200, 38 days ahead of my previous fastest 200. I knew that this was my chance to break the record, that everything had gone so well, and I might not get another chance.

Every winner counted, even Family Business at Southwell on 23rd January. It was only a Class E novices' chase, but Family Business was odds-on for it, and I was thinking, another winner, so I wasn't a bit happy when he made a mistake at the second-last fence on the first circuit – he jumped to his left and just slithered a little, and I fell off him. I picked myself up off the ground, disgusted with myself for falling off, and walked across to the inside of the track to the road where the cars and the ambulances go around following the horses, hopped my helmet off the ground in disgust, and got into one of the Jeeps to get a lift back to the weigh room.

It was a seven-horse race, and two of the horses had fallen before I had been unseated. Then, going down the back straight, two others fell. I was out of the Jeep at this stage, about to go back into the weigh room, but I had a look back down to the second-last fence and saw that one of the lads had caught Family Business. There were only two horses left racing at that stage, so I thought, you know, I might just get back up on this fellow.

By the time I got back down to where Family Business was, back down to the second-last fence, the two horses that had been left were gone as well. They had unseated and refused at the fourth-last. I got back up on Family Business and popped him over the second-last fence again. I don't know why I did that. He had already jumped the fence, I had fallen off him on the landing side, I didn't need to jump that fence again, but I did anyway, just to be sure. Then I jumped the last and headed out to do another circuit.

I kept on looking ahead and behind me to see if anyone else was remounting. A couple of them did, but all of them had either fallen or refused even after remounting. No horse had got past the fourth-last. I just popped Family Business around, down the back straight, over the fourth-last, up the home straight and past the winning line to record one of the most bizarre wins of my career. To me it was win number 210.

I won the Tote Gold Trophy on Copeland. Martin did run two others in the race as well, but they were 40/1 shots; there was no choice to be made like there had been in the William Hill Hurdle two years previously between Copeland and Rodock. I was always riding Copeland. Or at least I was when we decided not to allow Valiramix to run in the race. Martin had the Tote Gold Trophy in mind for him, he thought he could win it with him, a Champion Hurdle contender, as he had with Make A Stand in 1997, but he would have been burdened with top weight, so we all thought that it would be best to skip it and go straight to the Champion Hurdle as a fresh horse. It looked like a very good decision when we won the Tote Gold Trophy anyway with Copeland. We were chased home by Rooster Booster, winner of the County Hurdle the following month and of the Champion Hurdle the following year.

I went out in London the night I won the Tote Gold Trophy on Copeland. I had also won the Game Spirit Chase on Lady Cricket. I was up to 235 winners for the season, 269 was in view, and I wasn't feeling too bad about life. There wasn't any racing on a Sunday in the UK back then, so I felt that I was allowed go out on a Saturday night sometimes if I had a big winner. I would go out with David Manasseh a lot. His uncle had a club in London, so we used to go there quite a bit, myself, David and some of the other jockeys – Graham Bradley and Jason Titley and a few of the other experienced partiers.

David had just started out as a football agent then, so some of the footballers would be around as well. It was good to be able to blend in. It was nice to be able to think, nobody knows me here, I can do what I like. In Lambourn if you scratch your nose, everybody knows about it. Walk into a nightclub in London with Brian Lara though, you could be wearing a pink leotard and nobody would pay a blind bit of notice.

I rode a double at Plumpton the following Monday, I rode a treble at Taunton the following Thursday, another treble at Ascot the following Saturday, a four-timer at Ludlow the following week. That was the kind of season I was having, doubles and trebles and four-timers coming out my ears, and a five-timer to boot, but that was the type of season you needed to be having if you were going to ride more winners in a season in the UK than any other jockey who had ever lived.

And it wasn't just the low-grade races I was winning. I was winning the top-class races as well. Martin Pipe had a reputation for only doing well with low-grade horses, for winning lots of bad races with bad horses. It is true, he did win lots of bad races with bad horses, with horses who were just less bad than their rivals, or more fit, but he could also win the top-class races as well. Seven winners at the Cheltenham November meeting, five winners on Ascot Ladbroke Hurdle day, a Bula Hurdle, a Tote Gold Trophy, you don't win those races with bad horses.

I rode a treble at Huntingdon on 2nd March and broke my own best-ever total for a season. I started the day on 252 winners and ended it on 255, two better than my previous best. I only had three rides on the day, all for Jonjo O'Neill, and all three won.

I always liked riding for Jonjo. He was very good to me and he used me whenever I wasn't tied up with Martin, and we had a lot of success together. But if you had asked me then if I could see myself riding as his stable jockey, I would have said, no way. Two years later? No chance. No offence to Jonjo, but at the time he just didn't have enough horses, and he didn't have enough good ones to give him even a chance of challenging Martin's dominance. You just couldn't see a shift happening. It's like in any sport, you can't see how the dominant players are going to loosen their grip. Like a couple of years ago, you could not see a point where Tiger Woods would not be the number one golfer in the world, or where Roger Federer would not be the number one tennis player in the world. Things change.

I went into Cheltenham on the crest of a wave. Like the previous year, I was going into the week thinking how many. I wasn't thinking, God the racing here is so competitive, I hope I can ride a winner early in the week, then I can relax. Nope. All I could think was how many.

Cheltenham was a disaster. I finished second on Westender in the first race, the Supeme Novices' Hurdle, behind Like-A-Butterfly, I finished second in the second race, the Arkle, on Seebald behind Moscow Flyer, and then I rode Valiramix in the third race, the Champion Hurdle.

I loved Valiramix, I thought he was the next big thing, and I thought he had a massive chance of winning what I thought was going to be a weak enough Champion Hurdle. He hadn't run since he had won the Bula Hurdle, but he had strengthened up again since then.

Istabraq was going for his fourth Champion Hurdle, but he was never travelling, and Charlie Swan pulled him up just after we passed the stands on the first circuit. Outside of Istabraq, I was sure we could beat everything else. Valiramix travelled really easily for me, down the far side, over the fourth-last, over the third-last, and we swung down the hill, cantering, he was running away with me. I was just sitting up on him, just behind the leaders, running down the hill towards the second-last, when wham! He just disappeared from under me and I was fired headlong into the ground.

People said afterwards that he clipped the heels of the horse in front of him, but he didn't. Something went on him on the run down the hill, probably his shoulder, and he just dropped to the ground like a half-ton sack of potatoes.

I took a heavy fall, but I wasn't concerned for me. My concern was for the gorgeous grey horse who lay beside me, all the potential seeping out of him. Gloria Victis all over again, two years on. Nothing could be done for him. I tried to fight back the tears and failed.

As with Gloria Victis, for something like this to happen to a six-year-old horse, a potential champion, who hadn't even reached his prime, who had his whole racing career, his whole life stretching out in front of him, was simply devastating. It was exactly the same as Gloria Victis but with one key difference: Gloria Victis happened on the last day of the Cheltenham Festival, there were only a couple of races to get through before I could run away from the crowd and hide, deal with it on my own, as best I could, away from the public glare. Valiramix happened on the third race on the first day. There were two and a half more days of races left, two and a half more days of the highest-profile race meeting of the year, where everyone has a camera, microphone or a Dictaphone, and where your words and demeanour are recorded and analysed, and you are diagnosed as a miserable git.

I admit that I didn't handle it right. But I was devastated, and I made the mistake of allowing my emotions loose. The truth is, I didn't give a shit what people thought. I was feeling crap, I was distraught at having lost such a good horse, and the last thing I wanted was to have a camera shoved in my face and have somebody say, right, perform. People telling me to cheer up.

If something similar happened today, I think that I would be a lot better at dealing with it. I'd probably come out with the usual stuff, ah it's not the worst thing that could happen, it could have been a jockey. Back then, though, I didn't care what anyone said to me or what they thought of me. To me, it was the worst thing in the world. I was going to win the Champion Hurdle on this horse, I might have won two Champion Hurdles on him, maybe three, he was potentially that good, he could have won three Champion Hurdles, and now he's gone. That was how it affected me, and I was the most important person in the world.

I got plenty of criticism over how I was at that Cheltenham Festival, over my general demeanour. It didn't bother me one way or the other. That was just the way it was, I figured, that was just the way I was. What I did find strange, though, was that people were criticising me for being miserable; they thought it was because I wasn't riding any winners, because I was having all these second and thirds, near misses and no winners. The reality was that I was just so upset about Valiramix, and I wasn't going to bother my arse trying to hide it.

I was supposed to be a guest on *Morning Line*, Channel 4's preview show of the day's racing, every morning. I did it the first morning, but then Valiramix happened and I just didn't fancy it, so I cancelled the last two days. I had absolutely no desire to be going on national television, going through my rides for the day, what I fancied, what I didn't fancy, what I thought of the other horses, what were the main dangers. Worst of all, I was going to have to look back on Valiramix. I didn't fancy doing any of that, so I just thought, no, I've had enough of that.

Nothing happened on the second day to improve my form. I finished fourth in the Champion Chase on Edredon Bleu, and I finished second on Iznogoud in the Sun Alliance Chase. I chose to ride Golden Alpha instead of Ilnamar and a couple of other horses of Martin's in the Coral Cup. Golden Alpha finished last of the 26 finishers, Ilnamar won the race under Rodi Greene. I chose to ride Lady Cricket in the Mildmay of Flete, Ruby Walsh got the ride on my old friend Blowing Wind, and he got up on the run-in and beat me by a length. You couldn't have written this stuff.

I wasn't big friends with Ruby at the time, but I knew him all right. I thought he was a brilliant rider, but I wasn't good friends with him like I am now. I would say hello to him in the weigh room when he'd be over from Ireland, but we had never really had a conversation until the 2001 Grand National, when we remounted Blowing Wind (ironically) and Papillon and hunted around together until the second-last fence.

It was in December 2001, when Ruby was over to ride and school a few horses for Henrietta Knight – during the time that Jim Culloty was out of action with his broken arm – that he phoned me wondering if he could stay with me for a couple of nights. James Nash was a good friend of Ruby's and mine, it was through him that Ruby got my number and made the connection, and I had no hesitation in putting Ruby up. We grew very friendly very quickly. I suppose we are like-minded in lots of ways; he knows how I feel after a bad day at the races, after a winnerless day, because I'm sure he feels exactly the same. There aren't many people who can empathise with you like Ruby can.

However, Ruby's solution was to slag me. None of this putting his arm around my shoulder, it'll be okay AP. No way. Plenty of I-can't-believe-you-got-beaten-on-that though. And he has an opinion, that's for sure. You could be talking about the tactics employed by the Russian ladies' netball team, and Ruby would have an opinion on it. You'd get to hear it too, solicited or not.

Ruby has a permanent pass to our house now, whatever house we happen to be inhabiting. We don't call the main spare room the main spare room, we just call it Ruby's room, and the sad reality is that Eve often seems to be more excited by Ruby's arrival than by mine. He's a top bloke though. I have a lot of respect for him, both as a rider and as a person. I'd say he is the best rider that I have ever ridden against, and I have ridden against a lot of very good riders.

Day three of the Cheltenham Festival continued with the same theme. Third on It Takes Time in the Stayers' Hurdle, second on Exit Swinger in the Grand Annual, beaten less than a length by Fadoudal Du Cochet and David Casey, of all people. I should have charged him more rent.

Then I went out to ride Royal Auclair in the Cathcart Chase. He was the 2/1 favourite and he really was the most likely winner of the race, so I was intent on getting him home. It was the second-last race of the meeting, and the last thing I wanted was to be walking out of Cheltenham that evening without a winner.

I kicked Royal Auclair out in front as soon as the tape went up, and we weren't headed. It was just one of those rides – we weren't going to be beaten. It wasn't a great race, Ruby finished second on Cregg House, who was rated about two stone inferior to Royal Auclair. Even so, it was one of those, bang, take that, races. Now. There. A winner. Hah. Big deal. I was like a spoilt child. I went into the meeting with designs on the Champion Hurdle and the leading rider's trophy, I came out of it with a Cathcart. I was like an athlete going to the Olympic Games thinking I might win four or five gold medals but coming away with one for synchronised swimming. I couldn't wait to get out of the place.

Bad as I was feeling, Martin went through an even rougher time of it.

His dad died soon after Cheltenham. Martin and his dad didn't always see eye to eye, but Martin thought the world of him. It was his dad, a very shrewd bookmaker and a very clever man, who got Martin into racing in the first place, and I see a lot of similarities between the relationship that Martin has with his son David now, and the relationship that Martin's dad, also David, had with him. Martin's wife Carol told me that after his dad died, Martin used to spend hours up there, just sitting there and remembering him. It shook his world.

Martin also had the Valiramix fallout to deal with, the fact that he had lost this potentially top-class horse, and he had the Magnus issue. The stewards had Martin in over the running of his horse Magnus in the Coral Cup. Magnus carried top weight in the Coral Cup, with the result that he kept the weights down, and some of Martin's horses got to carry less weight than they would have carried if Magnus hadn't been in the race. The winner Ilnamar, for example, carried just 10 st 5 lb; my horse, Golden Alpha, carried just 10 st 2 lb. A lot of the horses in the race – 14 of the 27 runners, to be precise – were out of the handicap as a result.

Magnus finished 25th of the 26 finishers and the stewards had Martin in, suspecting him of just running the horse in order to keep the weights down for his other horses. But that wasn't the case. Magnus was there to do his best, obviously, it was the Cheltenham Festival. The fact that his handicap rating was so high that some of Martin's other horses got to race off a nice weight was obviously a positive, but there was no question of Magnus not doing his best. As it happened, he finished clinically abnormal, he burst a blood vessel, so Martin was completely exonerated. And even with a burst blood vessel, he could still finish in front of me and Golden Alpha.

Royal Auclair was winner number 263, Running Times at Chepstow the following day was number 264, Noisetine was 265, Polar Champ was 266, Carandrew was 267. That was 1st April.

All the while I was thinking, don't get injured, don't do anything stupid. You've done the hard bit, you've put yourself in a position to do it. It felt like I'd potted 15 reds and 15 blacks (not that I ever have), I'd got perfect position on the yellow and all the colours were on their spots. I had potted the six colours from their spots a million times in practice and never missed. Don't miss this time.

I had a good book of rides at Warwick on 2nd April. It was possible that I would equal or beat Sir Gordon's record there, but I didn't allow myself to think about it. I wasn't calling my family or my friends and saying, get yourself to Warwick on Tuesday, I think I might just beat this old record. In fact, Marcus Reiger, the owner of Valfonic, one of the horses I was riding, called me the evening before. He was a city boy, one of these London whizz kids, nice guy though and he loved a punt.

'I'm thinking of going racing tomorrow,' he said, 'and having a decent bet on my horse. What do you think?'

'I wouldn't bother really, Marcus,' I said. 'He was disappointing on his first run when I rode him, and he wasn't much better on his last two, by all accounts. The better ground might help him, but I wouldn't be that hopeful.'

I won the second race on Shampooed, a mare of Robin Dickin's. 268. I won the fourth race on Shepherd's Rest for Charlie Morlock. Charlie was my next-door neighbour in Kingston Lisle, so I was delighted to ride a winner for him. I don't think I've ridden another for him since. That was 269. I had equalled Sir Gordon's record, which was fantastic. But I didn't dwell on it, I had to beat it. There would be no let-up until I had.

I went out on Valfonic in the novices' handicap hurdle, and I was right, the better ground did help him. Martin told me to ride him in midfield, but I was almost last in the early stages of the race. We were able to make good headway down the back straight though and he kept running on. We got to the front on the run-in, and he kept at it to get home by about a length.

That was 270. I had broken Sir Gordon's record! I couldn't believe it. It had been a goal for ages, it had been on my radar, but I hadn't really allowed myself to think that I was going to break it, so then when it happened, when I did actually go through the 269 barrier, it felt quite incredible, almost unreal. This was the record that I had had my sights on since I had beaten Scu's record for most wins by a jump jockey, and that had been four years previously.

I felt that I had actually achieved something. To this day, more than breaking Scu's record, more than breaking Dunwoody's record, more than riding my 3,000th winner, more than winning the Gold Cup, more even than winning the Grand National, I think that this was and is the greatest achievement of my career. I thought I had achieved something special, to beat a record that Sir Gordon Richards had held, and all that he achieved.

I was presented with a bottle of champagne and I wasted most of it by spraying the lads and the crowd. We went to The Pheasant that evening – Gee had organised for a few people to come and have a celebratory drink. It was a good night – most of my good friends were there and lots of people just called in to say well done.

It wasn't all a bed of roses though. I missed the ride on Ravenswood in the two-and-a-half-mile handicap hurdle at Aintree, the last race on the Friday, which was a bit disappointing. Iznogoud fell with me in the previous race, the novices' chase, and I got a bang on the head which had me seeing stars. I remember hiding from the doctor in case he stood me down for 21 days with concussion – I didn't want to miss riding in the Grand National the following day, but I did realise that I couldn't go out and ride in the next.

I remember telling Martin that I couldn't ride Ravenswood, which was a difficult thing to tell him – Ravenswood was a certainty, another of those Martin Pipe handicap hurdlers with a stone or two in hand. Tom Scudamore, Peter's son, rode Ravenswood, and he won with his head in his chest. I rode Blowing Wind in the Grand National the following day, and we finished third, miles behind Bindaree and What's Up Boys. He ran well, but that was as good as he was that year. 2001 was his year, not 2002.

I also missed the ride on Take Control in the Scottish National at Ayr two weeks later. Well, I didn't miss it so much as chose not to take it. I chose to ride Cyfor Malta in the race instead. Guess who rode Take Control? Ruby Walsh. Ruby actually rode four winners that day, the other three for Paul Nicholls. And guess who won the race? Take Control. And guess who was pulled up? Cyfor Malta.

The season did end on a high for me though, when I rode Bounce Back to win what used to be the Whitbread, now called the Attheraces Gold Cup, at Sandown on the last day of the season. Bounce Back was only six, and he wasn't a great jumper of fences, but he went around Sandown as if he was on springs, passed another of Martin's horses, Dark Stranger, after the second-last, and he stayed on well to win nicely.

I ended up with 289 winners, 20 more than Sir Gordon had ridden. Dave says that that total will never be beaten, that so many things went right for me that season – Martin's horses were dominant, I had remained largely injury- and suspension-free for the entire season, the weather had been good, there were relatively few cancelled meetings – that it is unlikely that it will ever happen like that for someone again.

I'm not sure that it will never be beaten. Never is a long time, and I am sure that, as much as racing has changed, it will change again, the planets will line up and someone will ride more than 289 winners. For now though, I am happy that I have set as high a total as I could possibly have set, that I reached up and set the bar as high as I could. Now, beat that.

CHAPTER 22

It's All About the Stats

The thing about breaking a record and setting a statistic is that in years to come, there can be no argument about it, it's there in the record books. You hear arguments all the time over who is the best rider, Richard Dunwoody or John Francome or Peter Scudamore or Ruby Walsh or Jonjo O'Neill or Charlie Swan. Everybody will have their own opinions, nobody will be wrong. But ask somebody for the statistic of who rode the most winners ever, who won the most winners in a season, and it's there in black and white. Irrefutable.

Statistics are everything to me. I'm sure there have been, and will be, many jockeys who are better than me, but in years to come, when I finish riding and people can't remember who AP McCoy or John Francome or Richard Dunwoody were, if they look up the record books, they will see my name there. If they check up to see who rode more winners, Peter Scudamore or AP McCoy, it will say AP McCoy. That's more important than looking good or than winning any big race.

Thank God I was lucky enough to win the Grand National, because if I hadn't managed to win it before I retired, it would have been a glaring omission from my CV, that's for sure. However, as I have said before, lots of jockeys win the Grand National, whereas not many jockeys have been champion. Since 1980, 28 different riders have won the Grand National. In the same period of time, only four have been champion jockey.

That was why Sir Gordon's record meant so much to me. It was a big deal to break Peter Scudamore's record of most winners in a season by a National Hunt jockey, but beating Sir Gordon's record – most winners in a season by a flat or National Hunt jockey – was much bigger. And I beat it. That's a fact.

I accept that it was probably much tougher for Sir Gordon back in the 1940s: he had to travel to races by train, there was none of this flitting by helicopter between racecourses, and riding at more than one meeting in a day. As against that, though, he probably got to ride whatever he wanted in pretty much any race.

Beating his record was the most important thing in my life at the time. I never discussed it with anyone. I didn't sit down with Dave Roberts at the start of the season and say, right Dave, I want to beat Sir Gordon's record, here's what we're going to do. I didn't tell Martin to ready as many horses as he could for the easy races during the summer, that I was going to go all out to beat Sir Gordon. It was just something that lived with me, an idea that existed in my head and nowhere else. It didn't make for a very peaceful existence. It led to me regarding 245 winners in the 1999/2000 season as a disappointment. Only one rider before me had ridden more than 200 winners in a season, and I was regarding 245 as a disappointment.

I had lots of dark days during my record-breaking season. If I came home from the races without a winner, it wasn't good. Chanelle says that she knew what kind of a day I had by the way I put my keys down on the table after coming in the door. I was counting the days and I was counting the winners; I knew exactly how many winners I needed to have in order to break the record at every point, so if I came home with no winners, I was on the same number of winners at the end of the day as I was at the start, but another day's racing had passed by. That used to freak me out.

I was getting up in the morning, going racing again, hoping that those three or four hours that I spent on the racecourse were going to yield a couple of winners to add to the tally. The rest of life didn't matter. It was all about those three or four hours on the racecourse, how many winners it would bring. Then I'd come home in the evening, think about the day's racing, think about tomorrow's racing, go to bed, get up in the morning and do it all again.

It was a fairly depressing way of life. My head would be wrecked. After the bad days, the bad rides and the winnerless days, I'd just want to be on my own. People would try to make me feel better about it. Chanelle would try her hardest to cheer me up, but the reality was that I didn't want to be cheered up. I was happy wallowing in my misery, dealing with it as I had always dealt with it, on my own. Nobody else could understand it, and I didn't have the patience to try to explain it to people, even to those closest to me.

There was probably a part of me that felt that I needed to be miserable, that I needed to suffer for my poor rides or the mistakes that I had made that day. I was much happier at home on my own being miserable than being out and having other people see me being miserable. I couldn't just put it to the back of my mind and go out and have a nice meal. I could never do that.

It caused a lot of friction between Chanelle and me. She would have arranged to go out with friends, go out for a meal or for a drink or just to someone's house, and I'd come home, no winners, bad day, and just tell her that I didn't fancy it, that I wasn't going anywhere. It wasn't fair on her, she wouldn't know if we were going out in the evening before I came home, before she knew what type of day I'd had.

There were evenings when I just got home and went to bed. I wouldn't watch television or anything; I'd just come home, go upstairs to my bedroom, close the curtains and get into bed. Usually, I wouldn't sleep. I'd just be churning things around and around in my head. Sometimes I would just sit on the bed in the dark. Or just sit in the kitchen, in silence, in darkness.

I never thought about all the things I had going for me. I never thought about the fact that I was champion jockey, or that I had the best job in the country, or that, whether I wanted to admit it to myself or not, I had obviously been blessed with some kind of talent for riding horses. I would only think about how shit I was, how bad a ride I had given a horse.

I put myself under a lot of pressure that season because it was all about time. I had to ride 270 winners before the season ran out. Every winner was precious, every potential suspension or injury was crucial.

There were days when I thought I was mad to be going racing at all, but I never didn't go. I would be in so much pain from different injuries, I would hardly be able to walk to the car, but if I was able to put one foot in front of the other at all, I was going racing. I couldn't not go.

I wasn't miserable all the time, mind you. If I rode two, three or four winners at a meeting, I was happy going home that evening. That was a good day a worthwhile day. The only thing was, the following morning, that day was over, we were back to zero and starting all over again.

Anyway, it was all worth it. I broke the record. The day I broke it was really the first time that I felt that I had truly achieved something.

It was my seventh championship in a row as well. Peter Scudamore had won seven in a row in the late 1980s and early 1990s, but he had shared one with John Francome as well in the early 1980s, so he had a total of eight. Francome had won seven, so I was in good company. Nobody had ever ridden 300 winners in a season though. I had a new goal.

CHAPTER 23

Chasing 300

2 0th July 2002: I had six rides on a seven-race card at Market Rasen. I won on the first five, including on Chicuelo in the feature race, the Summer Plate, and I was challenging at the third-last fence in the last race on Passereau, when the leader Barnburgh Boy jumped across us and we came down.

I wouldn't have gone through the card because I didn't have a ride in one of the races, the novices' chase, but I had never before ridden six winners at one meeting, no National Hunt rider has, and it would have been nice to do it. Still, I remounted Passereau to finish second, so five winners and a second wasn't a bad haul.

There were other positives to take from the day as well. There was Chicuelo for one, an ex-French horse that Martin had got from another trainer, Ian Williams. He was sure to get a fair hike from the handicapper for winning the Summer Plate as easily as he did but, even so, he had jumped really well for a horse that had been labelled a poor jumper, and he had won so easily that he was shaping up to be our Thomas Pink Gold Cup horse.

The other positive was that those five winners put me on 1,676 wins in my career, just two behind Peter Scudamore, who rode 23 fewer winners than Dunwoody. Three more winners and I would be the second winning-most National Hunt jockey of all time; 26 more and I would be the most.

Four days later I rode a double at Worcester, four days after that I went to Newton Abbot and rode Polar Champ to win the first race, the novices' chase. He was a 1/6 shot, it was only a three-horse race in the end, but it didn't matter to me – it was another winner and it took me past Peter Scudamore's total.

It was nice to pass Scu. When he set his total of 1,678, it looked like it might not be beaten for a while, but then Dunwoody came along and posted 1,699. Dunwoody would have liked to have posted a higher total, he wasn't ready to retire when he was forced to, but I wasn't going to be happy until I had caught him. I rode three more winners at Newton Abbot that day and trained my sights on Dunwoody.

I tied his total on 27th August when I won the first race at Uttoxeter on Dream With Me, and I passed it a half an hour later when I won the second race on Mighty Montefalco. That was a big one, 1,700 winners – more winners than any other jump jockey in history. Without being blasé about it, there was a sense of inevitability about it. With summer jumping, there is now more racing these days than ever before. If you ride through the whole year, if you ride for Martin Pipe, if you remain largely injury-free and keep your wits about you a bit, inevitably the milestones will be reached. If I hadn't beaten Dunwoody's record on 27th August 2002 at Uttoxeter, I would have beaten it on 31st August at Market Rasen, or on 1st September, or on 1st October, or in 2003, or 2004.

That said, it was great to pass Dunwoody. Richard Dunwoody was the most complete rider in my book; he raised the standard for jockeys single-handedly, both in terms of riding style and in terms of professionalism. And then when I started to ride with him, I got friendly with him and came to realise what a good guy he was.

As well as his riding, there was also his pain threshold. I used to see him get up after so many bad falls, and go out and ride in the next race, and I got to thinking, that's what I needed to do. I received a congratulatory text from him. I'm sure he meant the words of congratulations, but I'm sure it killed him as well. Just like it would have killed me, just like it will probably kill me if and when I have to send the same text to someone else.

It was nice as well that Jonjo O'Neill trained Mighty Montefalco. Of course I owe so much to the winning machine that was Martin Pipe, but I was riding a fair bit for Jonjo at the time. I didn't know how closely I would be associated with him later in my career, but it was good that he could be part of the milestone.

I pulled up after passing the winning post on Mighty Montefalco, delighted, turned the horse around and was walking him back towards the exit from the racecourse when I saw Dave Roberts coming towards me.

'Brilliant!' he said as he extended his hand upwards, and shook mine.

'Thanks a million Dave,' I said. 'I didn't know you were coming.'

'I wouldn't have missed this,' he said.

Dave never goes racing. Nobody ever gets to see Dave. He is like this ever-present force in the weigh room, at the racetrack, that nobody ever sees. He is just so busy at home with his phones and his televisions and his computers and his declarations.

There was one evening we were all out in the Queens Arms, a pub that a friend of mine, Tom Butters, used to own. Andrew Thornton was there, and Norman Williamson, and a few of the other lads, and Dave came down to join us. There were a few of us standing up at one of the pillars in the pub, Norman and me and Dave and Andrew Thornton, plus Brian Crowley, who was riding for Venetia Williams at the time and who also had Dave as his agent.

'Is this fellow Dave Roberts coming then or not?' asked Brian.

I looked at Norman and swallowed a laugh. Dave looked at Brian, poker-faced.

'He said he was coming in, didn't he?' continued Brian, digging away. No Brian, dig up. 'He's meant to be coming to see us.'

Brian probably spoke to Dave every day on the phone. Dave had been there half an hour. I'm not sure who Brian thought Dave was. We didn't tell Brian for a while, but we all had a good laugh when we did.

It isn't an easy game these days, what Dave does. Not that it was easy before, but at least when he started doing it, he was more or less the only one doing it. Now there are quite a few jockeys' agents. Like most successful activities, it is more competitive now than it used to be.

Dave always wanted to work in racing. By his own admission, he wasn't great at school; he used to skive off a lot to go to the races. He went down a couple of journalism avenues, most of which were cul de sacs, but he did manage to convince Bath Racecourse that he should write a form guide for their racecards. Through that work, he met Geoff Lewis, and he also met an Indian businessman who had a couple of horses and who asked Dave to be his racing manager. The horses were in training with Geoff, so when the Indian businessman left the scene, sold his horses and went to America, Geoff suggested to Dave that he become a jockeys' agent.

There were hardly any agents at the time, two or three maybe, but the idea appealed to Dave a lot. He started off as agent for Geoff Lewis's apprentice at the time, Jason Swift, and it just went from there. (Table quiz question: who was Dave Roberts's first client? A. Adrian Maguire B. Norman Williamson C. AP McCoy or D. Jason Swift?)

That was in 1986. Dean Gallagher was living with Jason Swift, so he joined Dave. Dean Gallagher was friendly with Richard Guest, so he also joined Dave, and once people started to notice that Dean Gallagher and Richard Guest were getting more rides and having more winners than they had had in the past, they started thinking that there might be something to this Dave Roberts bloke. Richard Guest was riding for Toby Balding, so that was how the Toby Balding connection came about, that was how the Adrian Maguire connection happened and, ultimately, how the AP McCoy connection happened. Lucky it did.

*

In a strange way, the fact that Mighty Montefalco was my 97th winner of the season was almost as important to me at the time as the fact that he was the 1,700th winner of my career. At the same point during the previous season, my record-breaking 2001/02 season, I had ridden 87 winners. I was 10 winners ahead of myself and I thought that 300 winners in a season was a realistic target.

That was me all over. It was great to beat Dunwoody's record, but it was done, it was history, 300 winners in a season was the future, and I thought that I could do it, so I kicked on. On 4th September, when I rode Toi Express for Philip Hobbs to win a four-runner novices' chase at Newton Abbot, I clocked up the fastest century ever, beating my own record by 13 days. I reached the 200-winner mark by Boxing Day, when I won the first race on the day, the two-mile novices' hurdle, on Lord Sam, beating my previous fastest 200 by 16 days. Actually, as it turned out, Lord Sam was my 201st winner. I had finished second on Bongo Fury in a handicap hurdle at Cheltenham on Thomas Pink Gold Cup day, but the winner, Classic Note, was disqualified because morphine was found in his sample, so that was another winner.

I went to Chepstow on 27th December, rode Claymore to win the handicap chase and rode Control Man to win the bumper. Control Man was my 300th winner of 2002, my 300th winner of the calendar year. There wasn't that much made of it, milestones were all about the number of winners you ride in a season, not in a calendar year, but I was happy that it was a landmark of sorts and, just as importantly, it told me that, if I could ride 300 winners in a calendar year, I could ride 300 winners in a season. I rode five more winners before the end of December, 305 winners in 2002.

In terms of the season, I was 21 days ahead of where I had been the previous season when I won on Native Man at Huntingdon, and remember, I had ridden 289 winners the previous season. Could I ride 11 extra winners in 21 extra days? Of course I could. The bookmakers agreed – they made me a 1/2 shot to do so. I just needed to remain injury- and suspension-free. But that was where the deal fell down. The day before Racing Post Chase day, Kempton, 21st February, race one, a Class C handicap hurdle, I was riding a horse called Neutron for Martin. He had a chance, he was the 11/2 favourite, but he stepped at the second flight and came down, firing me into the ground. I knew it was bad; the pain went shooting up through my shoulder as soon as I hit the ground. Dr Turner, the racecourse doctor, came up to me as I picked myself up off the ground slowly, holding my shoulder.

'All right?' he enquired.

'Yeah all right,' I said. There was no way I was going to tell him that I thought I had broken my collarbone. Not when I was on track for 300 winners, not when the Racing Post Trophy was the following day, not when there were just two and a half weeks to the Cheltenham Festival.

I weighed out for Wahiba Sands in the second race, the two-mile chase, and I gave Martin the saddle.

'Are you okay?' he asked.

'I think I've broken my collarbone,' I told him. 'But I'm fine. I'm able to ride.'

Martin knew me. He knew that I would ride through the pain, and he knew that, once I felt that I was able to ride, he would have needed one of those construction cranes to get me off the horse.

Wahiba Sands finished third, that was as good as he was.

I rode Puntal in the next race, the Dovecote Novices' Hurdle, and we won. The next race was the Rendlesham Hurdle, three miles and half a furlong, on Deano's Beeno. Deano's Beeno was not one for doing anything on the bridle, anything he did, including consenting to race, he did because he finally succumbed to your urgings, not because he especially wanted to do it, not because he wanted to please. The last thing you want to be doing when you have a suspected broken collarbone is riding Deano's Beeno in a three-mile hurdle.

It didn't help that he got a kick from another horse as we circled at the start either, but he started okay, and he never saw another horse. We led the whole way, came clear in the home straight and won well. Then I won the three-mile novices' chase on Stormez. So I was happy with my haul for the day: three winners and a suspected broken collarbone.

I went home, took some painkillers and went to bed. The right thing to do would have been to go to hospital, get my collarbone x-rayed, confirm that it was broken, and take some time off, but I was riding

Montreal in the Racing Post Chase the following day, and I thought he had a chance.

I didn't win the Racing Post Chase, it was all just a bit much for Montreal, and we finished fifth behind Warren Marston on La Landiere, but I did win the previous race, the Adonis Hurdle, on the exciting juvenile hurdler, the French import Well Chief. It was my first time riding him in a race, and I loved him. There was no question, but he was going to be my Triumph Hurdle horse.

After racing Martin asked me how my shoulder was.

'It's fine,' I told him. 'A bit sore.'

'Come down to us tomorrow,' he said. 'We can have Ray x-ray it.'

I nodded my head. Then I thought, Ray is the vet. Is Martin going to have a vet x-ray me? He was. The next day, there I was, lying on the kitchen floor in Martin's house with Ray putting an x-ray machine over me, a machine that was no doubt designed for horses and cows, and examining the x-rays. I was right, fractured collarbone.

There isn't really much you can do for a fractured collarbone but rest it, and I probably hadn't done it any good by riding for two days. I decided that the main thing was to be ready for Cheltenham. I knew that if I had had another fall, I would probably smash it up good, and it would probably put me out of the Cheltenham Festival.

Taking time off was not something that I ever wanted to do, but it was almost certain that this collarbone was going to force me onto the sidelines for at least a little while. If I took a week or 10 days off, it would decrease my chance of riding 300 winners for sure, but it was going to happen anyway. If I had a fall I would be on the sidelines for even longer, so in my warped mind I decided that it was better to take the break then, before Cheltenham, and hope that that would be it, that I wouldn't have to take any more time off. That way, it meant that I could ride at Cheltenham and that 300 winners was still a possibility.

I decided to go to Dubai for a little while, relax, get away from racing so that I wouldn't be tormented by the winners that I was missing, and give the collarbone a chance. So I headed off to Dubai for a week with Chanelle, and we had a great week together. It was exactly the right thing to do, and I was back 10 days later, ready to go again for Cheltenham.

As it turned out, I should have stayed in Dubai. Cheltenham was a disaster. Le Roi Miguel fell at the third fence in the Arkle, the second race – buried me. Copeland fell at the third last in the Champion Hurdle, the third race – buried me. I was sore, dosed up to my eyeballs

with painkillers that Chanelle had got for me through her pharma-
ceutical business without prescription, so I decided to take the rest of
the day off.

The next day wasn't any better. Puntal wasn't mapped in the Sun
Alliance Hurdle, It Takes Time finished last of the six finishers in the
Sun Alliance Chase, Tiutchev fell in the Champion Chase, another sore
one, Korelo was paceless in the Coral Cup, and Lady Cricket had too
much weight in the Mildmay of Flete. At least I did win the bumper on
Liberman, he was the 2/1 favourite and we only just got home. Just as
well.

But the last day could hardly have been any worse. It started with a
head defeat on Well Chief in the Triumph Hurdle, and ended with a
mother and father of a fall from Golden Alpha at the third last in the
Grand Annual. As soon as I hit the ground I felt the shooting pain in
my shoulder again, and I knew that my collarbone had had it again.

I was brought back into the ambulance room. Tony Dobbin was there
as well, lying on a bed, wires coming out of him from everywhere. If
Dobbs was a normal person, you would have been worried, but Dobbs
is as big a hypochondriac as you ever would have found in the weigh
room. Once he was airlifted by ambulance off a racecourse after falling
in the first race, and he was back at the races with his arm in a sling by
the last. No joking.

The doctor came in and asked me if I was on any medication. After a
bit of interrogation, I caved and told him that I had got the drugs from
my girlfriend. Chanelle was in serious trouble. They paged her over the
public address system: could Chanelle Burke please go to the stewards'
room. It didn't sound good, I'm sure she would have been worried if
she hadn't been in the champagne bar all day. She sobered up quite
quickly though when she got an earful from the doctor, sourcing drugs
for a jockey without a prescription, without an x-ray, without even a visit
to a doctor. Imagine.

I had to go to the hospital then, having no option but to get it x-rayed.
So there I was leaving Cheltenham and all the celebrations, Best Mate
after winning his second Gold Cup, me with just one winner in the bag,
heading off to hospital to wait in line to have an x-ray done on my collarbone, which I knew was broken.

Unsurprisingly, I wasn't in great form as I waited for my x-ray. I'm
not sure that Chanelle was certain she had made the right choice, leaving her mates in the champagne bar to accompany a foul-humoured
me in the hospital waiting room. As we waited, there were these shrieks

and cries coming from one of the wards. It was incessant, going right through my head, and it was driving me and all the other patients mad. I called one of the nurses over and asked her what was going on.

'Oh that's a girl who tried to commit suicide,' she said to me. 'Tried to slit her wrists. It's not the first time she's done it, she's been in here before, and it's always the same, she's always cries and shouts like that.'

I said right, I got up, took my broken collarbone with me, and went into the ward where she was, surrounded by people.

'Here, that's ridiculous,' I said to her. She stopped crying and looked at me. All the other people around the bed stopped and looked at me.

'She's not trying to commit suicide,' I said. 'She's just an attention-seeker. Look, the next time you want to commit suicide, just give me a call and I'll come and make sure you do it properly.'

I'm not proud of that, it wasn't one of my best moments and I'm embarrassed thinking back on it now. But I was so out of it on the pain-killers, I was pissed off, Cheltenham over, only one winner, I was going to be on the sidelines for weeks, so sore with my collarbone and all my aches and bruises, so frustrated sitting there waiting to get my x-ray done. It was all too much for me, so I flipped.

Chanelle was gobsmacked. I turned on my heel and headed for the door. I couldn't take any more of the sitting around. I knew my collar-bone was broken, I didn't need a radiographer to tell me. I was out of there.

CHAPTER 24

Roller-Coaster Season

The November 2002 Cheltenham meeting was its own little mini roller-coaster. Martin had two winners on the Friday, but they were in an amateur riders' race and a conditional jockeys' riders race, neither of which I could have ridden obviously, so great. The winner of the amateurs' race, Iris Bleu, was actually ridden by Gordon Elliott, who would go on to train Silver Birch to win the 2007 Grand National, and is now one of the top National Hunt trainers in Ireland.

The Saturday didn't start off too badly. I won the first race on Tarxien and I finished third on It Takes Time in the second, the three-mile handicap hurdle. Then the roller-coaster started to go downhill. I chose to ride Shooting Light, the horse on whom I had won the Thomas Pink the previous year, in the Intervet Trophy but, while he travelled well for me, he didn't stay the near three and a half miles. To make things worse, Martin's other horse Stormez won the race, with Barry Geraghty riding.

I wasn't feeling great after that. I could have ridden Stormez. I had faced a similar quandary for the next race, the Thomas Pink Gold Cup itself, the feature race of the meeting. Chicuelo or Exit Swinger or Cyfor Malta? It was a no-brainer really; Chicuelo had been our Thomas Pink horse since he had won the Summer Plate at Market Rasen in June. The handicapper had raised him 16 lb for the performance that he put up in winning that, but Martin was confident that he had much more than that in hand. He didn't run him again between June and the Thomas Pink; he didn't want to give the handicapper another chance to assess him and raise him further.

He only had 10 st 1 lb to carry in the Thomas Pink; 10st 1lb was a struggle for me, but I had never before put up overweight, and I wasn't about to start. I wasn't inclined to ride at 10 st 1 lb very often, but I could do it as a one-off every now and again if I had enough notice and if it was worth it, and I was sure that it was worth it to ride Chicuelo in the Thomas Pink.

The week before was a week of fasting. Lots of hot sweet tea, a piece of chicken here, a Jaffa Cake there, plenty of water, some vitamin tablets and lots of hot baths. I wouldn't be in great form, that's for sure, but I could do it, like I say, if I thought it was worth it.

Turns out, it wasn't. Chicuelo was a disaster on the day. He rediscovered his old bad jumping habits, he lost his rhythm and everything started to unravel. He jumped the fourth fence poorly, he hit the eighth fence, and I lost my stirrup. Then he hit the fence going up the hill on the far side, and that was more or less that. He clobbered the fourth-last for good measure, and I pulled him up before the second-last, no point in making him jump the last two.

As I pulled him wide of the last two fences, I looked up ahead and I could see the finish of the race, I could hear the cheer from the stands as the horses up front landed over the last fence, me not involved, the 2/1 favourite for the race underneath me. I could see David Johnson's blue and green colours up there, it looked like he was in front and wouldn't be caught. It was Barry Geraghty again, riding another one of my horses, wearing the same silks as I had worn when I won the race on Lady Cricket in 2000 and when I won the race on the same Cyfor bloody Malta in 1998, four years previously.

I couldn't have chosen Cyfor Malta over Chicuelo though. He was nine, back from injury; Chicuelo was six, a young horse on the up, probably stacks in hand of the handicapper. It just shows you the power of Martin Pipe, against all the odds.

I could say that I was delighted for Barry, delighted for Martin and for David Johnson, but it would be a lie. I wasn't happy for Anthony McCoy, and that was all that mattered to me. I was out there, bumbling from fence to fence, survival odds-against, as Barry was zinging on Cyfor Malta, my horse, my ride, returning to the winner's enclosure, to another big-race winner and all the accolades. I skulked in, unsaddling in the place reserved for the also-rans. There isn't much in there to be happy about.

I did win the last race on Don Fernando, but my overriding thought that evening wasn't about the two winners that I had ridden. I should have been delighted to have ridden a double on Thomas Pink Gold Cup day, one of the most high-profile days of the season pre-Christmas, but I was gutted. All I could think of was the two that got away. I could have ridden four, and I should have won another Thomas Pink.

I rode a treble the following day, the Sunday, the third and final day of the meeting: one for Martin and two for Venetia Williams. But I was beaten by Ruby Walsh and Azertyuiop on Golden Alpha in the Grade 2 novices' chase, and I was beaten on Liberman in the bumper by the amateur rider JP Magnier, Coolmore supremo John Magnier's son, on Rhinestone Cowboy. Guess what I was thinking about that evening. (Hint: it wasn't the three winners.)

I was delighted to be on the shortlist for the 2002 BBC Sports Personality of the Year award, and I was thrilled to finish third. I can't remember any time, before or since, that I was thrilled to finish third in anything, but SPOTY was different.

As I have said before, racing is a minority sport. Unsurprisingly, racing had never done very well in SPOTY before. Lester Piggott, probably the greatest jockey of all time and the most established household name that there has ever been in racing, had received a Special Achievement Award in 1984 and in 1994, and, together with Nijinsky and Vincent O'Brien, had received the team award in 1970. Aldaniti and Bob Champion had received the team award as well in 1981, and Frankie Dettori had finished third in the overall competition in 1996, the year of his Magnificent Seven at Ascot. So for me to be even included among those people was a real honour.

It was a different set-up in 2002 to that in 2010. For starters, the event was held at Television Centre in the BBC studios at Shepherd's Bush, not in the LG Arena in Birmingham. It was on a much smaller scale back then; the audience consisted exclusively of sports people who had been invited to attend. It didn't include members of the public who could buy tickets and who swelled the attendance figure to 10,000.

For all of that, though, it was a really enjoyable event. I was humbled to be in the same room as so many great names, and I was gob-smacked when they called my name out in third position, behind David Beckham and Paula Radcliffe, who won the award by a distance. I received almost 88,000 votes, which bowled me over a bit, more than Jonny Wilkinson, more than Lennox Lewis. Jonny won the award the following year though, deservedly so, and Lennox Lewis had already won it in 1999, so fair is fair.

Back on the track, I was getting ready to have another crack at the King George on Best Mate. It was desperate luck for Jim Culloty that he was on the sidelines again for Best Mate's second attempt at winning a King George. He was injured in 2001 with a broken arm that just wouldn't heal on time (they're buggers like that), and suspended in 2002 for a misdemeanour, for not riding out for third place in a bumper at Doncaster. He missed out on the ride on the King George favourite for that. It would be like getting three years in prison for driving through an amber light.

In all honesty, I wasn't too concerned about Jim at the time; I was more concerned about me. Nothing new in that, I suppose. It wasn't certain that Henrietta Knight would ask me to ride Best Mate in the King George, but I knew there was a good chance she would. Jim had ridden Best Mate in all his races with the exception of the 2001 King George; I was the only other person who had ridden him in public, so I would have been disappointed had I not got the call. I was desperate to ride him, desperate to right the wrong of 2001, now that I knew how to ride him.

I did get the call, and Martin was great about it. He had Wahiba Sands and Shooting Light in the race, but Best Mate was the Gold Cup winner, a warm favourite for the King George from a long way out, and he wasn't going to make me ride a 25/1 shot instead.

There was no need for instructions this time. I knew now that Best Mate was a stamina horse, not a speed horse, and I was going to use his stamina. I was always handy on him, never too far away, he jumped on at the fifth last, and I let him stride away. He jumped the fourth-last well, the last fence in the back straight, and I asked him to stretch, use his stamina.

Marlborough got close to us over the last two fences, and he did get the last one wrong, which helped us. Even at that, we only got home by a length. But I am sure that, even if Marlborough had flown the last, Best Mate had a little more left to give. I'm sure we would have won anyway.

It was great to win the King George. The King George is one of the top prizes in National Hunt racing. Outside of the top three races at Cheltenham, the Gold Cup, the Champion Hurdle and the Champion Chase, and the Grand National, it is the one you want to win. Gold Cup, Champion Hurdle, Champion Chase, Grand National, King George. Now I had won them all except one. I didn't know it at the time, but the Grand National was going to take a while.

If you had told me then that that would be the last time I would ride Best Mate, of course I would have been disappointed, but it was. Jim was back for his next Gold Cup, and his next, and when Jim wasn't available for the William Hill Chase at Exeter in November 2004, Timmy Murphy was called up. Just after Jim had retired and when Best Mate was running in what, lamentably, turned out to be his final race, in the Haldon Gold Cup back at Exeter in November 2005, Paul Carberry got the ride.

It later transpired that Henrietta didn't think that I suited Best Mate. She didn't think that my riding style was good for the horse; she thought that he travelled and jumped better for a rider who was quieter than me. It's true, Jim always sat still on him over a fence, but that was simply because he was too scared to move. Jim will tell you that himself.

There has been plenty of discussion down the years about my riding style not suiting certain horses. When Paul Nicholls asked me to ride Denman in the 2010 Gold Cup, there was lots of talk about the fact that my riding style wouldn't suit Denman, that he was used to the quieter style of Ruby and Sam Thomas. Sure enough, I gave them plenty of fodder when I fell off Denman in the Aon Chase the month before the Gold Cup, but I think that he ran as well as he could possibly have run in the Gold Cup when he finished second to Imperial Commander.

I am certain that I am not the most naturally talented rider in the weigh room. No way. There are lads in there who have much more natural ability than me. Ruby has natural talent oozing from every pore. Carberry has such an understanding of horses that I wouldn't be surprised if they discover in years to come that he is part-horse. I have no doubt that I have achieved the success that I have through graft and endeavour. And I'm not just saying that, I'm sure that it's true.

My attitude is simple – I want to get my horse from one side of a fence to the other as quickly as possible. I could be a quiet rider, I could sit still over a fence and allow the horse do his own thing, and I have no doubt that the horse would jump the fence, but he wouldn't jump it as quickly as he would with me helping him. I am not knocking quiet riders. Ruby Walsh is as quiet a rider as you will ever watch, and he is the best National Hunt rider I have ever ridden against. Paul Carberry is a quiet rider. Carberry can sit so still on a horse that he looks like he is playing a game of musical statues and the music has stopped. Jim Culloty was a quiet rider, and he won three Gold Cups on Best Mate.

Riders develop their own style. Whatever works. Horses travel for Ruby Walsh and Paul Carberry without the need for them to be overly animated in the saddle. They look quiet, but you can be sure that there is lots going on underneath. They don't look busy, their upper bodies may be motionless and their arms may not be flailing around all over the place, but you can be certain that their legs are at work, encouraging their horse, cajoling.

That's not me. I like to wind a horse up, encourage him into the bridle, convince him that he wants to run, make him believe that he can, that he can run faster than all his rivals, so I look busy.

It's a similar story when I am riding over a fence. When I see a stride four, five, six or seven strides from a fence, I ask the horse to go and jump the fence on that stride, jump on the stride that I have seen and think that he can make. If you don't ask him, there is a chance that he will lose that stride, that he will meet the fence a half a stride short or a half a stride long. Then he is either reaching for the fence or he has to go in and pop it, neither is ideal as you lose half a length or a length if you don't end up on the floor; you come away from the fence further back in the field than you want to be, and it makes it all more difficult. True, a horse uses up energy when you ride him into a fence, but if he jumps that fence well, it is energy well expended.

I didn't learn that from Billy Rock or from anyone; it was just a notion that I developed along the way, and I still subscribe to it. The elementaries of riding, however, I learned from Billy, so it was a sad day when I got the call on 19th April 2003 to say that Billy had passed away. He was 59, far, far too young, but he had been suffering from cancer for years. I had ridden Jack High for him at Punchestown just that February in a three-mile handicap hurdle in which we finished third. It was great to ride for him again, but it was a shame that we couldn't have won.

Actually, Jack High, who joined Ted Walsh after Billy's death, went on to win the Troytown Chase at Navan the following year for Ted, and to win the Betfred Gold Cup at Sandown, the old Whitbread, in 2005, ridden by Gareth Cotter. On top of that, he was only just beaten in the 2005 Irish Grand National by the 2006 Aintree Grand National winner Numbersixvalverde, ridden by Ruby Walsh. It killed Ruby to beat one of his dad's horses, but he still did it.

Billy's funeral was on Easter Monday. It was a desperately sad day, but I was glad that I was there and to be able to go home and sympathise with Billy's wife Yvonne and their children Timothy and Lynn. My dad was devastated. Billy had been my mentor in my early days, he was someone to whom I always turned when I needed advice, but he and Dad had developed a deep deep friendship, cemented by their common interest in horses and in me. They were a huge part of each other's lives and, to this day, I know that Dad misses Billy terribly.

I said a few words at the funeral. It wasn't easy to find the right words and then being able to say them in front of all those people without breaking down and looking like an eejit.

'Nobody will ever know how much I owe this man,' I said. 'He was my lifetime mentor and nothing was ever too much trouble for him. I will sorely miss him as a friend.' I meant every syllable.

The Irish Grand National was on the same day – I was due to ride the well-fancied Winning Dream for Oliver McKiernan. I considered not riding him, but then had a chat with Ted Walsh about it, I also spoke to my dad. I thought about what Billy would have wanted, and I concluded that Billy would have wanted me to ride in the race. He would have hated it if he thought that I didn't ride in the Irish Grand National because I was at his funeral.

So Ted and I got a lift with Seamus Ross in his helicopter from Cullybackey to Fairyhouse. I was desperate to win the Irish National that year; I would have loved to have won it and dedicated the victory to Billy. Alas, although Winning Dream ran a cracker, he just wasn't good enough on the day. We finished third, two lengths behind Timbera, Dessie Hughes's horse, ridden by Jim Culloty.

I ended the season on 258 winners, my eighth championship in a row, the fastest century ever, the fastest double-century ever, and a King George thrown in for good measure. Martin won his 13th trainers' championship and David Johnson won his third owners' championship. The season was a huge success for all of us, yet when I was asked on the last day of the season, Betfred Gold Cup day at Sandown, what I thought of the season just gone, I said that it had been a disaster.

It's incredible looking back now to think how myopic I was, how self-centred. I'd had 258 winners, 111 more than the next-best (Richard Johnson, inevitably), my second-highest total ever, and I'm going around with a long face and telling everyone that the season had been a disaster. I needed a kick up the arse, the arrogance of it. I suppose I was disappointed that Cheltenham hadn't gone so well, but I was more disappointed with the fact that I hadn't ridden 300 winners. I really wanted to ride 300 winners and I had been bang on track for it until I did my collarbone that day at Kempton.

The new season started at Hexham the following Monday. I rode Wensley Blue to win the second race, a Class G selling hurdle, and I was on my way again.

CHAPTER 25

Pain in the Arm

I wasn't going around with a long face on purpose, I wasn't putting it on. I wasn't going around saying that it was a disaster, wanting people to say ah no it wasn't AP, look at all the good things that happened, look at all you achieved. It's difficult to imagine what kind of a frame of mind you were in to term 258 winners a disaster.

The reality was that I was spoilt riding for Martin Pipe. I used to go racing expecting to ride only winners. If I had no winners, it would be a disaster. Even if I only had one, I used to come home disappointed, only one winner today, shocking. I was really only happy if I had three or four, and even then I'd be looking at the ones that got beaten and thinking that I should have won on them. These days if I have a winner, I think that I've had a good day.

I used to look at entries, see the horses that Martin had entered up in novice hurdles and novice chases, horses that had already won one or two, and I'd be thinking, there's another winner. Two certain winners at Newton Abbot on Tuesday, three at Taunton on Thursday. You'd be chalking up the winners you'd ride during the week before the week had even started.

The previous year, the year I rode 289 winners, anybody could have won on most of the 189 winners that I rode for Martin. I'm sure that Martin himself could have won on a hundred of them. So it didn't matter who was riding them, I was just lucky to be sitting on them and steering them, to be the one clocking up the winners.

In June 2003 I received a letter telling me that I was going to be awarded an MBE. That was a bit of a bolt from the blue, and it was a huge honour, but I found myself stopping and thinking about it for a minute. When you are raised a Catholic in Northern Ireland, you don't really think that you will ever be awarded an MBE.

I called my mother to tell her the news and ask her what she thought.

'Martin O'Neill has an MBE, doesn't he?' she reasoned. 'And he's managing Celtic, isn't he?'

My mother was delighted, and that was good enough for me. It was a huge honour. Racing people like Lester Piggott, Richard Dunwoody, John Reid and Peter Scudamore had all been honoured by the Queen in the past, so it was wonderful for me to be among that group.

My only regret was that Billy Rock wasn't alive to see it. He would have been thrilled for me, as proud as punch, and he would have got great mileage out of it as well, the man who used to tease my mum about dressing me up in the Unionist regalia and taking me marching.

It might have been tricky for me to receive an MBE a generation ago, but not these days. Times have moved on. I think also, when the Queen visited Ireland in May 2011, she won over a lot of Irish people with her awareness of the history that the two countries have shared. I was awarded an OBE in 2011, and I was very honoured by that as well.

I have ridden for the Queen, I have ridden winners for the Queen, I rode my first winner for her on Barbers Shop in a novices' chase at Newbury in April 2008, and I have been proud to do so. I was lucky enough to be invited to Buckingham Palace for lunch with the Queen with Conor O'Dwyer and Nick Skelton.

Chanelle and I were invited to Zara Phillips's 21st birthday party in Windsor Castle. Zara, one of the Queen's granddaughters, went out with Dickie Johnson for a while, and Chanelle and I got to know her well during that time. We were at her 30th birthday as well in May 2011, and I had a good chat with her mother, Princess Anne, about racing. It was a bit bizarre because it was a fancy dress party, and there was I, in this mad seventies gear, gold medallion, under this big Afro wig, having this serious conversation with Princess Anne about racing.

I broke my arm at Worcester that summer, during Royal Ascot week actually. I was travelling well on a horse called Kymberlya, a horse of Martin's, owned by Peter Deal, who had owned Make A Stand and Blowing Wind. We were just going around the home turn when something went on the horse and he came down. I think he broke his shoulder.

When you are going around a turn, you are not expecting to fall. At least when you are jumping a hurdle or a fence, you know that you are leaving the ground, you know there is a chance that you will end up with muck in your mouth on the landing side of the obstacle, but when you fall galloping around a turn, you are taken by surprise. Thirty miles per hour, sitting pretty, then wham.

I got my arm caught in a divot on the ground or something and it just snapped. Like all these breaks, I knew it was gone straight away. It was my first proper break since that January morning when I broke my leg off Kly Green in Jim Bolger's. I had had injuries since then of course, and I had fractured vertebrae when Merry Gale buried me in the Marlborough Cup, but this was just my second proper break, and my first in 10 years.

So I got into the ambulance, went to Worcester Hospital and got some morphine, my old friend. They operated on my arm on the Thursday morning, I stayed overnight and went home the following morning. I wasn't feeling too bad when I got home, but by lunchtime I was getting a desperate pain in my arm, I was getting very hot and thinking, crap, my arm is sore, I didn't think it would be this sore. I didn't want to be ringing the doctor and telling him that my arm is sore, I had broken it after all, so I just kept pumping a few painkillers, and it wasn't too bad. Then at around six o'clock in the evening I felt light-headed and started sweating a lot. My arm was pumping. Again I'm thinking, don't say anything, don't ring anyone, you don't want to be soft, nobody ever died of a broken arm, so I popped a few more painkillers and went to bed.

I hadn't been in bed long when I started sweating again. I felt cold but I was dripping with sweat. On top of that, my arm was getting sorer and I was taking more painkillers. The more I took, the more I was sweating.

I did manage to fall asleep, and when I woke up the pain had eased a bit, so I was thinking, not too bad then. Then at lunchtime the following day, I started to sweat again. My arm started to feel very sore again, like it wanted to burst out through the plaster, and all I could think was that they put the plaster on too tight. I was sitting on the couch in the sitting room at around five o'clock, my arm on fire. I was eating more painkillers than you could imagine; I'd say my heart should have come out through my chest, I had that many of them.

It hadn't got any better by bedtime, and Chanelle was getting very concerned. She called Gee, and Gee called Doctor Pritchard. Doc Pritchard is my go-to doctor for just about everything. He is a top man and a thorough professional. I trust him implicitly. If he recommends a specialist, I know that I am getting the best, someone I can trust, and all of that is really important when you get as many injuries as jump jockeys get.

As it happened, Doc Pritchard was at a wedding when Gee called him, but it didn't matter, he diagnosed my problem there and then down the phone. He told Gee that it was Compartment Syndrome. He told her to get me to the Great Western Hospital in Swindon as quickly as possible, and that he would have a surgeon there waiting for me. Sure enough, there was a surgeon waiting for me at the Great Western. He cut the plaster open and said that I had to be operated on immediately. You get Compartment Syndrome, apparently, when the blood vessels get compressed in a part of your body, usually on your arm or your leg, and it leads to the death of tissue.

They operated on me that night. I remember being in the theatre and thinking, ah heaven. I just wanted to be knocked out, to escape from the sweating and pain. There were complications though, so they had to leave the wound in my arm open, so I was lying there with my arm under a cover – I couldn't move it. I had to stay in hospital.

That was on Saturday. I went back into theatre on Monday thinking they were going to close the wound, but that didn't work, they couldn't close it. That was my second anaesthetic on the Monday. Then they said on Wednesday they were going to try to close it, but again they couldn't. I was forming a close friendship with the anaesthetist at this stage, my third encounter with him in five days. He'd say count to ten, and I'd think, right, I'm going to beat this thing, I'm going to try to stay awake. One, two, three, four. Next thing I know, I'm waking up and they're telling me that they couldn't close my arm up.

I woke up Wednesday evening and felt really sick. I remember having a glass of water and throwing up straight away. And I'm never sick. Then I tried to eat something, which probably wasn't the cleverest thing to do, but I was starving. Unsurprisingly, it just came straight back up.

The only thing I was able to keep down was strawberries. I had a couple of strawberries and that was okay. All day Thursday I was just sick. I wanted to eat, I was starving, but I just couldn't keep anything down. I remember going into the anaesthetist on Friday to try to have my arm closed again, and they had a plastic surgeon there. They said that there was a chance that they would have to do a skin graft; the wound was so open.

Again I was delighted to see the anaesthetist. I wanted to be knocked out. I told him that since I had woken up on Wednesday, I wasn't looking forward to seeing anyone again as much as I was looking forward to seeing him. I'm sure he thought I was mad. Most people go in for an anaesthetic, a bit worried about going under, and here's me going, here I am Doc, knock me out again.

They managed to close it up on the Friday – it was fine. I woke up and

I didn't feel too bad. But the doctor who did the surgery told Chanelle that if I had waited another night I could have lost my right arm. If I had kept taking painkillers and waited until Sunday, she said it was that bad that you would definitely have lost the power in your right arm, and I could have lost the limb completely. Doc Pritchard saves the day again. I would only have been able to ride at left-handed tracks.

I was out for over two months, so that was that, no more records, no 300 winners in a season, another season gone. Actually, when I returned on 22nd August at Fontwell, Dickie Johnson had gone 18 winners ahead of me in the championship. I rode a winner for Gary Moore on my first day back, Flying Spirit in a novices' hurdle. I used to ride a lot for Gary and a lot of winners for him too, but that was before his son Jamie came along wanting to ride winners too. I can't believe that blood is thicker than water.

I got a bit panicked when Dickie went past me in the championship. The greatest fear I have in my career is that I won't be champion, so when another rider goes 18 clear of you, even as good a guy as Dickie Johnson, it has to cause you a certain degree of angst. You don't want to open the window even a little, you don't want to give anyone else the chance to drum up that wave of momentum. You want to snuff them out early in the season by going so far clear that it is not even a possibilty. Don't even think about it.

Ever since I won my first championship, I have always lived in fear that I would lose it. And if and when the time comes when I am not champion, then that will be the time for me to say enough. Unless I have missed a lot of time during the season through injury or something. I'm not taking anything for granted, but the way I look at it, if the time comes when I am not champion jockey, if I am beaten on merit, then it's because I am not as good as I once was, and it will be time to stop.

I wanted to win more championships than Peter Scudamore (eight), then I wanted to win more than Charlie Swan and Frank Berry had won in Ireland (10 each). I had drawn level with Scu that year, and I was going all out to win my ninth.

That's the difficulty with the championship. You go all out to win it, you win it, then it's back to zero for the start of the following season. The only time you can really relax about it is in April if you are lucky enough to have built up an unassailable lead. The early months of the season are the most difficult, when there is no champion jockey and all the clocks go back to zero. My valet Shane Clarke, who works for Chirs Maude, has great craic at that time of year.

'Not going so well this season Champ, are we?'

'Huh?'

'You're one behind. And the really worrying thing is that you're only six in front of Daryl.'

Daryl Jacob is a good rider. Shane knows that, he just likes having a laugh.

'Do you think I should tell Paddy Brennan that Gina Andrews has ridden more winners than him this season?'

I was asked after I rode 3,000 winners if I thought it was possible to ride 4,000 winners. In order to do that, all things being equal, I would probably have to go on riding until I was 39 or 40. Then you get to thinking, can I actually still be riding when I am 39 or 40? I always thought that I would retire when I was 35, yet here I am at 37, still riding.

How long should you go on? Physically, I don't think I have ever been in better shape, even now at 37. I have always looked after my body, I have always been fit. I am heavier than a lot of other jockeys, and I think that has protected me in a way. I think my body is quite hard.

For the last 15 years, I have ridden between 800 and 1,000 horses per year. That's a lot of rides, that's a lot of pushing and kicking, a lot of physical exertion, and that will get you fit and get your muscles hard. And I don't think the falls hurt any more now than they did when I was younger. I broke my leg in 1993, I broke my arm in 2003, I broke my back in 2008, and they were all sore. If anything, I think that I am better equipped to deal with the pain in the last few years. Sometimes it's a mental thing – how much pain can you stand?

Psychologically, I always think that as long as I am happy enough to crash, I can keep riding. Am I happy enough to drive a horse into a fence? Am I happy to put myself into a position where I could be involved in a pile-up, am I happy to push my horse into a fence in the middle of a load of other horses, and if we go down we go down, suffer the consequences if we do? And I think, yeah, drive on.

I see myself on the approach to a fence or a hurdle late on in a race, the third-last, second-last or last, and I'll be inclined to give a horse a kick into it. You can't do it every time, sometimes you are just meeting it on a wrong stride and you have to sit, but more often than not you can find that stride, and when I do I like to boot the horse into the obstacle.

As long as I am going forward, even on a tired horse, I think that we have a chance. That's my mentality now. I don't know if it will ever change, I don't know if there will come a time when I will think, hold on a second, I'm not sure about this, take a pull. At the moment, I can't ever see that happening, but who knows. I might get scared one day. At the moment though, I don't really see it as not being scared, I just see it as being realistic. It makes sense that if you get your horse going forward you have a better chance of getting over the fence than if you are slowing him up.

I don't think my mentality is any different now to how it was 10 years ago. I have never trusted a horse in my life. I have never trusted a horse to do the right thing; I have always felt that I needed to get him to do what I wanted him to do. I'd never go out on a bad jumper and think, this is going to fall. I'd go out on him thinking, I'll get you to jump around. I suppose an extension of that mentality is that I am happy to ride a bad jumper if he has a chance of winning. The flip side is that I wouldn't go out and ride a good jumper if he had no chance of winning.

It's not a case of being brave or being big-headed; I just always think that I can get a horse to jump. I am on the horse, I have control. I have always felt that I could get a horse to do what I want it to do.

It's difficult to teach mentality though. I was down at Sam Curling's place one day. Sam is a son of Peter Curling, the equine artist. He used to ride for Aidan O'Brien, he was St Nicholas Abbey's work rider in his younger days, and he started to keep horses over here when he left Aidan's. Anyway, he told me that one of his lads wanted to ask me to give his girlfriend a riding lesson as a birthday present. I said no problem, so Sam organised the horse and I met the girl in his indoor school.

She had ridden in a couple of point-to-points, but I was scratching my head, wondering how she ever completed it as I watched her ride around the indoor school. I was trying not to be too critical, to just tell her where I wanted her hands, where I wanted her feet in her irons, her heels. I told her to envisage herself on the horse, think of how she wanted to look and then put all her bits in those places.

I don't think I'm a very good teacher as she wasn't getting it, so I got her down off the horse and had her stand on the ground and put all her bits in the places that they should be on the horse. If it was difficult for her to get it right on the ground, so she had no chance on a horse. Like I say, I don't think I will be taking up teaching when I retire.

Actually, Chanelle was thinking a little while ago about going back to ride in a charity race. She enjoyed riding Bamapour, and thought she might enjoy a charity race. So I said right, if you're going to do this, you're going to do it right. I'm going to train you, and you're going to win. She seemed to go off the idea after that.

Three days after the riding lesson incident, I was playing golf with John Francome and I was telling him the story.

'A riding lesson, was it?' said Johnny in his drawn Francome accent. 'What kind of a riding lesson was that then?'

Typical Francome.

'She wasn't getting it at all,' I continued. (Ignoring Francome's innuendo is usually the best way to go.) 'I mean, how difficult can it be to ride a horse?'

Johnny stepped back from his ball.

'You know when you go down to Donnington?' he said.

Donnington Grove, where we often play golf. I nodded.

'And you know when Matt Woods gives you a lesson?'

Rhetorical.

'Well, you can be sure when you're there digging holes in his driving range, he's thinking, surely playing golf can't be that fucking difficult!'

CHAPTER 26

2000 Not Out

At Cheltenham, on New Year's Eve 2003, I got suspended for five days for my ride on Deano's Beeno before we lined up at the start.

Deano's Beeno wasn't everybody's cup of tea, but believe it or not, he was a horse that I used to love riding. I admired him. I often thought that if I was a horse, I would be Deano's Beeno. He had bundles of ability, but he wasn't going to use it just because somebody else wanted him to use it. He was going to use it if and when he wanted to use it, and on his own terms.

You wouldn't know what he was going to do though, or when he was going to do it, and this day it seemed that he was going to be particularly reluctant to line up at the start, so I wanted to keep him on the move as long as possible before we had to line up, otherwise there was an even greater chance that he wouldn't line up or consent to race. So I was cajoling him around at the start, squeezing him along, slapping him down the shoulder with my whip, just little slaps, just to keep him moving. Any time I stopped, he stopped, so I had to keep him on the go.

He did line up and he did consent to race, and I wasn't at all hard on him in the race itself, I didn't use my stick that much at all. He was up with the pace for most of the way, we were passed at the fourth last and he just faded up the home straight.

I couldn't believe it when the stewards had me in afterwards – I had no idea what I had done wrong. The horse wasn't marked or anything, I had just been slapping him gently down the shoulder before the start, just to keep him on the move. The stewards said that I hit the horse 50 times before the start, which was a joke. They weren't hits, it was more the noise of the whip than the physical impact on the horse. I'd hit myself 50 times down the leg in the same way.

William Nunnelly was the stipendiary steward that day. Coincidence? I didn't think so. I was sure that he had it in for me, that he had some kind of an agenda, a vendetta against me. I have changed my opinion

223

on that one, I get on great with William now, I regard him as a very good judge, and if I get suspended now when William is stewarding, I invariably deserve the suspension. Maybe he has changed, maybe my mentality has changed, maybe there's a little bit of both.

I'm not sure about the quality of stewarding in general in the UK though. William is now in the minority as a stipendiary steward who is able to apply common sense to a situation. Sometimes I feel that they just apply the letter of the law without using common sense. They pick up the book, yeah the book says he should get three days for that, here have three days. It appears to be different in Ireland, where stewards seem to apply more common sense.

That's not to say that racing in Ireland is better than in the UK. On the contrary, I don't really enjoy riding in Ireland that much, which is a shame. There are a couple of things that I can't work out about Ireland. The country is in a mess economically, but the prize money in racing is great compared to the UK. But here's what I can't understand. In the UK, jockeys are treated like professionals. We have physios at every track, we have caterers in all the weigh rooms, you can eat whatever you want, good food, you can have your dinner, you can have a salad. That's not the case in Ireland.

Also, in the UK, if you say that something isn't safe at a racetrack, they'll do something about it. They'll listen to the senior riders who know about these things. Maybe they are afraid of claims if something happens, but the reason is not important, the fact is that they act on the opinions of the jockeys.

That is not the case in Ireland. You could have 25 runners in a big race at one of the big meetings in Ireland, and you could have fallers on the flat. How is that safe? If you complain, they'll say your bottle is gone, McCoy has lost his nerve.

I went to Gowran Park on Thyestes Chase day last year, their biggest day of the year. I had four or five rides, but no winners. It lashed down all day and we got a right soaking every time we went out: bottomless ground, mud and shit everywhere. I went into the weigh room at the end of the day, got into the shower, put shampoo in my hair and turned the shower on. No water. I couldn't believe it. It wasn't just that the showers were cold, there was simply no water, hot or cold. I had to put my head in the sink to try to wash the shampoo out.

The biggest day of the year at Gowran Park, and there was no water for the jockeys to have a shower afterwards. Someone told me that there had been no water at the previous meeting either. So it wasn't that they didn't know about it, they had known about it from the previous meeting, it was just that nobody bothered to do anything about it. It wouldn't happen in any other sport at this level, and Ireland is supposed to be a world leader in thoroughbred racing.

I went to Wincanton on 4th January 2004 and rode Corporate Player for Noel Chance to win the first race, that was winner number 1,999, then two hours later I went out on another of Martin's, Magical Bailiwick, and won the three-mile handicap chase, number 2,000 – another milestone, another landmark.

You don't stay on a high for too long in this game though. Five weeks later I was riding Polar Red, the horse on whom I had won the Imperial Cup two years previously, in a novices' chase at Plumpton, when he made a mistake at the second fence and sent me flying. He didn't actually fall, but he knocked me out of the saddle and onto his neck. I tried to stay on him, I was hanging off his neck, but gravity was winning the battle. It's a horrible feeling. There you are, hanging off the horse's neck, knowing that you have passed the point of no return, the only way you can go is down, down into the horse's flailing hooves beneath you. You brace yourself for a good kicking, hope for the best and let go.

I didn't get the best. He kneed me in the face on my way down and then proceeded to trample all over me. I knew it wasn't good as I lay on the ground. My face swelled up like a football, my lip and gum went numb. I couldn't feel the left side of my face, blood was pouring from my cheek. Later I found out that I had fractured it in three places.

Luckily, though, it hadn't been displaced too badly. I didn't need an operation, I just needed to give it time to heal. But not too much time, this was 16th February – the Cheltenham Festival was only a month away. I rang Doc Pritchard.

'I've broken my cheekbone Doc,' I told him.

'How bad is it?' he asked.

'It's not too bad,' I said. 'It's not displaced, I don't need an operation.'

'What did they say?'

'They're telling me I'm going to be out for weeks,' I said. 'But look, I don't need my cheekbone to ride, do I?'

'Leave it with me,' said Doc. 'I'll see what I can do.'

Genius that Doc Pritchard is, he knew a guy in Blackpool who had made masks for a couple of football players who had broken cheekbones in the past. The worry with me was the kickback, the muck that comes flying back at you when you are in behind horses. My cheek was tender, the last thing it needed was to be hit with a piece of flying mud.

So I got this mask made and fitted to my face, and I was only out for less than two weeks. I did miss the ride on Our Vic in the Reynoldstown Chase at Ascot the following Saturday. Timmy Murphy rode him and won. I would say that that ride went a long way towards making the case for Timmy as David Johnson's retained rider after I left Martin's. I was back riding at Kempton the following Saturday, looking like Zorro and feeling a bit stupid, but I rode two winners, so not so stupid.

The feeling never came back to my face. To this day, my left cheek is numb. I put my hand up and touch my left cheek – it feels like I am touching something else. I can't feel a thing. My top lip is always numb as well. Most of the time it doesn't bother me, I don't notice it. It's only when it comes up in conversation, when my attention is drawn to it, that it annoys me. The doctor said that the nerves in your face grow back at the rate of a micrometre a year or something, so it takes a while.

I had a black eye for weeks. If I sneezed or coughed, or if I blew my nose, my eyes would go all bloodshot. I managed to get the mask off for Cheltenham, I just wore a plaster, which didn't look any less stupid but at least it wasn't as cumbersome under my goggles.

It is imperative for a National Hunt jockey to have a good doctor. We spend so much time dealing with doctors, it is important that we know that they know what they are doing. Doc Pritchard is fantastic in that regard; I will always ring him to ask him what he thinks of a particular doctor before I allow anybody near me. If he doesn't know himself, he will find out.

I won the Arkle on Well Chief at Cheltenham that year. He was really inexperienced over fences, he had only run in one chase before Cheltenham. I thought he had a chance, but I didn't fancy him that strongly. I was thinking, one run at Taunton and then the Arkle? That's a big ask.

I was supposed to ride him handily, that was the plan, but he was keen with me in the early stages, so I decided to drop him back just to get him settled, get him to drop the bridle and conserve his energy. Going down the far side, we started to pass one or two, and I was thinking, you know we might just go well here. I took it up from Barry Geraghty and Kicking King – who would go on to win the following year's Gold Cup – over the second-last, got the last all wrong, gave Barry another chance, but my fellow picked up well on the run-in and went away again. He followed up in the Maghull Chase at Aintree three weeks later. He was a good horse.

Well Chief was the only winner I rode at Cheltenham that year, but it didn't stop me going on a golf break with Carl Llewellyn, Mick Fitzgerald and Shane O'Donoghue, a very good friend of Fitzy's. It developed into an annual event. Between Cheltenham and Aintree, as long as I am far enough clear in the championship that nobody can catch me, the four of us head off to Portugal or somewhere warm to play golf and have a bit of craic. We invariably do both. It's hard not to play golf or have craic when Carl and Fitzy are on the team.

I chose to ride Jurancon, one of seven Martin Pipe representatives, in the Grand National. He was sent off as one of the 10/1 co-favourites, but we fell at the fourth fence. Another year down, another chance gone, another 12 months to wait.

I rode Stormez in the Whitbread Gold Cup on the final day of the season. Martin was running seven horses in it, and I thought that Stormez was the best of them. I certainly wasn't going to ride Puntal anyway, that was for sure. I thought that Martin was mad running him in it, as did David, Martin's son and effectively his assistant trainer at the time.

Puntal was a two-mile chaser, in my opinion, who probably got two and a half miles. On top of that, he was only a novice. But the Puntal case is just another example of the genius of Martin Pipe. There was a reason for everything that Martin did. Puntal won the Whitbread with Danny Howard riding him, he got home by a short head from Royal Auclair, the horse on whom I had won the Cathcart Chase two years previously, who was now with Paul Nicholls. I got to watch the finish all right, because little Stormez had unseated me at the third fence.

I won my ninth jockeys' championship that day though, with 209 winners, beating Richard Johnson by 23, beating Peter Scudamore's record of eight. Rewind eight days though. Something happened that meant that a completely different challenge awaited me the following season.

CHAPTER 27

Changing Horses

Cheltenham's April meeting is a fairly low-key affair compared with its March Festival. I suppose most things are low-key affairs compared with the Cheltenham Festival, but I still like their April meeting: the weather is usually good, the atmosphere is fairly relaxed, and it's nice to get back riding at the track where you were a month earlier, when you were in the middle of the crowds and the pressure cooker and when the significance of wins and losses was magnified by a thousand.

It was at the previous year's Cheltenham April meeting in 2003 that Jonjo O'Neill had first mentioned to me the possibility of riding for him and JP McManus. Jonjo is an amazing man. Born in Cork, he came to England as a young aspirant jockey in the early 1970s. He went home after a couple of months – he hated the place, he couldn't understand anyone ('Have you ever been to Cumbria?!') and nobody could understand him, so he packed his bag and headed home again. Gordon Richards managed to convince him to come back, and his first four rides for Gordon were winners.

He kicked on from there to become one of the best National Hunt riders of his generation: he was champion jockey twice, he won the Gold Cup on Alverton in 1979, the Champion Hurdle on Sea Pigeon in 1980, and, of course, famously, he won the Champion Hurdle and the Gold Cup on Dawn Run in 1984 and 1986, the only horse and rider to win both, ever.

Life has dealt him a couple of harsh blows, mind you. He was struck down with cancer when he was 34. He fell off Nohalmdun in the Scottish Champion Hurdle at Ayr a month after he won the Gold Cup on Dawn Run, and he knew that he wasn't well, that it was time to hang up his boots.

The doctors thought that it was glandular fever in the beginning. Jonjo had already starting training horses when he went in for more tests and was diagnosed with cancer. He had 24 horses in training at the time. He wrote to all his owners to tell them that he had to stop for a while. All of them told him to let them know when he was better, when he was ready to resume training, that they would send horses again. Two years later he was back training again and contacted all his old owners. Two of them sent him a horse. Just two. It was a lesson for Jonjo in how tough his new career was going to be.

But Jonjo is tough and he can train, and he got back going again. When he learned that Colin Smith, owner of Jackdaws Castle when the late David Nicholson trained there, was putting the place up for sale, Jonjo spotted an opportunity. He loved Jackdaws Castle, he loved the set-up, the facilities, and thought it was ideal as a centre for training racehorses. With the help of JP McManus, he got the funds together and bought the place. Now, even though JP owns a lot of the horses that Jonjo trains, Jonjo is very much his own trainer. He has other owners there besides JP, and he would love to have more.

JP McManus is a unique individual. He has always been a punter; one of his earliest bets was in the 1962 Cesarewitch, a bob each way at 25/1 on Orchardist, who won the race, but was disqualified and placed second. He made his way as a bookmaker and a punter, and he bought his first horse in 1976, Cill Dara, who won the Naas November Handicap and the Irish Cesarewitch later that year.

More than anything else, JP is a horse-racing fan. You couldn't under-estimate the amount of time that he spends studying racing, thinking about racing, his horses, potential targets, prospects. He simply loves the game. He can ring me at any time of the day or night to discuss a horse or a race, and I am frequently amazed at the depth of his knowledge, not only of his own horses, but also of others.

He is obviously a huge supporter of National Hunt racing. There are a lot of trainers who would have fewer horses, fewer staff, bleaker prospects, were it not for JP's investment. Also, he is an unsung hero of many charities. He is a silent donator. It isn't that he doesn't seek publicity for his donations, he actively shuns it. Like I say, he is quite a unique individual. And he couldn't have married a nicer person than Noreen. She is one in a million.

When Jonjo asked me about riding for him and JP in April 2003 though, I didn't think it looked like a good move. I always liked Jonjo a lot as a person, and I always thought he was a good trainer and loved riding his horses, but all I cared about was riding lots of winners, winning lots of races, winning championships, breaking records, and nobody could compete with Martin Pipe in that regard at the time. When he mentioned it to me again though, 12 months later, it was a different story.

On 14th April 2004, the first day of Cheltenham's two-day April fixture, I had just ridden Seebald to win a two-mile handicap chase when Jonjo came up to me and asked me if I would be interested in talking to the boss about the job. The boss, I presumed, was JP. The job, I presumed, was the job that he had spoken to me briefly about 12 months earlier, when I had politely shaken my head.

Things had changed a little in those 12 months though. There were signs that Martin's absolute dominance was being threatened. Paul Nicholls was on the move. Also, Jonjo was competing. In the previous couple of years he had established himself as a top three four trainer, he and Philip Hobbs were contending for the third spot in the trainers' ranks after Martin and Paul, and he was on an upward curve, he had some nice young horses and JP was investing in more.

I told Jonjo that I would meet with JP; it couldn't hurt to have a chat. So we agreed that we would meet in the Lygon Arms in Broadway the following day after racing.

I have to say, I was a bit nervous going into the Lygon Arms. For starters, I was nervous in case people saw me going in. Broadway is a quiet little village and people talk. As well as that, I had never really sat down and had a conversation with JP before. I had ridden for him plenty, but all of my encounters with him were in the parade ring before a race or in the unsaddling area afterwards. I don't think I had ever spoken to him when I wasn't wearing his green and gold hooped silks.

I met with JP in his suite. Jonjo was there, along with Frank Berry, JP's racing manager. It was all very pleasant, very straightforward: how would you feel about coming to ride for us, about being our retained rider? We're going to have a lot more good horses than we have had, we're building up our numbers, strengthening our team, that kind of thing. There's still a good chance that you'll be champion jockey. JP knew that that was my main focus. It was all very encouraging.

'So what do you think?' JP asked.

'It's very interesting,' I said.

'Are you interested in coming to work for us then?' he asked.

'I am,' I said.

I did a fair bit of humming and hawing, but by the end of the conversation, he had got me to commit to the job. That's JP's way, get things sorted, make a decision one way or the other. If my decision had been not to jump, that would have been fine too, but at least I would have made a decision and we all would have known where we stood.

'I'll have to speak to Martin before I speak to anybody else,' I told JP.

'No problem,' he said. 'Can you speak to him tomorrow?'

I was a bit taken aback. I was thinking that maybe I'd have a couple of days to think about this a little more, a week maybe, so that I could perhaps talk to a couple of people, make sure I was doing the right thing, before having to tell Martin. It was a bit naïve of me though. I was after committing to the job, I was after giving my word, I couldn't really be going back on it now even if I did realise afterwards that I had just traded a Maserati for a Morris Minor.

There had been a couple of rumours doing the rounds beforehand, linking me to Jonjo, linking me to JP, probably spawned by Jonjo mentioning the job to me the previous year. I heard them, and I was amazed that the ears of the racing world were so sensitive, and had so little else with which to be occupied. One mention from Jonjo to me, and suddenly the talk begins.

I hadn't really thought about it too deeply before I went to meet JP and Jonjo in Broadway that day, which was probably a bit of a mistake on my part. I had had a day and a half to think about it, but I didn't really use that time properly to deliberate on what was going to be a career-shifting decision. It was the most difficult decision that I have ever had to make in my life, professional or personal, by a million miles.

I didn't speak to my dad or Chanelle about it, or to Carl or Fitzy. I didn't even mention it to them. The only person I spoke to was Dave Roberts, and even then it was only after racing on the Thursday, about an hour before I was due to meet JP. I didn't seek Dave's advice, and he didn't give it. That's Dave for you. He just listened quietly.

'Which way are you thinking?' he asked.

'I don't know, Dave,' I said. 'I haven't got a clue.'

'Do you think you can still be champion jockey if you are riding for Jonjo and not Martin?' he asked.

Dave was great at asking the key questions.

'I think I can,' I said.

Before I walked into the Lygon Arms that day, I had no idea which way I was going to go. I should have known, I should have decided beforehand, but I didn't. During the conversation, though, it all seemed very attractive, it all seemed like a good idea. It was only when JP asked me if I could let Martin know the following day that it hit me – this was for real.

I walked out of the Lygon Arms in a daze. Was I crazy? Giving up the

best job in racing to jump into an unknown? What had I just committed to? And how the hell was I going to tell Martin?

I drove home that evening with a hole in my stomach. I hardly slept
a wink that night. Everything was turning around in my head, all I had
just agreed to give up, the uncertain future, how I was going to cope
with someone else winning on Martin's horses. How was I going to
cope if someone else was champion jockey?

I rang Martin the following morning and told him that I wanted to go
and see him that evening, that I had something I wanted to talk to him
about. I'm sure he knew. I arrived about seven o'clock in the evening,
Martin opened the door, shook my hand, how are you, into the kitchen,
Carol is there, David is there, and I'm thinking, they know.

'Cup of tea?'

If I drank at all, I would have asked for something stronger.

'Look,' I said after a couple of minutes. There was no point in delay-
ing this, no point in dancing around it, I just had to get it out there.

'I've been offered another job.'

Martin nodded.

'Is it JP?' he asked, straight away.

'It is.'

'And what are you going to do?' he asked.

'I'm going to take it, Martin,' I said, choking on the words. 'I've told
him I'm going to take it.'

There was a silence then. It probably lasted a second or two, but it
felt like hours. I didn't know what else to say. I had a million different
thoughts in my head, all he did for me, the times we had had, the victo-
ries we had shared, the trebles, the four-timers, the bad times, Valiramix
and Gloria Victis, always in it together, the wavelength we shared.

'He's obviously paying you a retainer?' he asked.

'He is,' I said. 'But it's not about the money.'

'If we speak to the owners,' Martin said. 'We have a lot of good owners here. I'm sure if I speak to them and tell them the situation, we
could come up with a retainer that will match what JP is paying you.'

'It's not about the retainer, Martin,' I said. 'It's not about the money.'

It wasn't about the money. Despite what was written in the papers
and what was said afterwards, it wasn't about the money. Sure, there
was a retainer, but people were saying that JP was paying me £1 million
a year. He wasn't, but it didn't matter. It wasn't about that. If it had been
only about the money, I would have taken up Martin's offer of a retainer
with him and kept on going the way I was going.

Some of the reporting afterwards annoyed me quite a bit. There was a tone in the reporting on my move that I was only doing it for the money, that I was selling out, that I was giving up on breaking more records and winning more championships, that I was giving up the challenge. Nothing could have been further from the truth.

I quite liked the idea of a new challenge, of coming out of my comfort zone and trying to kick on again for a new outfit. The way things looked at the time, I could have gone on riding for Martin Pipe and being champion jockey forever. But I wondered if I would be happy with that. The reality is that almost anybody could have been champion jockey riding for Martin Pipe. Martin was so dominant that his stable jockey was almost automatically champion. I was lucky that I was his stable jockey for seven years, and I was champion for those seven years, but I'm sure that if any one of the top 20 jockeys in the weigh room had been riding for Martin instead of me at the time, they would have been champion jockey as well. In a perverse kind of way, I quite liked the idea of proving to myself and to others that I could be champion jockey while not riding for Martin.

As well as that, I got on well with Jonjo and I admired JP – this was an opportunity to ride for people I liked. Not that I didn't like Martin or get on with him. Martin was a father-figure to me. But this was a new challenge and it was one that, on many levels, I was desperate to take on.

'I hated the idea of coming down here and telling you this,' I said to Martin. 'I'm really sorry. It's the worst thing I've ever had to do. It's the toughest decision I have ever had to make in my life.'

Then I had to go up and tell Martin's mother. That was nearly worse than having to tell Martin. I got on great with Betty Pipe. Her house was just up from Martin's home, and I used to call in to see her a lot. Sometimes I would stop to see her on the way home from Taunton; I'd just call into her house without going down to see Martin, although sometimes he'd see my car there and come up.

She knew that I loved grapes, and she used to send a little bag of grapes with Martin to the races for me. If I was doing a light weight, she would put a couple of wine gums in with the grapes, hidden in the bag disguised as grapes, just as a little sugar boost for me. Even after I moved to Jonjo's, even after I left Martin, Betty would still send a bag of grapes to the races with Martin for me. She was a great lady. It was very sad when she died a couple of years ago.

I stayed for a couple of hours with Martin, Carol and David, just drinking tea in the sitting room. We got to talking about all the win-ners and all the losers, all the good times and bad times we had been through together. It was like a wake. It was as if somebody had died.

We spoke about the fallouts, and I convinced them that they were all my fault. They were. That time I told Martin never to speak like that to me again – after I had been late to meet his owners at Cheltenham on the day that we won the Arkle and the Champion Hurdle – he should have told me to piss off, the little shit that I was. I would never speak to anyone like that now, least of all Martin Pipe.

I learned so much from Martin: about horses, about race tactics, about life. As well as that, he had become one of my best friends. It was a big operation, and winning was everything, but I never felt under pressure to perform. Everything was easy. I suppose that had a lot to do with the fact that we had a very similar mentality – we were almost always on the same wavelength.

It was late when I got up to leave. I hugged David, hugged Carol, hugged Martin. I got into my car and cried all the way home.

CHAPTER 28

Worst Day Ever

My life didn't change radically with the new job, but there were subtle differences. For starters, there was the retainer – it was the first time in my life that I had ever been given a retainer, and as a result I felt under pressure to perform.

I hadn't thought about that one much beforehand. I was getting paid just for my commitment to ride for Jonjo and JP, regardless of how I did. That was an unusual situation, but instead of allowing me to relax, safe in the knowledge that I had an income even if I never rode a winner, it had the opposite effect. It had me thinking, I'm getting paid this extra money, I need to perform.

The other change lay in the subtle difference in attitude between Martin and Jonjo. With Martin, every horse had to win every race. Every horse was very fit before it set foot on the racecourse, and every horse was ridden to exploit a fitness advantage that he often enjoyed over most of his rivals. With Martin, today was the day every day.

With Jonjo and JP though, it was a slower burn. JP is the most patient man I have ever met in my life. Don't be hard on them the first day. Horses were brought along gradually. JP didn't like the gun being put to his young horses' heads too early in their career; it was more important that they had a positive experience of racing.

People had started talking about my riding style, that I could only ride from the front, that I could only ride the Martin Pipe way, kick off and go hard early, and they wondered how that style would fit in with the JP ethos. After a while riding for JP, people told me that I was a better rider now since I started riding for JP, that I could ride differently, more patiently, that I didn't have to give horses a kick in the belly as soon as the tapes went up and go as fast as I could for as long as I could.

Bollocks. Absolute bollocks. I have always ridden horses in such a way as to suit the horse, to maximise his chance of winning. The thing with Martin's horses was that you usually maximised their chance of winning by going from the front, exploiting their fitness edge. But even when I was with Martin, I rode patient races when I needed to. I won an Arkle on Well Chief from the back, I won a County Hurdle on Blowing Wind from the back, I won a Gold Card Hurdle on Unsinkable Boxer from the back, and I was too patient on Best Mate in his first King George. I did whatever I thought was best for the horse I was riding, always.

Jonjo was different to Martin though. People are different. In life, everyone has a different way of doing things. Same in racing. For me, it was like starting a new job. I suppose it was because I was actually starting a new job. It was the first time that I really felt that I had a job and a boss, and I felt that I needed to perform.

That May I had my 30th birthday party at my house at Kingston Lisle. It was a good party. Most of my close friends were there, Carl and Fitzy, inevitably, most of the lads from the weigh room, Martin and Carol Pipe, Steve McManaman and a couple of other footballers. The party was in full swing when I became aware of the noise of a helicopter that was getting closer. Gradually the sound got louder until the helicopter was above my garden and it was obvious where it was going to land.

I had no idea who it was. There was great speculation among the guests, but my new boss JP McManus was long odds-on favourite, although the party was split about whether he was coming to join the party and give me a present, or whether he was arriving to tell me to stop partying.

The helicopter, it turned out, was paid for by Pat Curtain. It landed and Ray Parlour got out holding an Arsenal shirt with McCoy 30 on the back, signed by all the members of the Arsenal team. It was a fantastic present.

Later that evening, Ray was drinking brandy with Jim Culloty of all people. I have never seen anyone drink brandy like Ray, and I have never known Culloty to drink brandy, so it was probably a bit of a mismatch. Later in the night, they were just slagging and messing, and Ray gave Jim a little shove, as you do. Jim didn't have the wherewithal to adjust his feet, so he just crumpled to the floor. Ray said afterwards that it was as if someone had shot him – he just conked out and hit the floor. Actually, before he hit the floor he hit the Aga and split his head open.

So Culloty is lying there on the floor beside the Aga, blood pouring out of his head, and Ray is thinking, shit, people are going to think that I hit him. If he dies I'm going to be up for manslaughter at least. Luckily, Jim was all right. He did have a bit of a headache the following day, although we weren't sure whether it was the Aga or the brandy that did it. Whichever it was, it was the worst fall that Jim had all year. He wasn't really one for taking too many chances.

There was plenty of speculation about who was going to replace me as Martin's jockey. There was lots of talk about Dickie Johnson getting the job, which made a lot of sense: he is a top rider, a top guy, and he would have fitted in well with Martin. He would have fitted in well with anyone.

However, it would have been a disaster for me. If Dickie had been riding all of Martin's horses, he would have been long odds-on for the jockeys' championship. It would have been very difficult for me to have beaten him. But Dickie was very happy riding away for Philip Hobbs, and Philip was and is a top trainer, among the top three or four in the country then, as he is now. I'm not sure how close Dickie was to taking the job with Martin, but it may have been that Philip and his owners made it a little more attractive for him to stay with them. Whatever the reason, he decided to stay where he was. Dickie hasn't thanked me yet for getting him a better deal.

In May that year it was announced that Timmy Murphy had been appointed as David Johnson's rider. David had become the main owner in Martin's yard. A lot of the big winners that Martin had – Or Royal, Champleve, Lady Cricket, Cyfor Malta, Liberman, Well Chief – were all owned by David and carried his blue and green colours. I had ridden some memorable winners in those colours.

When I heard that Timmy had been appointed as David Johnson's rider, I heaved a sigh of relief. Not that Timmy wasn't a top rider, but the fact that he was riding David's horses meant, by implication, that he might not be riding the other horses in Martin's yard. So firstly, there was a chance that I would get to ride some of those horses when my commitments to JP and Jonjo allowed, and secondly, it meant that no one rider was going to ride all of Martin's horses, so no rider was going be jet-propelled towards the jockeys' championship.

Jonjo didn't have that many summer horses so, actually, I rode a lot for Martin that summer. As the season got going in October and November, I was riding more for Jonjo, but I was still riding for Martin when I was free. At Exeter on 2nd November 2004, I rode Seebald for him to finish second to Azertyuiop in the Haldon Gold Cup, one of the first big races of the new season, and I rode Tresor De Mai for him to win the three-mile handicap chase later on the card.

There were two stings in the tail though. The first was that the stewards decided that I had been too hard on Tresor De Mai, and they suspended me for one day. The second was that that one day was 13th November, Murphy's Gold Cup day, or Paddy Power Gold Cup day, as it had become. Disaster.

I was prepared for a frustrating time at the Paddy Power Gold Cup meeting. Just because I wasn't riding for Martin didn't mean that he didn't have a truckload of horses readied and bouncing out of their skin for the meeting. I knew it would be bad, and it turned out to be as bad as I had imagined. I rode The Rising Moon for Jonjo and JP in the first professional riders' race of the meeting on the Friday, and we finished fourth as Timmy Murphy won the race on Marcel, owned by David Johnson, trained by Martin Pipe. I rode Upgrade, a 16/1 shot, Martin's second string, in the two-mile handicap chase as Timmy finished second on Well Chief, my horse. I rode Limerick Leader for Philip Hobbs in the three-mile novices' chase and was unseated at the second fence as Timmy won the race on Comply or Die.

I was suspended the following day, so I watched it all unfold on television. I should have played golf or something, but it was difficult not to watch it. The day started badly and got progressively worse. Timmy won the first on Over The Creek, he won the second on Vodka Bleu, he won the fourth, the Paddy Power Gold Cup, on Celestial Gold, and he rounded off the day by winning the fifth on Stormez.

What did I expect? I knew what I was doing when I joined JP and Jonjo – I knew what I was giving up. I knew that Cheltenham's November meeting would roll around, that Martin would have a clatter of winners and that I couldn't expect to be riding them. I did come back the following day and ride a winner for Jonjo and JP, Manners in the bumper, the last race on the last day of the meeting, but it didn't make me feel a whole lot better about things. Martin had had seven winners, including the feature race – Timmy Murphy had ridden seven winners, I had ridden one. All was not right in my world.

Shortly afterwards, I did an interview with *The Sunday Times*. In it I said that things would have to get better at Jonjo's, things would have to move up a gear; I meant both in terms of the quality of horses and the number of horses, and I said that I knew that that was what Jonjo wanted too. I meant every word. I wasn't having a go at Jonjo or at JP, I just knew that things would have to get better.

Jonjo was and is in a difficult situation, in that the perception is that he is JP's trainer. People think that, if Jonjo gets a good horse, JP will automatically get it, and that if he is trying to find an owner for a horse, it means that JP didn't want it. That isn't the case. Jonjo isn't a private trainer for JP or anything like it, and he has had some top-class horses, like Iris's Gift, Exotic Dancer, Albertas Run and Black Jack Ketchum, for owners other than JP. And if people knew JP, they would know that he is just as happy, possibly even happier, when Jonjo has a big winner for another owner. Jonjo would love to get more owners into Jackdaws Castle, and JP would love it if he could, but it's difficult because of the perception that people have.

I never really thought of what would happen if things didn't get better, I just knew that they had to, and I knew that they would. Thankfully, they did, but not before they got a little bit worse.

I was cantering down to the start on a horse of Gary Moore's, Flying Patriarch, before the first race at Folkestone on 15th November, the juvenile hurdle. I was just tying my reins when another horse came past, my horse spooked, jinked, and sent me out the side. It was bad timing. My thumb became stuck in my reins as I came off. As I got to my feet I could feel my hand and my thumb tingling like mad. I thought, ah I'll be all right, until I looked down at my hand and saw blood pouring through my glove.

I was thinking that I didn't really need my thumb to ride, but when I went to take my glove off I realised how bad it was. Basically, the top of my thumb was coming off – you could actually see the bone. So I told the starter that I was in trouble, the horse had to be withdrawn, and they wanted to take me straight to hospital. I wouldn't let them though. I phoned Doc Pritchard, and he recommended a hand specialist, Dr Ian Lowdon, who sorted me out. I desperately wanted to be back for Newbury's Hennessy meeting at the end of December, when I was due to ride Baracouda for the first time in the Long Distance Hurdle.

Baracouda was one of JP's best-established horses at the time. He was trained in France by François Doumen, not at Jackdaws Castle by Jonjo O'Neill, but he was still my ride. I don't think Mr Doumen was overly happy with my appointment as JP's rider. His son Thierry used to ride Baracouda. The pair of them had beaten me a couple of times, including when I rode Mr Cool in the Ascot Hurdle in November 2002, but I had beaten him on Deano's Beeno in the Long Walk Hurdle a month later.

Baracouda's racing style was to be held up out the back early and come with a run through horses, just getting up on the line. I thought that the hold-up tactics were often exaggerated on Baracouda. Thierry is a nice lad, I liked him. He went training shortly after he gave up riding, and I rode a Grade 1 winner for him, Foreman, to win the Maghull Chase at Aintree in 2006.

I couldn't understand why they used to hold Baracouda up as far out of his ground as they did. There was no way Deano's Beeno should have ever beaten him, and when he beat Mr Cool, he had a much harder race than he should have had. If he had been ridden closer to the pace, he wouldn't have had to make up so much ground so quickly, and would have had an easier race.

The first time I rode Baracouda was in that Long Distance Hurdle at Newbury at the 2004 Hennessy meeting in November. I held him up well out the back as Monsieur Doumen had asked, we made our ground easily and won well enough, even if I had to ride him out on the run-in. He was never a horse who wanted to be in front for too long.

The second time I rode him, though, was in the Long Walk Hurdle the following month, which had been switched from Ascot to Windsor. We don't race over hurdles at Windsor any more, but when we did, it was a sharp track, a figure-of-eight, a track at which it was difficult to make up a lot of ground from the back. On top of that, there wasn't likely to be much pace in the race, so I decided that I would ride Baracouda closer to the pace than usual.

So that was what I did. It was a messy race, there was no pace, we were all on top of each other at the second last, and Baracouda hated that. Despite that, we managed to win. His class got him home on the run-in by three parts of a length. Monsieur Doumen wasn't very happy with me afterwards. I don't think he was my greatest fan. I'm not sure why. Luckily, it didn't really bother me what he thought of me.

Baracouda was my best ride going into Cheltenham 2005. He was really my only ride with a big chance. It was a fair comedown from previous years, when I was going into Cheltenham with an arsenal of Martin Pipe horses and thinking how many winners. Going into Cheltenham 2005, I was thinking hopefully one.

In spite of this, I was still well clear in the jockeys' championship – I had ridden 170 winners before Cheltenham, Timmy Murphy was second with 125. Timmy had ridden some big winners: Celestial Gold had gone on to win the Hennessy after winning the Paddy Power, he had won the Tolworth Hurdle on Marcel and won the Victor Chandler Chase on Well Chief. All my horses, all Martin Pipe horses, David Johnson horses. Still, at least I was looking good for another championship, and that was vital.

I didn't have a winner at Cheltenham. It was the first four-day Festival, 24 races, and I couldn't even win one of them. Graham Lee on Inglis Drever beat me and Baracouda in the World Hurdle. I remember passing Inglis Drever at the top of the hill, Graham was flat to the boards, but I knew that Inglis Drever was a horse who kept finding for pressure, I remember thinking, keep your eye on him, he's not beaten yet. We were going well jumping the second last, but I had to ride Baracouda to challenge at the last, by which stage Inglis Drever had built up a head of steam behind us, and he came past on the run to the last and ran away from us up the hill.

Baracouda was 10, Inglis Drever was six. It was just a case of the younger horse beating the older horse, and Inglis Drever was a bloody good younger horse who went on to win two more World Hurdles after that. Only one horse aged 10 or older has ever won the World Hurdle, and poor old Baracouda was coming towards the end of his tether. He raced just twice after that, and he was beaten both times.

Aintree was a bit better. I won on two of JP's Irish-trained horses on the Thursday and Friday. I rode Fota Island, who was trained by Mouse Morris, to win the Red Rum Chase on Thursday, and I rode Like-A-Butterfly, who was trained by Christy Roche, to win the Mildmay Chase on the Friday.

I liked Fota Island. I had ridden him to finish second behind the classy Watson Lake in a beginners' chase at Navan the previous November. I thought he could have been well handicapped over fences, and I actually suggested to Mouse that he run him in the Grand Annual Chase at Cheltenham. The problem was that he was too well handicapped for me; he got into the race with just 10 st on his back. I couldn't do that weight, and Paul Carberry rode him to win.

It shows you how well handicapped he was though, because I was able to win the Red Rum Chase on him off a 12 lb higher mark.

I was riding Like-A-Butterfly for the third time at Aintree. I had ridden her to finish fifth behind Trabolgan in the Sun Alliance Chase at Cheltenham the previous month, and then I went to Fairyhouse and rode her to win the Grade 1 Powers Gold Cup at Fairyhouse's Grand National meeting. Christy had been really good to me when he was stable jockey and I was just one of the lads at Jim Bolger's, so I was delighted to ride a Grade 1 winner for him.

I rode Clan Royal in the Grand National. Clan Royal loved Aintree. Put him anywhere else, and he was just an ordinary horse, but bring him to Aintree, put those big green spruce fences in front of him, lots of them, and he was different. He had run three times at Aintree before Jonjo legged me up on him in the parade ring that year; he had won a Topham Chase, he had won a Becher Chase, and he had finished second in the National itself the previous year.

My breast-girth broke early on in the race, which wasn't ideal. The breast-girth helps to keep the saddle in place; it goes around the horse's chest and attaches to the saddle in order to stop it from slipping backwards. Not all horses wear them as it isn't an essential piece of equipment, but Clan Royal had a tendency to pull quite hard, so it was a help on him. Anyway, it broke and my saddle slipped back a little, so I wasn't able to restrain him as much as I would have liked.

He was racing a little keenly, so keenly that I allowed him to stride on over the water jump and past the winning post with a full circuit to go, but I was still happy with him on the run to Becher's Brook on the second circuit. He was being Clan Royal at Aintree, he was loving the place, jumping from fence to fence, he had settled into a lovely rhythm. We were six lengths clear of our field on the approach to Becher's, travelling well, as we eyed up the fence.

There were two loose horses on my radar as well, one in front of me and one to my left, so I decided to stay wide, jump the fence on the outside, so that the loose horses could go to the inside if they wanted. As I did, however, the horse that was on my left moved across in front of me to my right, so I had to shape up to jump the fence inside him. As I did that, the horse in front of me decided that he didn't want to jump the fence and moved to his left so that he could run down along the fence, and the horse that was now on my right decided to follow him. The net result was that he carried me and Clan Royal with him.

So I'm sitting on Clan Royal's back, a helpless passenger, powerless as we gradually turn to our left and get carried down along Becher's Brook, the fence gradually going past us on my right-hand side, the chance to jump it painfully evaporating, and with it my chance of winning the Grand National for another year.

I was distraught, dumped on my arse at Becher's Brook while leading the Grand National. At the time I thought I was going to win. It was only afterwards when I looked at the video and saw how easily Hedgehunter won the race that I thought maybe I wouldn't have beaten him, but maybe I would. I'm certain we would have at least challenged him, that we would have at least finished second.

Not that I wasn't happy for Ruby, who rode Hedgehunter, or for Willie Mullins or Trevor Hemmings who trained and owned him, but

I just wanted to be somewhere else. I knew that, despite all the excitement that there would be around the winner, there would be lads there who would want to grab me and ask what happened at Becher's Brook. I didn't want to talk about it. I didn't want to even think about it.

And there were other lads who were asking if I thought I would ever win a Grand National. That was where it started really, the 'is-McCoy-destined-never-to-win-the-National' idea. Blowing Wind was before that, and Butler's Cabin would come later, but Clan Royal was really when that notion started to gather momentum. If I could have escaped from the racecourse through some other exit, if I could have sneaked off out a gate at Becher's Brook and gone home, that's what I would have done.

I met Jonjo when I came back in. I expected him to be as down as I was, but he seemed remarkably upbeat.

'That's the way it goes,' he said.

I looked up at him, I was almost in tears.

'This is the worst day ever,' I said, as I yanked the saddlecloth from the saddle.

'No, it isn't,' said Jonjo.

I stopped what I was doing and looked him straight in the eye.

'When you are lying in a hospital bed,' he said, 'waiting for a doctor to come in to tell you if you are going to live or die, that's the worst day ever.'

CHAPTER 29

Black Jack Beauty

Jonjo was great like that, at putting things into perspective. A horse doesn't win a race, big deal, it's nothing in the broad scheme of life, it's nothing compared with what Jonjo himself had to go through. It put things into perspective for me and I was a little less gloomy about not winning the Grand National as a result.

I went into the final day of the season, Betfred Gold Cup day at Sandown, on 199 winners, desperate to ride 200. I had got to thinking that 200 would be a fair total. If you reach 200 winners in a season, you will probably be champion jockey, so it's a fair target to set. I won the first race of the day on Yes Sir for Peter Bowen. That was 200 winners in my first season with JP, my first season away from Martin, and another championship, 58 clear of Timmy, who just beat Dickie Johnson for second place. Thankfully, I had had the jockeys' championship sewn up from a long way out, but the trainers' title went right down to that last day at Sandown. Martin and Paul Nicholls were at it again, each of them running whatever they could in order to earn more prize money than the other.

There were nine runners in the Celebration Chase, the second race on that day – five of them were trained by Martin and four by Paul. With £58,000 to the winner, the destination of the trainers' championship more or less rested on the outcome of that race. It was quite a spectacle; four of Martin's horses were owned by David Johnson, so the riders had to wear the same colours, just with different-coloured caps, while three of Paul's four were owned by Andy Stewart. There were hardly enough different-coloured caps in the weigh room.

As it turned out, Timmy Murphy rode Well Chief to win the race for Martin, beating Paul's horse Azertyuiop into second place, with me back in third on another of Martin's horses, Contraband. That more or less secured the championship for Martin. So he managed to win the trainers' championship without me.

Dave Roberts called me early the following week and asked if I could ride Brave Inca in the Grade 1 Champion Hurdle at the Punchestown Festival that Friday. I was a bit surprised as Barry Cash was Brave Inca's rider as far as I was concerned; he had been ever since Brave Inca emerged as a high-class hurdler. He had only been beaten a half a length on him in that season's Champion Hurdle at Cheltenham. Brave Inca and Barry went to Aintree after that, and fell at the third-last when looking like a winner in the Aintree Hurdle.

It appeared that the owners, the Novices Syndicate, wanted a change of jockey, not the trainer Colm Murphy. It was desperate for Barry, but at the same time, I was delighted to be asked to ride such a classy horse. And if it hadn't been me, if I had turned them down in a display of solidarity, it would have been someone else. They had obviously decided that Barry wasn't the man any more.

Brave Inca looked like a slow horse, but he obviously wasn't. I rode him prominently at Punchestown; Harchibald came to me under Paul Carberry, looking like he would go past me easily, and I'm sure that Harchibald headed me on the run to the final flight, but Brave Inca was well named, he battled back and we got back up to win by a head.

I committed to riding Brave Inca for the season, including in the Champion Hurdle at Cheltenham, as long as my commitments to JP allowed. I spoke with JP and Jonjo before I did that, although it was unlikely that there would be any conflict as we didn't have an obvious Champion Hurdle horse at the time.

That was before Lingo won the Greatwood Hurdle at Cheltenham the following November. Lingo had been a high-class novice hurdler two seasons before that; he had won two of his three races, including the Grade 1 Tolworth Hurdle at Sandown in January 2004, but injury had plagued his career, and he had been off the track from then until November 2005 when I won the Greatwood Hurdle on him.

The Greatwood Hurdle is only a handicap, but it is often a good pointer to that season's Champion Hurdle. Lingo carried just 10 st 6 lb in the race, and it probably wasn't the best Greatwood Hurdle ever run, but I still liked him a lot. He impressed me that day; he won it like a potential Champion Hurdle horse. He was a lot like Binocular in looks, and he was a fast hurdler like Binocular with loads of pace. He had the potential to improve a lot and, if he did, he was going to make up into a live Champion Hurdle prospect.

I was delighted for Jonjo and for JP that they had a Champion Hurdle possible, even if it meant that I wasn't going to be able to ride Brave Inca if Lingo lined up in the race. I did want to ride Brave Inca, I thought he had a hell of a chance of winning the Champion Hurdle, and I told JP as much, but my commitments were to JP, so Lingo was the horse I was going to ride if he improved enough to take his chance in the race.

The following week I went to Punchestown to ride Brave Inca in the Morgiana Hurdle. Actually, the journey there was more eventful than the race. My flight was at eight o'clock in the morning, the race was at 2.15, so I figured loads of time. Then the fog came down. My flight was delayed, nine o'clock, then 10 o'clock, and I thought, that's cutting it fine. Then they said, delayed again, and I thought there was no way I was going to make it. I was still sitting on the tarmac at Heathrow at 12 o'clock.

I called Frank Berry and told him that I was unlikely to make it. Frank phoned JP, and JP sent his helicopter to Dublin Airport so that it could pick me up and take me to Punchestown. I was riding a couple of horses for JP on the day as well, but Brave Inca was my first ride – JP didn't need to do this to have me ride a horse with which he had no connection. But that's the type of guy JP is.

We took off at 12.15. I was long odds-against to make it. Fair play to the pilot, though, a fellow called Se Pardy. He organised it so that as soon as the plane stopped I could get off, and he had a fellow there to take me across the runway to the helicopter. I got into the helicopter at a quarter to two, the race was due off half an hour later. It took us 12 minutes to get to Punchestown from Dublin Airport. We landed in Punchestown 12 minutes before the race was due off and, fair play to the stewards, they allowed me to weigh out five minutes after the deadline. There was hardly time to say hello to Colm Murphy or the owners in the parade ring. I just got legged up and legged it down to the start.

Brave Inca put up a similar effort in the race itself. It was a typical performance, gritty from the front, passed by Ruby Walsh and Essex on the approach to the last, but he stuck his head out and battled back up on the run-in to win by a half a length. At least the travel stress was worth it. These days, if I am riding in Ireland, I try to go over the night before and stay with Ruby and his wife Gillian to cut out the possibility of getting fogged in.

Sadly, my Champion Hurdle quandary was sorted the following February, when Lingo broke a leg on the gallops at Jackdaws Castle and had to be put down. It was desperate for everyone: for JP and Jonjo to have such a promising young horse's career ended like that, and for the girl who looked after him at Jonjo's, Becky Turner. It's always sad when a young potentially top-class horse is cut down before he has the chance to fulfil his potential, and it was no consolation to me that I was free to ride Brave Inca as a result.

I was in the wars myself. Risk Accessor slipped up with me in the Robin Cook Memorial Gold Cup, the two-and-a-half-mile handicap chase, the feature race of Cheltenham's December meeting, named that year after the late Robin Cook, the Labour Party politician who had been a vocal supporter of racing in the House of Commons all his career, and who, tragically, the previous August at the age of 59, died of a heart attack.

Risk Accessor just slipped up on the bend turning into the home straight on the first circuit. He didn't clip heels or anything, he just slipped up and went down. I must have smashed my mouth off his head on the way down, or maybe I banged it off the ground, but when I came to my senses I realised that my two front teeth were pushed up into the roof of my mouth.

I don't wear a gum shield. I never have. A lot of the lads wear them now, Barry Geraghty swears by them, but I could never wear one. The doctor had a look at me, there was blood pouring from my mouth, and said that he wanted a dentist to check me out to make sure I could ride for the rest of the day. Black Jack Ketchum was running in the last race – there was no way I wasn't going to ride him, teeth or no teeth.

They put a call out over the PA system for a dentist to come to the weigh room. Amazingly, there were four dentists at the races that day! The first one to arrive had a look at my mouth and said I was okay to ride. I think if he had said that I wasn't okay, I would have gone to the next one, and then the next one, until I found someone who said that I was. Black Jack Ketchum won the last without coming out of a canter.

I loved Black Jack Ketchum. He had won his only two bumpers when JP Magnier rode him, and I had won two hurdle races on him before that day. He just oozed class, he did everything so easily. He was a gorgeous-looking horse, just like Cyfor Malta, but there was something about Black Jack Ketchum. It might sound a bit barmy, but I always felt that he understood me. If ever there was a horse that wouldn't have surprised you if he'd opened his mouth and spoken to you, it was Black Jack Ketchum. He had an unbelievable way about him, a great temperament, like a kid's pony. You could put your child up on his back and not worry about him.

As well as that, he had tremendous ability. I remember when I rode him for the first time at Uttoxeter the previous October thinking, this is a good horse. After I won on him for the third time at Cheltenham then, with my teeth up in the middle of my gums, I thought this horse will win here in March. I couldn't see him beaten in the new three-mile novices' hurdle at the Festival.

He did win the Brit Insurance Hurdle at the Festival that year, and he won the Relkeel Hurdle back at Cheltenham on his debut the following season, but he was never the same horse after that. I'm not sure why, he just never gave me the same feel in his races after that. I think he was bursting blood vessels, the poor fellow. I got beaten on him in the Cleeve Hurdle in January 2007, and then we fell at the third flight in the 2007 World Hurdle when we were sent off the 2/1 favourite.

That was a bit gutting at the time, but it didn't diminish the regard in which I held him. I'd say he was my favourite horse. If there is one horse that I could have taken home with me, and had in a paddock out the back of my house, it is Black Jack Ketchum. He is enjoying his retirement now, out in Barbados sunning himself. He's lucky that he was trained by Jonjo O'Neill and owned by such good owners and Derrick and Gay Smith. He's having a great retirement, much better than the retirement he would have out in a field behind my house, I'm sure.

Things were looking up. My book of rides going into the 2006 Cheltenham Festival was significantly stronger than it was a year earlier. JP's plan was coming to fruition. Jonjo's young horses were progressing, and some of them were making up into genuine contenders.

There were plenty of others as well as Black Jack Ketchum and Brave Inca, two horses that I thought had big chances in their respective races. There was Reveillez, who was owned by JP but trained by James Fanshawe. The first time I rode Reveillez was in the previous year's Sun Alliance Hurdle, when we finished sixth behind No Refuge. After that, the Jewson plan was hatched. JP, Frank Berry and I had a chat about it and, the way we figured, he could run an absolute blinder in the Sun Alliance, and finish third or fourth, or we could train him to peak for the Jewson, which he could win off a decent handicap mark.

He ran in a couple of novice chases during the season. I got beaten on him a couple of times and I won a beginners' chase at Folkestone on him a month before Cheltenham. All the while I could feel that he was improving with every run; James was bringing him to the boil for Cheltenham.

There was also Straw Bear, a novice hurdler, who had won a couple

Chanelle, Rachel Reidy and Emma Spencer.

With Anne Marie, Roisin, Kelly, Jane and Colm

(l to r) Ruby Walsh, Jamie Spencer, Graham Lee, me, Carl Llewellyn, Mick Fitzgerald, Willie Supple

Peadar and Claire McCoy,
best parents, on their fortieth
wedding anniversary

Princess Eve

JP and Noreen McManus's A Team at Martinstown

My PA, Gee, with husband Mark

Dream Team: Chanelle and me with Martin and Carol Pipe

With Billy and Yvonne Rock

Me with Martin Pipe

Eve on Gee's pony Nibbles – at least one of us looks like a jockey

Wichita Lineman pursuing Nenuphar Collonges at Cheltenham, 2009 (Press Association)

Binocular and me en route to winning the 2010 Champion Hurdle

Don't Push It and
me safely negotiating
Becher's Brook
(John Grossick)

Grand National
presentation:
JP McManus and
Jonjo O'Neill

Don't Push It coming into
the winners' enclosure.
My brother Colm in the
blue and white striped
shirt is clapping us in.

The morning after. Now we can relax, Don't Push It and me at Jackdaws Castle, the Grand National hoodoo laid to rest. (Press Association)

of times for Sir Mark Prescott on the flat, trained now by Nick Gifford, and on whom I had won two novice hurdles.

I thought I was going to win the Supreme Novices' Hurdle on Straw Bear, the very first race of the Festival. We were clear at the final flight, where we made a bit of a mistake, but I still thought that we had enough in hand to last up the hill. That was before Ruby conjured a mighty run from Noland to get up and beat us by a neck.

It got better though. The Champion Hurdle was the third race, and Brave Inca was massive for me, simply because I had convinced myself that he was a certainty. I just rode him at his own pace, it didn't matter how quickly or how slowly the others went, I was always just going to ride him at a pace that suited him. We took it up at the second-last and I went for home. We led over the last and, although Macs Joy and Barry Geraghty came at us, he was never going to get past Brave Inca.

It was an incredible feeling. Not just to win the race, not only because it was the Champion Hurdle, another Champion Hurdle, not only because it was my first Cheltenham Festival winner in two years, but because I had been thinking about winning it for almost a year. You plan these things from that far out, then when you do actually go and win the race, you get some kick out of it.

I was delighted for Colm Murphy as well, he is a top trainer, he is very much in the Aidan O'Brien mould, relaxed and softly spoken, but with an innate understanding of horses, and it is no surprise that he spent his formative years with Aidan.

I was delighted for the owners at the time as well, but that one didn't end happily ever after. I rode Brave Inca when I could, when my commitments to JP and to Jonjo allowed – that was always the arrangement. I couldn't ride him a couple of times the following season, I couldn't ride him in the December Festival Hurdle at Leopardstown, and Ruby stepped in for the ride and won. I couldn't ride him in the Champion Hurdle the following season, I had to ride Straw Bear for JP, and Ruby stepped in and finished second behind Sublimity.

Then the following season, 2008/09, I thought that I was riding Brave Inca in the December Festival Hurdle when Dave called me to tell me that I wasn't. The owners wanted Ruby to ride him. Fuck them, I thought, but I wasn't surprised. If they jocked Barry Cash off as quickly as they did, after him winning a Deloitte Hurdle and a Champion Novice Hurdle and a Supreme Novices' Hurdle for them, then I was certain that they weren't going to think twice about jocking me off either, despite the fact that I had won a Champion Hurdle for them on him, and four other Grade 1 races besides.

I liked Brave Inca a lot, he was as honest and as tough as they made them, and I liked Colm Murphy, he is a good trainer and a good fellow, but I ended up not having a great deal of respect for the Novices Syndicate, the people who owned the horse. There were too many experts in the group, too many people who knew it all.

I won the Jewson Chase, the first race on Thursday, on Reveillez. That was another plan that was a long time in the hatching, and it was a brilliant training performance by James Fanshawe to get him to peak on the day. My job was easy, I just had to stay on him and keep him pointed in the right direction, and we won well.

JP also won the Pertemps Final that day with Kadoun, but I didn't ride him. He was a 50/1 shot, trained by Michael O'Brien, and Tom Ryan rode him. I rode Jonjo's horse, Olaso, but he went wrong early on and I pulled him up. Sadly, he had broken a leg and had to be put down. Friday was Gold Cup day, but for me it was Black Jack Ketchum day. He was brilliant; he hardly put a foot wrong in winning the Brit Insurance Hurdle.

I rode Clan Royal again in the Grand National that year. I was in good form going into the race; I had already ridden two winners that day, Foreman for Thierry Doumen, as I have mentioned, in the Maghull Chase, and Refinement, the mare owned and bred by Michael Tabor and trained by Jonjo, to win the three-mile handicap hurdle.

Clan Royal was 11 that year, but again he ran his heart out to finish third behind Numbersixvalverde and Hedgehunter. He was desperately unlucky not to win a Grand National. He deserved to win one, but I knew that his chance had probably gone now; there was very little chance that he would be able to go back as a 12-year-old the following year and win it.

I did win the championship again that year, but it was a close shave – I rode 178 winners to Dickie Johnson's 167. Eleven winners, it was as close as Dickie has got to me so far, as close as anyone has ever got to me so far, and it was much too close. I was aware of him the whole season. He wouldn't go away.

And I did look at the table. I always look at the table. Everybody does. I always knew how many winners Dickie had, how many I was in front of him. Actually, I always knew how many winners everybody had, or everybody who I considered to be a threat, which was pretty much everyone in the weigh room. Just because you are paranoid, it doesn't mean that everyone isn't out to get you.

I didn't reach my target of 200, and that was the problem. I had spent a little more time that season going to Ireland to ride Brave Inca and for JP. As well as that, Tom Scudamore had established himself at Martin Pipe's. He was riding almost all of the horses that weren't owned by David Johnson and ridden by Timmy Murphy, so that had cut off a fairly consistent supply of winners for me.

I was asked to go on *Morning Line* on Betfred Gold Cup day, the last day of the season. I was sitting there just before we went on air, when one of the producers said that Martin Pipe was going to be coming on by telephone. He hadn't been in the original schedule, but he had rung in to say that he would like to go on, to talk through his runners in the Betfred Gold Cup. He had plenty of them.

I thought it was a bit odd all right, Martin ringing into *Morning Line* wanting to go on, but I didn't think much more of it. So they got him on, he congratulated me on winning another championship and he talked through his runners, Puntal, Therealbandit and It Takes Time. Then he dropped the bombshell: he was retiring. I nearly fell out of my chair.

'I've not been in the best of health,' he said, 'and I've taken the decision that it's time for David to take over.'

I was surprised at how sad I felt, sitting on my chair and listening to Martin sharing the announcement of his retirement with an entire viewership.

'I'd like to be remembered for training horses who tried their best,' he continued. 'I got a great thrill out of getting horses to enjoy their racing and to try their best.'

Dave Roberts phoned me after the programme, in shock. It was a shock to me as well at the time, but when I thought about it a little afterwards, it shouldn't have been that big a surprise. His health was a little bit of a worry – he had a muscle-wasting disease that he needed to get under control. Also, David was getting to the point at which he was ready or almost ready to have a go on his own. He told me afterwards that he had asked David to take over a year before that, but David didn't want to, he didn't think he was ready.

On top of that, Martin wasn't as dominant as he used to be. Actually, that season, Paul Nicholls had beaten him to the trainers' championship. It might have been just a blip, but it might also have been the case that Martin saw the writing on the wall. Paul was just getting stronger and stronger, and maybe Martin just thought that it was time for him to say enough was enough.

It hasn't been easy for David, taking over from his dad, but he has done really well, he is a good guy and he has established himself as a top trainer. He has won a lot of the big races already, including a Hennessy with Madison De Berlais and a Grand National with Comply Or Die. Martin is still very much involved, he is always around, he says that he is always there annoying David, but he loves it, and I'm sure that his advice to David is invaluable. I slag David still when I ride a winner for him:

'Your dad must be training this one then, is he?'

CHAPTER 30

The Butler Did It

I knew from a fair way out that I was riding Far From Trouble in the 2006 Galway Plate. He was a horse who I had ridden quite a bit, even though he was trained by Christy Roche in Ireland. He was travelling well for me when he came down at the sixth-last in the Irish Grand National the previous April. He could have won an Irish National off a mark of 127, and he was only 1 lb higher for the Galway Plate. He was a young horse, and improving type, so I thought he had a big chance of providing me with my first win in the race.

Far From Trouble was going to have a light weight to carry, 10 st 4 lb if Ansar stayed in the race. It didn't bother me too much, I can do 10 st 4 lb when I have enough notice and I will do it when I think it's worth it, which I did in this case.

I rode Sporting Limerick in the two-and-a-half-mile handicap hurdle in the second race that day. Sporting Limerick was a nice horse that JP had in training with Noel Meade, but there were lofty expectations of him and he hadn't really fulfilled them. I hadn't ridden him before, but he had won his maiden hurdle at Roscommon three weeks previously.

He was travelling well enough for me going down the hill on the far side towards the second-last flight. I remember it like it was yesterday. I still thought I had a chance going to the flight, but he stepped at it and came down. That's never a nice feeling. You know that there are probably about 60 hooves coming behind you, that if the fall doesn't get you there is a big chance that at least one of the hooves behind you will.

I put out my hands to break my fall. The ground was fairly firm, but I didn't think it was too bad when I hit the ground. But within a fraction of a second I went from, I'm all right, to, I might be all right, and finally to, actually I'm not all right at all. I could feel the pain in my hand, then my wrist, then shooting up through my right arm. I lay on the ground and thought, ah this is not good. The paramedics came over to me and I told them my wrist was broken. Dr Adrian McGoldrick came up to me and I told him that I just needed morphine, which he gave me as soon as he was happy that my head was all right.

I walked to the ambulance holding my wrist, and they cut my glove off.

'It's pretty bad, isn't it?' I asked the doctor.

'It is,' he said. 'There are ligaments holding your wrist together.'

They took me off to Galway Hospital, but I rang Ruby on the way to get him to make sure that whichever doctor was looking after me was all right.

Chanelle was at the races and came to see me in hospital later, as did JP and Frank Berry. They didn't operate on me until the following morning, so I had plenty of time on my hands to think stupid thoughts like, how did it happen?

People were telling me that if there was a good time to break my wrist, it was now. I wouldn't miss Cheltenham or Aintree or any of the big meetings during the winter. Bollocks. There is never a good time to break your wrist, or anything else for that matter. I was going to be out for weeks, and that was no good when you wanted to ride winners and be champion. And guess what? Far From Trouble won the Galway Plate, with Roger Loughran deputising for me.

At least I fared better than Sporting Limerick, the poor fellow. He broke his leg in the fall and had to be put down.

I was going to be out of action for six or eight weeks, so with our wedding arranged for September, Chanelle and I decided that we would go on our honeymoon before the wedding, use the time that I was out of action anyway. It was easy enough to convince Chanelle, as long as we agreed that we could tell people we were on our honeymoon.

'We're on our honeymoon.'

'Oh great, congratulations, when did you get married?'

'In two weeks.'

JP very kindly arranged for us to spend the two weeks in the Sandy Lane Hotel in Barbados. Another perk of the job.

We got married that September in Majorca, just outside Palma. We both wanted to get away, we both wanted something small with just our closest friends and families there, and that was how it worked. My brother Colm was my best man, and the legendary TJ Comerford was my groomsman. All my family were there, all Chanelle's family, just about 14 or 15 friends each, and just a handful of people from racing: JP and Noreen McManus, Jonjo and Jackie O'Neill, Martin and Carol Pipe, Emma and Jamie Spencer, Conor Everard, Willie Supple, Ruby Walsh,

Mick Fitzgerald, Carl Llewellyn, Graham Lee, Steve McManaman, David Manasseh, and their wives (well, all their wives except Carl's wife, who doesn't exist, never has, I'm sure he'll set about looking for one when he decides that he was not put on this earth to keep lots of girls happy instead of just one) – all our very closest friends.

It was exactly what we wanted, apart from the weather. One of the reasons we went away was that we would have nice weather, but on the morning of our wedding, it lashed rain. Proper rain now, not the wishy-washy rain that you get in the west of Ireland. Thunder and lightning to go with it and all.

TJ knew a guy who knew Liam Reilly, the lead singer with Bagatelle, and, unknownst to me, he arranged through his friend to have Liam play at the wedding. I loved Bagatelle when I was younger. Conor Everard used to have a Bagatelle tape in his car, which we used to listen to all the time, and I really got into them.

The one worry about Liam was that he would have too much to drink before the evening and that he wouldn't be able to perform, so TJ got one of the lads to look after him, make sure that he didn't have too much to drink during the day. Inevitably, the lad failed.

I don't know how much Liam had to drink or what he did before he went on stage, but whatever it was, he should do it every time (he probably does). He was brilliant. Absolutely fantastic. He played all the old Bagatelle songs, Summer in Dublin, Trump Card, Second Violin, the whole lot. I went up on the stage to sing with him, Colm and Willie Supple went up too. Then Ruby and Jamie Spencer got up and started trying to sing The Streets of New York. Halfway through the song, as they bludgeoned it to death, Liam stopped and took the microphone from them.

'You wouldn't let me ride one of your horses,' he said, 'so there's no way I'm letting you do that to one of my songs.'

I got chatting to Liam during the night. I asked him how he was going, said it was nice to chat to him, although I'm not sure how much sense he was making. I asked him if he wanted a drink.

'Oh no,' he said, 'I never drink when I'm working.'

I looked at him, I'm sure he was taking the piss, but he just looked back at me, deadpan.

It was a great wedding, it could hardly have been better. The next morning, at the airport on the way home, Chanelle's brother and his wife met Liam Reilly who was wearing his cowboy boots on the wrong feet.

*

I was back riding on 28th September, eight weeks and one day after my fall from Sporting Limerick. In my absence, conditional rider Tom O'Brien had gone to the head of the jockeys' championship and was going great guns, but he was only a few winners ahead of me, which was fortunate. It would have been difficult if he or anyone else had been 20 or 30 winners ahead of me and I had to start playing catch-up. I had ridden 49 winners before I had gone to Galway, which was just as well.

My first ride back was on Absolutelythebest for John O'Shea in the first race at Hereford on 28th September, which won, number 50 for the season. I won the last race as well, the bumper, on Bouncy Castle, for Jonjo and Gay Smith, Black Jack Ketchum's owner. 51.

I went to Carlisle on 6th November to ride Exotic Dancer in a graduation chase. The field cut up a lot, and we were left with just three runners, none of whom wanted to lead. So we were left with this situation where, when the tape went up, we stood still for about 20 seconds – myself, Tony Dobbin and Timmy Murphy all waiting for one of the two others to go on. Timmy eventually did go on on Turnstile, and Dobbs and I settled in behind him, but he slowed up almost to a walk after jumping the third fence, wanting one of us to go past him, which Dobbs duly did.

The farcical pace didn't suit Exotic Dancer, but I was still disappointed to get beaten by Turpin Green. You could easily use the slow pace as an excuse, and Turpin Green was a talented horse on his day, but Exotic Dancer was shaping up to be my Paddy Power Gold Cup horse, and it wasn't ideal that he was beaten by such a distance.

Exotic Dancer wasn't owned by JP, he was owned by Sir Robert Ogden, whose famous pink and purple check colours have been carried by some top-class horses like Voy Por Ustedes, Ad Hoc, Marlborough and Star De Mohaison. Sir Robert is a great guy. He invited me and Chanelle out to Monte Carlo one year for the Monaco Grand Prix. Of course I couldn't go, I was riding at Fontwell, so Chanelle took her friend Rachel with her and I joined them the following day. I remember having a discussion with him that day about Prince Albert of Monaco, about whether or not he was ever going to get married. There's no fear of Sir Robert anyway, you rarely see him without a beautiful girl on his arm.

JP had a horse in the Paddy Power, Butler's Cabin, but he was set to carry 10 st, and that was just too light for me, so I rode Exotic Dancer. The plan was to drop him right out the back – he had a fair amount of weight to carry, and he was a little bit of a thinker. He was a classy horse with a turn of foot; we thought that he was well handicapped on the best of his ability, and Jonjo and I thought that, if they went hard up front, it just might suit him to be out the back, he just might like passing tired horses.

Bad luck, I dropped him in and they didn't go fast at all up front. The last position you want to occupy when they are not going fast in a 15-runner handicap is 15th, yet that's where we were. Even so, I decided to stick to the plan. Going down the back straight, just after we had jumped the water jump, I noticed that Johnny Farrelly was beside me riding Jonjo's other horse, JP's horse Butler's Cabin.

'You'd better get a move on there Johnny,' I shouted over to him. 'They're not going that hard up front and it's going to be difficult to win from the back. The leaders may not come back.'

I could see him looking over at me, baffled, maybe thinking that I was trying to pull the wool over his eyes.

'Well what the fuck are you still doing out the back then?!'

We were still last going down the hill to the third last, but I knew that I had plenty of horse under me. He made his ground fairly easily and rapidly down the hill. Timmy went for home around the home turn on Vodka Bleu, but I just gave Exotic Dancer a squeeze and he made up the three-lengths deficit fairly readily. We actually jumped the last marginally in front, and he stayed on really well up the hill.

It was a nice one to win; I was delighted to win a Paddy Power for Jonjo. I was happy for Sir Robert Ogden as well as he invests a lot in the game.

I was congratulated afterwards for the ride I gave Exotic Dancer. I didn't think it was a good ride. To have a horse so far out of his ground when they were dawdling up front does not amount to a good ride. The reality was that the horse saved my blushes. He was so talented and he was so well handicapped that he was able to win despite the fact that I had got the tactics all wrong. He won the Paddy Power off a mark of 139. Two runs and seven weeks later he was rated 167, so he probably had that 28 lb in hand. Two stone ahead of the handicapper, that's why he won, not because of the quality of the ride I gave him.

I didn't ride Exotic Dancer in the Boylesports Gold Cup, the old Tripleprint, the previous year's Robin Cook Memorial Gold Cup, the race that would be named the Vote AP Gold Cup, God help us, the one that has had more names than Prince, the feature race at Cheltenham's December meeting. JP had Reveillez in the race, and I couldn't really get off him to ride Exotic Dancer. I didn't even try, much and all as I thought that Exotic Dancer was still well handicapped off just a 10 lb higher mark.

Black Jack Ketchum made his seasonal debut on Boylesports Gold Cup day, 9th December, in the Relkeel Hurdle, which we won doing handsprings, and I won the novices' chase on the same day on a horse called Don't Push It. More of him later, obviously, but I liked him then even as a novice chaser. I was surprised and disappointed that he hadn't been able to win the novices' chase at Cheltenham's November meeting four weeks previously. Of course I didn't know at the time that the horse who beat him would turn out to be the monster that we now know as Denman, Cheltenham Gold Cup winner, dual Hennessy Gold Cup winner.

Reveillez didn't jump well in the Boylesports Gold Cup – he had fallen on his seasonal debut at Ascot three weeks previously. He was never a factor and Exotic Dancer won again, this time with Tony Dobbin on board.

Exotic Dancer was an unlucky horse in that he was born into the Kauto Star/Denman era. Kauto Star was just about the best steeplechaser of this generation. He had the speed to win two Tingle Creek Chases over two miles, the pace to win an unprecedented four King Georges over three miles, and the stamina to win two Cheltenham Gold Cups over an extended three and a quarter miles.

Denman was just a freak. The Tank, they called him. He was your typical traditional staying steeplechaser; he had a relentless gallop that took him to victory in two Hennessys and a Cheltenham Gold Cup.

Every era has its best horses, but these two were head and shoulders above most best-of-their-era steeplechasers of recent times and, while having the pair of them around together was great for racing, it wasn't great for Exotic Dancer, who was the exact same age as the pair of them.

Poor Exotic Dancer. He was second to Kauto Star in the 2006 King George, he was second again to Kauto Star in the 2007 Cheltenham Gold Cup, he was second to Kauto Star in the 2007 Betfair Chase, and he was third behind Kauto Star and Denman in the 2009 Cheltenham Gold Cup. He finally managed to land the Grade 1 prize that his talent thoroughly deserved when we went to Ireland and won the Lexus Chase at Leopardstown in December 2008.

I rode him in all his races after the 2006 Boylesports except for one, the 2007 Betfair Chase at Haydock, when I had to go to Ascot instead and when he was beaten a half a length by Kauto Star under Barry

Geraghty. He was a great warrior. He finished outside the first three just once in 20 runs over fences, most of them at the highest level.

I had just one winner at the Cheltenham Festival that year, Wichita Lineman in the Brit Insurance Hurdle, the race I had won the previous season on Black Jack Ketchum. I liked Wichita Lineman, he had a real engine, and I really fancied him for the Brit Insurance. He got a little outpaced going down the hill, it looked like Ruby was travelling much more easily on Black Harry, but I knew that my fellow would respond well, and we were back well in command when Black Harry fell at the last.

Two years later, my ride on Wichita Lineman to win the William Hill Chase received plenty of accolades, but my ride on him four weeks later in the Sefton Hurdle at Aintree was one of the worst rides I have ever given any horse. I got into a kamikaze duel with Dickie Johnson on Massini's Maguire that ended up flooring the pair of us.

I thought that he was the one we had to beat in the race, I thought that he had more pace than Wichita Lineman, but there was no doubt that we had more stamina, so I decided that I would turn it into a test of stamina rather than speed, and I joined Dickie in the lead fully six flights from home. I couldn't wait to get him off the bridle, and hassled and harried him into going faster until I broke him and I went on at the third-last.

I had the better of him all right, but the problem was that my horse was out on his feet, a sitting duck for Fitzy and Chief Dan George to come lolloping along from miles back and take it up at the last. We did keep on to take second place, 20 lengths in front of the third horse, who happened to be subsequent Gold Cup winner Imperial Commander, with Massini's Maguire well back in fourth, but I'm sure I should have won that race. It was a really brainless ride.

JP had three other winners at that year's Cheltenham Festival as well as Wichita Lineman: Drombeag in the Foxhunters', a race for amateur riders, so I obviously couldn't have ridden him, Heads Onthe Ground in the Cross-Country race, a race in which I don't generally ride, and Butler's Cabin in the four-mile National Hunt Chase, another race for amateur riders.

The plan for Butler's Cabin after that was the Irish Grand National at Fairyhouse on Easter Monday, 9th April that year. Jonjo fancied him quite a bit, and the more time passed, the more I realised that to not take on board Jonjo O'Neill's opinion when it came to staying handicap chases was to be an absolute idiot.

Jonjo is lethal in staying handicap chases. If I had a staying chaser and I wanted to win a big staying handicap chase with him, a Midlands National, a Welsh National or an Irish National, or even an Aintree Grand National, no disrespect to Paul Nicholls, Nicky Henderson, Willie Mullins or even Aidan O'Brien or Jim Bolger, but I would give it to Jonjo all day long. His record in Grand Nationals and in staying handicap chases is incredible for the number of horses that he runs in them.

The Irish National was on the day after Zach Johnson won the US Masters and been presented with the green jacket, as is tradition, in The Butler Cabin at Augusta. As we circled at the start, I remember David Casey messing with me.

'Sure you're a certainty, AP,' he was saying. 'Butler's Cabin, after Zach Johnson last night, he has to win.'

He did. Everything went right through the race, he travelled well and he jumped well, we got the gaps at the right time, and we hit the front on the run to the final fence. He did idle a bit on the run-in, but he stayed on well to win by a length.

It was a pity that JP wasn't there to see it. His son Ciaran and Ciaran's wife Anne Marie were there though, and Jonjo was there. Remarkably, it was Jonjo's first time at Fairyhouse. He had never ridden there, he had had runners there before, but he had never been there himself, not before the day that he won the Irish Grand National.

There were two main reasons why Butler's Cabin's win in the Irish National was special to me. Firstly, it was my first big win for JP and Noreen McManus. I had ridden a few good winners for them – I had won the Powers Gold Cup on Like-A-Butterfly and I had won the Jewson Chase on Reveillez – but the Irish Grand National is one of the big ones, it's one of the biggest National Hunt prizes in Ireland. And it was great to win on him for Jonjo as well as for JP. It was the first time that I thought that I was actually earning the job that I had, that I was giving something back to my employer.

Secondly, I was able to dedicate the win to Billy Rock. Billy was the first person I thought of when I pulled up after crossing the winning line. Maybe it was because he was buried on Irish National day four years previously, maybe it was because the Irish National was such a big race for him. I made sure to mention Billy in my post-race interview on television. I knew that Billy's wife would be watching and that my dad would be watching, and I'm sure that Billy himself was watching, so I made sure to give him a good mention.

'Billy will be looking down now,' I said to Ted Walsh, 'and hopefully he will be proud of me.'

'I think,' said Ted, quick as a lightning bolt, 'that he would have been proud of you long before now.'

CHAPTER 31

Freezing

So the 2006/07 season wasn't bad: an Irish Grand National, my first really big win in JP McManus's green and gold hooped colours, a Racing Post Chase on Innox, also in JP's green and gold hooped colours, and, crucially, another championship with 184 winners.

But no amount of winners, no amount of championships, no amount of Gold Cups or Grand Nationals could come close to what happened on 8th November 2007. Eve McCoy was born.

She had taken her time. She had taken us through the wringer and back again, but then she arrived in our lives, the gorgeous little baby that she was, and everything was okay. Our child, our little daughter.

It had been some journey, from the depths of despair when we were told that it was unlikely that I could ever have kids to the elation when we were told that Chanelle was pregnant to the trauma of the rocky road that was Chanelle's pregnancy, the scares, the worries, to 8th November. We had been ready to adopt – Chanelle was brilliant, she was just amazing, to have that mentality to consider that the fact that she probably wasn't going to be able to have kids with me wasn't an issue at all. We would have been delighted to adopt, we would have considered ourselves lucky to have been able to adopt, but both of us really always wanted to have our own children, so Eve's arrival was just about the best thing that you could ever have imagined.

She has her moments though, she has her tantrums (she must have got that trait from her mum). Actually, she reminds me a lot of me when I was small. If she doesn't get her way, she'll stomp up the stairs, making as much noise as possible, making sure that you know she's not happy with you.

But she is the most amazing child. She is affectionate, she's all cuddles. It doesn't matter how many winners you rode or how many favourites you got beaten. Although she has started to take an interest recently.

'How many winners did you have today, Daddy?'

'None, Evie.'

'Well do you think you will have any tomorrow?'

I miss her terribly when I am not at home in the evenings, during the summer when I am riding at evening meetings, or even when I am riding at a meeting that is a couple of hours away, and she is my first port of call when I get home. I try to get home in time to read her her bedtime story. I think she likes it when I do. Mommy reads two stories, that's all, whereas if she plays her cards right, she can get Daddy to read as many stories as she wants.

She was off getting her new dress for her uncle's wedding and her date with the Queen to help Daddy collect his OBE, and she happened to choose the most expensive dress in the shop.

'What about this one, Evie?' Chanelle asked, holding up the one without the zero on the end of the price tag.

'Daddy says I can have whatever dress I want.'

Twenty days after Eve's birth, I had a fairly bad fall off a mare of Jonjo's called Mem O'Rees in a mares' novices' hurdle at Lingfield. I had ridden her in two bumpers the previous season, but it was her first time to try to jump hurdles in public, and she failed. We fell at the first one. I was up in the firing line in a field of 12, I hit the ground and braced myself for the kicking that might follow, and it did, right in the back, full on.

A searing pain shot up through my back and my ribs and I thought, that's it, I'm dead. I lay on the ground and struggled for breath. I gasped and gasped and tried desperately to get air into my lungs. Gradually I got the hang of it, slowly, easing oxygen into my body, carefully getting my lungs to function without causing my back or my ribs to be affected at all. Suddenly I was aware that there was a doctor beside me asking me if I was all right. I'm fine, I told him, just winded. I crawled over to the rail, eased myself up into a standing position, and I actually walked to the ambulance. I climbed into the ambulance, lay down on the bed there and thought, I'm gone. There's no way I'm going to be able to ride again today.

Then I got to thinking though; I was riding an odds-on shot of David Pipe's in the next race, Pauillac in the novices' chase. He was a certain winner, all I had to do was get put on the top of his back and stay on him, and I thought, look, I'm walking to the ambulance, I must be all right, and if I was all right at all, I wasn't going to not ride an odds-on shot.

I did manage to haul myself up onto Pauillac's back and I did manage to stay on him. He fulfilled his part of the bargain as well, he won, another winner, although I had to be a little more forceful on him than I really wanted to be or thought I would have to be.

I had three more rides at Lingfield that day, all for Jonjo. I wanted to give them up, I should have given them up, but I thought that I would look like a right prick if I rode the odds-on shot and then gave up the rest of my rides, so I rode the three of them. Coconut Beach finished second in the handicap hurdle, but the other two didn't count.

Straw Bear was working after racing, I was due to ride him, so I thought I'd better do that. I thought it would be bad form if I didn't. He worked well, I was happy with him, but I was in agony afterwards.

I didn't sleep a wink that night. Painkillers served to dull the pain a little, but not enough to allow me to sleep. I didn't sleep well for about six weeks actually. Chanelle was up a lot with Eve during the night those days, and I'm sure the last thing she needed was to hear me complaining about my back and my ribs, but that was what she got.

I won the Christmas Hurdle on Boxing Day at Kempton that year on Straw Bear. I was fairly happy with that ride. I kept him wide the whole way for the better ground, kept him wide into the home straight. I could see Paul Carberry easing up to me on Harchibald at the second-last but, having seen Harchibald in action and ridden against him plenty, I thought that we might beat him in a battle, so I saved a bit for that battle. Straw Bear found plenty, and we got up to win by a head.

My season was turned upside down though at Warwick on 12th January. I got the ride on the favourite Arnold Layne for Caroline Bailey in one of Warwick's feature races of the year, the Classic Chase. He wasn't travelling that well early on, but that was his way. I still thought we had a chance as we went out on the final circuit, but we got the fence down the side of the track wrong, he wasn't meeting it on a stride and we were among horses. He couldn't get himself organised and he hit the fence and came down.

It wasn't a bad fall, but I knew I was in trouble as soon as I hit the ground. Usually the first thing I do after I fall, after I am sure that all the other horses have passed, is try to get up. This fall was different though. Instinctively, I thought that the best thing for me to do then was remain still.

I lay there, motionless, for about 30 seconds. A doctor came over and asked me where the pain was, and I told him it was in my back.

'How bad is the pain?' he asked.

'Very bad,' I said.

'Do you want me to give you something for it now?' he asked. 'Do you want morphine, do you want gas?'

'Not yet,' I said.

I had four more rides, and I thought there was a small chance that I might be okay.

'Not yet.'

They put me on a spinal board straight away, which was the correct thing to do, just in case there was serious damage to my back. They put a block on my head and they taped it across so that I couldn't move my head, or my legs or my arms for that matter. That's what a spinal board does.

The bad news is, I'm claustrophobic. I think it started when Conor Everard locked me in the boot of his car when I was at Jim's, in with all his riding gear and his tack, and I thought I was going to lose my life. When you are claustrophobic, a spinal board on which your movement is completely restricted is just not the thing for you.

Neither is an MRI scan, when you have to go into this little tunnel in which there is barely room for your head and your breath. I was okay with my first couple of MRI scans, but I think my claustrophobia got worse with every MRI scan I had to undergo.

So I'm in the ambulance on the way back to the weigh room, pinned down on this spinal board, and I start to panic.

'Doc,' I say, 'you have to get me off this spinal board. I'm claustrophobic, I can't stand it any longer.'

The doctor took me off it carefully – the medical staff at Warwick Racecourse were excellent – and rolled me onto my side and started to press gently on my back and neck. I shrieked with the pain.

'You'd better get me some morphine Doc, I ain't going to be riding again today.'

They brought me to Coventry Hospital and x-rayed me, and the doctor came out and said, Mr McCoy, I'm afraid you have some broken ribs. I'm thinking, is this guy for real? Broken ribs? If it was only broken ribs, I'd be out riding in the next.

'Has there been some damage to your ribs before?' he asked me.

'There has,' I said, still high as a kite on morphine. 'I broke them about five weeks ago. This isn't my ribs though. This is my back.'

'I think you might be all right,' he continued as if I hadn't said anything. 'I think you might be able to go home. Try to get off the bed there.'

'Doc,' I said. 'Listen, I'm not trying to be a martyr here, I'm not say-ing I'm paralysed or anything, but believe me when I tell you, I cannot get off this bed. There is nothing that I would like better than to get off this bed and go home, but I'm telling you I can't.'

I rang Doc Pritchard. Default position. I asked him to recommend a good back specialist for me. As usual, Doc came good, he organised everything so that I could go to the John Radcliffe Hospital in Oxford the following day.

That night in Coventry was hell. I was lying on my back, unable to move, unable to get up, even unable to go to the toilet. Jonjo's wife Jackie had rung Chanelle to tell her. She was in London with Eve, but she arrived at Coventry Hospital just after I had got there.

I got to the John Radcliffe the following day, and they did an MRI scan. I had fractured both sides of my T12 vertebrae and I had shattered my T9 and T10.

And that's why Doc Pritchard is such an invaluable asset for jockeys. These things are too important; jockeys get injured too often, your health and well-being are too important to leave in the hands of someone you don't know or hasn't been recommended by a trusted source.

Dr James Wilson-MacDonald was the surgeon; he was a spinal expert and he was excellent. He was assisted by Abi Zubovic, who was big into his racing. He was brilliant as well; he came in the morning after, even though he was off-duty, just to make sure that everything was okay. I had two options: have a body cast for three months and hope that the vertebrae would knit back together in that time, or have an operation, put some metal in there, a metal strip down each side of my spine to stabilise the vertebrae. That would probably take three months as well.

Of the two options, the body cast was the safer but also probably the slower. The operation was more dodgy, they told me that they didn't like operating on backs willy-nilly, to be poking around the spine. They were also concerned that T9 and T10 were so badly shattered that maybe even the metal strip wouldn't be able to stabilise the vertebrae.

I asked them which they thought would be the quicker, and they said probably the operation, but there was no guarantee.

'Well, it will have to be the operation then,' I said. 'I need to be back for Cheltenham.'

'It is very, very unlikely,' he said slowly, 'that you will be back for Cheltenham.'

Chanelle was thinking, oh Jesus, they don't know what they are dealing with here. She spoke to the doc outside.

'You are going to hear this from him a lot,' she said. 'He is going to tell you lots of times that he wants to be back riding for Cheltenham. He can be quite determined.'

I went into theatre on Monday morning. The usual, the anesthetist telling me to count to 10, I never get further than five or six, and I woke up on Tuesday morning at seven o'clock with the two doctors standing beside my bed looking at me.

'Do you know McCoy, you have bones like iron!' said Abi in his Croatian accent. That was the first thing he said. Not good morning, how are you, do you feel sore, are you alive. Bones like iron.

'What's that now?' I still wasn't sure where I was or what had just happened.

'I was sweating drilling into your back yesterday!'

Dr James Wilson-MacDonald was smiling, standing there beside him. He asked me how I was feeling. I wasn't sure – alive, able to breathe, a little sore.

'You know, you are very lucky that we did operate on you in the end,' he said. 'The two parts of your T12 are so far apart that they probably wouldn't have come back together with just a body cast.'

Thank God for that.

'The physiotherapists will be around tomorrow to help you walk again.'

That was weird. Why did I need physios to get me walking again? I could walk on my own.

But I couldn't. It was bizarre. I thought I'd roll out of bed and that it would be grand, I'd be away again, not a bother on me, but there was. The physios came around the next day and they lifted me out of the bed and I was stiff as anything. I felt like I was a hundred years old. They lifted me up and I tried to put my legs out of the bed. I couldn't stand up. Even when they lifted me up I couldn't get myself to stand.

It must have been a mental problem. It couldn't have been physical as I wasn't paralysed or anything, it was just as if I had forgotten how to walk. My brain wasn't allowing me to think that I could stand on my own legs. It was one of the weirdest feelings I have ever had. They put an arm either side of me and got me to put one foot in front of the other, taught me how to get going again. I kept thinking that my legs were going to fall from underneath me.

They walked me down the corridor of the hospital and back again.

Once they were happy that I was able to put one foot in front of the other with their help, they got me a Zimmer frame, and I was able to get around on that okay the following day. I stayed in hospital for a week, me and my Zimmer frame, ambling around the hospital corridors, annoying everyone no doubt, but all the while getting stronger, until they decided that I was strong enough to go home.

Chanelle and I took the opportunity to go to Dubai for a couple of weeks. We stayed with Willie Supple for a couple of days before moving to the Jumeirah Beach Hotel. I walked a lot. It was pretty much all I did in Dubai, walked up and down the beach. I thought that it would do me good, keep up my fitness levels, and that the sun on my back might help it heal.

Mick Kinane was out there as well for a little while, and I remember meeting him for lunch. As I have said, Mick was the one jockey that I always thought young riders should imitate. He is as close to the perfect rider as I have ever seen. If you were ever trying to teach someone how to ride, you should just get a video of Mick Kinane. So I always enjoy spending time with Mick, I always looked up to him and I was always interested to hear what he had to say.

Johnny Murtagh was in Dubai at the time as well. This was February 2008, and Johnny was just about to embark on his first season as first jockey to Aidan O'Brien at Ballydoyle, so it was interesting to talk to him about what he had to look forward to there. I told him about my early time with Martin Pipe, about how I was worried to begin with. But then, I thought he was a genius so I just decided that I was going to do whatever he asked me to do, especially in the beginning.

I wasn't giving Johnny advice, I would never think that I could give a top-class jockey like Johnny Murtagh advice, but it was interesting to have that discussion with him. In many ways he was facing a similar situation with Aidan to the one I had faced into with Martin, starting riding for a genius, a brilliant trainer. It was an exciting time for Johnny.

I went back to see the doctor about four weeks after my operation. He told me that I was doing well and that I could step up my exercise a bit. I said fine, but I still want to be back for Cheltenham. Cheltenham started on 11th March that year, earlier than usual, typical, and realistically I needed to be back riding at least three or four days before that – you want to get your eye in and you want to be fair to the owners and trainers who are putting you up. Doc was still dubious, but he didn't rule it out.

A couple of days later, the former trainer Charlie Brooks contacted me and asked me if I had considered cryotherapy. I'd never heard of it, but Charlie explained to me that it was a form of medical therapy that used extremely low temperatures to aid and accelerate the healing process. Champneys Health Farm in Tring had a cryotherapy chamber in which Charlie had invested, and he suggested to me that I go down there and give it a try. Champion flat jockey Ryan Moore had used cryotherapy in 2007 to help him recover from a broken arm, and I was happy to try anything to help me get back riding again as quickly as possible.

I was also trying everything anyway. I was taking calcium tablets, aloe vera, the works, anything I thought would help the bones heal more quickly. I read up on cryotherapy a little, and decided that it was well worth trying, that I had nothing to lose. The owner of Champneys, Stephen Purdew, very kindly invited me to come and stay in one of the suites. He said that I would need to undergo one or two sessions a day for 10 days, and that it would make sense for me to stay.

Charlie said he would go into the chamber with me on the first day. He had done it a couple of times before, no bother to him. You start off in a pre-chamber, which is minus 65 degrees Celsius, you stay there for about 30 seconds so that your body can begin to adjust, then you move into the main chamber and stay there for three minutes. Most people start off at minus 100 degrees in the main chamber, but because I was only there for 10 days, it was a bit of a rushed job, so I thought that I would start off at minus 110 and move to minus 120 quickly.

When I first went into the pre-chamber, I thought, this isn't so bad. I had obviously never experienced such cold before, but it was tolerable. You strip off, put on a pair of shorts, a pair of gloves, a pair of long socks, a headband to cover your ears, and you wear wooden clogs so that your feet don't stick to the floor.

Then we moved to the main chamber – I thought I was going to lose my life. I was kind of thinking, minus 65, that's cold, but I can bear that, so minus 110 shouldn't be too bad. How much colder than minus 65 can it get?

A lot, is the answer. It was unbearable. I was thinking, there is no way I'm going to be able to stick this. You can see your body starting to go red and you can feel it becoming numb. You see it going all pimply, with little white spots appearing, and you think your body is going to crack in places, like in cartoons. It was all pretty scary. I'm sure if Charlie hadn't been in with me the first day, I wouldn't have stuck it, I would have got out. But I stuck it out in there for three minutes with Charlie.

When you get out, you have 30 or 45 minutes on a power fitness machine. The girl who was looking after me, Renata, was brilliant. Over the next few days, I got down to minus 125 degrees, then to minus 130 degrees. I asked Renata what was the coldest anyone had ever done, and she told me that the football player Shefki Kuqi, who was playing for Newcastle at the time, had got down to minus 145. So I told her that, before I left, I would get down to minus 145.

The colder I was going, the more pairs of shorts, gloves and socks plus headbands I was wearing. My nose began peeling and I started getting burn marks all over my body. And the shorts didn't stop me getting burned downstairs either, the last place any man would want to get burned, and it was fairly painful. However, I felt that it was all doing me a lot of good. Physically I was able to exercise more as time went on, so I was able to build up my body. And mentally, I felt okay because I was doing something, I was being proactive about recovering. I wasn't just sitting at home waiting for my bones to heal. And being on a health farm, I was eating properly.

I was attracting attention. A few racing journalists were onto me, the two racing channels sent their cameras, Sky News and BBC filmed me a little and a couple of reporters got into the chamber with me, which was all a bit of fun.

On the last day I said to Renata, right, minus 150. She said you're crazy. You're going to burn your body really badly. I said fine, but if Shefki Kuqi can get down to minus 145, I can get down to minus 150. And I did. I was in there for three minutes at minus 150. Renata was right, I did get burned, frostbite all over my body, including the tender bits. It wasn't pleasant, I was suffering for days afterwards, but I was happy that I had set another record.

I went back to see the doctor on 1st March, 10 days before the start of the Cheltenham Festival, and he was amazed at how well I had healed. He told me that beforehand he'd thought me coming to see him was a waste of time, that there was no way my injury could have healed in seven weeks, but he was bowled over at the results of the MRI scan.

'It has healed well,' he said. 'It has healed very well.'

'So can I ride again now?'

'If you're asking me if you are physically able to ride a horse now,' he said slowly (I was), 'I would have to say yes, you probably are. Obviously there's a chance that, if you have a bad fall or get a kick, your back won't take it as well as it might have before, but the metal is in place. I couldn't say to you now that you shouldn't be riding, but it's not for me to say that you're perfectly fit to ride.'

I didn't hear too much after he said yes.

'I need you to say all this to Dr Turner,' I said (the British Horseracing Authority doctor).

'Okay,' he said. 'I don't see any reason why you shouldn't be riding, that's what I'll tell him.'

Dr Turner wasn't as positive. He wasn't sure that this was right, he wasn't sure that I should be riding again seven weeks after breaking my back. He could have said no, and that would have been it, but he sent me to a neurosurgeon in London, and he said that if he said I was okay to ride, then it was up to me.

I remember going into the neurosurgeon and telling him that I wanted to be back riding at Cheltenham nine days later. Like everybody else, he was amazed at how quickly the bone had healed. He looked at the MRI scan, he pointed out to me where you could still see where I had broken my vertebrae, but he agreed that I should be all right. That was all I needed to know.

I was back riding out on the Tuesday, 4th March, seven days before the Festival began. I schooled a couple of horses at Jonjo's, and I felt great. I was back riding at Sandown on Imperial Cup day, three days before the Festival started.

Fortunately, I was still long odds-on to win another championship. I had been lucky enough to ride 129 winners that season before I got injured, and I was lucky again that Richard Johnson chose that season to have a bit of a lull, by his standards. By the time I came back, he had just broken through the century mark, so I still had a fair cushion going into Cheltenham. It is remarkable how the ball hops sometimes. I won the championship with 140 winners that season. Dickie had ridden more than 140 winners in four of the five seasons before that, and in the year that he didn't, Timmy Murphy did.

I got great satisfaction from returning when I did though, getting back before Cheltenham. I had set that as my goal, people said I couldn't do it, that it was too soon, I kept saying I could, even if there were times in private when I doubted it. There was still something in the back of my mind that said, this might not be the cleverest thing to be doing. If I had a bad fall at Cheltenham, I could be in trouble, and you are highly likely to get falls at Cheltenham. I don't think I've ever ridden at a Cheltenham Festival and not got buried – you have to take risks at Cheltenham.

JP had three top-class novice hurdlers that year in Binocular,

Franchoek and Captain Cee Bee. Franchoek was going for the Triumph Hurdle, Captain Cee Bee was going for the Supreme Novices', and Binocular, as a four-year-old, could have gone for either. As it turned out, he ran in the Supreme Novices' – I chose to ride him in front of Captain Cee Bee, which was a very difficult decision. Captain Cee Bee was trained by Eddie Harty in Ireland and Binocular was trained by Nicky Henderson in Lambourn. Captain Cee Bee had a lot of pace, he had won over 11 furlongs at Killarney on the flat, but I had been impressed with Binocular at Kempton. So had Mick Fitzgerald, who rode him that day, and who said that he was even better than that. And I thought that the Kempton meeting is a good one for producing Cheltenham winners.

So I chose Binocular. I chose wrong. I came out the wrong side of a driving finish with Choc Thornton and Captain Cee Bee. It was great for JP, it was a 1-2 for him in the first race on the first day of the Cheltenham Festival, but it was 0-1 for me.Then I went out and finished second in the second race, the Arkle, on the mare Kruguyrova for Charlie Egerton. Two seconds, no good. 0-2.

The problem for me was that, with hindsight, we ran Binocular in the wrong race. If we had run him in the Triumph Hurdle, I would have ridden Captain Cee Bee in the Supreme, and I would have won that, and I'm sure that Binocular would have won the Triumph. Franchoek finished second to Celestial Halo in the Triumph, and we always thought that Binocular was better than Franchoek, which he was, as he proved when he hammered Celestial Halo at Aintree three weeks later.

That was the year of the high winds at Cheltenham, which resulted in the abandonment of the second day, the Wednesday, and Wednesday's races being dispersed through Thursday and Friday, so we had 10 races on Thursday and nine races on Friday. I managed to win one of them, the Sun Alliance Chase on Albertas Run. That was it, just one winner at Cheltenham. At the time I was disappointed that Binocular and Franchoek didn't win, and I had finished second on Kruguyrova in the Arkle and on Refinement in the Mares' Hurdle, but deep down I was genuinely happy to have one winner, and happy to be riding there at all. And importantly, I didn't think that any of my horses that were beaten got beaten because I didn't give them a proper ride or because I was lacking match-sharpness.

I fancied Butler's Cabin like mad for the Grand National three weeks later. He had the ideal profile for the race: an Irish National winner, like Bobbyjo and Numbersixvalverde, a National Hunt Chase winner at

Cheltenham, and Jonjo had been training him all season with just one race in mind.

I was delighted with Butler's Cabin on the first circuit, he really took to the place, he jumped the fences well and he travelled superbly with me. He wasn't an overly big horse, and he made a slight mistake at Becher's Brook on the first circuit, but he had got into a lovely rhythm by the time we came around to Becher's again on the second and final circuit, the 22nd fence, the ninth last.

He just got in a little deep to the fence, which wasn't ideal. He rubbed the top of the fence with his belly, and just sent his centre of gravity forward. By the time his front hooves landed on the ground, his centre of gravity had gone beyond the point of no return, and he toppled over. A typical Becher's fall.

I was gutted again. Same fence, same point in the race as Clan Royal, my chance of winning the Grand National over for another year, the usual questions from the press afterwards: how did it feel, how many more Nationals could I ride in, why hadn't I ever won it, was I ever going to win it.

I remember walking out of Aintree that evening and wondering the same thing.

CHAPTER 32

Wichita Hardman

I had scraped home in the 2007/08 championship – 140 winners is not a total that should be winning any championship. I got away with it. I know that I was out for seven weeks with my back, but I had been out with injury in previous seasons. I was out for longer with my arm, and I still managed a respectable total. I was lucky to win the championship that season. I resolved that I would do better the following term.

I rode four winners for Nicky Henderson at Newbury on Hennessy Gold Cup day, 29th November 2008. The job as stable jockey at Nicky's had come up that summer after Nicky's perennial jockey, Mick Fitzgerald, had been buried at the second fence in the Grand National by L'Ami, one of the horses that I rejected in order that I could ride Butler's Cabin.

Fitzy is one of my really good friends. He was a top-class rider; he took over from Richard Dunwoody as first rider at Nicky Henderson's, and his relationship with Nicky brought them both huge success at the highest level. Fitzy calls a spade a spade, he just says what he thinks, which is probably why he told Des Lynam, live on BBC television, after he won the Grand National on Rough Quest in 1996, that after that, even sex was an anticlimax.

L'Ami gave him a horrible fall in the 2008 Grand National – he was lucky that he wasn't killed, and at one point it was 50–50 whether he was going to be able to walk again. There was no question of him ever riding again. I still miss him in the weigh room, I miss his dry wit and his banter, but he remains one of my very best friends, and he is a huge addition to our television screens.

Nicky asked Barry Geraghty if he would ride for him. Barry is one of Ireland's top riders, he had already won just about every top race in Ireland and the UK at that stage, and his ride on Punjabi to win the Champion Hurdle at Punchestown in April 2008 probably influenced Nicky's decision to ask Barry to ride for him on a more permanent basis. Barry was based in Ireland; the understanding was that he would commute between Ireland and the UK to ride for Nicky, and that I would help out when my commitments to JP and Jonjo allowed.

That year, as is the case most years, Hennessy day at Newbury clashed with Fighting Fifth Hurdle day at Newcastle. Punjabi was going in the Fighting Fifth Hurdle, so there was no real question of Barry not going up to ride him. That meant that Nicky had some good horses going to Newbury who needed a rider. Me. Unfortunately for Barry, Newcastle was abandoned because of fog, but he had already gone up there and probably wouldn't have had time to get back down to Newbury to ride Nicky's horses. Even if there had been time, I'm not sure that Nicky would have taken me off his horses.

Any day that you ride four winners is a good day, but to ride four winners at Newbury on Hennessy day – Shouldhavehadthat, Petit Robin, Duc De Regniere and Classic Fiddle – was big. I should have been bursting with pride and a sense of achievement on my way home that evening, but all I could think about was the shocking ride I gave Albertas Run in the Hennessy itself. I was terrible on him. Albertas Run is a horse who likes to have a bit of space around him; he doesn't like being crowded in his races or at his fences. If he does, he gets agitated and doesn't perform.

I suspected this before the Hennessy, yet I proceeded to go down the inside. The ground was a bit dead on the day, but they had moved the inside rail inwards from the previous day's racing, with the result that there was a strip of ground, about eight or 10 feet wide, all the way around the inside, on which they hadn't raced the previous day and which was therefore better than the rest of the track. There was room for about three horses on that strip, and I thought, that's where I'll go. Albertas Run hated it, he never travelled through the race, and I ended up pulling him up at the top of the home straight. I have never ridden Albertas Run down the inside since.

I got three phone calls on the way home from Newbury that day. The first was from JP McManus congratulating me on riding a four-timer on Hennessy day. It didn't matter that none of them were for him, they were all for Nicky Henderson and JP owned none of them, that's the type of person JP is – he was just happy for me and he called me to tell me.

The second was from Dave Roberts, telling me that he wouldn't be surprised if I was asked to ride Master Minded in the Tingle Creek Chase the following Saturday. The third was from Paul Nicholls, asking me if I would be able to ride Master Minded in the Tingle Creek Chase the following Saturday.

Master Minded was being widely acclaimed as the best two-mile chaser we had seen in decades, and he was due to make his seasonal debut at Sandown the following Saturday. He was trained by Paul Nicholls, so was Ruby Walsh's ride, but Ruby was on the sidelines with a ruptured spleen, sustained after he fell on Pride of Dulcote at Cheltenham's November meeting.

This game never ceases to amaze me. Ruby was on the sidelines at exactly the same time the previous year after dislocating his shoulder in a fall at the same Cheltenham November meeting, and Paul Nicholls's second rider Sam Thomas stepped in. Sam won the Betfair Chase on Kauto Star, he won the Becher Chase on Mr Pointment, he won the Hennessy on Denman and he won the Tingle Creek on Twist Magic. Even when Ruby came back and chose to ride Kauto Star in the Cheltenham Gold Cup, Sam got the ride on Denman, and he won the Gold Cup. It was a truly remarkable season for Sam, who was just 23 at the time.

The contrast with 2008 could not have been more stark. Sam got unseated off Kauto Star at the final fence in the Betfair Chase when he might or might not have won, he got unseated off Gwanako in the Grand Sefton Chase at Aintree's November meeting, he got unseated off Big Buck's at the last fence in the Hennessy when he still had a chance of winning, and now it looked like he was going to be sent to Chepstow on Saturday when Master Minded was due to run in the Tingle Creek.

I felt sorry for Sam, I really did. He's a great lad. Paul said that it might be good for Sam to get out of the limelight for a while, but the reality was that there was no upside for Sam to be riding at Chepstow when the television cameras were on Master Minded at Sandown. I'm not sure he ever really recovered from it, reputationally at least. Of course I was delighted to be in the frame for the ride, and I didn't feel bad about taking it. It was like Barry Cash and Brave Inca, Sam wasn't getting the ride anyway; if I hadn't been in the frame, somebody else would have been.

Paul said to me that Sam hadn't done a lot wrong, but he had had a couple of mishaps, and that Master Minded's owner Clive Smith was talking about getting somebody else to ride the horse at Sandown. He was just ringing me to let me know that he might be offering me the ride, and wondering if I would be in a position to take it if he did. I told him that I would have to speak to JP.

I called JP.

'Ah yes,' said JP, almost before I had finished my first sentence. 'You should be riding Master Minded.'

I was a bit stumped.

'I'm not sure what we have running next Saturday,' I said. 'I'm not sure if we'll have runners at Sandown or if I'm needed to go to Chepstow instead.'

'Ah no,' said JP. 'I think you want to be riding Master Minded, you know. I don't think we have anything that important. If you're asked to ride him, tell him you'll ride him.'

I got off the phone thinking what a brilliant boss I had.

Sure enough, the next day Dave called me to tell me that Paul wanted me to ride Master Minded, which was great. I was lucky that I rode those four winners at Newbury. It's a fickle business, what's current is what's good, and 13 championships probably didn't count as much in my favour when it came to being offered the ride on Master Minded in the 2008 Tingle Creek as four winners on Hennessy day did.

I really enjoyed riding Master Minded in that Tingle Creek. He was a super horse, and he was at his best that year. I still think that the best type of horse you can ride is a top-class two-mile chaser, and the best track in Britain for a good two-mile chaser is Sandown. Two-mile chasers didn't get much better than Master Minded in his prime. To ride him around Sandown, over those seven fences down the back straight, over the three Railway Fences, kick on from the home turn over the last two fences – exhilarating.

I rode three other winners on the day as well as Master Minded: Clay Hollister, Sunnyhillboy and Kilbeggan Blade, so that was two Saturdays in a row, Hennessy day and Tingle Creek day, two really high-profile days, that I had ridden four winners. Inevitably, people said that I was riding better than ever.

Ruby was back to ride Kauto Star in the King George, which he won, again, beating me and Albertas Run into second place by eight lengths. Jonjo had obviously decided that he was sick of finishing second to Kauto Star with Exotic Dancer, so he sent Albertas Run to Kempton to finish second to him instead, and he sent me and Exotic Dancer to Leopardstown, where we won the Lexus Chase, notching a deserved first Grade 1 win for Exotic Dancer. It was the first time I had won the Lexus as well, so that was another landmark for me.

I reached an even more notable landmark at Plumpton on 9th February 2009, an innocuous wet and miserable Monday afternoon.

I had ridden the 2,998th winner of my career on Stradbrook at Wincanton on 29th January, and then I hit a flat spot. I couldn't ride a winner for days. The weather was desperate and meetings kept being abandoned.

I couldn't believe that Plumpton went ahead on 9th February. The weather was awful, the ground was atrocious, almost unraceable I would have thought, or actually unraceable. There was surface water lying on the track, we were splashing through puddles on the way around, and I'm sure if I hadn't been on for 3,000 winners, if there hadn't been a marketing opportunity, a chance for Plumpton to make the main evening news, they would have called the meeting off.

I won the fourth race, the handicap hurdle, on Hello Moscow for Jim Best. That was 2,999. Then I went out in the next race, the mares' novices' hurdle, on Miss Sarenne, a mare of Nicky Henderson's. She travelled well for me, we came clear at the second last, went down to the final flight, race in the bag, number 3,000 coming up, when she just stepped at the hurdle and landed on her head.

I couldn't believe it. What a time for a horse to fall. I should have been in the winner's enclosure with a bottle of champagne spraying everybody; instead I was lying on my face in the muck at the back of the final flight. I picked myself up, made my way back to the weigh room and thought, this just isn't going to happen.

I went out on Restless D'Artaix in the next race, the beginners' chase, my last ride of the day, another horse trained by Nicky. Timmy Murphy made the running on The Package, my horse travelled well and we joined Timmy at the second last. From there, it was nip and tuck, but Restless D'Artaix put his head down and he battled all the way to the line for me to get home by a length.

I was a bit blown away. There in the muck and the rain at Plumpton, my 3,000th winner. I would never have thought starting out that I would have 3,000 rides in my life, let alone 3,000 winners. And there, as soon as I crossed the line, just like he was at Uttoxeter on 27th August 2002 when I rode my 1,700th winner on Mighty Montefalco and became the winning-most National Hunt rider ever, the first person I saw when I pulled up was Dave Roberts.

Dave had been at home when I won the handicap hurdle on Hello Moscow and he thought, he could do it today you know, AP could ride his 3,000th winner – I'd better get myself along. He got into his car and drove to Plumpton. As it happened, if I had won the previous race on Miss Sarenne, Dave wouldn't have made it on time.

I was delighted that Dave was there because, more than any other person, more than anybody else, it is Dave who has been with me through every one of those 3,000 winners. Dave has been with me since the beginning. I couldn't have reached such a milestone without the help of so many people: Toby Balding, Martin Pipe, JP McManus, Jonjo O'Neill, Nicky Henderson, and a lot of my winners were for them, but every single one of my winners was for Dave, so it was pretty special that he made one of his rare forays to the races to be there.

*

I loved Wichita Lineman. He was hard, tough; he was like one of those boxers who wouldn't lie down no matter how hard you hit them. He wasn't the fastest horse in the world, but he was one of the most genuine.

Jonjo had sent him chasing that season. He was small, wasn't the ideal build for jumping fences, but his toughness counted for a lot. Jonjo's plan for him at the 2009 Cheltenham Festival was always the William Hill Chase, the handicap chase, where he would be meeting more experienced horses, not the Sun Alliance Chase or the National Hunt Chase, even though he was a novice and was therefore eligible for both of those. If you are targeting the Sun Alliance with a young chaser, you really want to be thinking that you have a future Gold Cup horse on your hands. Wichita Lineman was a lot of things, but he wasn't a future Gold Cup horse. The handicap route was the right route for him.

He only ran three times over fences during the season, winning twice, and the handicapper gave him a mark of 142 over fences, which was exactly a stone lower than his mark over hurdles.

Jonjo fancied him quite strongly for the William Hill; he thought he was well enough handicapped to win it. I could see that he had a good chance, but I thought he might struggle at Cheltenham, the size of him, in a big field of experienced chasers, 24 runners, his first run in a handicap. But I kicked him off in a nice position, on the inside about halfway down the field, but even running up past the stands for the first time, I had to nudge him into the bridle just to keep his position. It wasn't easy for him. Even when he was meeting a fence on the perfect stride, he had to put in a huge effort to get over it, he had to jump out over it, whereas some of his more experienced and physically bigger rivals were able to just glide over their fences effortlessly.

We were travelling okay when we made a fairly significant mistake at the second-last fence on the first circuit. We were hard up against the inside rail; Lacdoudal, who was immediately in front of us, jumped across us a bit, nearly putting us into the side of the fence, and my horse nodded on landing.

He had lost a little bit of his confidence. He was slow jumping the last fence on the first circuit, and as a result we dropped back to about 15th or 16th, about 12 lengths behind the leaders setting out on the final circuit. He made another mistake at the last fence before turning down the hill. I gave him two smacks of the whip and set about getting after the leaders.

Turning to go down the hill with just three fences to jump, there must have been at least 10 horses in front of us and we were about 15 lengths behind the leaders. I still thought we had a chance though. When I pulled him out to try to get him running, I could feel him pick up under me, and I thought, we have a chance here. He made another mistake at the third-last, and I pulled him to the outside, but when I did he picked up again, so much so that I allowed him to drift back in behind horses – I wanted to save a little bit for the final climb up the hill.

He jumped the second-last well in among horses, and suddenly we were sixth going around the home turn with one fence to jump. I pulled him to the outside as soon as we straightened up so that he could get a good view of the final fence, but by that stage Maljimar and Daryl Jacob had kicked on on the far side, and I thought shit, I might not get there. We jumped the last pretty well, but Maljimar had gone clear.

I thought Maljimar had gone, I wasn't sure that we could catch him, but I concentrated on getting my horse running up the hill, about clawing back the five or so lengths that the other horse had on us. It looked like a tough ask, but I knew that Wichita Lineman would give everything he had. We didn't start gaining on Maljimar until about 100 yards from the winning post, but when we did, we closed quickly.

It seemed to take an age to get past Choc Thornton on Nenuphar Collonges on my left, we must have only had about 50 yards to run when we finally got past him into second place, but once we did, my horse could see the other horse in front of him and he could see that he could catch him. I asked him for one final lung-bursting effort. Every stride we took brought us closer to the leader, but also closer to the line. One stride took us up to his quarters, then his withers. Almost there. I didn't even look up to see where the winning post was, I just drove with all my strength, helping my willing partner as much as I could. Stride, stride, stride, one, two, three. Gotcha! There's the winning post. Yes!

It was only after we crossed the winning line that I was aware of the noise coming from the stands. It was Cheltenham, Wichita Lineman was a well-backed favourite, and the punters were cheering. I got a kick out of it as well and I couldn't help but smile.

I was a bit high on the emotion of it all, carried by the crowd and the occasion, but also I suppose by the fact that victory seemed unlikely from a long way out. It was probably one of the better rides that I have given any horse; in fact, I'd say that in my own little head I thought it was probably the best ride I have ever given a horse.

I thought I made a difference. It was similar to Pridwell in the 1998 Aintree Hurdle in that regard. I have ridden plenty of winners that anybody could have ridden. There are plenty of rides that have been acclaimed in the press as top-class rides that simply weren't. Wichita Lineman was different. I don't think that everybody could have won on him. I thought to myself afterwards, and I don't think I was being arrogant, you know what, you did all right there.

The following February I received a Lester award for Jumps Ride of the Year for it, which meant a lot to me. Ironic that my best ride and my worst ride so far were both on the same horse.

The postscript to the Wichita Lineman story is desperately sad. We went to Fairyhouse the following month for the Irish Grand National. I thought he had a big chance, but our race ended at the very first fence. He just clipped the top of the fence and came down. I got a pretty heavy fall but I was all right, he was all right as well, but then a following horse jumped right in behind him, had nowhere to go, tried to jump over him just as he was getting up, and kicked him in the back. I could hear Wichita Lineman groaning with the pain. It didn't look good. I went over to him and leaned on his head just to keep him calm until the vet arrived.

The vet confirmed my worst fear – broken back. Dead. I cried as they put the screens up around him and I walked away. I just had to get out of there. He didn't deserve that. If any horse deserved to be retired, and have the retirement at JP's place at Martinstown that he would have had, it was Wichita Lineman.

He was one of my favourite horses, he was so brave, he would have run through a brick wall for you. And there he was lying at the back of the first fence just away from the stands at Fairyhouse, dead. It can give you some kicking, this game.

Back at Cheltenham, I didn't have time to wallow in his William Hill Chase win either. The next race after the William Hill was the Champion Hurdle, and I thought that Binocular was a certainty. In much the same way as I had thought that Brave Inca was a certainty in the race three years previously, I just couldn't see Binocular getting beaten.

Coming down the hill to the second-last flight, I thought he would definitely win, but when he jumped it, I went to give him a squeeze and go after them and he just flattened out. The previous year in the Supreme Novices' Hurdle, I thought that he had been outstayed by Captain Cee Bee, so I was wary about committing him too early. So when he came off the bridle at the second-last, I thought he had no chance of getting up the hill, so I just nursed him away, trying to get him home. Then in the last 50 yards he seemed to get his second wind and he started to stay on again, but he just couldn't get back up to beat Punjabi and Celestial Halo.

We were beaten by just a neck and a head, but we were beaten, and that was the important thing, that was the sickener. Punjabi and Celestial Halo were very good horses, but there was no way they should have beaten Binocular. Punjabi, like Binocular, was trained by Nicky Henderson, and there was no doubt in any of the lads' minds at Nicky's which of them was the better horse. And Binocular had beaten Celestial Halo easily at Aintree the previous season and again in the Boylesports International, so he shouldn't have been finishing in front of us either.

Amazing how I could be so buoyed by the high of winning on Wichita Lineman and then a half an hour later be so deflated by defeat on the Champion Hurdle favourite. It deadened the whole day. That evening, I didn't want to talk about Wichita Lineman. In my strange psyche, his win was a distant second to Binocular's defeat.

Wichita Lineman was my only winner at that year's Cheltenham Festival. I was second on Karabak in the Ballymore Hurdle, and I was third on Exotic Dancer in the Gold Cup, behind Kauto Star and Denman, but I didn't have another winner.

I rode Butler's Cabin in the Grand National again, but it just didn't happen for him and we finished seventh behind Mon Mome. Like Clan Royal and Blowing Wind before him, it was difficult for Butler's Cabin on his next attempt at the National after looking unlucky the previous year. I did ride a horse called Don't Push It to win the race before the National though, the three-mile handicap chase. Of course, I could never have known that a year and an hour later, winning a different race on the same Don't Push It would have such an impact on my career and even my life.

We lost Exotic Dancer at that Aintree meeting. He again ran a cracker to finish second behind Madison Du Berlais in the Totesport Bowl, after Denman had fallen at the second-last fence. He was fine after, if a little tired. Back in the stables, his lass Hannah thought he was a little more tired than usual, so she brought him down to the vet, where he just lay down and died of a heart attack. It was very sad, he was a wonderful horse. We took some consolation from the fact that he didn't suffer.

Three weeks later at Sandown, on the last day of the season, I rode Hennessy in the Bet365 Gold Cup. Hennessy was owned by Malcolm Denmark and trained by my good friend Carl Llewellyn. I didn't ride that much for Carl, which was surprising given that he was and is such a good mate, and Eve's godfather. He had his own riders and I had my commitments, so I suppose there wasn't really that much opportunity. I was delighted to ride Hennessy for him though in the big race that ended the season.

Hennessy was small and narrow, he wasn't a natural chasing type, similar to Wichita Lineman in that way. The similarities didn't end there either, because he was off the bridle from a long way out, and he didn't jump well down the back straight final time. But the leaders had gone pretty hard up front and, jumping the Pond Fence, the third-last, even though we were about 10 lengths behind the two leaders, Church Island and Lacdoudal, I still thought that we had a chance.

I love riding horses like this. I like trying to build it into their head that they are going to get there. It's important not to start beating up on them; if you do, you sour them and they simply won't run for you. But if you can build them up gradually, encourage them – look, I know it's not happening for you at the moment, but stick with it, it will happen for you yet, just keep doing what you're doing and it will be okay, the others will come back – it will happen, trust me.

Going to the second-last, I knew that I had Hennessy racing. Briery Fox and Mark Bradburne, my PA Gee's husband, had made ground from the back as well, and he probably looked set to win when he jumped to the front over the last, but I switched Hennessy to the stands side and just managed to get him going up the hill. He stayed on really well and got up to beat Briery Fox by a neck.

It was tough on Mark, but I was delighted to have won the race, and I was delighted for Carl. The job wasn't going great for him, he was employed by Malcolm Denmark to train for him, and the Bet365 Gold Cup was a big race for him to win, the feature race on a Saturday, live on Channel 4. Malcolm Denmark was also delighted, as he should have been, high-profile race, £94,000 for the winner. I got chatting to him afterwards, and he told me that it was great for Carl; he seemed to be genuinely delighted for him.

'Things haven't been going great for him,' he said. 'He has to do better. But he wants to do better, and this will do him a lot of good.'

'He's a good lad,' I said. 'He's a real trier. He just needs a break.'

'I'm all for changing things for him, if that's what he needs,' he said. Two weeks later, I heard that Carl had been sacked.

I couldn't believe it.

'Malcolm Denmark's horses are not for me.' I said. 'I don't think I'll be bothering riding his horses any more. Friendships are more important than riding a few winners.'

Warren Greatrex took over from Carl. Warren is a nice lad, and he was on to Dave a bit about me riding a couple of horses, but Dave turned him down. I met Warren shortly afterwards and I told him that it was nothing to do with him. I have ridden for Warren, I have ridden winners for him, but I haven't ridden any of the horses that he has for Malcolm Denmark.

I might one day ride for Malcolm Denmark again, but it will probably be up to Carl if it ever arises again. I thought I wouldn't ride for Charlie Mann again, but I did. You get over these things.

Hennessy was my 186th winner of the season. I didn't reach the 200 landmark, but it wasn't a bad total, it was 64 more than Dickie Johnson, and we missed a lot of days with the weather, I had also broken through the 3,000 winner mark and I had landed another championship. My 14th.

CHAPTER 33

Not in the Top 10

The Professional Jockeys' Association (PJA) doesn't do a bad job. They look out for jockeys' interests, they make sure that jockeys have a voice in the world of British racing politics when sometimes you need to jump up and down a little in order to get anywhere. Also, they look after jockeys' well-being and health, and if ever a jockey has a problem, it can always go to the PJA.

Michael Caulfield was chief executive when I arrived in the UK. Michael was great for jockeys, and he became a good friend. He left in 2003 to set up his own sports psychology clinic, and is now a very successful sports psychologist. A fellow called John Blake took over from Michael, but I'm not sure what John Blake really did.

Josh Apiafi succeeded John Blake in 2007. We thought that Josh Apiafi would be good for the organisation, he had been an amateur rider and he had worked for the betting exchange Betfair for a bit, but he seemed enthusiastic. I was joint president when he was appointed; they usually have a National Hunt jockey and a flat jockey as joint presidents, so I represented the jumps lads while Steve Drowne was the flat representative.

One of my main objectives as joint president was for jockeys to have their own doctor. Have one person appointed, create a full-time position so that we would have our own doctor who knew the jockeys and knew the injuries. I thought that Doc Pritchard would be the perfect person for the job. Even if he wasn't interested, there was nobody better positioned to advise us on the type of person we should recruit.

The first thing most jockeys did when they were injured was call Doc Pritchard. His advice is top class, his referrals are sound, and it doesn't matter what time of the day or night you call him.

Betfair and the Injured Jockeys' Fund kindly put up the funding for the job, and it was quite a well-paid position. I didn't really have a lot of interest in the other things that were going on with the PJA, but I thought the doctor was crucial – it was the one thing that I was sure we needed to get right. I told Josh Apiafi this, so he was well aware of my view. I also told him that he should keep Doc Pritchard informed as to how things were developing, and he said he would. I wanted to be sure that, before any appointment was made, Doc Pritchard was happy with the person. I thought that that was important. I am well aware that not everyone would have agreed with this. Not everyone outside the weigh room would have agreed with what Doc Pritchard did or said, even patrons of the Injured Jockeys' Fund, who were part-funding the position.

It transpired that Doc Pritchard was actually interested in the job. I thought, perfect. He used to ride himself, he knew what it was like being a rider, he knew all the lads in the weigh room, he had worked a lot at the races, he had been in the weigh room, he knew the type of injuries that the lads would have, and he knew specialists all over the country, back specialists, hand specialists, face specialists, people who he could trust and recommend to us.

I know that some people on the British Horceracing Authority wouldn't have shared my opinion, and fair enough – I respected that. If he wasn't the right person for the job, then he wasn't the right person for the job, but I still wanted him to be kept informed. Before we employed someone, I wanted to make sure that Doc Pritchard was happy with who we employ, whether it's him or someone else.

A few weeks passed and I heard that another person was going to get the job, Dr Anna Louise Mackinnon. I thought fair enough, obviously they decided that she was better for the job than Doc Pritchard, fine. She's a nice woman, she should be good, I have no sides. I didn't have any problems with her as long as Doc Pritchard was happy. Josh called me.

'Yes, Doc Pritchard is fine with everything,' he said. 'I spoke to him and he's happy that Anna Louise is getting the job.'

All fine. I met Doc at the races a couple of weeks later.

'So you were happy enough with Anna Louise getting the job,' I said.

'What?' Doc looked confused.

'Josh Apiafi spoke to you,' I said. 'You were happy with Anna-Louise.'

Doc looked at me blankly.

'Josh never spoke to me.'

I was livid at first. Then I started doubting myself. I rang Gee and asked her what had happened here, if I told her that Josh told me that he had spoken to Doc Pritchard.

'Yes you did,' Gee said. 'And Josh told me as well himself, told me just what you are telling me now, that he spoke to Doc and that he was happy with Anna Louise.'

That was it for me.

'I'll tell you what,' I said to Gee. 'Can you ring the PJA and tell them to take my name off their books. Tell them that I'm resigning as joint president, they can get someone else. I want nothing more to do with it. And I'm not paying into any insurance schemes any more. I'm finished.'

I have no personal issues with Anna Louise, I'm sure she's very good at her job, but I still think to this day that Doc Pritchard should have got the job. Because I'm still in the position where I'm ringing Doc Pritchard looking for advice or recommendations, and I'm still referring other riders to him when they ring me with an issue, which they often do. Even so, if I had been told that Anna Louise had got the job because she was the better candidate, that she had a better CV, was better qualified for the position, fine. But I wasn't. I don't think I was being precious either, I think as joint president it was reasonable to expect that you be told the truth.

Kevin Darley took over as chief executive in 2009, and he asked me back as joint president, so I went back, but only because Josh Apiafi had left. I sometimes see Josh at golf days and the like, and I say hello, but as far as dealing with him goes, he's just not for me.

*

I had a pretty sore fall off Teeming Rain in the Sussex National at Plumpton on 3rd January 2010. We got the second-last fence wrong and he got rid of me, he didn't actually fall, and the fall that I got off him wasn't that bad, but a following horse kicked me in the ribs. I don't think any of my ribs were broken, but it wasn't pleasant.

In January 2010, a big freeze gripped the UK and Ireland, and it looked like all racing was going to be abandoned for a while. JP called me from Barbados that evening and asked me if I wanted to go out for a couple of days, bring Chanelle and Eve, Jonjo was there, just relax, allow my ribs to heal. I told Chanelle. This was a Sunday evening. Before I got off the phone, Chanelle had booked flights for six o'clock on Monday morning.

It was just after Christmas and a lot of the Magnier kids were there as well. JP Magnier, Coolmore supremo John and Sue's son, asked me to look after his little nephew Max Wachman, David and Kate Wachman's son, John and Sue Magnier's grandson. Max was about four or five. I said no problem. JP told me that he was afraid of the water, so not to take him close to the water. Fine.

The problem was that I thought that if I took him into the water and played with him in it, he would get over his fear. So I took him down to the water's edge, holding his little hand, and we had a little paddle. There were waves coming in and the little guy seemed to like letting the waves wash over his feet. Then I picked him up, time to be more daring, and brought him out into the water. There were waves about, but it was fine, and little Max seemed to be fairly happy.

Next thing, this massive wave caught us, came right over us and turned us upside down. So I'm twirling around under the water, under this wave, I have no idea if I still have a grip of Max or not, and all I can think of is, Jesus Christ I'm after drowning this young lad, I'm after killing the heir to the Coolmore estate, and that after I was told not to let him near the water!

Thankfully I found Max under the waves. He was grand. It must have been a little scary and a little exhilarating for him at the same time. I concentrated on the exhilarating part when I discussed it with him, and asked him not to tell his dad.

'You won't tell your dad, will you?'

'No.'

'You won't, will you?'

'No.'

He told his dad. The first thing he did when he saw him: Dad, guess what. We had a good laugh about it, succession lines were still intact, and I think I cured little Max's fear of water.

*

Professional gambler and racehorse owner Harry Findlay called me shortly after racing resumed and asked me if I would be free to ride Denman in the Gold Cup. Denman is trained by Paul Nicholls and is obviously Ruby's ride, but Harry and Paul Barber wanted a jockey sorted early for Denman for the Gold Cup, and Ruby was obviously going to ride Kauto Star, so they asked me to ride Denman. Whoever rode Denman in the Gold Cup would ride him in his prep race as well, the Aon Chase at Newbury on Totesport Trophy day, 13th February. JP didn't have a Gold Cup horse that year, nor did Jonjo, so after checking with them, I let Harry know that I would be able to ride Denman. He was a super ride to get in the Gold Cup.

There was a lot written about the fact that I had been offered the ride. Not everybody thought that I was the right man for the job. Tom Segal, for example, Mr Pricewise in the *Racing Post,* one of the most respected tipsters in the business, said that I wasn't the right man for Denman. He wrote that, actually, I couldn't ride over a fence and that I wouldn't be in his top 10 jockeys for Denman.

I wondered where he was going with it. I respect him as a tipster and I always read his *Racing Post* column every Saturday. But I don't know where he was going passing judgement on someone's ability to ride over fences. He's good on form, on assessing value, but I'm not sure that he's an authority on the nuances of riding over fences. Maybe he wanted to get first-mover advantage, maybe he thought that I was gone at the game, that I was going to retire soon, and he wanted to be able to say that he was the first person to have spotted it. Who knows?

Did I give a toss about whether a tipster thought that I could ride over fences? Did I heck. I couldn't have cared less. It was irrelevant. Barstool talk. Also, I know myself, I knew that I was riding as well as ever; I knew that, deep down, I was the best judge of how well I was riding.

The statistics don't lie. I'm not being big-headed but it's a fact that I have ridden more winners over fences than any other rider, ever, so how did that happen if I can't ride over a fence? Tom Segal did come back after I won the Grand National and admit that he was wrong, but it was all completely irrational. It was absurd to come out with the statement in the first place, and then it was a bit daft to admit he was wrong after the Grand National. Just because I won the Grand National, it didn't make me a good jumps jockey. If I wasn't a good jumps jockey before I won the National, then I wasn't a good jumps jockey afterwards either.

Denman was long odds-on to win the Aon Chase, as he should have been. I didn't feel under any major pressure going out. I had been beaten on Best Mate, for God's sake, it doesn't get much worse than that. The way I look at these things, the worst thing that can happen is that you get beaten, and every horse can get beaten, so that helps you handle the pressure a little bit. I had to amend that one after the Aon Chase though: the worst thing that can happen is you fall off him.

I was never really happy with Denman through the race, I could never really get him going and stretching. I thought we had gone a fair pace, but when I had a look around on the approach to the cross-fence, the fifth-last, the fence before you turn into the home straight, I was surprised at how close to us the other horses were.

Off the bend and going to the fourth-last, I was thinking these horses are a lot closer to me than they should be. Niche Market was actually almost alongside when we took off at the fourth-last. Then disaster. Denman hit the fence, and staggered like a drunk on landing. We lost five or six lengths, we were away to the left, suddenly Niche Market had flown. I tried to get Denman organised for the next fence, the third-last. He was a bit shaken, but we had to make up the ground. Defeat was a real possibility. We were meeting the fence on a stride. One, two, up. I asked him, he wasn't sure, his confidence rocked. He stepped at it a bit, tentatively, put his front legs into the fence, almost bunny-hopped over to the far side. I lost my balance, bobbled on his back, and fell off.

Ah fuck. What just happened? Did I just fall off Denman? Of all the horses to fall off. Ah fuck. They're going to have plenty to write about now, aren't they?

I dreaded walking back in, facing the crowds, facing the reporters, facing the connections. But I have to say, Paul Nicholls was brilliant, Harry Findlay was brilliant, Paul Barber, who owned the horse in partnership with Harry, was brilliant. It was just one of those things.

I was gutted for Harry. He was the one who put his neck on the block, he was the one who wanted me to ride the horse, and then I rewarded him by falling off. However, there was never any question of me not riding Denman in the Gold Cup as a result. Paul Nicholls never even hinted that there was a chance of that happening, and I appreciated that.

Half an hour after I fell off Denman, I won the Totesport Trophy on Get Me Out Of Here. That's the great and the terrible thing about this game. One minute you can be flying high, the next you can be sitting in the muck, and the reverse is also the case. It was nice to win the Totesport Trophy, it was great that it was for Jonjo and JP, but it was the Denman debacle that occupied my thoughts that night.

The Totesport Trophy was really my first big win of the season. I had won the Summer Plate at Market Rasen on Nostringsattached, and I had won the Amlin Chase at Ascot on Albertas Run in November, plus the Henry VIII Chase at Sandown in December on Somersby, but the Totesport Trophy was the first real headline race that I won that season. I had ridden plenty of winners though – Get Me Out Of Here was my 162nd – and I was on track for another championship and possibly another double century.

I got down to 10 st 3 lb to ride Qaspal in the Imperial Cup on the

Saturday before Cheltenham. That was tough. When you get down that low, every extra ounce is a struggle. Qaspal was owned by JP but he was trained by Philip Hobbs, so Dave rang Philip and asked him if it was worth it for me to get down to 10 st 3 lb to ride him, and Philip said yes, it really was. So it was sweet tea and Jaffa Cakes for the week.

Philip was right, it was worth it. Qaspal won with plenty in hand, providing me with my fifth win in the Imperial Cup. In so doing, as well as picking up a good prize, he put himself in line for the bonus for any horse that can win the Imperial Cup and then at Cheltenham. Alas, even though he was entered in just about every race at Cheltenham except the bumper, and even with the 5 lb penalty he received for winning the Imperial Cup, he was balloted out of everything. He went wrong after that, and didn't run again until the following year.

I rode Get Me Out Of Here in the first race at the Cheltenham Festival, the Supreme Novices' Hurdle. I thought he had a chance of winning it, but everyone was going on about Dunguib, the Irish banker, for the week. We finished second, beaten by a head, not by Dunguib, but by Menorah and Dickie Johnson. That was a real sickener. It was the third time in five years that I had finished second in the first race at the Cheltenham Festival. Beaten by a neck on Straw Bear in 2006, beaten by two lengths on Binocular in 2008 and now beaten by a head on Get Me Out Of Here in 2010.

I was riding Binocular in the Champion Hurdle again. It had been a rocky road to Cheltenham for Binocular that year. I had been well beaten on him in the Fighting Fifth Hurdle at Newcastle on his seasonal debut, we had been beaten again in the Christmas Hurdle at Kempton, and then he had been absolutely unimpressive in winning the Contenders Hurdle at Sandown in February on his prep race for Cheltenham.

When I rode him at Sandown, I thought that he would have come forward from Kempton, be nearing his peak, but, despite the fact that he won, I felt that he had gone backwards. He jumped to his left and he gave me no feel at all. I spoke to JP afterwards.

'Something wasn't right with the horse,' I said. 'There was something bothering him, something hurting him, maybe his back, maybe his shoulder. If he runs like that in the Champion Hurdle, he'll get lapped.'

Nicky had lots of people examine Binocular. Every vet that he could lay his hands on, every person who had ever had anything to do with a horse's well-being, and nobody could find anything wrong with him. JP called me late the following week.

'I don't think Binocular is going to be running at Cheltenham,' he said. 'Everyone has looked at him and they can't find anything wrong with him, but we know he's just not right. I'm going to bring him home here to Martinstown.'

I was gutted. We deserved another shot at the Champion Hurdle, the horse deserved another shot at the Champion Hurdle, and we were going to miss out again. I had no doubt that a fully fit Binocular could win a Champion Hurdle. Alas, it wasn't to be.

Late the following week, JP called again.

'He's coming back,' he said.

'What?' I asked, shocked.

'Binocular is on his way back,' said JP quietly. 'I had the lads here look at him and they think they've sorted him out.'

'The lads' were John Halley, Coolmore's vet, and Ger Kelly, who works with John, and the back specialist Mary Bromiley. I didn't care at the time who had got him back, all I heard was that he was coming back and he was back in the Champion Hurdle picture, which was great news for me and Jonjo and JP, but bad news for those punters who laid him at 999/1 on Betfair.

I went in to Nicky's the week before the Champion Hurdle to school Binocular, see how he was, if he was well enough to run in the race. I schooled him alongside Stravinsky Dance, who was ridden by the amateur rider Sam Waley-Cohen, who in the 2010/11 season would go on to ride Long Run to win both the King George and the Gold Cup.

'I'm going to be going fast here,' I said to Sam. 'I'm sorry, but I want to find out if this fellow is good enough to run in the Champion Hurdle, and the only way I'm going to find that out for sure is if I go flat out. Nicky likes his horses to be ridden upsides when they school, so if you could keep up with me, that would be great.'

Sam just nodded and fastened the chin-strap on his helmet.

Fair play to Sam, he did keep up, and he did well to do so, because we flew. I don't think I've ever gone as fast over five flights of hurdles before, and Sam was right with me. Unfortunately, it may not have been the best Cheltenham preparation in the world for Stravinsky Dance. She ran in the Mares' Hurdle, and she took off with Sam. She went about 12 lengths clear over the first five hurdles before she faded. She must have thought she was still schooling.

I got off Binocular with a smile on my face.

It was still difficult to be confident in Binocular before the Champion. He hadn't had the ideal preparation. He had been over to Ireland and back literally a couple of weeks before the race, which wasn't ideal, and we still couldn't be certain that whatever had been ailing him wouldn't return during the race.

It didn't. After we jumped the second-last, he was travelling so well up on the outside of old nemesis Celestial Halo that I took a pull on him. I sat on him until after we had straightened up for home, then I said go, and I could feel him picking up underneath me, like I had just changed gear. He pinged the final flight, met it right in his stride, and stayed on really well all the way to the line.

It was a year later than I thought it would be, but I always thought that Binocular was a Champion Hurdle horse, and now, finally, he had won it. JP owned Istabraq, of course, he was no stranger to winning Champion Hurdles, but it still meant the world to him to win it. For me, it was almost as if I was justifying my position again, as if I was letting JP know that he didn't make a mistake when he asked me to ride for him.

I became a bit annoyed at the post-race press conference. One of the journalists started asking Nicky leading questions about the doubts about Binocular's participation in the lead-up to the race: did you not think about the punters, that type of thing, did you not think about keeping them informed? What about the person who laid Binocular at 999/1? What about the person who backed him?

The very definite implication of the questioning was that Nicky knew all along that Binocular was running, and because he was owned by JP McManus, there was a betting angle that might just make a story for his newspaper.

I'm not even sure that JP backed Binocular. I don't think he did. He was as much in the dark as everyone, as me, as Nicky. We just didn't know if he was going to run, and even when he was running, we didn't know for sure that he was fully right.

Nicky, being the gentleman that he is, was trying to give this journalist an explanation, but I just got annoyed with the insinuation, so I butted in.

'Look,' I said. 'Nobody has to justify what happened to Binocular to you or to anyone else. I was convinced he wasn't going to run. I was getting ready to ride Zaynar. We knew as much as everyone else knew, so don't try to be making out that there was something untoward in this, because there wasn't.'

I got a fairly good thumping from Jered in the first race on the Thursday. He fell at the first and I got a kick on the head and a kick on the knee from a following horse. I was dazed. I knew where I was but my head was spinning. I nearly got to a point where I was happy to lie there on the grass. I would have gladly gone to sleep right there on the turf, had a little nap and then got ready for the next race.

However, the last thing you want to do when your head is spinning is let the doctor know. You don't want to run the risk of being stood down, so when the doctor got to me I told him about my knee, got him concentrating on that, give me a couple of minutes to get my head together in case he starts asking me questions in order to try to determine if I am concussed or not. It's a bit like a boxer getting knocked to the floor; you take the count to eight in order to get your wits about you.

I started thinking of the answers to the questions he might ask me. Where are you? Easy one. The back of the first fence at Cheltenham. What is the name of the horse you were just riding? Easy as well. Jered, the bugger. If he had remained upright I wouldn't be in this position. What won the Champion Hurdle yesterday? Was that a dream?

I convinced the doctor that I was okay and got back to the weigh room. Shane, my valet, took one look at me when I got back to the weigh room and got me a cup of tea with lots of sugar.

I wasn't feeling great before I went out to ride Albertas Run in the Ryanair Chase two races later, but I had taken plenty of painkillers and I was feeling much better. I rode him handily, we were always in the front rank, we took it up at the fourth-last and he stayed on really well to beat Poquelin and J'y Vole.

It rained on Gold Cup day. People said that the softer ground would suit Denman, but I thought that it was neither an advantage nor a disadvantage. Paul Nicholls told me beforehand that he was very happy with Denman, that he expected him to run a big race, and he duly did. Kauto Star fell at the fourth last and gave Ruby a fairly nasty fall. Actually, he gave himself a fairly nasty fall. If the ground hadn't been on the easy side, it could have been a disaster.

I had Denman prominent throughout, I had him galloping, and we led into the home straight with Paddy Brennan and Imperial Commander on our outside. I knew that Denman would stay the trip, but I wasn't sure about Imperial Commander, he had never run over three and a quarter miles before, so I was hoping that our stamina would win out. Regrettably, Imperial Commander did stay the trip. He passed us at the second-last and we just couldn't get back at him.

It was a good Cheltenham for me, but it could have been a great one.

As well as winning the Champion Hurdle and the Ryanair Chase, I had finished second on Denman in the Gold Cup, I had finished second on Forpadydeplasterer in the Champion Chase, and I had finished second also on Burton Port in the RSA Chase, the old Sun Alliance. Then I won the Midlands National at Uttoxeter on the Saturday after Cheltenham on Synchronised.

Mathematically I had another championship in the bag, so I headed off to Portugal for a bit of golf for a few days with Carl, Fitzy and Shane, and set my sights on Aintree.

CHAPTER 34

That's Pushing It

I am a patron of Alder Hey Children's Hospital in Liverpool, and all the jockeys visit there during Aintree every year. It's tradition now, we have been doing it for about 10 years on the Friday morning of the Grand National meeting. We meet the children, chat to them, talk to their parents. It puts everything into perspective, seeing the kids there with cancer, and how happy they are, how nothing seems to faze them. And their parents. I know I wouldn't be so brave.

The day before the 2010 Grand National, I met Luca Nash. Luca was a great kid, so happy and full of life. He had a brain tumour and only had a very slight chance of recovery, but his parents Vicky and James were clinging to that chance.

I kept in touch with them. They are great people and are into racing too. I had photos taken with Luca, and I emailed them regularly, just to check in and to find out about Luca's progress.

Last Christmas, 2010, Luca's scan results revealed that the tumour had almost fully cleared. The treatment was working; the chemotherapy had had the desired effect. Vicky and James couldn't believe it – their little boy had a chance at life. Then he went in for another scan in March, and the tumour was back worse than ever.

Before the 2011 Grand National meeting, I phoned the girls at Alder Hey to ask them how Luca was doing, to get them to tell him that I would be around to see him during Aintree week as usual, but they told me that he had gone home. Vicky and James had basically taken him so that he could die at home.

I called to see him at home on the Wednesday before Aintree started, and it was just the worst thing ever. He was in the living room, just lying on his bed, with the curtains pulled. Whatever drug he was on, morphine or whatever he was taking to relieve the pain, just had him listless, a three-and-a-half-year-old little boy with the life draining out of him.

When I had seen him in Alder Hey, he looked like a cancer patient, he was on chemotherapy and had lost all his hair. When I saw him lying on his bed in his living room though, he looked like a healthy little boy, he had all his hair and his face didn't look drawn or gaunt. And he had grown since I had seen him. He looked like a normal three-and-a-half-year-old boy, except that he was just lying there lethargically, and you knew that the life was being sucked out of him by this cursed tumour.

It was the saddest thing I have ever experienced, sitting there with Vicky and James, helpless. It's unimaginable, sitting there, not being able to do anything, just watching, knowing that your child is dying. Vicky was pregnant again, but the fact that Luca would probably never get to meet his little brother or sister made it even sadder. I choked back tears as I spoke to Vicky and James.

I'm not sure why Luca got to me more than any of the other children that I used to visit. I had been going to Alder Hey for 10 years before I met Luca, and I always thought, yes it's desperately sad, all these kids with cancer, you couldn't imagine anything worse. But then I'd get myself along to the races and all I would think of was riding horses, riding winners, winning the Grand National.

Luca touched a nerve with me though. Something clicked. He was just the nicest little fellow, so happy, and his parents were brilliant. Maybe it was because he was more or less the same age as my own daughter Eve, maybe it was easier for me to imagine what Vicky and James were going through, maybe it was easier for me to empathise and think, there but for the grace of God go any of us. How does it happen that one child has a brain tumour and another doesn't?

I had thought I would stay for 20 minutes, that I would just go in and say hello because I wouldn't be able to see Luca in Alder Hey on the Friday as usual. I thought going in, this is going to be horrible, this is going to be awkward, but I need to do it. It wasn't awkward at all, and the only horribleness was in the sadness of Luca's sickness. I stayed for two hours before I peeled myself away, said goodbye to Vicky and James, said goodbye to Luca.

Three weeks later, Luca Nash died.

*

JP was set to have four runners in the 2010 Grand National: King Johns Castle, trained by Arthur Moore, Arbor Supreme, trained by Willie Mullins, and Don't Push It and Can't Buy Time, both trained by Jonjo. I was never going to ride King Johns Castle, even though he had finished second in the race in 2008. There were just too many doubts about him. And Arbor Supreme just wasn't for me either. I just didn't think he was a National horse. So I had decided from a long way out that I was going to ride one of Jonjo's horses – I just didn't know which one.

I thought that Can't Buy Time was the safer option. I thought he would jump around, and he had won a good chase at Cheltenham for me on New Year's Day. That said, Don't Push It was the classier horse. He was travelling well in the 2007 Arkle when he came down at the second-last fence – Can't Buy Time would have been lapped in an Arkle – and he had got to within three parts of a length of Denman in a novices' chase three months before that. Also, he had won the handicap chase at the 2009 Aintree Grand National meeting over the normal Mildmay fences.

However, he had disappointed me when he had got beaten at Warwick that December, and he was desperately disappointing in the Pertemps Hurdle at Cheltenham. I didn't ride him in that, I rode Ainama instead, but Alan Berry, Frank's son, rode him and he pulled him up when he was tailed off at the last flight.

As well as riding him in the Pertemps, Alan Berry also looked after Don't Push It at home in Jonjo's, and he did a fantastic job with him between Cheltenham and Aintree. Don't Push It is a bit of a character, he has his own ideas about life, but Alan knows him intimately, he understands his whims, and between him and Jonjo, they worked on getting him spot on for Aintree.

The Pertemps was only three weeks before the National, and Jonjo hadn't been able to find any reason why he ran so badly. If he hadn't run at Cheltenham, I would have chosen him over Can't Buy Time. But that run made me think that maybe the other horse was the better ride.

I was in the bath at the Radisson Hotel in Liverpool on Thursday morning when Dave Roberts called. It was about 8.30 am.

'What are you riding in the National?' he asked.

'I don't know, Dave,' I said. I was being honest. 'It will be either Don't Push It or Can't Buy Time. I'll call you in an hour and let you know.'

I called Jonjo.

'I have no idea which one of them I'm going to ride, Jonjo,' I said.

'It's nothing to do with me,' he said. Helpful. 'I just don't know why Don't Push It ran so badly at Cheltenham. He seems fine now though. He's in good shape.'

'I think we should toss a coin,' I said.

'Okay,' he said, 'I'll toss it.'

'Grand.'

Silence for a moment. I was thinking, it probably doesn't matter which of them I ride, neither of them really has a chance of winning the thing. Both of them were 50/1 shots so I was going to be riding a 50/1 shot in the Grand National whatever the coin said.

'Well?' I asked.

'I'm going to toss it again,' said Jonjo, laughter in his voice.

Silence.

'Well?' I asked again. This was getting ridiculous.

'Don't Push It,' said Jonjo. 'You're riding Don't Push It.'

'Grand,' I said.

I don't know for certain, but there was probably no coin. Truth be told, I knew that Jonjo wanted to steer me towards Don't Push It. He just thought he was the classier horse. He was sure that Can't Buy Time would run a good race, but if one of them had a chance of winning it, it was Don't Push It, not Can't Buy Time. I reckoned tossing a coin at the other end of a telephone was a good way to decide it. JP said after the race that he wouldn't mind getting a lend of the coin that Jonjo used.

I was relaxed on the Friday night. I was after riding a double on the day at Aintree, Albertas Run in the Melling Chase and Ringaroses in the three-mile handicap hurdle. I went down to the hotel bar with Chanelle in the early evening, then had a bath and was in bed by nine o'clock.

I had done an interview with Helen Chamberlain on Soccer AM on Grand National morning every year for the previous six or seven years, but I didn't do it in 2010. It just never happened, I'm not sure why, she just never asked me. Maybe they were sick of me going on every year and then not riding the winner. (I spoke to Helen a couple of days after the race and told her that, all these years I was wondering why I couldn't win the Grand National, and now I knew: it was her fault all along. I'm not superstitious, but I had to turn her down in 2011. There was no way I was going to do it in 2011, just in case!)

I got to the course early and took things easy. I felt relaxed, no major pressure, no panic. I didn't think that I was any more or less relaxed than other years, but maybe I was a little more relaxed, because I didn't think that I had a great chance of winning the race.

Fitzy was working for the BBC on the day, and he did an interview with me early in the morning. He told me afterwards that he had never seen me so relaxed on Grand National day. If it wins, it wins. If it doesn't, it doesn't. Fretting about it wasn't going to change anything.

Actually, everyone was very relaxed in the parade ring beforehand. JP is always quiet before a race, he doesn't want to get too involved, especially for the bigger races. He just wished me luck. Jonjo is quiet as well, we didn't have too many tactics, he never ties me to instructions. We discuss the race, what might happen, but he leaves it up to me to see how the race develops, which is how it should be. If you are tying a jockey to strict instructions, if you are not allowing him to work it out for himself, you are employing the wrong jockey. Then he legged me up.

I did get butterflies when I got to the start though. I always do. You can't help but get carried away by the atmosphere. You're circling at the start just in front of the grandstand; you can hear the hum of the stands, the cheering, the anticipation before the most famous horse race in the world. This is why you do what you do. If you can't get butterflies as you circle at the start before the Grand National, you are doing the wrong thing.

Don't Push It was getting butterflies too. He was sweating like mad. I didn't mind too much. It is usually a negative sign when a horse sweats up before a race – it usually means that he is anxious, too anxious to run his race. But Don't Push It always sweated up, it was just him. I took my feet out of the irons and patted him down the neck. Jonjo had inserted a pair of earplugs into his ears, just to insulate him a bit from the noise, to help him relax. We didn't want him wearing them in the race as we hadn't declared them, but I wanted to leave it until as near to start time as possible before I took them out. I didn't want him getting buzzed up too early.

I looked up at the big screen to check on the betting. That was something that Martin Pipe had always told me. If you are circling at the start and you are close to the stands or close to a screen on which they are showing the betting, always have a look. It's no harm knowing what is being backed in the race, what else is fancied, what your dangers might be. I couldn't believe what I was seeing, Don't Push It was plummeting in price: 20/1, 16/1, 14/1, 12/1.

I couldn't believe it. I don't know how he was sent off as joint favourite given that he was 50/1 the previous week. It didn't make sense. The fact that I was riding him couldn't have had that much of an impact and I don't know who was backing him. I don't think his owner backed him at all.

For the previous four or five years, I had always tried to follow Ruby in the early stages of the Grand National. I figured, he had won it twice, he knew what he was doing, he knew how to win one of these things, so I should be doing whatever he was doing. I used to say to him, I'll be your shadow. Wherever you go, I'll be right behind you. And he'd be laughing at me during the race, you weren't joking were you?

This year though, Ruby had had a bad fall off Celestial Gold in the Aintree Hurdle earlier in the day and broken his arm. Poor Ruby was on his way to Fazakerley Hospital while we were all heading down to the start in the Grand National. It was desperate for Ruby. His intended ride Big Fella Thanks, now the mount of Barry Geraghty, had been favourite. I'm sure he was listening to the race or watching it in hospital, hoping Big Fella Thanks wouldn't win it. It's terrible, but it's human nature. Deep down, you don't want the horse you were supposed to ride to win it. It would be like me – if Can't Buy Time had won it, I would have found it very difficult to say afterwards that I was delighted for the owner and the trainer. If you were being honest, you would say it was the worst possible result.

I used to get a lot of coverage in the build-up to the Grand National because I had never won it. It used to annoy me a bit in the first few years, but then I just used to laugh it off. And then you think to yourself, I'm not the only person who has never won the Grand National. John Francome never won it, Peter Scudamore never won it, Jonjo never won it. They are three of the best jump jockeys of recent times, and none of them won it. Poor Jonjo never got around. On the morning of the 2010 race, Jonjo took his two young fellows around the track. They got to the Foinavon fence, the one after Becher's Brook.

'Okay lads,' he said to them, 'this is where the race ends.'

They looked at him, a little confused.

'I don't know what happens after this,' he said with a chuckle. 'I've never got further than this.'

The starter asked us to line up, and a couple of lads started charging towards the tape. I could see that King Johns Castle and Paul Carberry were way behind us, and there were a couple of other horses that weren't ready. We circled for another minute or so, and then the starter called us in again. King Johns Castle was still being a bit reluctant, but this looked like it could be it.

'Come on then!'

As the starter released the tape, the crowd roared behind us.

When I was younger, I used to go down the inside. I figured it was the shortest way around. The fences were bigger down the inside, so you were saving ground. As I was got older, though, I was looking at the riders who had won the race a couple of times, Carl Llewellyn, Richard Dunwoody and Ruby Walsh, they all went down the middle of the track. There was no need to be brave; better to get your horse jumping and keep him safe, you can be too brave as well, you know. Also if you are in the middle, you have more options, you can go left or right if a horse falls in front of you.

So I was in the middle of the track and towards the rear, crossing the Melling Road on the way to the first fence. Don't Push It jumped the first well, jumped the second well, then he came to the third fence, the big ditch, probably the most difficult fence on the course, coming, as it does, so early in the race, and he sailed over it. He was taking to these fences, he was enjoying himself over them. He could just run a big race here, I thought, he has every chance of getting around at the very least.

He jumped Becher's Brook in his stride. I settled in and started enjoying it. Down the side of the track, over the Canal Turn and Valentine's Brook, and back around to the main racecourse, over the Chair and the water jump and back up past the stands, we were about ninth or tenth now. I heard the cheers from the grandstand as we passed the winning post for the first time and headed out again, just one more circuit, and my feeling of God I'm enjoying this turned to, you know what, we could win this.

At the second fence on the second circuit, I saw a stride, gave him a squeeze, but he didn't see the same stride, he put in a little short one and popped over it. It could have been disaster, I could have put him on the floor and that would have been it for another 12 months. He was cute, he knew what he was doing, and that was great. I was happy that he was cleverer than me.

Becher's Brook second time, the scene of the Clan Royal and Butler's Cabin disasters, and I just thought, just get him over it, don't let any of those other fuckers run in front of you or bring you down. They didn't, he sailed over Becher's and suddenly we were in fifth place, the five of us were clear, the field was stretching out behind us and it was beginning to get serious.

There were only two or three horses that were travelling well in front of me. Barry was going well on Big Fella Thanks, Denis O'Regan was going well on Black Apalachi, but he had been forcing a strong pace with Conna Castle for a while, Daryl Jacob was going well on Maljimar, but I wasn't certain that he would stay. Of course, there was a long way to go, there would be other horses staying on from behind, but there couldn't have been many others with a chance. Over Foinavon, towards the Canal Turn, I angled him out so that he could jump it at an angle and he flew it, just as he had done on the first circuit.

Maljimar started to drop away, and suddenly there were only four of us. Of the four, Big Fella Thanks was the one that I feared most. Barry seemed to have plenty left in the tank, and Black Apalachi and Hello Bud had been up there with the strong pace from the start. At the second fence down the side of the course, Hello Bud jumped in front of us and we made a mistake. It halted our momentum a bit, but he still had plenty of energy left, and we were still upright.

Black Apalachi made quite a bad mistake at the last on the side of the track, the third-last overall, which can't have helped him. He did well to stand up actually. Then we joined the racecourse again, crossed the Melling Road on the way back, and I'm thinking, not yet. Hold onto him. There is still a long way to go.

Going to the second-last, I gave him a squeeze and asked him to make ground up on the outside of the other three. He picked up nicely and we landed over the second-last alongside Black Apalachi, almost in front. I could see Barry wilting, and I knew my fellow would keep going, but I was still thinking, not yet, it's a long way from the last to the line. Down to the last, and I was just looking for a stride, got one, I asked him to pick up and he did, jumping the fence perfectly.

Black Apalachi was still there on my inside, and I was squeezing away, and I thought I had him. As we approached the Elbow, I was thinking, if I have to get down on the ground and carry this fellow over the line, that's what I'll do. I'm not losing this now. I have come too far.

We got to the Elbow and Black Apalachi was still there on my inside, dogged as you like – he just wouldn't go away. When the rail appeared, I moved my horse in towards it. I didn't want to cut the nose off Black Apalachi, I didn't want to risk a stewards' inquiry, but I did want to get the rail in front of him, to give him a reason to down tools, just sicken him a little.

I got onto the rail in front of Black Apalachi, and just sat down and drove for the line. I had a little look under my right shoulder and could see Black Apalachi getting further behind me. I looked ahead and could see the winning line getting closer. I wanted to scream. I thought, is this really happening? Could this be it? After all these years? Is this really the Grand National? Is this dreamland?

CHAPTER 35

Dreamland

I didn't know whether to scream, jump, cry, cheer or laugh. What do you do when you've just won the Grand National? I had no idea, I had never won the Grand National before.

I remember standing up in the irons as if I was standing on the ground. I forgot for a minute that there was a horse underneath me. I turned to the grandstand, fist clenched, and had this irrepressible urge to scream, which I did.

I don't know what it's like to score a goal in a World Cup Final, but it couldn't have been any better than this. I remember pulling my horse up and thinking, God, I can't believe this is happening. But people were congratulating me, so it must have been real. Richard Johnson and Denis O'Regan and David Casey and Davy Russell. Paddy Brennan, our travelling head lad, came running over. I can remember Martin Pipe running up towards me. I can't say that there were tears in his eyes, but it looked like there had been. He just said brilliant, brilliant AP, you've just won the Grand National, and I said something like I wish I had won one for you.

And I remember Ted Walsh coming up to me, he was the same as Martin, his eyes were red, and he just said brilliant, I'm delighted for you, it's the best thing ever. And I'm there thinking, Martin Pipe and Ted Walsh, two of the biggest names in racing, and they're nearly in tears because I have won the Grand National. If you were a young lad and someone said to you, Martin Pipe and Ted Walsh were congratulating you after you won a big race, well then you'd feel special wouldn't you?

It hit me. Have I really won the Grand National? Have I really conquered it on my 15th attempt? Suddenly Rishi Persad from the BBC is there and he's putting a microphone up to me and asking me how it feels. I had never thought about an interview, I had never thought about what I would say. When I dreamt about winning the Grand National, the dream ended at the winning line.

I said something like, oh well I've done all right now or something. I wasn't going to be a failure any more. I have a reason to be proud. I hope Eve will be proud of her daddy now. I got all choked up. Totally uncool.

Then I wanted to get water for Don't Push It. The first couple of minutes after winning it were all about me, but then I started to think, the poor horse, he's after carrying me to victory. Suddenly he became the most precious thing in the world. Get Don't Push It water, get Don't Push It whatever Don't Push It wants.

We were walking down the chute towards the winner's enclosure, and the crowd was cheering like I hadn't heard before. Everyone was shaking my hand. Paul Nicholls came over to say well done, then Timmy Murphy and Barry Geraghty. Then just before we reached the winner's enclosure, some prick tried to pull me off the horse. Everyone was shaking my hand, I was leaning down to shake hands, and this prat tried to pull me off the horse. Great lad, very funny. I was furious. In a way, I wish he had, because I would have boxed his head in. I lost it for about 30 seconds. I would have killed him. It would have been hilarious, I would have spent the night in prison, that's for sure. Grand National-winning jockey done for assault. Then I forgot about it and got carried away on the wave of elation.

I jumped off the horse in the winner's enclosure and gave Noreen McManus a hug, gave JP a hug, gave Jonjo a hug. My brother Colm was there in the winner's enclosure. Colm is the most unemotional person you will ever meet, but there were tears in his eyes as well when he put his arms around me. Chanelle was there too, I gave her a kiss, then I weighed in, 11 st 5 lb – fine. It was official.

I did more interviews, then went back to the weigh room. My valet Chris Maude was there, congratulated me, then gave out to me because he wouldn't be able to slag me any more for not winning the Grand National. I rode in the last race, a horse called Amuse Me, who didn't show at all, I think he broke a blood vessel, then I had a shower and made my way up to JP's box. It took me a while to get there. People were stopping me and asking me to sign things and having their photo taken with me, and I figured, I should do this. Why wouldn't I do this? You could be a prick and refuse, but it wouldn't be the right thing to do.

I called my mother from the car on the way back into Liverpool. I hadn't been able to get her all afternoon, but I eventually got her from the car, but there were so many people in the car, Chanelle and her friend Rachel and a few others, that I couldn't have her on hands-free. So I had the phone up to my ear when I was pulled over by a copper.

I was thinking, ah crap, I'll get a few penalty points now and we'll move on, but your man asked me to get out of the car. So I'm standing beside my car, getting a dressing down from this copper, and Rachel and Chanelle are shouting from the car, ah leave him alone, he's just won the Grand National. Unfortunately, the number plate on my car was M6 COY, so he must have known who I was. People were walking past and they were stopping, wanting their photo taken with me, which I don't think impressed the copper. I shouldn't have been on the phone, but he wasn't overly nice about it.

I called Ruby and met him and his broken arm in the Radisson as he was getting his stuff together to go home. He put his good arm around me.

So many other things happened – it was all a bit of a haze. Like I remember Richard Hughes and his dad Dessie coming up to me and saying well done. Hughesie is a good mate and his dad is a gentleman, and I appreciated their good wishes, but it wasn't until afterwards that I copped that Dessie trained Black Apalachi, who finished second. What kind of a prat was I? Well done AP. Ah thanks, yeah. It was great. And no mention of them finishing second? That wasn't good.

I received about a million text messages, and I appreciated every one. Frankie Dettori sent me one – he knew exactly how I felt having ridden in so many Epsom Derbies; he attempting his 15th when he finally won one on Authorized. Liam Brady, my childhood hero, sent me a text, Sir Alex Ferguson sent me a text, Jim Bolger sent me a text.

I didn't sleep very well that night. I went to bed at around two o'clock, but I just lay awake, awake with adrenalin, turning over all the events of the day in my mind, reliving every moment, the race itself, after the race. Some difference to the other Saturday nights when I had come out of Aintree wondering if I was ever going to win this race, thinking I don't care if I never ride in that race again.

Chanelle was asleep, so it was the first time that I had been on my own since I won the race, it was the first time I had the opportunity to fully consider what had happened, how it had happened, and appreciate the enormity of it.

My conclusion was that it was all down to Jonjo. It was his decision that I should ride Don't Push It. He put me on the right horse. The whole lot should be dedicated to him. If he hadn't put me on Don't Push It, I wouldn't have won the Grand National. My overriding feeling? I would say relief more than ecstasy. That I could relax about the Grand National now. And fulfilment – that was some feeling.

I wanted to go to Jackdaws Castle the next day, go and see Jonjo and see the lads in the yard and the horse, do the right thing, but I also wanted to be at Southwell, where I had a decent book of rides. Just because I had won the Grand National, it didn't mean I wasn't going to go to Southwell. The way I looked at it, if I didn't go to Southwell, I didn't win the Grand National. So I called Gee and asked her to organise a helicopter for me from Jackdaws Castle to Southwell. I rode a winner at Southwell, so it was well worth the trip.

There were plenty of Grand National parties. JP had a great party at Martinstown, he held another at his local GAA club, South Liberties, and they had one for me at home in Moneyglass, also in the local GAA club. Hundreds of people turned up, people I hadn't seen in 20 years but who I still recognised, and other people whom I hadn't seen in 20 years, who were just children when I left, whom I didn't recognise. That was a bit embarrassing, I hope I didn't come across as a prat, not knowing these people, not seeing them in 20 years and then suddenly when I win the Grand National, I'm back milking it. It wasn't like that. I really appreciated the fact that they wanted to celebrate the win, and I loved seeing everyone again.

Chanelle organised a party at home in Lodge Down as well. Chanelle doesn't believe in doing things by half, so when she organised a Grand National party, you could be certain that it was going to be a monster. I think she spent all my Grand National winnings on that party, I'm not joking, but it was worth it, it was a hell of a party. I wanted to have a party for the lads in the weigh room, all the lads I rode with regularly, and for the valets. We ended up with about 300 people, which was more than we thought we would have, but once you start inviting people, where do you draw the line?

I was riding at Perth the following day, as were a couple of the other lads, Graham Lee and Paddy Brennan. I hired Richard Hannon's plane to take us up, so I had to sneak off to bed at about four o'clock in the morning when the party was still in full swing. About 10 minutes after I got to bed, my door opened.

'What are you doing in bed this early?' Kieran McManus, JP's son.

'It's four o'clock in the morning, Kieran. It's past my bedtime.'

'You're very boring,' he persisted. 'The party is still in full swing. You're the host – you can't be going to bed.'

'Look,' I said, 'I'm riding at Perth tomorrow. If you don't piss off, I'm going to tell your dad that you wouldn't let me go to sleep.'

*

JP was hosting his pro-am golf event at Adare Manor in Limerick that July. He hosts the event every five years, invites most of the top professional golfers as well as an A-list of celebrities from sport, entertainment and all walks. It is an unbelievable event where everybody gives up their time for free, and which raised over €40 million for charity in 2010.

Tiger Woods was coming. That was the big news in 2010. He always does, he is a good friend of JP's and when JP asked him to come in 2010, he said of course he would without even checking his diary. This wasn't long after the incident that had made world headlines, and some people were wondering about whether he was coming or not, but any time anyone asked JP if Tiger was coming or not, JP just said that he presumed he was because he hadn't heard that he wasn't.

JP invited me to play in the event. To be even included among those people, all the top golfers, legends of the sport like Tiger, Padraig Harrington, Jose Maria Olazabal, Tom Lehman, Ernie Els and just about every top golfer you could name was a huge honour. And celebrities like Samuel L. Jackson and Michael Flatley and Hugh Grant and Michael Douglas... It was all a bit surreal.

It wasn't enough for me though. I probably felt a little brave after winning the Grand National for the host, but every opportunity I got, I asked JP if I could be paired with Tiger. I was like an annoying little child. Any time I was chatting to JP, or any time the event came up in conversation – can I play with Tiger?

JP assured me that it was an open draw, that the draw was made by the European Tour and that he had nothing to do with it. I didn't relent though. I wasn't sure that JP couldn't influence the draw. I'm not sure that there are many things in life that JP can't influence. I was a real nuisance. Can I play with Tiger, can I play with Tiger? It wasn't as if the other top golfers in the world weren't there, but all I wanted was to play with Tiger.

I played a practice round at Adare Manor on the Saturday with Fitzy and Mick Kinane and Chanelle's dad, Michael Burke. The draw was being made on Saturday evening, but we were quite late finishing, I didn't have any smart clothes with me, and I had to get to Tralee anyway, where a friend of Chanelle's was having a cancer research fundraising evening that I had promised I would attend. I was about to leave Adare Manor when I met JP.

'Are you not coming in for the draw?' he asked me.

'Ah no,' I said, 'I thought I'd head on down the road. I need to get to

Tralee. And I'm not dressed for the draw anyway.'

'Sure everyone is dressed like that,' he said. 'Come on in.'

So myself and Fitzy went in with JP, us in our golf gear, the gear we'd been wearing on the golf course all day, into the drawing room where the draw was being made, everyone in their smarts, and sat with JP at his table.

The draw started. They drew two amateur teams and then drew two professionals. It was a two-day event, so each amateur team played with the two professionals that they drew, one on the first day, one on the second day. There were 54 amateur teams of three players – our team was made up of Fitzy, Jim Brewer, a friend of JP's who was celebrating his 70th birthday, and me, and it was very generously sponsored by Derrick Smith – and 54 professionals. I was trying to work it out, I think I had a one in 27 chance of drawing Tiger, that's a 26/1 shot, and not many of those win.

The teams were being drawn, no sign of our team yet, no sign of Tiger. Ten teams were drawn, 12 teams, 14 teams, 20 teams and still no sign of us or of Tiger. I looked at JP, this is looking fairly promising. JP just smiled. We had gone from 26/1 to just about 16/1. Then JP Magnier's team was drawn, and our team. I held my breath as I waited to hear who we would play with. Steve Webster was the first professional drawn for us, a good guy who plays on the European Tour, a great golfer and great craic, as we found out. Our odds of getting Tiger had just plummeted though.

And Tiger Woods!

I couldn't believe it. I just went, yessss! I looked over at JP and he was looking at me, laughing. Fantastic! To this day, I don't know if JP influenced the draw. I'm not sure how he could have, the draw was made in full view of everyone, this guy swirling these balls around a glass bowl and picking one out. I didn't care if it was fixed or not, I just got the right result, in the same way as when Jonjo tossed the coin for Don't Push It or Can't Buy Time, I got the right result.

I started texting everybody I knew to let them know, to do some gloating. The first person I texted was Richard Hughes, a huge golf fan, a huge Tiger fan, and he's a bloody good golfer.

'We got Tiger!' was all I said in my text.

Hughesie came back:

'What, eaten by one?!'

I got Ruby to caddy for me. I had asked Carl and Sam Thomas as I knew they would both get a big kick out of it, but neither of them could do it. Ruby was walking around with his arm in a sling, he's not a massive golf player and I wasn't sure how much he would be into it, but when I asked him if he wanted to do it, he jumped at the chance. He was delighted.

It was as good as I imagined it would be. We played the first day with Steve Webster. It was amazing. People everywhere. Normally you stand up on the first tee in these pro-ams and you think, I'd better hit this drive right, everyone is watching, pressure on. Then once you get off the first tee you're fine because there aren't many people out on the course. This was completely different, the spectators were everywhere. Every shot was like your first drive.

Then playing with Tiger the second day was just incredible. If I thought there were a lot of spectators around the first day, it was nothing compared to the second day. Everybody wanted a piece of Tiger. And he was amazing, he was very chatty, very interested in what Ruby and I did for a living, interested in the psychology that went behind it and the physical pressures.

The craic was good as well, we had a lot of funny moments. Like I seemed to find every bunker that was on the course. It seemed that every time I hit a shot, it would end up in some bunker. Tiger was laughing.

'Does your caddy not point out where the hazards are for you?' he asked.

He obviously didn't know Ruby Walsh very well.

Then on the 14th green, I had this putt that was breaking about four different ways. Ruby thought he saw an opportunity.

'How much do you bet that my man gets down in two?' he asked Tiger.

'Whatever makes you nervous, buddy,' said Tiger.

Ruby just laughed. No bet. I three-putted.

Any time I duffed a shot, Ruby would throw the bag on the ground in a huff. That would usually get a good laugh from the crowd. And then there was a little girl who broke past the security guards on the ninth tee and came running out to Tiger to get him to sign her hat, which he did willingly. Then another little boy ran out with a cap, and he signed that as well. He was just a star. Then there was this stampede. I'm not joking, it was as if someone had dropped a million pounds at his feet.

I told him about me begging JP to arrange it so that I could play with him. I wasn't embarrassed to tell him that. There is no point in trying to be cool when you are dealing with Tiger Woods. And I was telling him that there were doubts among some about him turning up at all, with the turbulent couple of months he had had to endure. I told him that I thought that JP really appreciated the fact that he came.

'Ah,' he said nonchalantly, 'when JP asks you to do something, you just do it, don't you?'

CHAPTER 36

Personality High

I t had been some year. Win the Champion Hurdle, win the Grand National, win another championship, play golf with Tiger Woods. It wasn't because I had played golf with Tiger Woods, though, that people started talking about me as a contender for the BBC Sports Personality of the Year 2010.

I remember watching *Sports Personality of the Year* as a kid, sitting on the sofa with my mom in Moneyglass. I remember Barry McGuigan winning it in 1985, beating Steve Cram and Ian Botham. That was huge, an Ulsterman, a man from Monaghan, winning the BBC's top sports award. And it's a strange thing. It's not like any other prize, it's not like the Grand National or the Gold Cup or the Champion Hurdle, you can't win it yourself, you have to rely on other people's votes, you have to allow other people to win it for you.

Of course, it is the culmination of everything, you can't win it if you haven't excelled in your sport, but it's out of your hands, and that's a strange feeling. I'm privileged that so many people wanted me to win it. It's a deeply humbling feeling. Just as humbling as looking at the engravings on the trophy of the past winners: Sir Steve Redgrave, Ryan Giggs, Steve Davis, Nick Faldo and Jackie Stewart, all the way back to Bobby Moore, Henry Cooper and Stirling Moss. How could Anthony McCoy belong in the same ball park?

The first jockey? Sir Gordon Richards, Lester Piggott, Frankie Dettori. It is unbelievable that none of them ever won it.

I appreciated the support that Racing For Change had given me, but I am not naïve enough to think that it was purely for my benefit. On the back of a push for me, they saw an opportunity to get articles about racing into the main newspapers, onto the radio, onto the television, and they exploited it.

I found it all a little bit of a pain, to be honest. It was all a little embarrassing. Not because I didn't appreciate it, because I did, but because

I was everywhere, and it was the same stuff everywhere. I was being asked the same questions by different journalists and I was giving the same answers.

The racecourses got behind me as well. There was the Vote AP Gold Cup at Cheltenham in December and several other Vote AP races around the country, very kindly organised by Andy Stewart. There were life-size cardboard cutouts of me all over the place with the reminder, don't forget to vote for AP. The lads in the weigh room, my colleagues, my supposed friends, wouldn't let you get too far ahead of yourself. They had drawn moustaches and glasses on the cutouts, and worse.

It was all a little cringey. No matter who you are in life, no matter how good or bad you are at what you do, not everybody is going to have the same opinion of you. Some people are going to like you, some people are going to dislike you. We definitely provided lots of fodder for the latter group. Who does this guy think he is? Cardboard cutouts? C'mon.

*

Sunday morning, I was on Radio 1 with Sarah Cox. I'm sure she had no idea who the hell I was, but she was very supportive. I had spoken to lots of different people, different television channels, different radio stations; I remember Chris Evans and Johnny Saunders on Radio 2 were very supportive, as was Alan Brazil on TalkSport. Ed Chamberlin on Sky Sports News told everyone to vote for me. I did an interview on Sky News on Sunday morning before I left home for Birmingham, and Eve was delighted because she saw herself on television.

I was the favourite for the award with the bookmakers, but that counted for nothing. My overriding thought was that the bookmakers are racing people, they are coming at it with a racing hat on, and people who are betting on it are most likely racing people. So the vast majority of people who had been involved in setting and influencing the odds were racing people; of course they were going to think that I had a chance. The wider world probably had no idea who I was.

I didn't think for one moment that I would get enough votes to win it. I remember looking and seeing that Ryan Giggs got about 150,000 or 160,000 votes when he won it in 2009, and I thought, how the hell am I going to get 150,000 votes? If you had told me then that I would get over 290,000 votes, over 40 per cent of the vote, four times as many votes as the runner-up got, I would have said you were getting me mixed up with a golfer.

Admittedly, I had won the Sports Journalists Association award a couple of days beforehand, and that was a good omen. I had beaten Graeme McDowell by one vote. One of the journalists told me that I was the only person for whom all the sports journalists had voted. That was a fairly amazing feeling, to have all the sports journalists vote for you. Of course it doesn't have even nearly as wide an audience as the *BBC Sports Personality of the Year* programme, but as a sports person, it meant almost as much to me.

A couple of days before that award, I was honoured with a couple of Derby Awards, the National Hunt Jockey of the Year Award and a special President's Award. Unfortunately, I couldn't attend the presentation lunch. The Horse Racing Writers' and Photographers' Association, which runs the awards, contacted Gee the previous week and asked her if I could be there, that I had won two awards, including the prestigious President's Award. It was a Monday afternoon and racing wouldn't be that good, they reasoned. No chance, Gee told them.

'What if we were to ring JP or Jonjo,' they asked, 'and ask them if AP could get off for the day to attend the lunch? It really is a very prestigious award.'

'If you could get them to ring God,' Gee said, 'and ask God if he could sort out something, that would be their only chance.'

Racing was abandoned that Monday because of the snow and the frost. It looked like they had actually got through to God. But the BHA put on a replacement meeting at Southwell, a mixed card, three flat races and three bumpers, and I was riding in one of the bumpers. Again the organisers of the Derby Awards got on to Gee.

'Can he come to the awards now, racing has been abandoned, it's only bumpers at Southwell. Surely he'll come to the awards.'

'He can't,' Gee told them. 'He's riding at Southwell.'

She was right. If I didn't go to Southwell, I didn't get any awards in the first place. It has always been my job to go and ride, not to go to lunch, even if it is to go and accept an award. Much and all as I appreciated winning the awards, I wouldn't have gone to lunch 10 years ago, and I wasn't going to start doing it then.

Actually racing was abandoned on the Wednesday, so I was able to go to the Sports Journalists' Association Awards. It was nice to be able to go to that. Sir Michael Parkinson presented me with the award; it was nice to meet him and to be presented with the award by him.

That evening I was invited to the Emirates Stadium by Arsenal to see them play Partisan Belgrade in the Champions' League. I did an interview for their match day programme and I got to go out onto the pitch, which was fantastic.

The weather really was bad in mid-December, so the BBC was worried about getting people to Birmingham for the *Sports Personality of the Year* show. I said I was going to get there for 5.30 or 6.00, but the people at the BBC wanted me there for about 3.00, just to be sure that we would be there. So they sent a car for me, Chanelle, Dominic Elsworth and Louise, Jonjo's daughter, Dominic's wife. We stayed in the hotel until about 6.00, and then went down to the NEC where they had a bit of a drinks reception for us.

We were all there, nine of the ten people who were on the shortlist. David Haye didn't make it to the event on the night. Graeme McDowell was there, and Phil Taylor, Tom Daley and Mark Cavendish. Lee Westwood was one of the first people I saw when I went in, so we chatted to him for a while. Lee has a couple of horses, so I knew him from seeing him at the races, but it was all very daunting. JP McManus and Jonjo O'Neill arrived later.

I got chatting to Dwight Yorke. I had met him for the first time about seven years previously on a flight to Dublin to ride at Leopardstown, and I actually ended up going out with him, Wes Brown and Fabien Barthez that night.

Slight digression. Dwight is great friends with his compatriot Brian Lara, the cricketer, whom I had met previously through David Manassch, who was Brian Lara's agent. I had played golf with Brian a couple of times, and I had been out for dinner with him and David before. That was in 2002, actually just a couple of days after I had finished third at that year's Sports Personality of the Year. I had told Chanelle that we were going out for dinner with David and a friend of his, Brian. I'm not sure why I didn't tell her who Brian was, maybe I said Brian Lara, maybe I didn't. Maybe I expected that she would know who he was.

So we were sitting in the Mandarin Oriental Hotel in Knightsbridge, me and Chanelle and David and Brian. We were chatting away, the craic was good, when I thought I heard Chanelle asking Brian what he did for a living.

'I play a bit of cricket,' said Brian.

'Do you play for a club?' asked Chanelle.

At this stage David and I stopped talking. Whatever we had been talking about, it couldn't have been as interesting as Chanelle's conversation with Brian Lara.

'Are you any good?'

I looked at David. Did Chanelle just ask Brian Lara if he was any good?

'I'm okay,' said Brian. 'I play for the West Indies.'

In fairness to Chanelle, when we had sat down at the table to eat, she had noticed that a lot of people were looking in our direction. She thought it a little odd; there was no way Anthony's profile could have gone up by that much just by finishing third in Sports Personality of the Year.

At that stage I decided to save Chanelle.

'Do you not know who Brian is?' I asked her.

Blank look.

'His hands are in Madame Tussauds.'

'Oh right,' said Chanelle. 'So you're obviously a very famous cricketer?'

'I suppose I am,' said Brian. 'Why, what did you think I did?'

'I thought you were into fashion.'

Back to 2010, LG Arena in Birmingham, and I'm chatting with Dwight Yorke when Chanelle arrives with Zara Phillips.

'Oh hiya Brian!' Chanelle says to Dwight.

'Hi Chanelle, how are you?' says Dwight warmly.

Chanelle is taken aback a little by the warmth of Brian's greeting.

'I can't believe you remember me,' says Chanelle. 'It must be about six or seven years since we met.'

'Of course I remember you,' says Dwight. Charmer.

Then Chanelle turns to Zara.

'Zara, meet my friend Brian.'

Zara looks at Chanelle, looks at me, looks at Chanelle's friend Brian.

'That's Dwight Yorke.'

It was an amazing night. The atmosphere in the room was fantastic, and for me, it was down to the fact that David Beckham was there. He just had this aura about him. It was a bit like playing golf with Tiger Woods, everyone was looking at Beckham. I'm not a Manchester United fan, but you have to admire him. He's a global superstar.

I had never met him before, but he couldn't have been nicer, more down to earth. He's just a person at the end of the day. He was a normal bloke. He just happens to be a global superstar. He made the night, he made the occasion.

When we were being photographed at the end of the night, I was holding the trophy with Beckham on one side of me, Jessica Ennis on the other, and I'm looking at the pair of them, two of the most beautiful people in Britain, and I'm thinking, this isn't making me look too good. Phil Taylor was on the other side of Beckham, so I called over to him:

'Phil, would you mind coming over here and standing beside me – at the moment this photo isn't going to present me in a very good light!'

I wasn't nervous beforehand. I was really quite chilled. I had it in my head that there were 10 of us on the list, any one of the 10 of us could have won it. We were taken to our seats before the show started. We were right there in the front row, ringside seats. It was quite incredible. Me and Chanelle on one side of the front row, with Jonjo and JP behind us, and David and Victoria Beckham and their kids on the other side. Nobody knew the result, so I'm not sure how it was decided that we would be in the front row, but we were. Even if you weren't there hoping to win an award, it was a fantastic show at which to be present, at which to have front-row seats.

Beckham's award was huge. The ovation he received was quite incredible, people would have stood and clapped all night if they had been allowed. Half an hour after Beckham's award, Freddie Flintoff read out my name. It was slow-motion stuff. The 2010 BBC Sports Personality of the Year is AP McCoy. The words hit me like a brick. I was stunned, rabbit in the headlights, 10,000 people in the arena and 12 million people in their sitting rooms. I didn't really know what to do. I just looked down at the ground for a second, allowed it to wash over me for a moment. Chanelle gave me a kiss, she was smiling, beaming, and hugged me. I stood up, everyone else stood up, I looked behind me to see JP and Jonjo in the two seats behind us clapping and smiling and I hugged them both in turn. Then I thought, shit, I've won, I'm going to have to get up on the stage and make a speech. How am I going to do that?

Chanelle had said to me earlier that day that I should have a think about what I would say if I did happen to win, but I had dismissed that. I wasn't going to win, and if I did I would figure something out. She had persisted though. Make sure you thank all the people who voted for you, she had said, and JP and Jonjo and everyone else who has helped you.

I remembered this as I turned to look at the stage. I remember Chanelle's words and I thought, right, better not forget anybody. It's very different when you are actually in the situation. I looked up at the stage and exhaled. It wasn't that long a walk, we were in the front row for God's sake, I knew I could make it.

The crowd were still clapping and cheering when I reached the stage, with lights flashing, music blaring, quite incredible. Overwhelming really. I shook Freddie Flintoff's hand first, then Cesc's. I had never met Cesc Fabregas before. People told me afterwards that I had blanked Freddie Flintoff. I didn't mean to, I didn't think I had, but I was star-struck in the presence of Cesc Fabregas. Cesc handed me the trophy. Amazing.

I moved over to the right of the stage, towards the podium, shook Phil Taylor's hand, kissed Jessica Ennis on both cheeks, and then I noticed that the music had stopped but the crowd were still cheering. So I'm standing there like an eejit, Gary Lineker and Sue Barker are smiling over at me, everyone is smiling and clapping and cheering, everyone is watching me, and all I want is that they will stop cheering so that I can say a few words and sit back down again. David Beckham had stood on the same spot a half an hour ago for an age as we had cheered, but he was at ease with the adulation, he just seemed to be able to allow it to wash over him, wait for it to stop before he started to speak. I couldn't.

'Thank you,' I said. They kept cheering. 'Thank you.' Again. They cheered even louder. Someone whistled. 'Oh dear.' I actually said 'Oh dear' out loud. I didn't mean to be ungracious or ungrateful, I wasn't, quite the opposite, I was overwhelmed, unworthy; it was one of the most humbling experiences of my life.

'Thank you,' I said again. The cheering began to die down. Thank God.

'This is an unbelievable feeling to be standing in front of so many amazing sports people,' I said. 'So many people who I look up to, who I watch all the time on television. To win this award, well, it's just very surreal. Obviously, with the help of so many people. I've got so many people to thank, I don't even know where to start.'

As I spoke, I saw David Beckham looking up at me and smiling. That made it even worse. Why did I have to notice him? Why did I have to look at David Beckham? He's probably looking up here wondering who I am.

'I work in a wonderful sport in horseracing, and I would like to thank everyone in the sport, because I know that most of them probably spent most of the night voting for me. Without Jonjo O'Neill I wouldn't be standing here, because I definitely wouldn't have ridden the winner of the Grand National without him. Obviously, to win it for JP and Noreen McManus was an unbelievable feeling, because I knew that they want-ed to win it as much as I did.'

It was all down to them. JP and Noreen for having the belief in me to get me to ride for them, Jonjo for putting me on the right horse, whether there was a coin-flip involved or not.

'To my wife Chanelle, my mother and father, my brother and sisters, all the other lads in the weigh room who I work with every day and who I know I drive mad. Mostly, even more amazing than winning this trophy, my daughter Eve at home. She's three. She was shouting at me today when she realised I was on television this morning. I know she's going to be watching and I just want to say how amazing she is. Thank you everyone.'

I was about to wrap it up, but I was sure I was forgetting lots of people.

'Another person, my agent Dave Roberts, he has put me on all the horses that I have ridden throughout the years. Octagon who have supported me. BGC. There are so many people to thank that I could be here all night.'

I would have been, and I'm sure people were well sick of me by then.

'And obviously,' I turned to Cesc with my Arsenal cap on. 'Cesc, I'll be the idiot in the crowd shouting at you whenever we're not winning, so, I apologise.'

Cesc just looked back, smiled and nodded. God knows what he was thinking.

'Thank you.' The crowd clapped again as all the while I held the microphone with both hands. Security blanket.

'Ladies and gentlemen,' Sue Barker was saying. Somebody else was speaking, the limelight was removed from me. I heaved a sigh of relief. 'The 2010 BBC Sports Personality of the Year is AP McCoy.'

CHAPTER 37

As Good As Ever

I could never have expected to hit the highs of the 2009/10 season the following year, but I was intent on giving it a shot. People said that I was more relaxed heading into this season than normal, that I was a little different after winning the Grand National, but I don't think I was. It was a big relief for sure, it was a big weight off my shoulders, I definitely didn't want to be remembered as a good jockey who didn't win the Grand National, but I don't think I faced into the new season with a decreased intensity as a result. My number one goal was to win the championship, as ever, and that quest began as usual on the first day of the season.

JP wanted me to ride Finger Onthe Pulse in the Galway Plate at the end of July 2010, I wanted to ride Dancing Tornado. JP owned them both, Finger Onthe Pulse was trained by Tom Taaffe, Dancing Tornado was trained by Michael Hourigan, and I was all set to ride Dancing Tornado when he was injured the day before the race and had to be withdrawn.

Frank Berry, JP's racing manager, called me when I was in the car with Graham Lee between the airport and the races to tell me. I was disappointed, but at least I was able to switch to Finger Onthe Pulse, the horse that JP thought I should ride all along, and we won it, my first Galway Plate. It was tough on Mark Walsh, who was supposed to be riding him, but he'll bounce back. He's a good young rider with a future.

I also had my first win in the Welsh Grand National that season on Synchronised, the horse on whom I had won the Midlands National at Uttoxeter the previous March. I thought he was the ideal type for a Welsh National. He wasn't overly big, but he would gallop and stay all day – a lot like Wichita Lineman in that respect – and he loved soft ground, which you almost always got on Welsh National day at Chepstow in late December.

As it turned out, the ground was too soft and the race was postponed for a week, from late December to early January. Jonjo had planned to take a holiday after the Welsh National – he and Jackie were off to stay with the boss for a week or so in Barbados, so he headed off anyway. He told me afterwards that they all went up to John Magnier's house in Barbados to watch the race. It must have been about nine o'clock in the morning, but they cheered him home.

I remember Rishi Persad from the BBC interviewing me afterwards, and asking me where Jonjo was. I said he was at home in the yard working. Actually, as he was asking me where Jonjo was, Frank Berry was just over to my right. Kieran McManus is always slagging Frank and Jonjo, he says they look like identical twins. He is forever calling Frank Jonjo. 'How are you Frank,' he'll say to Jonjo. 'Where's Jonjo today?'

So for a split second, when Rishi asked me where Jonjo was, I thought of pointing to Frank and saying, 'Sure there he is.' I'm not sure how Rishi would have reacted. He might have gone off to interview him. Maybe it's as well that I didn't. It was probably more an in-house joke than anything else. I'm not sure too many other people would have got it.

Ruby got badly injured again that season – he broke his leg in a fall off Corrick Bridge at Down Royal in early November, just an hour after he had ridden Kauto Star to win the Grade 1 JNWine.com Champion Chase. It was desperate luck for Ruby again, and it meant that a lot of those high-profile rides on the Paul Nicholls horses were up for grabs. Noel Fehily was in the frame for them, he was riding a lot of them, but then he got injured as well.

Paul and owner Andy Stewart asked me to ride Big Buck's in the Long Distance Hurdle at Newbury in November and in the Long Walk Hurdle, also at Newbury, rerouted from Ascot, in December, and I was delighted to do so. Big Buck's is one of the best staying hurdlers ever and it was a privilege to get to ride him in two races. Fortunately, we won both of them.

I rode Master Minded again for Paul in the Victor Chandler Chase at Ascot in January and I nearly got him beat. I thought he would win easily, so I kicked on from the fourth-last, thought I'd just kill the others for pace and put the race to bed from a long way out. He did pick up well, but then he got tired, and we only just held on from Somersby in the end. I said afterwards that I had committed him too early, but I also think that he probably wasn't fully wound up. January is probably a quiet enough time for Paul Nicholls's yard, you have to let horses down a little sometimes, so it makes sense that you let them down a little in January and then build them up for Cheltenham and Aintree in March and April.

Paul also asked me to ride Kauto Star in the King George. That presented me with a bit of a problem because Albertas Run was also on track for the race. Even though Albertas Run is trained by Jonjo, he is owned by Trevor Hemmings, not by JP, so I was under no obligation to ride him, but when you have ridden a horse to win a Sun Alliance Chase, a Ryanair Chase and a Melling Chase, there is a degree of expectation there.

Kauto Star was quite unique though. It wasn't as if I was getting off one horse to ride a slightly better horse in an ordinary race, or even in a good race. This was Kauto Star, the opportunity to ride probably the best staying chaser of our generation, and this was the King George, one of the most prestigious races on the calendar. More than that, Kauto Star was bidding to make history: he had already won four King Georges, the same number as Desert Orchid, and he was odds-on to win his fifth, more than any other horse ever. I had never ridden him in a race before, and I was dying to team up with him.

I rang JP and told him my predicament. He just told me that I should call Jonjo. So I did. Jonjo was great about it, as I knew he would be. Jonjo rang Mick Meagher, Trevor Hemmings's racing manager, and he was fine, but then he called Jonjo back to tell him that Trevor wasn't happy, which was understandable. Jonjo called me back to tell me.

I decided that I would call Trevor. It was a difficult phone call to make, but I knew that it was the right thing to do. The difficult phone calls are the ones that you should make. I didn't ring him straight away though. What was I going to say? It took me about three hours to pluck up the courage. Eventually I did, trying to explain as well as I could that it wasn't that I was being disloyal, but Albertas Run was a 33/1 shot and this was the opportunity of a lifetime to ride a horse like Kauto Star who was on the brink of history in the King George. Trevor was great, he said he understood. I think he appreciated that I called him.

The King George was postponed from 26th December to 15th January because of the weather, but it didn't seem to affect Kauto Star. I went down to Paul's to school him the week before the race, and he was good, but, although he was an odds-on shot for the King George, I knew that it was going to be tough. He was 11 years old. At some stage, age catches up with even the best of them.

We got beaten. We finished just third behind Long Run and Riverside Theatre, although if we hadn't made a horrendous mistake at the second-last, I'm sure we would have been second. We wouldn't have beaten Long Run though, Nicky Henderson's horse, owned by Robert Waley-Cohen and ridden by his amateur son Sam. He was just too good and, five years Kauto Star's junior, too fast. I was never really comfortable on him at any stage in the King George, I just always felt that Long Run was going a stride too quick.

I was disappointed that we got beaten, but I didn't think that I could have done anything differently. I think he was, at best, the second-best horse in the race on the day. Two and a half months later Kauto Star came out and ran a cracker in the Gold Cup, but he still only finished third behind Long Run and Denman. He was a superstar, one of the best horses I have ever had anything to do with, but there is no question that his superpowers were on the wane.

It was a pleasure to be associated with Kauto Star. It was an honour to be given the chance to ride him in a race, especially on his date with history, his bid to become the first horse ever to win five King Georges. Before Kauto Star came along, I always thought that Desert Orchid was the best and most versatile steeplechaser that I had ever seen. Kauto Star was similar. He had the speed to win two Tingle Creek Chases over two miles, the pace to win four King Georges over three miles, and the stamina to win two Cheltenham Gold Cups, becoming the only horse ever to win the Gold Cup back two years after winning it for the first time and losing it in between.

The only shame was that he was past his best when I did get to eventually ride him. Of course there were people who said that I didn't get on with him in the King George, that it was my fault that he didn't win, but I don't agree. The evidence that he was in decline was there for all to see, as befits an 11-year-old, and it was confirmed in his later efforts at Cheltenham and Punchestown.

I suppose it is hardly surprising that I don't agree with those people, but I genuinely don't. Fortunately, the talk didn't bother me that much. There are people in life and in racing whose opinions I deeply respect, but at the end of the day, I do believe that you have to make up your own mind about things. You can listen to people, you can listen to reasons, arguments and rationale, but in the end you have to make up your own mind about any course of action you are going to take or about any opinion you are going to form. Without being arrogant about it, regarding Kauto Star's run in the King George, I am happy that that he was as good as he was on the day.

I did ride a treble on King George day: Kazzene in the juvenile hurdle, Ski Sunday in the handicap hurdle, and Binocular in the Christmas Hurdle.

Binocular's main target, of course, again, was the Champion Hurdle in March, the defence of his title, and Nicky and JP and I were all very happy with his Christmas Hurdle win as a stepping stone to Cheltenham. His next stepping stone, as it had been the previous year, was the Contenders Hurdle at Sandown in February, and he was desperately disappointing in that. He won the race all right, but he was not good in so doing. He started jumping out to his left again, and he only just scraped home from a mare of Nicky's who was rated 55 lb his inferior.

It was the same as the previous year, disappointing in the Contenders Hurdle despite winning. He is obviously not an easy horse to train, he obviously has his problems, more with his back than anything else, and something was obviously hurting him that was causing him to jump to his left, but he was a million miles off what was going to be required to win the Champion Hurdle again.

But it didn't really matter how he was at Sandown, what mattered was how he was at Cheltenham, and everything seemed to be going right in the build-up. Nicky seemed happy with him before I went down to school him the week before Cheltenham, and I was delighted with him when I did. I rang JP to tell him that everything was great.

Binocular was by far my best ride at Cheltenham 2011. I had some good rides, Captain Cee Bee in the Champion Chase, Get Me Out Of Here in one of the handicap hurdles, Albertas Run was back to defend his Ryanair Chase crown, Noble Prince in the Jewson Chase, Spirit Son or Sprinter Sacre for Nicky in the Supreme Novices' Hurdle, and I had a couple of other bits and pieces, but Binocular was head and shoulders above everything else, he was the Champion Hurdle favourite, the reigning champion.

I was sitting in my house on the Saturday evening before Cheltenham, it must have been around 10 o'clock, when I got a text message from JP asking me to call him at his house. He had tried to call me and couldn't get through – the signal wasn't great in the house – so he sent me a text, which was unusual, because I always called him back anyway when I saw that I had a missed call from him. It must have been urgent.

'I don't think Binocular is going to run in the Champion Hurdle,' he said when I called him back.

The words hit me like 12 bricks. I couldn't speak.

'He was given some medication for a rash,' JP continued, 'but the substance is still in his system. He had some tests today and there is twice as much of the substance in his system as there should be. He can't race with that substance in his system, he would be disqualified afterwards, and there is no chance that it will have enough time to leave his system before Tuesday.'

I went upstairs to find a darkened room in which I could sulk. Chanelle saw me going up.

'What's wrong?'

'Binocular isn't running in the Champion Hurdle.'

I didn't even go into our room; I went into one of the spare rooms and just sat there in the dark. Why am I bothering? I was finding it difficult to get over this. With Binocular, I was going to Cheltenham with the Champion Hurdle favourite and a couple of other rides with chances. Without him, my book of rides looked fairly threadbare.

Nicky was gutted, JP was disappointed. The rash that he had was just a superficial rash, it didn't look good, but it might not have affected his performance. And the drug he was given wasn't a performance-enhancing drug, it was just medication to clear up the rash, but it contained one of the substances that were banned for racing under British Horseracing Authority rules, so there was no option but to withdraw him.

He might not have beaten Hurricane Fly anyway. Hurricane Fly was a very good Champion Hurdle winner, he could be the best we have seen since Istabraq, but he might have, you never know. An on-song Binocular is very good too, and it looked like he was going to be on-song at Cheltenham. Hurricane Fly did beat us well when we met at Punchestown six weeks later, but that wasn't the real Binocular.

I had a few good rides at Newbury on 12th February, Totesport Trophy day, including Get Me Out Of Here in the Totesport Trophy itself, bidding for back-to-back wins in the race, and Kid Cassidy in the opening novices' hurdle, but I didn't get to ride any of them, as things transpired. It was a quite bizarre day.

I didn't get to see what happened initially, it had all happened before I got out to the parade ring before the first race. When I got there, Nicky Henderson told me that Kid Cassidy had fallen over and got up again.

It just looked like he stumbled and fell over. He seemed fine, but he was dragging his lass around the parade ring. So I decided I would just take him down to the start early, get him to relax.

He was trying to run away with me the whole way down to the start. He was sweating like mad, I couldn't believe how worked up he was, charging everywhere with me. It wasn't like him. I had ridden him a couple of times and he had never done this before. When he won his bumper he was the most laid-back horse in the world.

Simon McNeill, the starter that day, told me that there was going to be a delay, that two horses had collapsed in the parade ring. I thought no more of it, I was just concentrating on getting my horse to relax down at the start. Then a few minutes later, Simon told me that a few horses had been electrocuted in the parade ring. One of them was Jonjo's and two of them were JP's, which was desperate.

I didn't want to allow Kid Cassidy to run when I heard this, I was afraid that he had been electrocuted as well. Nicky came down to the start and we decided not to run. The first race was run, but racing was abandoned after that on health and safety grounds. It really was quite a surreal day, and I think that it took Kid Cassidy a long time to get over it. I like him a lot, he won well at Punchestown in early May, and he could be a nice novice chaser next season.

Cheltenham 2011 wasn't that bad in the end. No Binocular – I watched the Champion Hurdle from the weigh room – but I did win the Jewson on Noble Prince and I won the Ryanair Chase again on Albertas Run just over an hour later. Going into the meeting I genuinely thought that there was a chance I would have no winners at Cheltenham, so I was delighted with two.

I went back to try to win the Grand National again on Don't Push It, but it was just too much for him. It's almost impossible to win back-to-back Grand Nationals; Red Rum was the last horse to achieve that feat in 1973/74, and he was a National institution. Hedgehunter went close, Comply or Die went close, and Don't Push It went close. He had 7 lb more to carry than he had in 2010, he had to shoulder 11 st 10 lb, but he ran his heart out again to finish third behind Ballabriggs and Oscar Time. I was proud of him.

I won my 16th jockeys' championship last season, I rode 218 winners, my highest total in eight years so, given that statistics are everything, I must be getting better again.

Ever since I won the Grand National, people have been asking me about retirement.. It has been the only downside to winning the Grand National. Before that, I can't remember anybody ever asking me about retiring. Now I can hardly have a conversation with somebody without retirement coming up.

A few years ago, I thought that I might retire when I was 35. I thought, if I can win the championship every year between now and then, I will have won 15 championships, and I'll retire when I'm 35, all nice numbers. As I got closer to 35 though, I started to think that maybe it wasn't such a good idea. I'm 37 now, and I think I am still riding as well as ever. I am certainly enjoying it as much as ever. So why give up something you love and something you believe you are still good at?

And what would I do? I always said that I would never train horses. I know that you should never say never, but I don't think I have the right mentality for it; I'm not sure I'd be able to deal with owners properly. I don't think I would be very diplomatic. Strangely, if I did take out a trainer's licence, I would be more interested in training on the flat than over jumps. Who knows though? Whatever I do, I hope that it will be something to do with racing, sport or media, and I would hope to do something that I am good at. I would hate to be doing something that I didn't think I was good at.

Of course, time is the enemy of every sportsperson; it isn't nice to watch someone who used to be good at what they do turn into someone who isn't so good, an old sportsperson carrying on too long. I hope that doesn't happen to me. I hope I will be able to recognise when I start to decline. I think I will. I think, if they are being honest, most people do.

Hopefully I won't be forced to retire, God forbid that injury ends my career. It can happen. Every horse is capable of falling, even the best jumper, and I never go out to ride thinking I am definitely not going to fall or I am definitely not going to get hurt. I know it's a possibility. Every day, when you put on your boots and leave the weigh room, it's a possibility.

But I think the same way as I did when I started riding, I have the same thought process. It's all about riding the next winner. You do what you can to maximise your horse's chance. It's only when you actually hit the ground that you feel the pain. If it's a bad fall it can hurt for days, weeks or months, but you heal and you start again. As Lance Armstrong said, pain is temporary.

If I were to lose my bottle though, that's a different thing. If you go out on a horse afraid of falling, afraid of pain, then it's time for you. If you don't want to go out and ride that horse in a novice chase because it's a bad jumper, then it's time for you to think about what you are doing. As long as you are happy to ride the bad jumper once it has a chance of winning, as long as you are happy to get up on the horse that has fallen in its previous three races knowing that if you get it around it will probably win, then kick on.

I'm very fit, and I don't feel like I have had a hard career. I have a brilliant agent, I have a fantastic PA, a driver who will take me anywhere at the drop of a hat, I have a wife who would do anything for me, a daughter who adores me, all I have to do is go and ride the horses. I don't think I have ever done a day's work in my life.

People ask me if my next target is 4,000 winners, and I laugh – 4,000 seems so far away, it's a bit depressing, but I would be lying if I said that the thought has never crossed my mind. And then I get to wondering, is it that far away really? I have ridden just over 3,500 winners now. I need 500 more or thereabouts. If I can ride 200 winners a season, that's just two and a half more seasons. I'm 37 now, and as I say, I feel like I am riding as well as ever. Could I go on riding until I am 39 or 40?

I tell Chanelle that I am going to try to ride 4,000 winners and she gets frustrated with me. She just wants me to retire now in one piece, to get out with my head, neck and back intact, so that we can enjoy the rest of our lives together. Life after life as a jockey, whatever that may be.

I tell her sometimes that I am going to try to ride more winners than Martin Pipe has trained. That's 4,182. I am joking though. Really I am. Honestly.

Index

Davis, Richard 70
Deal, Peter 216
Deano's Beeno 204, 223–4, 239, 240
Deep Bramble 93–4
Delaney, Mrs 27, 32, 35, 37
Denman 75, 212, 258, 276, 283, 288–90, 294–5, 323
Dennis, David 176
Derby Awards 314
Derrymoyle 156
Desert Orchid 323
Desert Style 42, 46
Dettori, Frankie 1, 177, 210, 306, 312
Dewhurst, the 42
Dickin, Robin 194
Direct Route 167, 168–9
Dobbin, Tony 206, 256, 258
Dr. Devious 41
Dr Jekyll 23
Dom Samourai 137, 183
Don Fernando 209
Don't Push It 94, 168, 179, 258, 282, 297–303, 305, 306, 326
Dorans Pride 124, 149
Doumen, François 239–40
Doumen, Thierry 239–40, 250
Down Royal 23
Downey, Dave 28, 36–7
Doyle, Jack 176
Dream With Me 201
Dreaper, Jim 156
Drombeag 259
Drowne, Steve 285
Dubai 101, 205, 268
Dubai Spring Carnival 51
Dublin Flyer 132
Dunwoody, Richard 12, 25, 48, 49, 56, 56–7, 60, 61, 68, 71, 76, 79, 82–3, 85, 92, 95, 119, 126, 129, 149, 164, 175–6, 194, 196, 200–1, 216, 274, 302
Durack, Seamus 185–6
Durcan, Ted 37, 52
Durkan, Ted 31, 38
Dwyer, Mark 48
Easthorpe 91

Eddie Wee 16, 23
Edredon Bleu 148, 150–1, 167–9, 178, 191
Edwards, Gordon 64
Egerton, Charlie 272
Elementary 51
Ellery, Sean 71
Elliott, Gordon 208
Elsworth, David 64, 146
Elsworth, Dominic 315
Elsworth, Louise 315
Ennis, Jessica 3, 316–17, 318
Epsom Derby 41
Errant Knight 77
Eskimo Nell 74
Essex 246
Eudipe 144, 161, 162
Eva Luna 42, 42–3
Evans, Chris 313
Evans, Jamie 131–2
Everard, Conor 27–8, 32, 32–3, 38, 265
Exit Swinger 192, 208
Exotic Dancer 256, 256–7, 257–8, 277, 282, 282–3

Fabregas, Cesc 2, 318, 319
facilities, race courses 68
Fadoudal Du Cochet 192
Family Business 187–8
Fanshawe, James 183–4, 248, 250
Far From Trouble 253, 254
Farrant, Rodney 69, 74
Farrelly, Johnny 257
Fataliste 153
Ferguson, Alex 36
Ferguson, Ian 53, 306
Fiepes Shuffle 134
Findlay, Harry 288–90
Finger Onthe Pulse 320
Finian's Rainbow 49
Fire Forest 6, 12
Fitzgerald, Jimmy 54
Fitzgerald, Mick 61, 64, 68, 103, 184, 227, 272, 274, 299, 308–9
Flaked Oats 123–5
Flame of Tara 26